RETURN DISTRIBUTIONS IN FINANCE

Butterworth-Heinemann Finance

QUANTITATIVE
FINANCE SERIES

Aims and objectives

- books based on the work of financial market practitioners and academics
- presenting cutting edge research to the professional/practitioner market
- combining intellectual rigour and practical application
- covering the interaction between mathematical theory and financial practice
- to improve portfolio performance, risk management and trading book performance
- covering quantitative techniques

market

Brokers/Traders; Actuaries; Consultants; Asset Managers; Fund Managers; Regulators; Central Bankers; Treasury Officials; Technical Analysts; and Academics for Masters in Finance and MBA market.

series editor

Dr Steven Satchell

Apart from being an economics/finance academic at Trinity College, Cambridge with many publications to his credit, he also works in a consultative capacity to many firms and edits the journal *Derivatives: use, trading and regulations* published by Henry Stewart Publishers. He has edited two finance books published by Butterworth-Heinemann: *Forecasting Volatility* with John Knight and *Advanced Trading Rules* with Emmanuel Acar. He is currently writing, with Frank Sortino, a new book, *Downside Risk in Financial Markets: theory, practice and implementation* and editing a new book, with John Knight, *Performance Measurement in Finance: firms, funds and managers*. His latest edited book with John Knight is *Return Distributions in Finance*. He is a regular speaker at professional conferences.

series titles

Return Distributions in Finance
Downside Risk in Financial Markets: theory, practice and implementation
Performance Measurement in Finance: firms, funds and managers
Global Tactical Asset Allocation: theory and practice

RETURN DISTRIBUTIONS IN FINANCE

Edited by

John Knight

Stephen Satchell

BUTTERWORTH HEINEMANN

OXFORD AUCKLAND BOSTON JOHANNESBURG MELBOURNE NEW DELHI

Butterworth-Heinemann
Linacre House, Jordan Hill, Oxford OX2 8DP
225 Wildwood Avenue, Woburn, MA 01801-2041
A division of Reed Educational and Professional Publishing Ltd

A member of the Reed Elsevier plc group

First published 2001

British Library Cataloguing in Publication Data
Return distributions in finance
1. Asset allocation 2. Financial engineering 3. Investments Mathematics
I. Knight, John II. Satchell, Stephen E.
332.6′0151

ISBN 0 7506 4751 5

Printed and bound in Great Britain by MPG Books Ltd, Bodmin

Contents

Preface

The purpose of this book is to bring together research on the question of how to model the probability of financial asset price returns. There is now a consensus that conventional models that assume normality need to be broadened to deal with such issues as tail probabilities, pricing derivatives and outliers, to name some more obvious cases.

The first chapter, by Bingham and Kiesel, discusses the modelling of stock returns and interest rates using a family of stochastic processes called hyperbolic Lévy processes. They demonstrate that such an approach can be estimated empirically and applied to option pricing problems. Bond surveys and discusses the use of asymmetric density functions in finance and their usefulness in modelling conditional skewness. Lizieri and Ward present a detailed investigation of UK commercial property returns. Hwang and Satchell discuss how to build capital asset pricing models when the data is non-normal and described by coefficients of skewness and kurtosis. They apply this methodology to emerging markets data. Rogers, Satchell and Yoon present an analysis of returns when conditioned in various ways on volume. By changing clocks from Newtonian time to volume time they find that seemingly non-normal data is, in effect, normal. This work was completed some years ago but is being published in this volume as, recently, other scholars seem to be discovering this result afresh. Jun Yu presents a chapter that addresses issues of hypothesis testing for asset returns. In particular his test procedure allows one to discriminate between finite and infinite variance distributions. Jiang presents an analysis of option pricing when the underlying asset return process is both predictable and discontinuous. This extends existing results in this literature and emphasizes how the properties of the underlying process can influence the options price. In a similar vein, Knight, Satchell and Wang investigate the impact of different distributional assumptions on the future option prices and Value-at-Risk calculations. Knight and Satchell discuss the pricing of options when the values of skewness and kurtosis of returns are known to the investigator. Finally, Fritsche computes distributional results for moving average trading rules under different distributional assumptions.

Taken together, these ten chapters should communicate to the reader the importance of distributional assumptions for financial modellers and the wide variety of applications available to those wishing to undertake research in this area.

John Knight and Stephen Satchell

Contributors

Nicholas Hugh (Nick) Bingham took his degree in mathematics in Oxford in 1966 and his PhD in Cambridge in 1969. His thesis, written under David Kendall, was on limit theory and semi-groups in probability theory. He spent thirty years teaching mathematics at the University of London, at Westfield College (Lecturer 1969–80, Reader 1980–84), Royal Holloway College (Reader 1984–5, Professor of Mathematics, 1985–95) and Birkbeck College (Professor of Statistics, 1995–9). He joined Brunel University as a Professor of Statistics in 2000. His interests centre on probability and stochastic processes, pure and applied, particularly limit theorems, fluctuation theory, branching processes, probability on groups and other algebraic structures, and links with analysis. He also works in analysis (regular variation, Tauberian theory, summability theory), statistics (non-parametrics), mathematical finance and the history of mathematics.

Shaun Bond is currently an assistant lecturer in Finance in the Department of Land Economy at the University of Cambridge. Prior to commencing this appointment, Shaun was a graduate student in the Economics Faculty at Cambridge. Before undertaking graduate studies at Cambridge he was employed as a senior economist with the Queensland Treasury Department and also holds a first-class honours degree in Economics from the University of Queensland.

Alexander Fritsche is a research associate in the Economic Forecasting Group at The Conference Board of Canada. He has an MA in Economics from the University of Western Ontario and is currently pursuing the CFA designation. He has interests in forecasting and financial trading strategies with applications to quantitative and programme trading.

Soosung Hwang is currently a lecturer in the Banking/Finance Department at City University Business School, London, UK. He has also worked as both an accountant and a fund manager. Among his degrees he holds a PhD from Cambridge. He has published in numerous journals including *Econometric Theory*, *Journal of Banking and Finance* and *Applied Mathematical Finance*. His interests include all aspects of empirical finance and financial econometrics.

George J. Jiang is an assistant Professor of Finance in the Schulich School of Business, York University, Canada. He is also a SOM Research Fellow of the Faculty of Business and Economics at the University of Groningen, the Netherlands. He received his PhD from the University of Western Ontario in 1996. His research interests are in the areas of derivative valuation, term structure modelling and risk management with publications in leading journals, including *Econometric Theory*, *Journal of Financial and Quantitative Analysis*, and *Journal of Computational Finance*.

Rüdiger Kiesel was educated at the University of Ulm, Germany, where he received his PhD (1990) and Habilitation (1995) in Mathematics. After spending three years as a lecturer in statistics at Birkbeck College, he is presently Reader in Financial Mathematics and Actual Science in the Department of Statistics at the London School of Economics. His academic work focuses on pricing and hedging of derivative securities (in complete markets) and aspects of credit risk (measurement and management of credit risk, credit risk models, credit derivatives).

John Knight is Professor of Economics at the University of Western Ontario. His research interests are in theoretical and financial econometrics, areas in which he has both published extensively as well as supervising numerous doctoral dissertations.

Colin Lizieri is Professor of Real Estate Finance at the University of Reading where he is director of postgraduate research in the Department of Land Management. He has an undergraduate degree from the University of Oxford and a doctorate from the London School of Economics. He is a fellow of the Royal Geographical Society and a member of the Investment Property Forum. Prior to joining Reading, he was reader in international real estate markets at City University Business School and visiting professor at the University of Toronto. In his research and consultancy, he has specialized in the analysis of office markets, in international real estate investment and in the application of quantitative and statistical models to commercial property market problems. He has written many academic and professional articles and is co-author (with Ball and MacGregor) of *The Economics of Commercial Property Markets* published in 1998 by Routledge.

Chris Rogers is Professor of Probability at the University of Bath. His MA and PhD degrees are both from the University of Cambridge. He is the author of more than 90 publications, including the famous two-volume work *Diffusions, Markov Processes, and Martingales* with David Williams. Many of his papers deal with topics in finance, such as the potential approach to term structure of interest rates, complete models of stochastic volatility (with David Hobson), portfolio turnpike theorems (with Phil Dybvig and Kerry Back), improved binomial pricing (with Emily Stapleton), infrequent portfolio review, and high-frequency data modelling (with Omar Zane). Professor Rogers is an associate editor of several journals, including *Mathematical Finance*, and was the principal organizer of the 1995 programme on Financial Mathematics held at the Isaac Newton Institute in Cambridge. Chris Rogers is a frequent speaker at industry conferences and courses, and consults for a number of financial clients.

Stephen Satchell is a lecturer in Economics at the University of Cambridge, and a fellow of Trinity College. He has a keen empirical and theoretical interest in most areas of finance and is particularly intrigued by all issues of asset management, risk management and measurement. He advises a number of city companies and has published extensively in both academic and practitioners' outlets.

Guoqiang Wang is currently completing a PhD in Economics at the University of Western Ontario. His research interest are in the area of financial econometrics with particular emphasis on risk management. Before coming to Canada he gained his MA and BA from Nankai University, PR China.

Charles Ward has MA degrees from Cambridge and Exeter and a PhD from Reading. He is a Fellow of the Institute of Investment Management and Research and a member of the Investment Property Forum. Before moving to the University of Reading, Charles was Professor of Accountancy and Finance at the University of Stirling and Deputy-Principal from 1989 to 1991. His teaching and research has ranged over a wide area and includes investment performance, financial reporting, accounting, finance as well as the behaviour and performance of the property market. He published the first CAPM-based study of UK Unit Trust performance (1976), the first application of option pricing to property (1982) and the first analysis of the smoothing effect in appraisal-based indices (1987). His recent work has been mainly concerned with investment performance and pricing issues. The second edition of his book on *British Financial Institutions and Markets* (co-authors Piesse and Peasnell) was published in 1995 by Prentice Hall.

Youngjun Yoon completed his Phd in financial economics at Cambridge University. He is currently working in the asset management industry in Europe.

Jun Yu is a lecturer in Economics at the University of Auckland, New Zealand. He obtained his PhD in Economics from the University of Western Ontario in 1998. His research interests are in the fields of financial and theoretical econometrics with particular interests in time series modelling, estimation and forecasting.

Chapter 1

Modelling asset returns with hyperbolic distributions

N.H. BINGHAM AND RÜDIGER KIESEL

ABSTRACT

In this chapter we discuss applications of the hyperbolic distributions in financial modelling. In particular we discuss approaches to model stock returns and interest rates using a modelling based on hyperbolic Lévy processes. We consider the structure of the hyperbolic model, its incompleteness, choice of equivalent martingale measure, option pricing and hedging, and Value-at-Risk. We also give some empirical studies fitting the model to real data. The moral of this survey is simply this: if one wants a model that goes beyond the benchmark Black–Scholes model, but not as far as the complications of, say, stochastic-volatility models, the hyperbolic model is a good candidate for the model of first choice.

1.1 INTRODUCTION

The benchmark theory of mathematical finance is the Black–Scholes theory, based on the Wiener process in the continuous-time setting or appropriate discrete-time versions such as binomial trees. This has the virtues of being mathematically tractable and well known, but the equally well-known drawback of not corresponding to reality. Consequently, much work has been done on attempts to generalize the Wiener-based Black–Scholes theory to more complicated models chosen to provide a better fit to empirical data, preferably with a satisfactory theoretical basis also. We focus here on models including the hyperbolic distributions. This family has been used to model financial data by several authors, including Eberlein and Keller (1995) and Bibby and Sørensen (1997); much of the underlying work derives from the Danish school of Barndorff-Nielsen and co-workers.

We mention briefly various other approaches to generalizations of the Wiener-based Black–Scholes theory. One of the more immediately apparent deficiencies of the Black–Scholes model is the tail behaviour: most financial data exhibit thicker tails than the faster-than-exponentially decreasing tails of the normal distribution. Replacement of the normal law by a stable distribution, whose tails decrease much more slowly – like a power $x^{-\alpha}$ – is an idea dating back to Mandelbrot's work in the 1960s; for a recent textbook synthesis of this line of work see Mandelbrot (1997). However, it is nowadays recognized that the tails of most financial time series have to be modelled with $\alpha > 2$ (see Pagan, 1996), while stable distributions correspond to $\alpha \in (0, 2)$.

In addition, stochastic volatility models and ARCH and GARCH models from time series have been used, e.g. by Hull and White (1987) and by Duan (1995); overviews are given in Frey (1997), Ghysels *et al.* (1996) and Hobson (1998).

We turn in Section 1.2 below to a description of the hyperbolic distribution and theory used in modelling financial data. The principal complication is that hyperbolic-based models of financial markets are incomplete (stochastic volatility models share this drawback; for a recent alternative approach see Rogers (1997)). Consequently, equivalent martingale measures are no longer unique, and we thus face the question of choosing an appropriate equivalent martingale measure for pricing purposes. We consider the relevant theory in Section 1.3. We discuss option pricing, hedging and Value at Risk (VaR) in the framework of a case study in Section 1.4.

1.2 HYPERBOLIC MODELS OF FINANCIAL MARKETS AND HYPERBOLIC LÉVY MOTION

We begin with the basic stochastic differential equation (SDE) of Black–Scholes theory for the price process $S = (S_t)$,

$$dS_t = S_t(\mu dt + \sigma dW_t) \tag{1.1}$$

where μ is the drift (mean growth rate), σ the volatility, and $W = (W_t)$ – the driving noise process – a Wiener process or Brownian motion. The solution of the SDE (1) is

$$S_t = S_0 \exp\{(\mu - \sigma^2/2)t + \sigma W_t\} \tag{1.2}$$

the stochastic exponential of the drifting Brownian motion $\mu dt + \sigma dW_t$. For proof and references see e.g. Bingham and Kiesel (1998, §5.6.1).

Now the driving noise process W is a Lévy process – a stochastic process with stationary independent increments (for a monograph treatment of Lévy processes see Bertoin, 1996). Stationarity is a sensible assumption – at least for modelling markets in equilibrium on not too large a timescale – and although the independent increment assumption is certainly open to question, it is reasonable to a first approximation, which is all we attempt here. What singles out the Wiener process W among Lévy processes is path-continuity. Now the driving noise represents the net effect of the random buffeting of the multiplicity of factors at work in the economic environment, and one would expect that, analysed closely, this would be discontinuous, as the individual 'shocks' – pieces of price-sensitive information – arrive. (Indeed, price processes themselves are discontinuous looked at closely enough: in addition to the discrete shocks, one has discreteness of monetary values and the effect on supply and demand of individual transactions.)

One is thus led to consider a SDE for the price process $Y = (Y_t)$ of the form

$$dY_t = bY_{t-}dt + \sigma Y_{t-}dZ_t \tag{1.3}$$

with $Z = (Z_t)$ a suitable driving Lévy process. Now a Lévy process, or its law, is characterized via the Lévy–Khintchine formula by a drift a, the variance σ of any Gaussian (Wiener, Brownian) component, and a jump measure $d\mu$. Since the form of $d\mu$ is constrained only by integrability restrictions, such a model would be non-parametric. While the modelling flexibility of such an approach, coupled with the theoretical power of modern non-parametric statistics, raises interesting possibilities, these would take us far beyond our modest scope here. We are led to seek suitable parametric families of Lévy processes, flexible enough to provide realistic models and tractable enough to allow empirical estimation of parameters from actual financial data. We refer to Chan (1999) for a thorough theoretical analysis of models of price processes with driving noise a general Lévy process.

One such family has been mentioned in Section 1.1: the stable process. There are four parameters, corresponding to location and scale (the two 'type' parameters one must expect in a statistical model), plus two 'shape' parameters, α (governing tail decay: $0 < \alpha < 2$, with $\alpha = 2$ giving Brownian motion) and β, a skewness or asymmetry parameter. Our concern here is the hyperbolic family, again a four-parameter family with two type and two shape parameters. Recall that, for normal (Gaussian) distributions, the log-density is quadratic – that is, parabolic – and the tails are very thin. The hyperbolic family is specified by taking the log-density instead to be hyperbolic, and this leads to thicker tails as desired (but not as thick as for the stable family).

Before turning to the specifics of notation, parameterization, etc., we comment briefly on the origin and scope of the hyperbolic distributions. Both the definition and the bulk of applications stem from Barndorff-Nielsen and co-workers. Thus Barndoff-Nielsen (1977) contains the definition and an application to the distribution function of particle size in a medium such as sand (see also Barndoff-Nielsen *et al.*, 1985). Later, in Barndoff-Nielsen *et al.* (1985), hyperbolic distribution functions are used to model turbulence. Now the phenomenon of atmospheric turbulence may be regarded as a mechanism whereby energy, when present in localized excess on one volume scale in air, cascades downwards to smaller and smaller scales (note the analogy to the decay of larger particles into increasingly smaller ones in the sand studies). Barndorff-Nielsen had the acute insight that this 'energy cascade effect' might be paralleled in the 'information cascade effect', whereby price-sensitive information originates in, say, a global newsflash, and trickles down through national and local level to increasingly smaller units of the economic and social environment. This insight is acknowledged by Eberlein and Keller (1995) (see also Eberlein *et al.*, 1998; Eberlein and Raible, 1998), who introduced hyperbolic distribution functions into finance and gave detailed empirical studies of its use to model financial data, particularly daily stock returns. Further and related studies are Bibby and Sørensen (1997), Chan (1999), Eberlein and Jacob (1997), Küchler *et al.* (1994) and Rydberg (1996, 1999).

To return to the Lévy process, recall (see e.g. Bertoin, 1996) that the sample path of a Lévy process $Z = (Z_t)$ can be decomposed into a drift term bt, a Gaussian or Wiener term, and a pure jump function. This jump component has finitely or infinitely many jumps in each time interval, almost surely, according to whether the Lévy or jump measure is finite or infinite. Of course, the latter case is unrealistic in detail – but so are all models. It is, however, better adapted to modelling most financial data than the former. There, the influence of individual jumps is visible, indeed predominates, and we are in effect modelling shocks. This is appropriate for phenomena such as stock market crashes, or markets dominated by 'big players', where individual trades shift prices. To model the everyday movement of ordinary quoted stocks under the market pressure of many agents, an infinite measure is appropriate. Incidentally, a penetrating study of the mechanism whereby the actions of economic agents are translated into market forces and price movements has recently been given by Peskir and Shorish (1999).

We need some background on Bessel functions (see Watson, 1944). Recall the Bessel functions J_ν of the first kind (Watson, 1944, §3.11), Y_ν of the second kind (Watson, 1944, §3.53), and K_ν (Watson, 1944, § 3.7), there called a Bessel function with imaginary argument or Macdonald function, nowadays usually called a Bessel function of the third kind. From the integral representation

$$K_\nu(x) = \frac{1}{2}\int_0^\infty u^{\nu-1}\exp\left\{-\frac{1}{2}x(u+1/u)\right\}du \quad (x>0) \tag{1.4}$$

(Watson, 1944, §6.23) one sees that

$$f(x) = \frac{(\psi/\chi)^{\frac{1}{2}\lambda}}{2K_\lambda(\sqrt{\chi\psi})}x^{\lambda-1}\exp\left\{-\frac{1}{2}(\psi x + \chi/x)\right\} \quad (x>0) \tag{1.5}$$

is a probability density function. The corresponding law is called the generalized inverse Gaussian $GIG_{\lambda,\psi,\chi}$; the inverse Gaussian is the case $\lambda = 1$: $IG_{\chi,\psi} = GIG_{1,\psi,\chi}$. These laws were introduced by Good (1953); for a monograph treatment of their statistical properties, see Jørgensen (1982), and for their role in models of financial markets, (Shiryaev, 1999, III, 1.d).

Now consider a Gaussian (normal) law $N(\mu + \beta\sigma^2, \sigma^2)$ where the parameter σ^2 is random and is sampled from $GIG_{1,\psi,\chi}$. The resulting law is a mean-variance mixture of normal laws, the mixing law being generalized inverse Gaussian. It is written $IE_{\sigma^2}N(\mu + \beta\sigma^2, \sigma^2)$; it has a density of the form

$$\frac{\sqrt{\alpha^2-\beta^2}}{2\alpha\delta K_1(\delta\sqrt{\alpha^2-\beta^2})}\exp\left\{-\alpha\sqrt{\delta^2+(x-\mu)^2}+\beta(x-\mu)\right\} \tag{1.6}$$

(Barndorff-Nielsen, 1977), where $\alpha^2 = \psi + \beta^2$ and $\delta^2 = \chi$. Just as the Gaussian law has log-density a quadratic – or parabolic – function, so this law has log-density a hyperbolic function. It is accordingly called a hyperbolic distribution. Various parameterizations are possible. Here μ is a location and δ a scale parameter, while $\alpha > 0$ and β $(0 \le |\beta| < \alpha)$ are shape parameters. One may pass from (α, β) to (ϕ, γ) via

$$\alpha = (\phi+\gamma)/2,\ \beta = (\phi-\gamma)/2,\ \text{so } \phi\gamma = \alpha^2 - \beta^2$$

and then to (ξ, χ) via

$$\xi = (1+\delta\sqrt{\phi\gamma})^{-\frac{1}{2}},\ \chi = \frac{\xi\beta}{\alpha} = \xi\frac{\phi-\gamma}{\phi+\gamma}$$

This parameterization (in which ξ and χ correspond to the classical shape parameters of skewness and kurtosis) has the advantage of being affine invariant (invariant under changes of location and scale). The range of (ξ, χ) is the interior of a triangle

$$\nabla = \{(\xi,\chi) : 0 \le |\chi| < \xi < 1\}$$

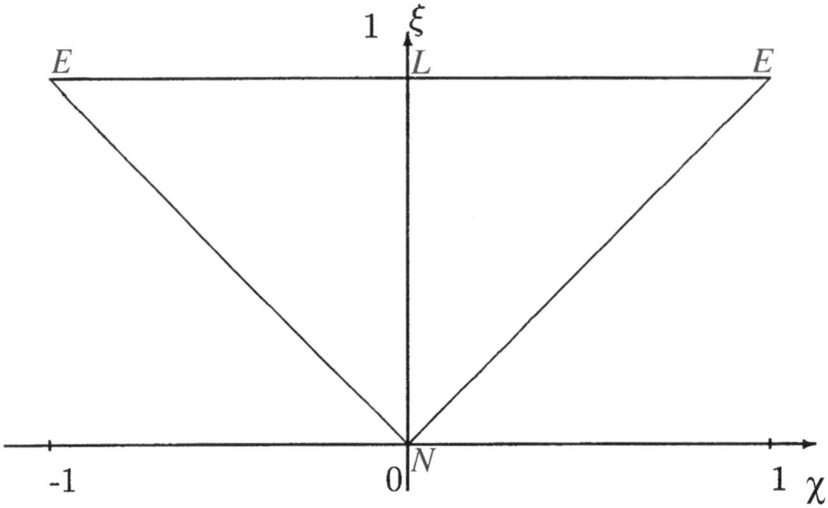

Figure 1.1 Shape triangle

called the shape traingle (see Figure 1.1). It suffices for our purpose to restrict to the centred ($\mu = 0$) symmetric ($\beta = 0$, or $\chi = 0$) case, giving the two-parameter family of densities (writing $\zeta = \xi^{-2} - 1$)

$$hyp_{\xi,\delta}(x) = \frac{1}{2\delta K_1(\zeta)} \exp\left\{-\zeta\sqrt{1 + \left(\frac{x}{\delta}\right)^2}\right\}, \quad (\xi, \delta > 0). \tag{1.7}$$

1.2.1 Infinite divisibility

Recall (Feller, 1971, XIII,7, Theorem 1) that a function ω is the Laplace transform of an infinitely divisible probability law on $I\!R_+$ iff $\omega = e^{-\psi}$, where $\psi(0) = 0$ and ψ has a completely monotone derivative (that is, the derivatives of ψ' alternate in sign). Grosswald (1976) showed that if

$$Q_\nu(x) := K_{\nu-1}(\sqrt{x})/(\sqrt{x}K_\nu(\sqrt{x})) \quad (\nu \geq 0, x > 0)$$

then Q_ν is completely monotone. Hence Barndorff-Nielsen and Halgreen (1977) showed that the generalized inverse Gaussian laws *GIG* are infinitely divisible. Now the *GIG* are the mixing laws giving rise to the hyperbolic laws as normal mean-variance mixtures. This transfers infinite divisibility (see e.g. Kelker, 1971; Keilson and Steutel, 1974, §§1,2), so the hyperbolic laws are infinite divisible.

1.2.2 Characteristic functions

The mixture representation transfers to characteristic functions on taking the Fourier transform. It gives the characteristic function of $hyp_{\xi,\delta}$ as

$$\phi(u) = \phi(u;\xi,\delta) = \frac{\xi}{K_1(\xi)} \frac{K_1\left(\sqrt{\xi^2+\delta^2u^2}\right)}{\sqrt{\xi^2+\delta^2u^2}}. \tag{1.8}$$

If $\phi(u)$ is the characteristic function of Z_1 in the corresponding Lévy process $Z = (Z_t)$, that of Z_t is $\phi_t = \phi^t$. The mixture representation of $hyp_{\xi,\delta}$ gives

$$\phi_t(u) = \exp\{tk(\tfrac{1}{2}u^2)\}$$

where $k(.)$ is the cumulant generating function of the law IG,

$$I\!E\left(e^{-sY}\right) = e^{k(s)}$$

where Y has law $IG_{\psi,\chi}$ (recall $\chi = \delta^2$), and Grosswald's result above is

$$Q_\nu(t) = \int_0^\infty q_\nu(x)dx/(x+t)$$

where

$$q_\nu = 2/(\pi^2 x(J_\nu^2(\sqrt{x}) + Y_\nu(\sqrt{x}))^2) > 0 \quad (x > 0)$$

(thus Q_ν is a Stieltjes transform, or iterated Laplace transform; Widder, 1941, VIII). Using this and the Lévy–Khintchine formula Eberlein and Keller (1995) obtained the density $\nu(x)$ of the Lévy measure $\mu(dx)$ of Z as

$$\nu(x) = \frac{1}{\pi^2|x|}\int_0^\infty \frac{\exp\left\{-|x|\sqrt{2y+(\xi/\delta)^2}\right\}}{y(J_1^2(\delta\sqrt{2y}) + Y_1^2(\delta\sqrt{2y}))}dy + \frac{\exp\{-|x|\xi/\delta\}}{|x|}y \tag{1.9}$$

and then

$$\phi_t(u) = \exp\{tK(\tfrac{1}{2}u^2)\}, \quad K(\tfrac{1}{2}u^2) = \int_{-\infty}^\infty (e^{iux} - 1 - iux)\nu(x)dx\,.$$

Now (Watson, 1944, §7.21)

$$\left.\begin{aligned} J_\nu(x) &\sim \sqrt{2/\pi x}\cos\left(x - \frac{1}{2}\pi\nu - \frac{1}{4}\pi\right) \\ Y_\nu(x) &\sim \sqrt{2/\pi x}\sin\left(x - \frac{1}{2}\pi\nu - \frac{1}{4}\pi\right) \end{aligned}\right\} \quad (x \to \infty)$$

So the denominator in the integral in equation (1.9) is asymptotic to a multiple of $y^{\frac{1}{2}}$ as $y \to \infty$. The asymptotics of the integral as $x \downarrow 0$ are determined by that of the integral as $y \to \infty$, and (writing $\sqrt{2y + (\xi/\delta)^2}$ as t, say) this can be read off from the Hardy–Littlewood–Karamata theorem for Laplace transforms (Feller, 1971, XIII.5, Theorem 2, or Bingham *et al.*, 1987, Theorem 1.7.1). We see that $\nu(x) \sim c/x^2$, $(x \downarrow 0)$ for c a constant. In particular the Lévy measure is infinite, as required.

1.2.3 From driving noise to asset returns

Returning to the SDE (1.3), with driving noise a hyperbolic Lévy process Z as above, the solution is given by the stochastic exponential

$$Y(t) = Y(0)\exp\{Z^{\xi,\delta}(t) + \rho t\} \prod_{0<s\leq t} (1 + \Delta Z^{\xi,\delta}(s))e^{-\Delta Z^{\xi,\delta}(s)} \tag{1.10}$$

(here the quadratic variation $[Z]_t$ is just

$$\sum_{s\leq t}(\Delta Z_s)^2$$

with no continuous component, as Z is a pure jump process). Passing to logarithms to pass from prices to returns, one obtains two terms, the hyperbolic term $Z_t + \rho t$ and the sum-of-jumps term. To first order, this is $\sum_{s\leq t}(\Delta Z_s)^2$. Now since the Lévy measure is infinite, small jumps predominate, and these become second order effects when squared, so negligible. Thus to a first approximation, the return process is hyperbolic.

1.2.4 Tails and shape

The classic empirical studies of Bagnold (1941) and Bagnold and Barndorff-Nielsen (1979) reveal the characteristic pattern that, when log-density is plotted against log-size of particle, one obtains a unimodal curve approaching linear asymptotics at $\pm\infty$. Now the simplest such curve is the hyperbola, which contains four parameters: location of the mode, the slopes of the asymptotics, and curvature near the mode (the modal height is absorbed by the density normalisation). This is the empirical basis for the hyperbolic laws in particle-size studies. Following Barndorff-Nielsen's suggested analogy, a similar pattern was sought, and found, in financial data, with log-density plotted against log-price. Studies by Eberlein and co-workers (1995, 1998), Bibby and Sørensen (1997), Rydberg (1997, 1999) and other authors show that hyperbolic densities provide a good fit for a range of financial data, not only in the tails but throughout the distribution. The hyperbolic tails are log-linear: much fatter than normal tails but much thinner than stable ones.

1.2.5 Hyperbolic diffusion model

We pointed out that the weakness of the hyperbolic Lévy process model lies in the independent-increments assumption. This is avoided in the hyperbolic diffusion model of Bibby and Sørensen (1997). They use a stochastic volatility $v(X_s)$, where $dX_t = v(X_t)dW_t$. For $v^2(.)$ log-hyperbolic, this gives rise to an ergodic diffusion, whose invariant distribution is hyperbolic. See Bibby and Sørensen (1997), §2 for the model, §3 for its fit to real financial data and §4 for option pricing.

1.3 EQUIVALENT MARTINGALE MEASURE

As in the other non-normality approaches mentioned above the drawback of the model is that the underlying stochastic model of the financial market becomes incomplete. We thus face the question of choosing an appropriate equivalent martingale measure for pricing purposes. We outline here two approaches to determining an equivalent martingale measure: the risk-neutral Esscher measure and the minimal martingale measure.

1.3.1 General Lévy process-based financial market model

Recall our Lévy process-based model of a financial price process:

$$dY_t = bY_{t-}dt + \sigma Y_{t-}dZ_t \tag{1.3}$$

with $Z = (Z_t)$ a suitable driving Lévy process on a probability space $(\Omega, \mathcal{F}, I\!F, I\!P)$. The characteristic function takes the form

$$I\!E(\exp\{i\theta Z_t\}) = \exp\{-t\psi(\theta)\}$$

with ψ the Lévy exponent of Z. The Lévy–Khintchine formula implies

$$\psi(\theta) = \frac{c^2}{2}\theta^2 + i\alpha\theta + \int_{\{|x|<1\}} (1 - e^{-i\theta x} - i\theta x)\mu(dx) + \int_{\{|x|\geq 1\}} (1 - e^{-i\theta x})\mu(dx)$$

with $\alpha, c \in I\!R$ and μ a σ-finite measure on $I\!R\backslash\{0\}$ satisfying

$$\int \min\{1, x^2\}\mu(dx) < \infty.$$

μ is called the Lévy measure.

From the Lévy–Khintchine formula we deduce the Lévy decomposition of Z, which says that Z must be a linear combination of a standard Brownian motion W and a pure jump process X independent of W (a process is a pure jump process if its quadratic variation is simply $\langle X \rangle = \sum_{0<s\le t}(\Delta X)^2$). We write

$$Z_t = cW_t + X_t . \tag{1.11}$$

Under further assumptions on Z_t we can find a Lévy decomposition of X (for details see Chan, 1999, §2 or Shiryaev, 1999, III §1b and VII §3c). This leads to the decomposition

$$Z_t = cW_t + M_t + at \tag{1.12}$$

where M_t is a martingale with $M_0 = 0$ and $a = IE(X_1)$. We shall assume the existence of such a decomposition (1.12). Then we can restate equation (1.3) as

$$dY_t = (a\sigma + b)Y_{t-}dt + \sigma Y_{t-}(cdW_t + dM_t) \tag{1.13}$$

where the coefficients b and σ are constants (though one can generalize to deterministic functions). Now equation (1.13) has an explicit solution

$$Y_t = Y_0 \exp\left\{\int_0^t c\sigma dW_s + \int_0^t \sigma dMs + \int_0^t \left(a\sigma + b - \frac{\sigma^2 c^2}{2}\right) ds\right\}$$
$$\times \prod_{0<s\le t} (1 + \sigma \Delta M_s) \exp\{-\sigma \Delta M_s\} .$$

In order to ensure that $Y_t \ge 0$ for all t almost surely, we need $\sigma \Delta M_t \ge -1$ for all t. A sufficient condition is that the jumps of X should be suitably bounded from below.

We also introduce the (locally) risk-free bank account (short rate) process B_t with

$$dB_t = r_t B_t dt \tag{1.14}$$

with r_t a suitable process.

1.3.2 Existence of equivalent martingale measures

To characterize equivalent martingale measures $\boldsymbol{Q}$ under which discounted price processes $\tilde{S}_t = S_t / B_t$ are (local) $\mathcal{F}_t$-martingales, we rely on Girsanov's theorem for semi-martingales. (See Jacod and Shiryaev, 1987, III §3d, for a thorough treatment, or Shiryaev, 1999, VII §3g for a textbook summary. Bühlmann *et al.* (1998a) provide a discussion geared towards financial applications.) We follow the exposition in Chan (1999), to which we refer for technical details. Define a process L_t as

$$L_t = 1 + \int_0^t G_s L_{s-} dB_s + \int_0^t \int_{IR} L_{s-}[H(s,x) - 1] M(ds, dx) \tag{1.15}$$

with functions G and H satisfying certain regularity conditions. Then

Theorem 1. *Assume* $\boldsymbol{Q}$ *is absolutely continuous with respect to* $I\!P$ *on* $\mathcal{F}_T$, *and*

$$\left.\frac{d\boldsymbol{Q}}{dI\!P}\right|_{\mathcal{F}_t} = L_t$$

with $I\!E(L_T) = 1$. *Under* $\boldsymbol{Q}$ *the process*

$$\tilde{W}_t = W_t - \int_0^t G_s ds$$

is a standard Brownian motion and the process X *is a quadratic pure jump process with compensator measure given by*

$$\tilde{\nu}(dt, dx) = dt \tilde{\nu}_t(dx)$$

where

$$\tilde{\nu}_t(dx) = H(t,x)\nu(dx)$$

and the previsible part is given by

$$\tilde{a}_t = I\!E_{\boldsymbol{Q}}(X_t) = at + \int_0^t \int x(H(s,x) - 1)\nu(dx)ds.$$

Using Theorem 1 we can write the discounted process $\tilde{S}$ in terms of the $\boldsymbol{Q}$ martingale $\tilde{M}$ and the $\boldsymbol{Q}$ Brownian motion $\tilde{W}$ and read off a necessary and sufficient condition for $\tilde{S}$ to be a $\boldsymbol{Q}$ martingale:

$$c\sigma_t G_t + a\sigma_t + b_t - r_t + \int \sigma_s x(H(s,x) - 1)\nu(dx) = 0. \tag{1.16}$$

Since the martingale condition (1.16) does not specify the functions G and H uniquely, we have an infinite number of equivalent martingale measures, i.e. the market model is incomplete. We hence face the problem of choosing a particular martingale measure for pricing (and hedging) contingent claims.

1.3.3 Choice of an equivalent martingale measure

We briefly discuss two widely used approaches (for an overview see Bingham and Kiesel 1998, Chapter 7).

Minimal martingale measure

Consider the problem of hedging a contingent claim H with maturity T (modelled as a bounded $\mathcal{F}_T$-measurable random variable) in an incomplete financial market model. Under an equivalent martingale measure $\boldsymbol{Q}$ we only can obtain a representation of the form

$$\tilde{H} = H_0 + \int_0^T \xi_t d\tilde{S}_t + L_T$$

where (L_t) is a square-integrable martingale orthogonal to the martingale part of $\tilde{S}$ under $I\!P$. ξ corresponds to a trading strategy which would reduce the remaining risk to the intrinsic component of the contingent claim. Therefore we try to find a martingale measure that allows for such a decomposition and preserves orthogonality. Such a measure is called minimal martingale measure.

Esscher transforms

The idea here is to define equivalent measures via

$$\left.\frac{dI\!P_\theta}{dI\!P}\right|_{\mathcal{F}_t} = \exp\left\{-\int_0^t \theta_s Z_s ds + \int_0^t \psi(\theta_s) ds\right\} \tag{1.17}$$

where $\psi(\theta) = -\log I\!E(\exp(-\theta Z_1))$ is the Lévy exponent of Z given by equation (1.3). One then has to choose θ_s to satisfy the martingale conditions. The use of Esscher transforms as a technical tool has a long history in actuarial sciences. Gerber and Shiu (1995) were the first to introduce it systematically to option pricing. Chan (1999) provides an interpretation of it in terms of entropy – the measure $I\!P$ encapsulates information about market behaviour, then pricing by Esscher transforms amounts to choosing the equivalent martingale measure which is closest to $I\!P$ in terms of information content. Equilibrium-based justifications have been given in Bühlmann *et al.* (1998b) and Gerber and Shiu (1995). Further background information can be found in Chan (1999), Bingham and Kiesel (1998, §7.3) and Shiryaev (1999, VII §3c).

We outline an approach suggested by Rogers (1998) (for a general discussion of optimal consumption/investment problems see Karatzas and Shreve, 1991, and Korn 1997). Consider a financial market defined as in Section 1.3.1 with a discount process $\beta(t) = e^{-\delta t}$, $\delta > 0$ a constant and introduce a representative agent with a utility function U. Suppose that the wealth process of the investor satisfies

$$dX_t = rX_t dt + \pi_t\left(\frac{dY_t}{Y_{t-}} - rdt\right) - C_t dt \tag{1.18}$$

with (π_t) resp. (C_t) the portfolio resp. consumption process of the investor. The return process dY_t/Y_{t-} is given as in equation (1.3) with a suitable driving Lévy process. The investor wishes to maximize

$$I\!E\left(\int_0^\infty \exp\{-\delta t\}U(C_t)dt\right). \tag{1.19}$$

We specialize to a utility function $U(x) = -\gamma^{-1}e^{-\gamma x}$ and solve the investors optimization problem following the standard Hamilton–Jacobi–Bellman approach (see Karatzas and Shreve, 1991, §5.8, or Korn, 1997). This leads to an optimal consumption process C_t^* (and an optimal portfolio process π^*).

Now the equivalent martingale measure is given by

$$e^{-rt}\frac{d\boldsymbol{Q}}{dI\!P}\bigg|_{y_t} = e^{-rt}L_t \propto e^{-\delta t}U'(C_t^*) \tag{1.20}$$

Solving equation (1.20) leads to

$$L_t = \exp\{-\theta^* Z_t + \psi(\theta^*)t\}$$

with an optimal parameter θ^*, which is exactly of the form (1.17).

1.4 CASE STUDY

1.4.1 Fitting the hyperbolic distribution

It is well known that the normal distribution fits stock returns poorly. In this section we compare the normal fit with the fit obtained by using the hyperbolic distribution (similar studies are contained in Eberlein and Keller, 1995, and Rydberg, 1999). As an example we consider daily BMW returns during the period September 1992–July 1996, i.e. a total of 1000 data points. We fit the normal distribution using the standard estimators for mean and variance. To estimate the parameters of the hyperbolic distribution we use a computer program described in Blaesild and Sørensen (1992). Under the assumptions of independence and identical distribution a maximum likelihood analysis is performed. The maximum likelihood estimates of the parameters are

$$\hat{\alpha} = 89.72 \quad \hat{\beta} = 4.7184$$
$$\hat{\delta} = 0.0009 \quad \hat{\mu} = -0.0015$$

Figure 1.2 shows the corresponding empirical density, the normal density and the hyperbolic density.

Figure 1.2 indicates there is more mass around the origin and in the tails than the normal distribution suggests and that fitting returns to a hyperbolic distribution is to be preferred. The same conclusion is made even more clearly

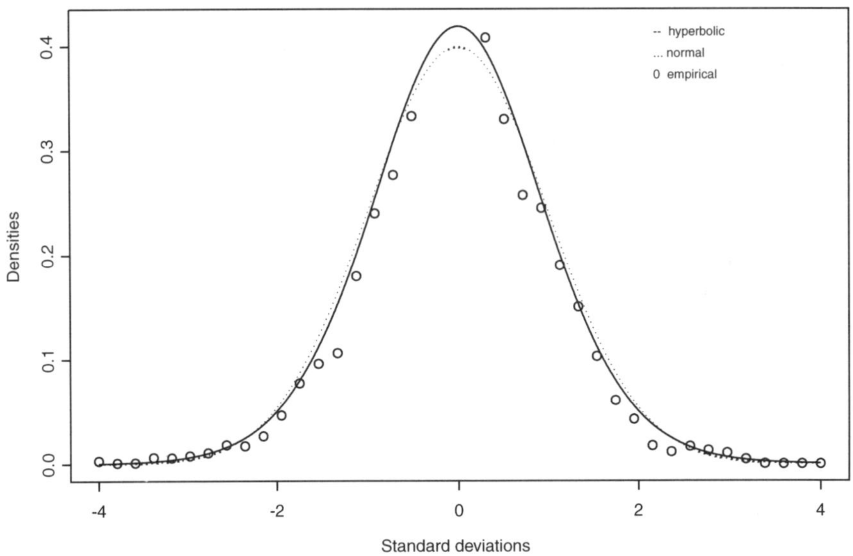

Figure 1.2 Density plots

in the wider range of empirical studies, and the accompanying density plots, given by Eberlein and Keller (1995).

1.4.2 Constructing the hyperbolic Lévy motion

Given the empirical findings in Section 1.4.1 it is natural to concentrate now on the symmetric centred case, i.e. set $\mu = \beta = 0$. This leads to modelling the stock-price process by (10) (i.e. equation (1.3) with driving noise a hyperbolic Lévy process). As mentioned above, the return process so generated is hyperbolic to a first approximation. To generate exactly hyperbolic returns along time intervals of length 1 Eberlein and Keller (1995) suggest writing

$$S(t) = S(0)\exp\{Z^{\xi,\delta}(t)\} \tag{1.21}$$

as a model for stock prices, and we shall work with this model in what follows.

1.4.3 The risk-neutral Esscher measure

To price contingent claims in the hyperbolic Lévy model we use Esscher transforms, which are defined via equation (1.17). Now in our model (1.21) the function $\theta(.)$ in equation (1.17) reduces to a constant. Therefore defining the moment-generating function of $Z^{\xi,\delta}(t)$ as

$$M(\theta, t) = I\!E\left[e^{\theta Z^{\xi,\delta}(t)}\right] \tag{1.22}$$

the Esscher transforms are defined by

$$L(t) = \left\{ e^{\theta Z^{\xi,\delta}(t)} M(\theta, 1)^{-t} \right\}_{t \geq 0} \tag{1.23}$$

(observe that L is a positive martingale). According to equation (1.17) we define equivalent measures via

$$\left.\frac{dIP_\theta}{dIP}\right|_{\mathcal{F}_t} = L(t)$$

and call IP_θ the Esscher measure of parameter θ.

The risk-neutral Esscher measure is the Esscher measure of parameter $\theta = \theta^*$ such that the process

$$\{e^{-rt} S(t)\}_{t \geq 0} \tag{1.24}$$

is a martingale (with r the daily interest rate). From the martingale condition

$$IE[e^{-rt} S(t); \theta^*] = S(0)$$

we find

$$e^r = \frac{M(1+\theta^*, 1)}{M(\theta^*, 1)}$$

from which the parameter θ^* is uniquely determined. Indeed, since the moment-generating function $M^{\xi,\delta}(u, 1)$ is

$$M^{\xi,\delta}(u, 1) = \frac{\xi}{K_1 \xi} \frac{K_1(\sqrt{\xi^2 - \delta^2 u^2})}{\sqrt{\xi^2 - \delta^2 u^2}}, \quad |u| < \frac{\xi}{\delta}$$

we have

$$r = \log \left[\frac{K_1\left(\sqrt{\xi^2 - \delta^2(\theta+1)^2}\right)}{K_1\left(\sqrt{\xi^2 - \delta^2\theta^2}\right)} \right] - \frac{1}{2} \log \left[\frac{\xi^2 - \delta^2(\theta+1)^2}{\xi^2 - \delta^2\theta^2} \right]. \tag{1.25}$$

Given the daily interest rate r and the parameters ξ, δ equation (1.25) can be solved by numerical methods for the martingale parameter θ^*.

1.4.4 Option pricing

A useful tool for option pricing in the hyperbolic model (1.21) (and indeed any model of type $S(t) = S(0)exp\{X(t)\}$ with $X(t)$ a process with independent and stationary increments) is the following (compare Gerber and Shiu, 1995)

Lemma 2 (Factorization formula). *Let g be a measurable function and h, k and t be real numbers, $\theta \geq 0$, then*

$$I\!E\left[S(t)^k g(S(t));\right] = I\!E\left[S(t)^k; h\right] I\!E[g(S(t)); k+h]. \tag{1.26}$$

We now value a European call with maturity T and strike K in the hyperbolic model, that is, we assume that the underlying $S(t)$ has price dynamics given by equation (1.21). By the risk-neutral valuation principle we have to calculate

$$\begin{aligned} I\!E\left[e^{-rT}(S(T)-K)^+;\theta^*\right] &= I\!E\left[e^{-rT}(S(T)-K)\mathbf{1}_{\{S(T)>K\}};\theta^*\right] \\ &= e^{-rT}\left\{I\!E\left[S(T)\mathbf{1}_{\{S(T)>K\}};\theta^*\right] - KI\!E\left[K\mathbf{1}_{\{S(T)>K\}};\theta^*\right]\right\} \end{aligned}$$

To evaluate the first term we apply the factorization formula with $k = 1, h = \theta^*$ and $g(x) = \mathbf{1}_{\{x>K\}}$ and get

$$\begin{aligned} I\!E\left[S(T)\mathbf{1}_{\{S(T)>K\}};\theta^*\right] &= I\!E[S(T);\theta^*]I\!E\left[\mathbf{1}_{\{S(T)>K\}};\theta^*+1\right] \\ &= I\!E\left[e^{-rT}S(T);\theta^*\right]e^{rT}I\!P[S(T)>K;\theta^*+1] \\ &= S(0)e^{rT}I\!P[S(T)>K;\theta^*+1] \end{aligned}$$

where we used the martingale property of $e^{-rt}S(t)$ under the risk-neutral Esscher measure for the last step. Now the pricing formula for the European call becomes

$$S(0)I\!P[S(T)>K;\theta^*+1] - e^{-rT}KI\!P[S(T)>K;\theta^*] \tag{1.27}$$

We now can use formula (1.27) to compute the value of a European call with strike K and maturity T. Denote the density of $\mathcal{L}(Z^{\xi,\delta}(t))$ by $f_t^{\xi,\delta}$ (compare equation (1.5) for the exact form). Then

$$\begin{aligned} E\left[e^{-rT}(S_T-K)^+;\theta^*\right] &= S(0)\int_c^\infty f_T^{\xi,\delta}(x;\theta^*+1)dx \\ &\quad - e^{-rT}K\int_c^\infty f_T^{\xi,\delta}(x;\theta^*)dx \end{aligned} \tag{1.28}$$

where $c = \log(K/S(0))$.

Eberlein and co-authors (1995, 1998) compare option prices obtained from the Black–Scholes model and prices found using the hyperbolic model with market prices. They find that the hyperbolic model provides very accurate prices and a reduction of the smile effect observed in the Black–Scholes model.

1.4.5 Risk management: hedging and Value-at-Risk

We consider hedging first, and focus on computing the standard hedge parameters, i.e. the so-called greeks. It is relatively easy to compute the delta of the European call C using formula (1.28). Now

$$\Delta = \frac{dC}{dS} = \int_c^\infty f_T^{\xi,\delta}(x;\theta^* + 1)dx - f_T^{\xi,\delta}(c;\theta^* + 1) + e^{-rT}\frac{K}{S}f_T^{\xi,\delta}(c;\theta^*)$$

Consider the last two terms. Using subsequently the definition of $f_T^{\xi,\delta}(.;.)$ and θ^* we get

$$\begin{aligned} & -f_T^{\xi,\delta}(c;\theta^* + 1) + e^{-rT}\tfrac{K}{S}f_T^{\xi,\delta}(c;\theta^*) \\ = & -\frac{e^{c(\theta^*+1)}f_T^{\xi,\delta}(c)}{M(\theta^* + 1)^T} + e^{-rT}\frac{K}{S}\frac{e^{c\theta^*}f_T^{\xi,\delta}(c)}{M(\theta^*)^T} \\ = & -\frac{K}{S}\frac{e^{c\theta^*}f_T^{\xi,\delta}(c)}{M(\theta^* + 1)^T} + e^{-rT}\frac{K}{S}\frac{e^{c\theta^*}f_T^{\xi,\delta}(c)}{e^{-rT}M(\theta^* + 1)^T} \\ = & \ 0. \end{aligned}$$

So we end up with the simple expression

$$\Delta = \int_c^\infty f_T^{\xi,\delta}(x;\theta^* + 1)dx$$

Other sensitivity parameters can be computed in a similar fashion; however, as above the evaluation has to be done numerically.

We study aspects of risk-management in terms of Value-at-Risk in a simple linear position in the underlying asset. We compare a normal fit and a full hyperbolic fit with a tail approximation via Extreme-Value theory. In particular, to compute high quantiles we use the Peak-over-Threshold method, which is outlined in Embrechts *et al.* (1997, §6.5). (A detailed study using the POT method has been done by McNeil, 1998.) As may be seen from Table 1.1, the EVT quantiles obtained using Extreme-Value theory are more accurate than either the normal or hyperbolic quantiles. This is to be expected: Extreme-Value methods, being specifically designed for the tails, outperform other methods there. By contrast, the hyperbolic approach is designed to give a reasonable fit throughout, and in particular a better fit overall than the normal.

1.5 CONCLUSION

The hyperbolic model has a good case to be regarded as the model of first choice in any situation where the benchmark normal, or Black–Scholes, model

Table 1.1 Comparison of quantiles

Quantile %	Empirical	Normal	Hyperbolic	EVT
0.1	−0.04743	−0.03670	−0.06257	−0.05388
0.5	−0.03490	−0.03051	−0.04927	−0.04180
1	−0.03004	−0.02751	−0.04138	−0.03655
5	−0.01873	−0.01931	−0.02543	−0.02430
95	0.01863	0.02028	0.02626	0.01863
99	0.03137	0.02848	0.045302	0.03140
99.5	0.03541	0.03148	0.053259	0.03894
99.9	0.06861	0.03767	0.069521	0.06332

is found inadequate. It has a sound theoretical basis, the independent-increments assumption being the one most open to question. Also, in its four- and two-parameter forms, it has a suitable set of readily interpretable parameters. Thanks to the already developed software (Blaesild and Sørensen, 1992), fitting the model empirically to actual data is quick and convenient. It gives a reasonable fit throughout, but is outperformed by methods based on Extreme-Value theory in the tails. (More examples can be found on the website of the Freiburg Center for Data Analysis and Modelling, http://www.fdm.uni-freiburg.de/UK/).

REFERENCES

Bagnold, R.A. (1941), *The Physics of Blown Sand and Desert Dunes*, Matthew, London.

Bagnold, R.A. and Barndorff-Nielsen, O.E. (1979) 'The Pattern of Natural Size Distributions', *Sedimentology*, **27**, 199–207.

Barndorff-Nielsen, O.E. (1977) 'Exponentially Decreasing Distributions for the Logarithm of Particle Size', *Proc. Roy. Soc. London A*, **353**, 401–419.

Barndorff-Nielsen, O.E., Blaesild, P., Jensen, J.L. and Sørensen, M. (1985) 'The fascination of sand', in A.C. Atkinson and S.E. Fienberg (eds), *A Celebration of Statistics*, Springer, New York.

Barndorff-Nielsen, O.E. and Halgreen, O. (1977) 'Infinite Diversibility of the Hyperbolic and Generalized Inverse Gaussian Distributions', *Zeitschrift für Wahrscheinlichkeitstheorie und verwandte Gebiete*, **38**, 309–312.

Bertoin, J. (1996) *Lévy processes*, vol. 121 of *Cambridge Tracts in Mathematics*. Cambridge University Press, Cambridge.

Bibby, B.M. and Sørensen, M. (1997) A Hyperbolic Diffusion Model for Stock Prices, *Finance and Stochastics*, **1**, 25–41.

Bingham, N.H. and Kiesel, R. (1998) *Risk-neutral Valuation*, Springer, London.

Bingham, N.H., Goldie C.M. and Teugels, J.L. (1987) *Regular Variation*, Cambridge University Press, Cambridge.

Blaesild, P. and Sørensen, M. (1992) 'hyp' – A Computer Program for Analyzing Data by Means of the Hyperbolic Distribution, Research Report no. 248, Department of Theoretical Statistics, University of Århus.

Bühlmann, H., Delbaen, F., Embrechts, P. and Shiryaev, A. (1998a) 'No Arbitrage, Change of Measure and Conditional Esscher Transforms', Preprint, ETH Zürich.

Bühlmann, H., Delbaen, F., Embrechts, P. and Shiryaev, A. (1998b) 'On Esscher Transforms in Discrete Financial Models', Preprint, ETH Zürich.

Chan, T. (1999) 'Pricing Contingent Claims on Stocks Driven by Lévy Processes', *Annals Applied Probab.*, **9**, 504–528.

Duan, J.-C. (1995) 'The GARCH Option Pricing Model', *Mathematical Finance*, **5**, 13–32.

Eberlein, E. and Jacod, J. (1997) 'On the Range of Option Prices', *Finance and Stochastics*, **1**, 131–140.

Eberlein, E. and Keller, U. (1995) 'Hyperbolic Distributions in Finance', *Bernoulli*, **1**, 281–299.

Eberlein, E., Keller, U. and Prause, K. (1998) 'New Insights into Smile, Mispricing and Value-at-Risk: The hyperbolic model', *J. Business*, **71**, 371–406.

Eberlein, E. and Raible, S. (1998) 'Term Structure Models Driven by General Lévy Processes', *Mathematical Finance*, **9**, 31–53.

Embrechts, P., Klüppelberg, C. and Mikosch, P. (1997) *Modelling Extremal Events.* Springer, New York.

Feller, W. (1971) *An Introduction to Probability Theory and its Applications, Volume 2*, 2nd edn. Wiley, Chichester.

Frey, R. (1997) 'Derivative Asset Analysis in Models with Level-Dependent and Stochastic Volatility', *CWI Quarterly* (to appear).

Gerber, H.U. and Shiu, E.S. (1995) 'Actuarial Approach to Option Pricing', Preprint, Istitut de Sciences Actuarielles, Université de Lausanne.

Ghysels, E., Harvey, A. and Renault, E. (1996) 'Stochastic Volatility', in G.S. Maddala, and C.R. Rao (eds), *Handbook of Statistics, Vol. 14, Statistical Methods in Finance*, North Holland, Amsterdam.

Good, I.J. (1953) 'The Population Frequency of Species and the Estimation of Population Parameters', *Biometrika*, 237–240.

Grosswald, E. (1976) 'The Student *t*-distribution Function of any Degree of Freedom is Infinitely Divisible', *Zeitschrift für Wahrscheinlichkeitstheorie und verwandte Gebiete*, **36**, 103–109.

Hobson, D.G. (1998) 'Stochastic Volatility', in D.J. Hand and S.D. Jacka (eds), *Statistics in Finance*, Arnold, London.

Hull, J. and White, A. (1987) 'The Pricing of Options on Assets with Stochastic Volatilities', *Journal of Finance*, **XLII**, 281–300.

Jacod, J. and Shiryaev, A.N. (1987) *Limit Theorems for Stochastic Processes* vol. 288 of *Grundlehren der mathematischen Wissenschaften*, Springer, New York.

Jørgensen, B. (1982) *Statistical Properties of the Generalized Inverse Gaussian Distribution Function*, vol. 9 of *Lecture Notes in Statistics*, Springer, Berlin.

Karatzas, I. and Shreve, S. (1991) *Brownian Motion and Stochastic Calculus*, 2nd edn, Springer, New York.

Keilson, J. and Steutel, F.W. (1974) 'Mixtures of Distributions, Moment Inequalities and Measures of Exponentiality and Normality', *Annals of Probability*, **2**, 112–130.

Kelker, D. (1971) 'Infinite Divisibility and Variance Mixtures of the Normal Distribution', *Annals of Mathematical Statistics*, **42**, 802–808.

Korn, R. (1997) *Optimal Portfolios*, World Scientific, New York.

Küchler, U., Neumann, K., Sørensen, M. and Streller, A. (1994) 'Stock Returns and Hyperbolic Distributions', Discussion paper 23, Sonderforschungsbereich 373, Humboldt-Universität zu Berlin.

Mandelbrot, B.B. (1997) *Fractals and Scaling in Finance. Discontinuity, concentration, risk, Selected works of Benoit B. Mandelbrot*, Springer, New York.

McNeil, A. (1998) 'Calculating Quantile Risk Measures for Financial Return Series Using Extreme Value Theory', Preprint, ETH Zürich.

Pagan, A.R. (1996) 'The Econometrics of Financial Markets', *J. Empirical Finance*, **3**, 15–102.

Peskir, G. and Shorish, J. (1999) 'Market Forces and Dynamic Asset Pricing', Working Paper No. 39, Centre for Analytical Finance, University of Århus.

Rogers, L.C.G. (1997) 'Stochastic Calculus and Markov Methods', in M.A.H. Dempster, and S.R. Pliska (eds), *Mathematics of Derivative Securities*, Cambridge University Press, Cambridge.

Rogers, L.C.G. (1998) 'Utility Based Justification of the Esscher Measure', Private communication.

Rydberg, T.H. (1996) 'Generalized Hyperbolic Diffusions with Applications Towards Finance', Research Report 342, Department of Theoretical Statistics, Institute of Mathematics, University of Århus.

Rydberg, T.H. (1997) 'The Normal Inverse Gaussian Lévy Process: Simulation and Approximation', Research Report, Department of Theoretical Statistics, Institute of Mathematics, University of Århus.

Rydberg, T.H. (1999) 'Generalized Hyperbolic Diffusions Processes with Applications in Finance', *Mathematical Finance*, **9**, 183–201.

Shiryaev, A.N. (1999) *Essentials of Stochastic Finance*, vol. 3 of *Advanced Series of Statistical Science & Applied Probability*, World Scientific, New York.

Watson, G.N. (1944) *A Treatise on the Theory of Bessel Functions*, 2nd edn, Cambridge University Press, Cambridge (1st edn 1922).

Widder, (1941) *The Laplace Transform*. Princeton University Press, Princeton, NJ.

Chapter 2

A review of asymmetric conditional density functions in autoregressive conditional heteroscedasticity models

SHAUN A. BOND

ABSTRACT

This chapter provides a review of the use of asymmetric density functions in models of Autoregressive Conditional Heteroscedasticity. Recent findings on the presence of skewness in financial returns are reviewed, and four parametric approaches to capturing skewness in the conditional density function are evaluated. Using data on small company returns in the UK, the skewed t model proposed by Hansen (1994) is found to perform well. The chapter ends with a discussion on the merit of attempting to capture skewness in financial returns.

2.1 INTRODUCTION

Are the returns of financial assets skewed? Such a question is not easily answered and indeed, it is likely that the answer will be highly dependent on the specific asset or class of assets examined. However, it is clear that it is a question that is worthwhile asking, as skewness in the returns process may have implications for asset pricing (Harvey and Siddique, 2000), portfolio construction (Kraus and Litzenberger, 1976; Markowitz, 1991) and risk management. In order to investigate this issue, one could begin by approaching the problem from a theoretical viewpoint, and examine economic models which may generate skewed outcomes under particular assumptions about, for example, elements of market microstructure or particular forms of institutional restrictions/incentives faced by rational agents (see, for instance, Aggarwal and Rao, 1990 or Blazenko, 1996). Alternatively the question could be tackled in a purely empirical way by, for example, calculating a sample skewness measure from market returns and assessing its significance. The latter, statistical based, approach has been applied much more frequently than the former in addressing the question of skewness in asset returns, although little consensus about the original question emerges from this body of literature (such as Simkowitz and Beedles, 1980; Badrinath and Chatterjee, 1988; Bekaert *et al.*, 1998; Peiró, 1999).

The statistical approach will be the focus of this chapter, though not so much as an attempt to prove or disprove whether returns are skewed, but more so to provide a review of dynamic models which allow for asymmetry in the conditional distribution of a stochastic process. Hence, the issue that is really under review is not whether returns exhibit skewness, but if there is skewness in returns what would be an appropriate model to capture that feature of the data. Naturally any review or comparison of models will be limited in scope and this chapter is no exception to that. The coverage of the models in this chapter is restricted to only considering discrete time generalized autoregressive conditional heteroscedasticity (GARCH) processes with asymmetric conditional distributions captured by known parametric forms. Hence, there is no discussion of asymmetry in stochastic volatility models. This is partly justified on the basis that GARCH models are still widely employed by both academics and practitioners in financial markets and also that the estimation technology required for asymmetric GARCH models is less demanding than a similarly specified stochastic volatility model. In addition, as the attention of this chapter is primarily on the distributions themselves, it may be expected that the density functions favoured by GARCH processes may also be the preferred ones if the comparison had been conducted assuming a different specification of the stochastic process (though such a claim may well need to be subjected to further research).

To date, the literature on conditional skewness in asset returns has received only modest attention in comparison to the number of papers focused on tests of skewness in the unconditional distribution of returns. This lack of attention is gradually changing and with the extensive volume of work devoted to conditional heteroscedasticity models, it is only natural that some authors have questioned the initial (possibly restrictive) assumption of conditional normality used by Engle (1982) and sought to extend the GARCH class of models to consider departures from normality.[1] Indeed some of the models

[1]Including conditional skewness though more commonly research has concentrated on models which capture the excess kurtosis normally found in asset returns.

discussed here are also able to capture time variation in conditional skewness, and as such are a valuable addition to the econometrician's toolkit. However, in this chapter, those models which permit time variation in the third moment are only considered in a form which displays constant (that is, time invariant) conditional skewness.[2] A further restriction on the selection of the models under review is that nonparametric or semi-nonparametric models, such as those of Engle and González-Rivera (1991) or Gallant *et al.* (1991) are not included, because of the emphasis in this chapter on parametric density functions. For those readers particularly interested in this aspect of volatility model, Pagan and Schwert (1990) provide some comparative results.

The ordering of this chapter is as follows. The next section provides a brief introduction to the previous literature on empirical aspects of skewness in financial returns. Following this the ARCH class of models are introduced before presenting the parametric density functions which are to be evaluated. The models are applied to data on small capitalization companies in the United Kingdom in Section 2.4. Section 2.5 provides an assessment of the contribution of conditional skewed models and Section 2.6 concludes the review.

2.2 THE LITERATURE ON SKEWNESS

Despite being a routinely made assumption, the returns on financial assets are generally not well described by the normal distribution. Early research found that extreme returns occur much more frequently than would be expected if the data-generating process was normal (for instance, Mandelbrot, 1963, Fama, 1965 or Kon, 1984 are commonly cited references). Another feature often observed in empirical studies of financial markets is that negative (or positive) returns may occur more than returns of the opposite sign, that is, the returns' distribution is skewed. For example, Simkowitz and Beedles (1980), using updated data from the study of Fama (1965), find extensive evidence that the returns of individual securities are positively skewed. This finding held whether the individual stocks chosen were from the Dow Jones Index or across a broader (random) selection of other US stocks. Interestingly, Fama had noted 'slight' evidence of positive skewness in his earlier study but chose to proceed with the assumption of symmetry.

Kon (1984), in a later study, also found positive skewness in the individual returns of the stocks that make up the Dow Jones Index and proposed a discrete mixture of normal distributions as a suitable framework for capturing the skewness. Singleton and Wingender (1986) also find evidence of skewness

[2] For a comparison of models displaying time-varying skewness see Bond (1999).

in individual stocks. However, in considering whether these findings of skewness were useful for the development of investment strategies, they find little evidence to suggest that the skewness in returns persists, limiting the applicability of the earlier findings. This is even more noticeable at a portfolio level, where skewness was found to be diversified away to a large extent in a portfolio of five stocks[3] and there was even less evidence to suggest that skewness could persist in a portfolio. Evidence for the presence of skewness in an index of security returns is provided by Badrinath and Chatterjee (1988). They also find that the evidence for skewness is not sensitive to temporal aggregation, so that similar skewness measures are found in both daily and monthly index returns. Alles and Kling (1994) show that skewness is present in both equity and bond returns. Their study covers three market indices (NYSE, AMEX and NASDAQ) and an assortment of bond indices (including Treasury, Mortgage and Government Agency Bonds). It is also found that skewness varies with size (small capitalization indices display more negative skewness than large capitalization indices) and across the business cycle, with relatively larger negative skewness found in times of favourable economic conditions and smaller negative (and sometimes positive) skewness evident in less favourable times.

Equity markets outside of the USA have also provided evidence for the presence of skewness in returns. Aggarwal *et al.* (1989) find that the proportion of shares on the Toyko stock exchange which exhibit skewness is higher than that found in US studies. They also find stronger evidence that skewness persists across time for individual stocks and small portfolios. Though, as would be expected, the skewness found in portfolios declines rapidly as portfolio size is increased. Theodossiou (1998) also notes that skewness is found across a range of stock exchanges, foreign exchange rates and commodities. In addition, recent research has indicated that the returns of emerging market securities (equities and bonds) display a high degree of skewness (Bekaert *et al.*, 1998 for equities and Erb *et al.*, 1999 in relation to Bonds). Bekaert *et al.* (1998) examine how fundamental variables may affect skewness and find that there is a negative correlation between skewness and GDP growth and country risk rating, and that is positively related to inflation, book-to-price and beta (where beta is measured against the MSCI world index). It should be noted that not all studies find evidence of skewness in international equity returns. A recent example of this is Peiró (1999), who finds that using 'distribution-free' statistical procedures provides little evidence of skewness in nine developed countries (covering the USA, Japan and Europe).

---

[3]The evidence of diversification of skewness is based on the work of Simkowitz and Beedles (1978).

The above survey suggests that, while differences of opinion exist, further investigation into modelling skewness in financial returns is warranted. In particular, as many of those studies listed have considered asymmetry in the unconditional distribution of returns, it is interesting to consider the evidence when a conditioning information set is included in the analysis. The next section introduces the GARCH class of models, which form the basis of the approach used in this paper.

2.3 DYNAMIC VOLATILITY MODELS

The Autoregressive Conditional Heteroscedasticity (ARCH) model of Engle (1982) was originally suggested as a method of capturing the time-dependent volatility observed in the rate of inflation. However the applicability of the ARCH model was soon found to be wider than the original application of inflation modelling and following the seminal work of Engle and then Bollerslev (1986), ARCH and generalized ARCH (GARCH) models have been applied extensively in empirical modelling in finance. The literature on ARCH models is vast and a number of good survey articles exist which provide a comprehensive summary of this field (see, for instance, Bollerslev, Chou and Kroner, 1992; Bera and Higgins, 1993; Bollerslev, Engle and Nelson, 1994; Diebold and Lopez, 1995; Palm 1996; Shephard, 1996). Given that ARCH models have now been discussed in the literature for almost two decades and such a large number of surveys have been written on this subject, only a brief introduction to the GARCH models used in this chapter will be given here.

The GARCH model of Bollerslev (1986) generalized the original autoregressive conditional heteroscedasticity (ARCH) model of Engle (1982). For a time series variable x_t, the model is expressed as

$$x_t = \sigma_t z_t \tag{2.1}$$

where

$$\sigma_t^2 = \alpha_0 + \alpha_1 x_{t-1}^2 + \beta_1 \sigma_{t-1}^2 \tag{2.2}$$

and $z_t \sim NID(0, 1)$, for $\alpha_0, \alpha_1 \geq 0$ and $t = 1, ..., T$.

The above model implies that $x_t|\Omega_{t-1} \sim N(0, \sigma_t^2)$, where the information set which exists at time t is given by Ω_{t-1}, although other (non-normal) forms of the conditional distribution have also been used (see, for instance, Nelson, 1991) and some of these are reviewed in the following section. The ARCH model has found a particularly strong following in financial econometrics as the structure of the model allows for x_t to be leptokurtotic and also captures 'volatility clustering', which are both features of financial data. The model can also be estimated by maximum likelihood techniques, which further adds to its appeal.

The above paragraphs presented the GARCH model in its simplest form, (called a pure GARCH process). Clearly there are a number of alternative choices for specifying the model. For example, a conditional mean equation could be added to capture a non-zero (conditional) mean or dynamic effects in the process. For example,

$$x_t = a_1 + b_1 x_{t-1} + \varepsilon_t \tag{2.3}$$

$$\sigma_t^2 = \alpha_0 + \alpha_1 \varepsilon_{t-1}^2 + \beta_1 \sigma_{t-1}^2, \tag{2.4}$$

which is sometimes referred to as the AR(1)-GARCH(1,1) model. Asymmetric effects in the innovation term can also be captured. Glosten, Jagannathan and Runkle (1993) have proposed the form

$$\sigma_t^2 = \alpha_0 + \alpha_1 \varepsilon_{t-1}^2 + \alpha_2 \varepsilon_{t-1}^2 I_{t-1} + \beta_1 \sigma_{t-1}^2 \tag{2.5}$$

where I_{t-1} is an indicator variable, such that

$$I_t = 1 \qquad \mathit{for}\ \varepsilon_t > 0 \tag{2.6}$$

$$= 0 \qquad \mathit{for}\ \varepsilon_t \leq 0. \tag{2.7}$$

This form of the model is consistent with the 'leverage effect' literature, first proposed by Black (1976), which is often found in empirical studies of equity returns. Zakoian (1994) has also proposed a similar model with threshold effects. The EGARCH model of Nelson (1991) is another model which captures the asymmetric linkage between the innovation term and the conditional variance, through a different mechanism than that listed above. Nelson's model has the form

$$\log \sigma_t^2 = \alpha_0 + \alpha_1(\phi z_{t-1} + \gamma[|z_{t-1}| - E|z_{t-1}|]) + \beta_1 \log \sigma_{t-1}^2 \tag{2.8}$$

which has the advantage that there are no restrictions to ensure non-negativity.

As stated above, the ARCH model originally proposed by Engle assumed that the conditional density of the stochastic process x_t was normally distributed. Many authors following Engle have allowed for conditional distributions other than the normal to be used. The most common of these alternative distributions are the Student's t-distribution (Bollerslev, 1987) and the generalized error density (Nelson, 1991). The use of asymmetric density functions in ARCH models has been more limited. Early attempts to capture asymmetry include Hsieh (1989) and Gallant, Hsieh and Tauchen (1991).

Engle and González-Rivera (1991) also found evidence of asymmetry in their semi-non-parametric model of individual stock returns and foreign exchange rates. Parametric density forms have also been used as a method for capturing skewness in the conditional distribution of returns. Four forms of skewed density functions have been selected for evaluation in this chapter. The four distributions: the skewed t of Hansen (1994); the non-central t of Harvey and Siddique (1999); the Gram–Charlier expansion proposed by Lee and Tse (1991);[4] and the recently proposed double gamma model of Bond (2000a) which was developed from earlier work by Knight, Satchell and Tran (1995).

2.3.1 Skewed t-distribution – Hansen's model

Hansen (1994) proposed the Autoregressive Conditional Density (ACD) estimator, as a means of incorporating not only leptokurtic behaviour in the conditional distribution, but also skewness. In fact, his model provides for skewness as well as variance to be indexed by time, although the presentation of the skewed t model is only considered in a time invariant form in this chapter. The model uses the Student's t-distribution as a starting point, which has the form:

$$f(z_t|\Omega_{t-1}, \eta) = \frac{\Gamma\left(\frac{\eta+1}{2}\right)}{\sqrt{\pi(\eta-2)}\Gamma\left(\frac{\eta}{2}\right)}\left(1+\frac{z_t^2}{(\eta-2)}\right)^{-\left(\frac{\eta+1}{2}\right)} \tag{2.9}$$

with $2 < \eta < \infty$. Furthermore, this distribution can be adapted to allow for skewness and excess kurtosis by re-writing the above distribution as:

$$f(z_t|\Omega_{t-1}, \eta, \lambda) = bc\left(1+\frac{1}{\eta-2}\left(\frac{bz_t+a}{1-\lambda}\right)^2\right)^{-\frac{(\eta+1)}{2}} \qquad z_t < -\frac{a}{b} \tag{2.10}$$

$$= bc\left(1+\frac{1}{\eta-2}\left(\frac{bz_t+a}{1+\lambda}\right)^2\right)^{-\frac{(\eta+1)}{2}} \qquad z_t \geq -\frac{a}{b} \tag{2.11}$$

where

$$a = 4\lambda c\left(\frac{\eta-2}{\eta-1}\right) \tag{2.12}$$

$$b^2 = 1 + 3\lambda^2 - a^2 \tag{2.13}$$

$$c = \frac{\Gamma\left(\frac{\eta+1}{2}\right)}{\sqrt{\pi(\eta-2)}\Gamma\left(\frac{\eta}{2}\right)} \tag{2.14}$$

[4]It is noted that the Gram–Charlier expansion is not strictly defined as a density function but rather an approximate density. However, it is included in this review because it provides a simple way of capturing skewness (and excess kurtosis) in financial returns.

and $-1 < \lambda < 1$, where λ is a parameter to control for the skewness of the distribution. It can be readily verified that if $\lambda = 0$, the distribution will collapse to the standardized *t*-distribution with η degrees of freedom.

2.3.2 Non-central *t*-distribution – Harvey and Siddique's model

Harvey and Siddique's (1999) non-central *t*-distribution is another model designed to investigate conditional skewness in asset returns. It is claimed by Harvey and Siddique that Hansen's model is an alternative parameterization of the non-central *t*-distribution. Nonetheless, it is worth presenting both models to highlight the different parameterizations available. While two different parameterizations of a density should produce the same outcome, there may be practical differences, such as sensitivity to initial values or speed of estimation. As in the previous instance, the model will only be presented with the skewness parameter in a time-invariant form. In this instance the η and δ parameters can be estimated directly, but, in the time-varying skewness form the parameters are obtained from solving a non-linear equation system linking the parameters with the first and third conditional moments. The density function has the form:

$$f(z_t|\Omega_{t-1},\eta,\delta) = \frac{\eta^{\eta/2}}{\Gamma(\eta/2)}\frac{\exp\left(\frac{-\delta^2}{2}\right)}{\sqrt{\pi}\left(\eta+z_t^2\right)^{(\eta+1)/2}} \tag{2.15}$$

$$\times\sum_{i=0}^{\infty}\Gamma\left(\frac{\eta+i+1}{2}\right)\left(\frac{\delta^i}{i!}\right)\left(\frac{\sqrt{2}z_t}{\sqrt{\eta+z_t^2}}\right)^i \tag{2.16}$$

where η is the degrees of freedom parameter and δ is a parameter which controls the shape of the distribution.

2.3.3 Gram–Charlier expansion

Another interesting implementation of a skewed conditional distribution in the ARCH literature is by Lee and Tse (1991). (See also Knight and Satchell in this volume.) These authors use a three-term Gram–Charlier Type A[5] series to model the conditional volatility of interest rates in the Singapore dollar market. For the standardized innovations z_t, the conditional distribution can be approximated by

$$f\left(z_t|\Omega_{t-1},\delta_3,\delta_4\right) = \phi(z_t)\left(1+\frac{\delta_3}{6}H_3(z_t)+\frac{\delta_4}{24}H_4(z_t)\right) \tag{2.17}$$

[5]See Stuart and Ord (1994) or Johnson, Kotz and Balakrishnan (1994) for a more detailed presentation of this expansion.

where $\phi(.)$ is the standard normal density function. $H_3(.)$ and $H_4(.)$ are Hermite polynomials defined by

$$H_3(z_t) = z_t^3 - 3z_t \tag{2.18}$$

$$H_4(z_t) = z_t^4 - 6z_t^2 + 3 \tag{2.19}$$

and δ_3,δ_4 are the standardized measures of skewness and excess kurtosis, respectively.

2.3.4 Double-gamma distribution

The double-gamma distribution was proposed by Knight, Satchell and Tran (1995) as a method of capturing asymmetry in the distribution of financial returns. The model was later used in a conditional volatility framework by Bond (2000a), in an application to the measurement of downside risk in exchange rate data. The double-gamma distribution has the advantage that it provides a convenient decomposition of the distribution into positive and negative components. Furthermore, it can be shown that an estimate of the semi-variance (a measure of downside risk) can be easily calculated from the parameters of the distribution. The double-gamma conditional density is represented by

$$\begin{aligned} f(z_t|\Omega_t, \alpha_1, \alpha_2, \lambda_1, \lambda_2, p) &= p\frac{\lambda_1^{\alpha_1}}{\Gamma(\alpha_1)} z_t^{(\alpha_1 - 1)} \exp(-\lambda_1 z_t) \qquad \mathit{for} \quad z_t > 0 \\ &= (1-p)\frac{\lambda_2^{\alpha_2}}{\Gamma(\alpha_2)}(-z_t)^{(\alpha_2-1)} \exp(-\lambda_2(-z_t)) \\ &\mathit{for} \quad z_t \leq 0 \end{aligned} \tag{2.20}$$

where

$$\Pr(z_t > 0) = p$$

Moment restrictions are typically placed on λ_1 and λ_2 during estimation to ensure that the density function has zero mean and a variance of one.

2.4 EMPIRICAL EVIDENCE

As discussed in Section 2.2, many studies have previously found evidence of skewness in the returns of stock market indices. This finding is particularly evident in the returns of small capitalization companies (Alles and Kling, 1994; Chelley-Steeley and Steeley, 1995). The empirical section of this chapter applies the four models listed above, along with two symmetric GARCH

Table 2.1 Statistical summary of dataset

FTSE Small Capitalization Companies	
Mean	0.0498
Variance	0.1967
Semi-variance	0.1184
Skewness	−2.3937
p-value	[0.00]
Kurtosis	23.2014
p-value	[0.00]
Minimum	−4.5649
Maximum	2.5498

models (using the normal and Student's *t*-distributions), to evaluate the most suitable framework for capturing asymmetry in the conditional density (if it is present). The data series chosen is the FTSE Small Capitalization Index.[6] Five years of daily observations from 18 January 1995 to 17 January 2000 are used in the analysis, providing a total of 1262 observations. Only the capital gains element of the index is used, no attempt is made to allow for the inclusion of dividends in the returns calculation or the calculation of the excess return over a risk-free rate of interest. This may seem like a limitation at first, but, Nelson (1991) has noted that only modelling capital gains appears to have little impact on the results of the model.

Summary statistics for the data are presented in Table 2.1. Using the approximation that the sample skewness coefficient is approximately normally distributed, such that

$$\widehat{sk} = \frac{m_3}{m_2^{3/2}} = \frac{\sum_{t=1}^{T}(r_t - \bar{r})^3/T}{\left(\sum_{t=1}^{T}(r_t - \bar{r})^2/T\right)^{3/2}} \tag{2.21}$$

where

$$\sqrt{T}\left(\widehat{sk} - sk\right) \xrightarrow{d} N(0,6) \tag{2.22}$$

the series appears to exhibit negative skewness. Peiró (1999) warns that an interpretation of the significant skewness coefficient may simply be that normality rather than skewness is being rejected (as the data also display excess kurtosis). However, using the Monte Carlo critical values for the sample

[6]The FTSE Small Capitalization Index consists of the UK Companies within the FTSE All Share Index which are not large enough to be constituients of the FTSE350 (FTSE International, 2000).

Table 2.2 LM ARCH and F-test (squared residuals from ARMA(1,2))

Lag length	4
LM	356.22
p-value	[0.00]
F-test	124.01
p-value	[0.00]

skewness coefficient generated by Peiró,[7] a rejection of symmetry also occurs.[8] A further issue in tests of the sample skewness measure is dependency in the dataset. As autocorrelation appears present in the series (discussed below), a more rigorous evaluation of the sample skewness coefficient would allow for the dependency.

Table 2.2 examines whether the data exhibit time-varying conditional heteroscedasticity. In this case the data reject the hypothesis of homoscedasticity and the process is modelled using the GARCH framework discussed in Section 2.3 above. Model-selection criteria suggest that the mean of the series is well captured by a ARMA(1,2) process, which was favoured by the Akaike and Schwarz criteria marginally above an AR(3) specification. This finding of autocorrelation in the returns of an index of small capitalization stocks is not surprising. Fisher (1966) was one of the first researchers to conclude the non-synchronous trading in illiquid small company securities may result in the appearance of autocorrelation in an index as the price of illiquid securities will respond more gradually to the arrival of news. Chelley-Steeley and Steeley (1995) have also observed the presence of autocorrelation in an equally weighted portfolio of small capitalization UK shares. The specification of the volatility dynamics was not as straightforward. Initial indications supported a GARCH(3,3) model, however estimation difficulties were encountered for some of the models using this specification. Finally it was decided to adopt the simpler GARCH(1,1) specification for all the models.

Asymmetry of the volatility process to innovations in returns (or news) is captured by using the specification of Glosten, Jagannathan and Runkle (1991). In each case, the volatility associated with negative innovations is much larger than that attributed to positive innovations. The significance of this leverage term has been noted in many studies examining equity returns. Also included in the model (in both the conditional mean and conditional variance equations) are day-of-week variables and a dummy variable to

[7]The critical value are developed for a random variable following a Student's t-distribution to allow for the excess kurtosis displayed by financial data.

[8]The 5% critical value of the sample skewness statistic for 1000 observations of a random variable distributed according to the Student's t-distribution with four degrees of freedom is 1.89.

Table 2.3 ARMA(1,2)-GARCH(1,1) parameters: normal distribution

Parameter	Estimate	Std error	t-ratio	p-value
a_0	0.0206	0.0094	2.196	0.0141
a_1	0.8614	0.0446	19.293	0.0000
b_1	−0.3381	0.0619	−5.460	0.0000
b_2	−0.1493	0.0592	−2.523	0.0058
Dum_mon	−0.0710	0.0249	−2.856	0.0021
Dum_tue	−0.0293	0.0230	−1.274	0.1014
ω	0.0109	0.0043	2.536	0.0056
Dum_hol	0.0548	0.0409	1.341	0.0899
α	0.5104	0.1465	3.483	0.0002
α^*	−0.3491	0.1407	−2.481	0.0066
β	0.6029	0.0774	7.791	0.0000
LL	−220.5903			

indicate when the market has reopened after a bank holiday. The day-of-week dummy variable is added to the model as there has been an extensive literature which finds that returns appear to vary systematically according to the day of week. Hsieh (1989) has also noted that volatility also appears to vary systematically according to the day, and further, that volatility is higher after the market reopens following a public holiday. To allow for this second effect a dummy variable, which takes the value of one when the market reopens after a bank holiday, is also included.

Estimation results for each model are displayed in Tables 2.3 to 2.8. The symmetric models using the normal distribution and the Student's t-distribution are presented first. Table 2.3 contains the parameter estimates

Table 2.4 ARMA(1,2)-GARCH(1,1) parameters: Student's t-distribution

Parameter	Estimate	Std error	t-ratio	p-value
a_0	0.0322	0.0060	5.351	0.0000
a_1	0.8334	0.0398	20.927	0.0000
b_1	−0.3974	0.0515	−7.714	0.0000
b_2	−0.1013	0.0420	−2.412	0.0079
Dum_mon	−0.0725	0.0169	−4.301	0.0000
Dum_tue	−0.0203	0.0158	−1.285	0.0994
ω	0.0082	0.0032	2.561	0.0052
Dum_hol	0.0375	0.0255	1.473	0.0704
α	0.4266	0.1138	3.749	0.0001
α^*	−0.1935	0.1082	−1.788	0.0369
β	0.6568	0.0672	9.773	0.0000
η	3.4713	0.3748	9.263	0.0000
LL	−104.8280			

Table 2.5 ARMA(1,2)-GARCH(1,1) parameters: Hansen's skewed *t*-distribution

Parameter	Estimate	Std error	*t*-ratio	*p*-value
a_0	0.0191	0.0055	3.486	0.0002
a_1	0.8839	0.0285	30.967	0.0000
b_1	−0.4773	0.0474	−10.074	0.0000
b_2	−0.1371	0.0344	−3.986	0.0000
Dum_mon	−0.0717	0.0160	−4.482	0.0000
Dum_tue	−0.0229	0.0168	−1.367	0.0858
ω	0.0079	0.0030	2.616	0.0044
Dum_hol	0.0452	0.0293	1.546	0.0611
α	0.4286	0.1065	4.024	0.0000
α^*	−0.1382	0.1092	−1.265	0.1029
β	0.6600	0.0623	10.592	0.0000
η	3.5427	0.3895	9.096	0.0000
δ	−0.2739	0.0378	−7.253	0.0000
LL	−79.0004			

from the ARMA(1,2)-GARCH(1,1) model with conditional normal density. An immediate issue that arises, as discussed by Engle and González-Rivera (1991) is that the quasi-maximum likelihood estimator (QMLE) may be inefficient when the conditional density function is skewed. However, more recently Newey and Steigerwald (1997) have suggested the addition of a location parameter to the conditional mean equation to make the QMLE estimators robust to skewness in the conditional density function. In the case of the normal distribution model, the additional parameter suggested by

Table 2.6 ARMA(1,2)-GARCH(1,1) parameters: Harvey and Siddique's skewed *t*-distribution

Parameter	Estimate	Std error	*t*-ratio	*p*-value
a_0	0.0364	0.0084	4.333	0.0000
a_1	0.8331	0.0399	20.870	0.0000
b_1	−0.3979	0.0512	−7.771	0.0000
b_2	−0.1022	0.0421	−2.427	0.0076
Dum_mon	−0.0722	0.0169	−4.285	0.0000
Dum_tue	−0.0201	0.0158	−1.268	0.1024
ω	0.0036	0.0014	2.584	0.0049
Dum_hol	0.0161	0.0107	1.510	0.0655
α	0.1797	0.0447	4.021	0.0000
α^*	−0.0741	0.0440	−1.682	0.0463
β	0.6459	0.0690	9.367	0.0000
η	3.4694	0.3709	9.355	0.0000
δ	−0.0504	0.0650	−0.776	0.2189
LL	−104.6491			

Table 2.7 ARMA(1,2)-GARCH(1,1) parameters: Gram–Charlier expansion

Parameter	Estimate	Std error	t-ratio	p-value
a_0	0.0127	0.0094	1.350	0.0885
a_1	0.8680	0.0316	27.440	0.0000
b_1	−0.4288	0.0550	−7.798	0.0000
b_2	−0.1370	0.0435	−3.145	0.0008
Dum_mon	−0.0582	0.0196	−2.968	0.0015
Dum_tue	−0.0187	0.0195	−0.954	0.1699
ω	0.0119	0.0062	1.920	0.0274
Dum_hol	0.0599	0.0310	1.933	0.0266
α	0.5289	0.1713	3.088	0.0010
α^*	−0.2433	0.1797	−1.354	0.0879
β	0.5747	0.0819	7.020	0.0000
μ_3	−0.6953	0.1516	−4.586	0.0000
μ_4	1.8334	0.2399	7.642	0.0000
LL	−128.3286			

Newey and Steigerwald is found to not be significant at a 5% critical value (estimation results not reported). When the parameter is included in the Student's t-model, it is found to be significant [parameter = 0.0344, p-value = 0.00].

The parameter estimates for the conditional mean equation are broadly similar between the normal and Student's t-models. The average return on Mondays is found to be 0.07% below the days later in the week, and there is also a slightly lower return on Tuesdays, though this is not significantly

Table 2.8 ARMA(1,2)-GARCH(1,1) parameters: double-gamma distribution

Parameter	Estimate	Std error	t-ratio	p-value
a_0	0.0273	0.0001	216.346	0.0000
a_1	0.8365	0.0019	451.096	0.0000
b_1	−0.4041	0.0027	−149.864	0.0000
b_2	−0.1279	0.0011	−112.374	0.0000
Dum_mon	−0.0786	0.0005	−152.623	0.0000
Dum_tue	−0.0380	0.0002	−155.255	0.0000
ω	0.0074	0.0026	2.785	0.0027
Dum_hol	0.0422	0.0254	1.664	0.0480
α	0.3764	0.0816	4.611	0.0000
α^*	−0.1296	0.0714	−1.817	0.0346
β	0.6392	0.0644	9.930	0.0000
α_1	1.5302	0.0707	21.629	0.0000
p	0.5607	0.0101	55.578	0.0000
LL	−76.0509			

different from zero for either model (it is retained for comparison with later models). There is some indication that volatility is higher after the market reopens following a bank holiday. However, there is no evidence that the expected return is any different when the market reopens and the term is dropped from the conditional mean equation. The leverage effect term is significant in both models, with the impact on volatility associated with positive news shocks being around half the level of a correspondingly sized negative shock. The stationarity conditions for the volatility process are more difficult to assess due to the inclusion of the leverage effect term. In common with many other studies using daily equity data, the volatility process appears to be highly persistent. While the sum of the α and β parameters is greater than one, this does not necessarily imply that the volatility process is explosive, because of the threshold structure of the equation (for example, Tong, 1990 has shown that when the model has a threshold form, the overall system may be stable even though an element of the subsystem is individually unstable). This remains an area for further evaluation.

Of the two symmetric density function, the Student's t model has a far higher likelihood function than the normal model, suggesting that the general preference for the Student's t-distribution over the normal distribution in the econometrics literature is not misplaced. One final issue to note with the GARCH-t model is that the η parameter (which represents the degrees of freedom of the distribution) indicates that the fourth moment of the conditional density function may not exist.

Table 2.5 contains the estimation results for the skewed t density of Hansen (1994). The parameters estimates are generally of comparable magnitude to the symmetric t model. An important exception to this is the significance of the skewness parameter δ. When δ is equal to zero, Hansen's model collapses to the standard t distribution. As the skewness parameter is significant, it suggests the importance of capturing this feature of the data. This is borne out by the higher log-likelihood value of -79.00 for Hansen's model, compared to -128.33 for the GARCH-t model (suggesting a significant rejection of the hypothesis that $\delta = 0$ using a likelihood ratio test).

Another version of a non-central t-distribution was proposed by Harvey and Siddique (1999). The parameter estimates for this model are displayed in Table 2.6. A number of features of the estimations results are apparent on inspection of the table. First, the magnitude of the parameters in the conditional variance equation are generally lower than all the other models. For example, the value of α is 0.1797, which is well outside of the range of 0.4–0.5 found in the other tables. A second feature is that the skewness parameter is not significantly difference from zero based on a t-test. This conflicts with the results of significant skewness found using the skewed t model of Hansen and the expectation that as the distributions are essentially similar, the resulting output should also be the same. However, such differences may be due to sensitivity to initial starting values.

A significant (negative) skewness parameter is found when the Gram–Charlier expansion is used as a conditional density function (results in Table 2.7). The Gram–Charlier expansion is equivalent to the normal distribution when μ_3 and μ_4 equal zero. This joint restriction is convincingly rejected by a likelihood ratio test. The estimated parameters μ_3 and μ_4 are consistent with the requirements for the Gram–Charlier expansion to be non-negative (see Draper and Tierney, 1972). Unlike the models listed above, maximum likelihood estimation of the Gram–Charlier model is quite sensitive to initial parameter estimates. When the estimation of the model took place it was found necessary to search over a wide set of initial parameters before selecting the model with the highest likelihood value. It is noted that the likelihood value is less than that of the skewed t and non-central t models.

Estimation of the double-gamma model also proved troublesome. Initial attempts to freely estimate all parameters proved futile. Kanno (1982) notes the sensitivity of maximum likelihood estimation of a double-gamma model to the starting values. However, even after covering a wide range of possible initial values the model estimates did not converge. Knight *et al.* (1995) also encounter problems in estimating the double-gamma distribution and used a grid search procedure over a range of values for one of the parameters to find a parameter set which maximizes the likelihood. A similar approach is used in this chapter. In the course of the initial attempts to estimate the model, it was noticed that α_2 was particularly slow to converge. A sequential grid search procedure was used to search over a range of values of α_2 at intervals of 0.1. When the value of α_2 which produced the highest likelihood was identified, a more local search over intervals of 0.01 was conducted. After finding the maximum, the procedure was once again repeated over intervals of 0.001. The resulting value of $\alpha_2 = 1.030$ was found to have the highest likelihood value. Clearly this procedure may not produce the model with the highest likelihood function if the likelihood surface is not well behaved. However, for the purposes of this chapter is it sufficient to illustrate the use of the double-gamma model in capturing asymmetry. It is particularly unfortunate that it was necessary to search over the parameter α_2, as this parameter controls the shape of the downside part of the distribution. The information on the downside shape of the distribution is important in providing information about the level of downside risk of a financial series (as discussed in Bond, 2000a, or Knight *et al.*, 1995), which may then be used in either portfolio management or risk management applications. Grid-search procedures were also attempted over the parameters α_1 and p. However, convergence problems

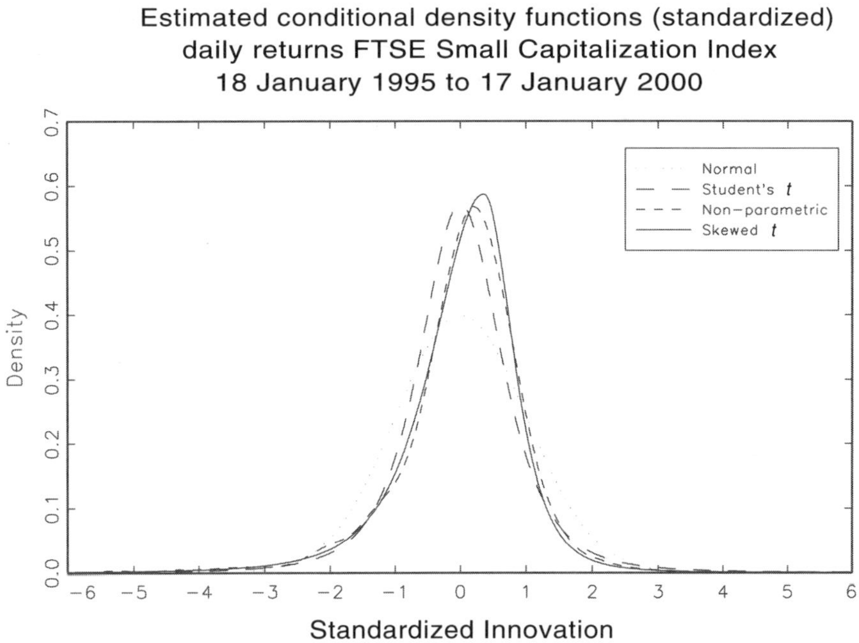

Figure 2.1 Hansen's skewed *t*

were still encountered. The model estimates obtained from the grid-search procedure are consistent with the results obtained for the other models, which provides some reassurance that the grid-search procedure has produced a plausible set of parameter estimates. However, the standard errors for the conditional mean equation appear downward biased, although this does not appear to have occurred in the conditional variance equation. Despite the difficulties involved in estimating the model, the double-gamma model produces one of the highest likelihood values of all the models used in this chapter (along with the skewed *t* model).

Graphs of the estimated (standardized) conditional density functions are presented in Figures 2.1–2.4. Each graph contains one of the four estimated density functions along with the two symmetric densities and a plot of the non-parametric density estimate.[9]

While no attempt has been made to provide a battery of statistical tests to assess the fit of each density function,[10] a comparison of likelihood functions

[9]Using a Gaussian kernel applied to the residuals of the skewed *t* model (see Silverman, 1986 for details)

[10]For example, the recent work of Diebold, Gunther and Tay (1998) may provide a framework for further research.

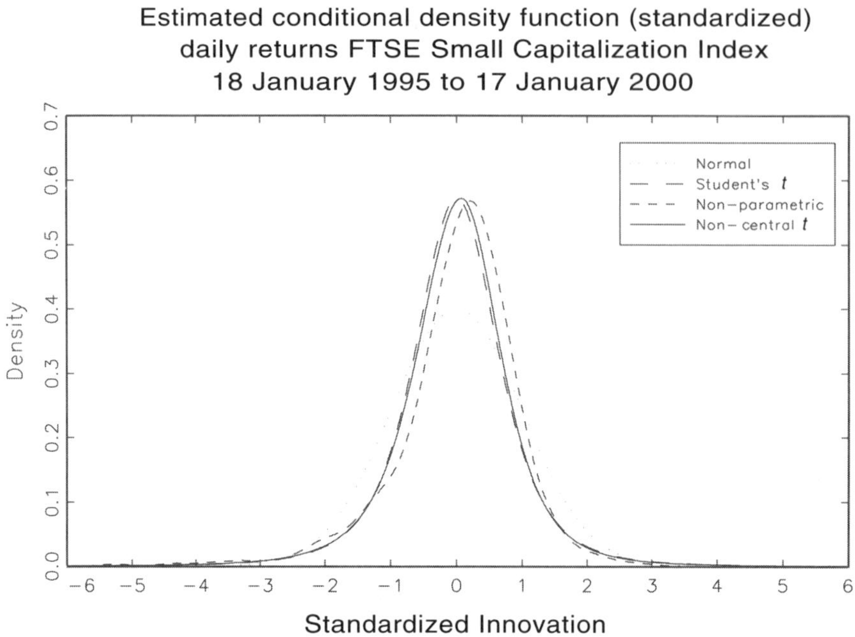

Figure 2.2 Harvey and Siddique's non-central *t*

and statistical tests on individual skewness parameters clearly show that the advantages of using density functions which incorporate skewness for modelling this dataset. Skewness has been found in many other studies of small company returns and this research provides further evidence for its existence. The implications of this finding and a discussion of the general issue of modelling skewness in financial data are contained in the next section.

2.5 THE ROLE OF DISTRIBUTIONS

The purpose of this section is to consider the wider role and also implications of using asymmetric density functions in financial econometric work. Of particular interest is the issue of whether explicitly modelling the skewness of the conditional density provides information which is useful in financial applications. That is, apart from the usual desire to obtain the most accurate statistical model, is there any benefit in employing the more complex statistical procedures necessary to capture skewness?

From the empirical application above, models which allow for skewness in the conditional density appear to provide a better fit of the data than symmetric models. While further statistical tests may be desirable before confidently asserting a superior fit, there is certainly little doubt that the

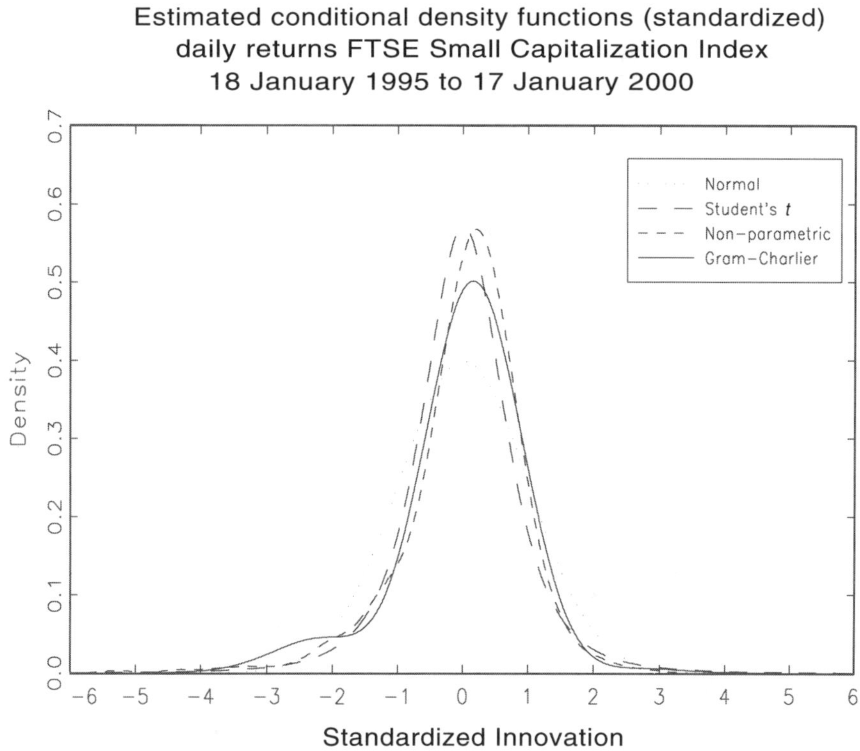

Figure 2.3 Gram–Charlier expansion

models which allowed for asymmetry produced a higher value of the likelihood function. Furthermore, when the asymmetric distributions are nested within symmetric ones (e.g. Gram–Charlier and normal distribution, GARCH-*t* and Hansen), a likelihood ratio test reveals the hypothesis of symmetry is rejected.[11]

In terms of the actual cost of estimating the skewed models, this is generally low.[12] The skewed *t* model of Hansen took only 1.6 minutes to estimate on a Pentium III 450MHz PC, only marginally longer than the symmetric *t* model (1.4 minutes). Harvey and Siddique's non-central *t* contains a slightly more complex parameterization of the conditional density, which results in an

[11]As a further check on the extent of asymmetry in the data, an individual dummy variable was introduced into the conditional mean equation for the five largest and smallest returns in the dataset. Hansen's model was re-estimated on this trimmed dataset, as a means of determining whether an appearance of skewness was induced by a few abnormally large observations. When the model was re-estimated the estimate of the skewness parameter was still significantly negative (parameter: −0.2918, standard error: 0.0381).

[12]All models were estimated using the Maxlik estimation package with GAUSS (Aptech, 1996).

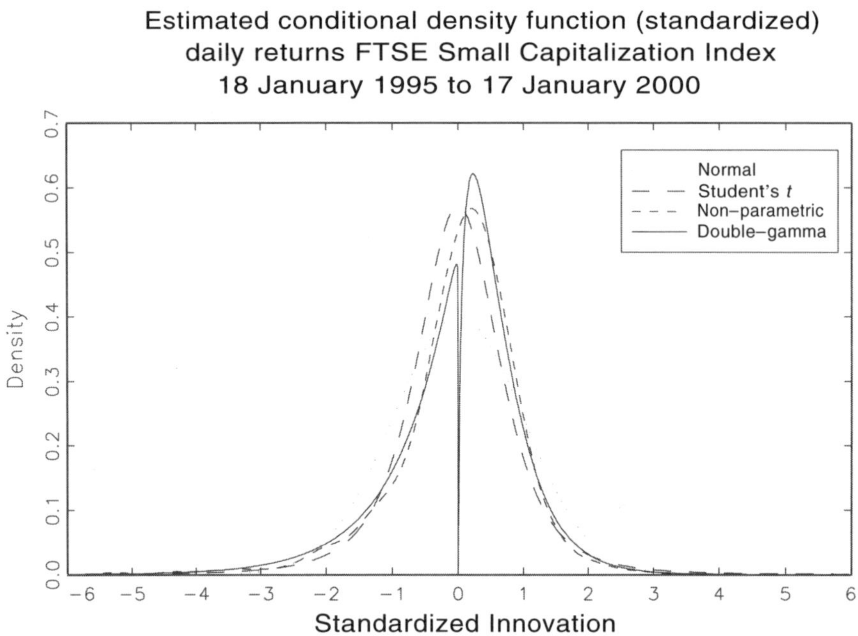

Figure 2.4 Double gamma

estimation time of 3.6 minutes. The remaining two asymmetric models are much slower to estimate. The estimation time for the Gram–Charlier model is 9.7 minutes. Because of the complex search routines needed for the maximization of the likelihood function for the double-gamma model, an accurate estimate of the time taken for this model is not available. Needless to say, the time component necessary here is significantly longer than all other models and is non-trivial (in excess of three hours). Hence, to allow explicitly for skewness in the density function, the actual costs involved are generally not large or excessive because of the low cost of computing resources (especially if the parameterization of the density function is chosen with care). Of course, if the skewness parameter is not of direct interest, and the conditional volatility is the main centre of interest, a quasi-MLE approach could be taken in estimation using the adaptation suggested by Newey and Steigerwald (1997). However, as Engle and González-Rivera (1991) found the price paid in efficiency terms may be high if the distribution is skewed.

So far the only criterion for the evaluation of explicitly modelling skewness has been a purely statistical one. Recent literature on the evaluation of econometric models has emphasized the importance of economic considerations in model selection, particularly when the true variable of interest is unobserved, making the usual 'fitted versus actual' comparisons more difficult (as in the case of conditional volatility or skewness). Such papers include Satchell and Timmermann (1995) and Pesaran and Timmermann (1995, 2000) for conditional mean prediction in a trading context, or West, Edison and Cho (1993) or Ang and Bekaert (1999) for a portfolio selection using a utility-based framework. Therefore, in evaluating the usefulness of explicitly allowing for skewness in asset returns, some form of portfolio or trading example may be useful. While no attempt is made to assess the economic value of the models described in this paper, some observations based on previous research may be made. Singleton and Wingender (1986) was an early attempt to consider the information contained in conditional skewness measures. They found that the lack of persistence in skewness hindered any chance of successfully constructing portfolios to take advantage of *ex-post* skewness found in returns, and conclude that '...portfolio strategies based on selecting skewed stocks are likely to fail'. Bekaert *et al.* (1998) is another example of an attempt to derive a trading strategy based on a conditional measure of skewness in financial markets. Consistent with the work of Singleton and Wingender, their results are mixed, with some evidence to suggest that the *ex-post* returns from selecting either a high or low skewness portfolio (based on *ex-ante* estimates of skewness) are essentially similar. In preliminary research, Bond (2000b) uses models incorporating time-varying conditional skewness to calculate a measure of downside risk and then from this calculate portfolio weights for an investor who displays loss aversion. It is found that the loss-averse investor derives higher expected utility for using some models incorporating conditional skewness. This suggests that while most results to date have found little in the way of economic value from modelling skewness, there may be some class of agents, particularly sensitive to asymmetric risks, for whom such an approach is of value.

2.6 CONCLUSION

This chapter has attempted to provide a review of the use of a small selection of asymmetric conditional density functions in models of conditional heteroscedasticity. The motivation for this is to provide an empirical comparison of alternative parametric assumptions about the conditional density in light of continued empirical evidence of skewness in financial asset returns. The chapter began by outlining possible approaches which may be taken to examining the issue of skewness in asset returns. It was decided to focus primarily on the empirical side of the debate although it was noted that theoretical arguments have been put forward as possible reasons why skewness may be present in financial returns. The literature on past empirical studies of skewness in asset prices was reviewed. Several studies confirmed the finding of skewness and this is common across both international markets and asset class. However, this is not an uncontested belief with evidence presented which criticizes the previous methodology employed along with evidence of symmetry in some major equity markets.

Four asymmetric forms of conditional density functions were compared in an application using data on small company returns in the United Kingdom. This dataset was selected as previous research had noted skewness appeared present in the returns of small capitalisation stocks. The four density functions, the skewed t of Hansen (1994), the non-central t of Harvey and Siddique (1999), the Gram–Charlier model of Lee and Tse (1991) and a model based on the double-gamma density function were applied in the context of the GARCH class of models. Initial attempts to allow for a richer set of volatility dynamics were not successful and an ARMA(2,1)-GARCH(1,1) was chosen as the preferred specification for the conditional mean and variance equations. Two symmetric density models (based on the normal and Student's t-distributions) were also estimated for comparison. The skewed t and the double-gamma density were found to provide the highest value of the likelihood function with the symmetric models appearing the least successful in fitting the data. A likelihood ratio test comparing the symmetric and skewed versions of the Student's t density function, convincingly rejected the hypothesis that the data was symmetric. In terms of recommendations for use in empirical applications, the skewed t model of Harvey is the most appealing as it provides a simple parametric form (which results is faster estimation times) and was found to perform well in capturing the skewness in the dataset.[13] However, this study only considered the constant conditional skewness forms of the models and the same findings may not hold if a time-varying skewness comparison were undertaken. While the double-gamma model performed well in terms of fitting the data, it proved particularly troublesome to estimate with this dataset, and so could not be recommended above the model of Hansen.[14]

Finally an examination of the benefits of explicitly modelling skewness was undertaken. While the dataset and models used in this study were not fully evaluated from this point of view, enough evidence exists in the literature to draw some conclusions from previous results to supplement the findings of this study. First, it was found that for some forms of the skewed distributions (notable the skewed t and non-central t), including a skewed parametric density function in the models, had little cost in terms of complexity or

[13]However, one problem which may cause difficulties in a forecasting environment is that the skewness parameter used in the density is not the same as the third moment of the distribution.
[14]It is noted, however, that the double-gamma model is an appealing model in terms of developing estimates of downside risk.

estimation time. A statistical improvement was noticed in models which allow for skewness over symmetric models. However, doubt is cast on the economic value of modelling skewness with previous studies finding little is gained, from an investment perspective, from the information on skewness obtained from the data. An exception to this is recent work which looks at a utility-based comparison of models of time-varying skewness used in the portfolio selection problem of a loss-averse agent. However, these results are preliminary and further research is required to identify fully (if at all) the benefits of explicitly incorporating skewness into dynamic models.[15]

ACKNOWLEDGEMENTS

The author would like to thank Steve Satchell for helpful comments.

REFERENCES

Aggarwal, R. and Rao, R.P. (1990) 'Institutional Ownership and Distribution of Equity Returns', *Financial Research*, **25**, 211–229.

Aggarwal, R., Rao, R.P. and Hiraki, T. (1989) 'Skewness and Kurtosis in Japanese Equity Returns: Empirical Evidence', *Journal of Financial Research*, **12**, Fall, 253–260.

Alles, L.A. and Kling, J.L. (1994) 'Regularities in the Variation of Skewness in Asset Returns', *Journal of Financial Research*, **17**, 427–438.

Ang, A. and Bekaert, G. (1999) 'International Asset Correlations with Time-Varying Correlations', NBER Working Paper, 7056.

Aptech Systems, Inc. (1996) *GAUSS: Mathematical and Statistical System.*

Badrinath, S.G. and Chatterjee, S. (1988) 'On Measuring Skewness and Elongation in Common Stock Return Distributions: The Case of the Market Index', *Journal of Business*, **61**, 451–472.

Bekaert, G., Erb, C.B., Harvey, C.R. and Viskanta, T.E. (1998) 'Distributional Characteristics of Emerging Market Returns and Asset Allocation', *Journal of Portfolio Management*, **24**, Winter, 102–116.

Bera, A.K. and Higgins, M.L. (1993) 'ARCH Models: Properties, Estimation and Testing', *Journal of Economic Surveys*, **7**, 305–366.

Black, F. (1976) 'Studies in Stock Volatility Changes', *Proceedings of the 1976 Meeting of the Business and Economics Statistics Section, American Statistical Association*, pp. 177–181.

Blazenko, G.W. (1996) 'Corporate Leverage and the Distribution of Equity Returns', *Journal of Business Finance and Accounting*, **23**, 1097–1120.

[15]Utility-based evaluation requires non-quadratic utility. There is no empirical consensus as to what are the appropriate parameters to use in a mean-semivariance or cubic utility function and any conclusions drawn from such an analysis will be sensitive to the parameters chosen.

Bollerslev, T. (1986) 'Generalized Autoregressive Conditional Heteroskedasticity', *Journal of Econometrics*, **31**, 307–327.

Bollerslev, T. (1986) 'A Conditionally Heteroskedastic Time Series Model for Speculative Prices and Rates of Return', *The Review of Economics and Statistics*, **69**, 542–547.

Bollerslev, T., Chou, R.Y. and Kroner, K.F. (1992) 'ARCH Modelling in Finance: A Review of the Theory and Empirical Evidence', *Journal of Econometrics*, **52**, 5–59.

Bollerslev, T., Engle, R.F. and Nelson, D.B. (1994) 'ARCH Models', in Engle, R.F. and McFadden, D.L. (eds), *Handbook of Econometrics*, Volume IV, Elsevier Science, Amsterdam, pp. 2959–3038.

Bond, S.A. (1999) 'Time Varying Skewness and Downside Risk Measurement: A Comparison of Models', paper presented to the Royal Economic Society Annual Conference, March–April 1999, University of Nottingham, Nottingham.

Bond, S.A. (2000a) 'Asymmetry and Downside Risk in Foreign Exchange Markets', mimeo, Department of Land Economy, University of Cambridge, Cambridge, UK.

Bond, S.A. (2000b) 'A Utility Based Comparison of Dynamic Semi-variance Models', mimeo, Department of Land Economy, University of Cambridge, Cambridge, UK.

Chelley-Steeley, P.L. and Steeley, J.M. (1995) 'Conditional Volatility and Firm Size: An Empirical Analysis of UK Equity Portfolios', *Applied Financial Economics*, **5**, 433–40.

Diebold, F.X., Gunther, T.A. and Tay, A.S. (1998) 'Evaluating Density Forecasts with Applications to Financial Risk Management', *International Economic Review*, **39**, 863–883.

Diebold, F.X. and Lopez, J.A. (1995) 'Modeling Volatility Dynamics', in K.D. Hoover, (ed.), *Macroeconometrics: Developments, Tensions, and Prospects*, Kluwer Academic Publishers, Boston.

Draper, N.R. and Tierney, D.E. (1972) 'Regions of Positive and Unimodal Series Expansion of the Edgeworth and Gram-Charlier Approximations', *Biometrika*, **59**, 2, 463–465.

Erb, C.V., Harvey, C.R. and Viskanta, T.E. (1999) 'New Perspectives on Emerging Market Bonds', *Journal of Portfolio Management*, **25**, Winter, 83–92.

FTSE International (2000) *Ground Rules for the Management of the UK Series of the FTSE Actuaries Share Indices*, mimeo, FTSE International, London.

Engle, R.F. (1982) 'Autoregressive Conditional Heteroscedasticity with Estimates of the Variance of United Kingdom Inflation', *Econometrica*, **50**, 987–1007.

Engle, R.F. and González-Rivera, G. (1991) 'Semiparametric ARCH Models', *Journal of Business and Economic Statistics*, **9**, 345–359.

Fama, E. (1965) 'The Behavior of Stock Prices', *Journal of Business*, **47**, 244–280.

Fisher, L (1966) 'Some New Stock Market Indexes', *Journal of Business*, **39** (suppl), 191–225.

Gallant, A.R., Hsieh, D.A. and Tauchen, G.E. (1991) 'On Fitting a Recalcitrant Series: The Pound Dollar Exchange Rate, 1974–1983', in W.A. Barnett, J. Powell and G. Tauchen (eds), *Nonparametric and Semiparametric Methods in Econometrics and Statistics*, Cambridge University Press, Cambridge.

Glosten, L.R., Jagannathan, R. and Runkle, D.E. (1993) 'On the Relation between the Expected Value and the Volatility of the Nominal Excess Return on Stocks', *The Journal of Finance*, **68**, 1779–1801.

Hansen, B.E. (1994) 'Autoregressive Conditional Density Estimation', *International Economic Review*, **35**, 705–730.

Harvey, C.R. and Siddique, A. (1999) 'Autoregressive Conditional Skewness', *Journal of Financial and Quantitative Analysis*, **34**, 465–487.

Harvey, C.R. and Siddique, A. (2000) 'Conditional Skewness in Asset Pricing Tests', *Journal of Finance* (forthcoming).

Hsieh, D.A. (1989) 'Modelling Heteroscedasticity in Daily Foreign-Exchange Rates', *Journal of Business and Economic Statistics*, **7**, 307–317.

Johnson, N.L., Kotz, S. and Balakrishnan, N. (1994) *Continuous Univariate Distributions, Volume 1*, 2nd edn, John Wiley, New York.

Kanno, R. (1982) 'Maximum Likelihood Estimation of Parameters for a Mixture of Two Gamma Distributions', *Reports of Statistical Application Research, Union of Japanese Scientists and Engineers*, **29**, 14–24.

Knight, J.L. and Satchell, S.E. (this volume) 'Pricing Derivatives Written on Assets with Arbitrary Skewness and Kurtosis'

Knight, J.L., Satchell, S.E. and Tran, K.C. (1995) 'Statistical Modelling of Asymmetric Risk in Asset Returns', *Applied Mathematical Finance*, **2**, 155–172.

Kon, S.J. (1984) 'Models of Stock Returns – A Comparison', *Journal of Finance*, **39**, 147–165.

Kraus, A. and Litzenberger, R.H. (1976) 'Skewness Preference and the Valuation of Risk Assets', *Journal of Finance*, **31**, 1085–1100.

Lee, Y.K. and Tse, T.K.Y. (1991) 'Term Structure of Interest Rates in the Singapore Asian Dollar Market', *Journal of Applied Econometrics*, **6**, 143–152.

Mandelbrot, B. (1963) 'The Variation of Certain Speculative Prices', *Journal of Business*, **36**, 394–419.

Markowitz, H.M. (1991) *Portfolio Selection: Efficient Diversification of Investments*, 2nd edn, Basil Blackwell, Oxford.

Nelson, D.B. (1991) 'Conditional Heteroskedasticity in Asset Returns: A New Approach', *Econometrica*, **59**, 347–370.

Newey, W.K., and Steigerwald, D.S. (1997) 'Asymptotic Bias for Quasi-Maximum Likelihood Estimators in Conditional Heteroskedasticity Models', *Econometrica*, **3**, 587–599.

Pagan, A.R. and Schwert, G.W. (1990) 'Alternative Models of Conditional Stock Volatility', *Journal of Econometrics*, **45**, 267–290.

Palm, F.C (1996) 'GARCH Models of Volatility', in Maddala, G.S. and Rao, C.R, (eds), *Statistical Methods of Finance. Handbook of Statistics*, vol. 14, Elsevier/North-Holland, Amsterdam, pp. 209–40.

Peiró, A. (1999) 'Skewness in Financial Returns', *Journal of Banking and Finance*, **23**, 847–862.

Pesaran, M.H. and Timmermann, A. (1995) 'Predictability of Stock Returns: Robustness and Economic Significance', *Journal of Finance*, **50**, 1201–28.

Pesaran, M.H. and Timmermann, A. (2000) 'A Recursive Modelling Approach to Predicting UK Stock Returns', *Economic Journal*, **110**, 159–191.

Satchell, S.E. and Timmermann, A. (1995) 'An Assessment of the Economic Value of Non-Linear Foreign Exchange Rate Forecasts', *Journal of Forecasting*, **14**, 477–497.

Shepard, N. (1996) 'Statistical Aspects of ARCH and Stochastic Volatility', in Cox, D.R.,. Hinkley, D.V. and Barndorff-Nielsen, O.E. (eds), *Time Series Models in Econometrics, Finance and Other Fields*, Monographs on Statistics and Applied Probability, 65, Chapman and Hall, London.

Silverman, B.W. (1986) *Density Estimation for Statistics and Data Analysis*, Chapman Hall, New York.

Simkowitz, M.A. and Beedles, W.L. (1980) 'Asymmetric Stable Distributed Security Returns', *Journal of the American Statistical Association*, **75**, 306–312.

Singleton, J.C., and Wingender, J. (1986) 'Skewness Persistence in Common Stock Returns', *Journal of Financial and Quantitative Analysis*, **21**, 335–341.

Stuart, A. and Ord, J.K. (1994) *Kendall's Advanced Theory of Statistics*, Vol 1, *Distribution Theory*, Edward Arnold, London.

Theodossiou, P. (1998) 'Financial Data and the Skewed Generalised *t* Distribution', *Management Science*, **44**, 1650–1661.

Tong, H. (1990) *Nonlinear Time Series: A Dynamical Systems Approach*, Oxford University Press, Oxford.

West, K.D., Edison, H.J., and Cho, D. (1993) 'A Utility-Based Comparison of Some Models of Exchange Rate Volatility', *Journal of International Economics*, **35**, 23–45.

Zakoian, J-M. (1994) 'Threshold Heteroskedastic Models', *Journal of Economic Dynamics and Control*, **18**, 931–955.

Chapter 3

The distribution of commercial real estate returns

COLIN LIZIERI AND CHARLES WARD

ABSTRACT

This chapter reviews the literature on the distribution of commercial real estate returns. There is growing evidence that the assumption of normality in returns is not safe. Distributions are found to be peaked, fat-tailed and, tentatively, skewed. There is some evidence of compound distributions and non-linearity. Public traded real estate assets (such as property company or REIT shares) behave in a fashion more similar to other common stocks. However, as in equity markets, it would be unwise to assume normality uncritically. Empirical evidence for UK real estate markets is obtained by applying distribution fitting routines to IPD Monthly Index data for the aggregate index and selected sub-sectors. It is clear that normality is rejected in most cases. It is often argued that observed differences in real estate returns are a measurement issue resulting from appraiser behaviour. However, desmoothing the series does not assist in modelling returns. A large proportion of returns are close to zero. This would be characteristic of a thinly-traded market where new information arrives infrequently. Analysis of quarterly data suggests that, over longer trading periods, return distributions may conform more closely to those found in other asset markets. These results have implications for the formulation and implementation of a multi-asset portfolio allocation strategy.

3.1 INTRODUCTION

In this chapter, we consider the distribution of returns in the commercial real estate market. By commercial real estate, we mean land and buildings owned by one party (an institutional investor, a specialist property company or private individual) and let to another party. Such real estate includes office, retail and industrial properties let to firms and apartments and homes let to private individuals, this last category being conspicuously absent from UK institutional investment portfolios. We, thus, distinguish commercial real estate from private residential markets, from owner-occupied corporate real estate and from loans secured on property (such as mortgage-backed securities). We focus largely on the UK and US markets, reflecting both available data and existing research. Initially we discuss definitional issues and measurement problems. We then review the published literature on return distributions and return-generating processes. Next, empirical evidence from the UK market is presented. Finally, we consider the implications of the findings for mixed-asset portfolio strategies.

3.2 DEFINITIONAL AND MEASUREMENT ISSUES

Within the real estate literature, research usually distinguishes between the private and public real estate markets. The private (or direct) market consists of buildings owned and managed by investors or their agents. Transactions are typically by private treaty, although lower quality ('secondary') property may be sold by auction. The public (or indirect) market consists of the securities of firms specializing in the management or trading of property: property companies in the UK, real estate investment trusts (REITs) and real estate operating companies (REOCs) in the USA. There are also some corporate or institutional vehicles that combine characteristics of both markets – property unit trusts and commingled real estate funds for example. The characteristics of each market are considered further below.

The commercial real estate market forms a small but significant part of institutional and private investors' portfolios. Despite this, real estate has been a comparatively neglected topic in the financial economics literature. There are a number of reasons for this lacuna. First, commercial real estate has characteristics that distinguish it from other asset markets. Properties, because of their locational fixity and size differentiation, rarely have near-perfect substitutes. Thus, the market is characterized by heterogeneity. This has implications for portfolio construction, particularly in the direct market where problems are exacerbated by large lot size and high transaction costs. Further, in the private market, the absence of a transparent marketplace leads to asymmetric information and the absence of transaction-based data. Reported returns are frequently based on appraisals of value rather than sales information. This has important implications for the modelling of returns distributions, as we shall see.

The distinct institutional structure of the real estate market has led to the development and preservation of analytic techniques and terminology which differ from those found in other asset markets. This is particularly true in the UK, where the Royal Institution of Chartered Surveyors holds a quasi-monopolistic position over professional advice (and education) in the real estate field. The RICS lays down a set of definitions and practice notes that professional members must follow if they are to avoid potential professional negligence claims. These enshrine certain practices and techniques, a process reinforced by court and tribunal decisions and precedents.

The estimation of returns in the private real estate market is much more complex than in bond and equity markets. The basic components are, of course, income return and capital growth. Each presents particular problems in calculation.

The income return comes from the rent paid by the tenant. The return must account for the timing of payments (typically quarterly in advance in the UK, monthly in the USA) and for the cost of rent collection. The latter is problematic and there is no common standard for calculation of net operating income. Direct costs (maintenance, repairs and insurance not chargeable to the tenant, professional fees, marketing charges, for example) are clear, but the indirect costs of managing the property may be obscured. This is particularly true for properties held and managed by an institution or property company with an in-house management function.

The estimation of the capital gain component of return is particularly difficult in real estate. Long holding periods and infrequent transactions mean that the capital value is an estimate provided in-house or by an external appraiser or valuer. There is insufficient space to discuss all the appraisal issues relating to property (for a review, see Ball *et al.*, 1998). Because the transaction market is so thin, the valuer has to resort to a formalized version of what is, essentially, a dividend discount model of valuation. He or she must consider the current and future income stream, the security of that income (that is, the probability of the tenant defaulting or vacating and the probability of securing a new letting), the investment demand for the property (which will include consensus estimates both of future market rental growth and of the covenant strength of the tenant), the legal terms of the agreement between landlord and tenant and any specific risk factors relating to the building. These risk factors, typically, are incorporated into a single 'initial yield' or capitalization rate. Asset heterogeneity and thin transaction markets means that the appraisal utilizes a very limited current information set.

Two consequences of this process are important. First, the appraisal process creates uncertainty as to the true value, and hence about both components of the return. There have been a number of studies concerning valuation and appraisal accuracy.[1] These are not conclusive but cast doubt on validity of conclusions drawn from appraisal-based data. That said, it is the appraisal-based returns that are used to measure fund performance and fund manager added value. Thus there is a case for using unadjusted returns. Second, because appraisers are faced with a limited information set, it is suggested that they use evidence over a time window around (but generally preceding) the notional date of the valuation and that they adjust prior valuations in the light of new evidence by an intuitive process of Bayesian adjustment. The first gives rise to temporal aggregation effects, the second to an autoregressive or exponential smoothing effect.[2] The consensus position from published research is that appraisal smoothing reduces the measured volatility of real estate. Further, appraisals may lag turning points and understate both peaks and troughs.

Unitized property investment vehicles such as Property Unit Trusts are similarly liable to appraisal uncertainty, since the value of each unit (and, hence, the notional return) is determined by independent property valuers. For larger funds, diversification may reduce this valuation uncertainty – or at least its random component. Additional uncertainty arises in poor market conditions as fund managers widen spreads and seek to defer redemption, reducing liquidity.

Performance in the public market is easier to measure, since share prices and dividend information are readily available. Two issues are worth mentioning. First, many REITs and property companies have relatively small market capitalizations and, in common with other small cap stocks, consequently have larger bid–ask spreads than large cap stocks and potential problems of illiquidity in difficult market conditions. Second, care must be taken in using published sector indices, in that very dissimilar types of firms may be included. For example, in the UK, many property sector indices include property investment companies, speculative developer-traders and property service providers, while the widely used US National Association of Real Estate Investment Trusts (NAREIT) index (see below) includes both property-owning and mortgage REITs. Although information on returns is readily available, investors are faced with the same appraisal problem as in the private market in attempting to estimate the net asset value of firms.

In the USA, the most frequently used index of private commercial real estate performance is that produced by the National Council for Real Estate Investment Fiduciaries (NCREIF). NCREIF provide income, capital and total returns disaggregated by sector and region based on a sample of

[1]For the UK, see, for example, Adair et al. (1996); Brown (1992); Lizieri and Venmore-Rowland (1993); Matysiak and Wang (1995)

[2]Discussions may be found in Barkham and Geltner (1994, 1995), Blundell and Ward (1987), Brown (1991), Geltner (1991), Quan and Quigley (1991) and Ross and Zisler (1991).

institutional-owned properties valued at \$73 billion as at 1999 Q2. The data runs from 1977 Q4 and is available on a quarterly basis. Many of the properties are only valued on an annual basis, creating seasonality in the data. The lack of high-frequency data is a particular problem in real estate, the high cost of appraisal precluding frequent reporting. In the UK, an equivalent benchmark performance service is provided by Investment Property Databank (IPD). The IPD databank contains property valued at £75 billion (\$126 billion) as at December 1998. Annual performance, again separable into sectors and regions, is available from 1980. IPD have produced a monthly index since December 1986. However, the properties in that index are predominantly held in unit trusts and, hence, may not be representative of the total institutional markets. A number of commercial agents produce similar appraisal-based indices. However, since these tend to contain small numbers of properties and, hence, high levels of specific risk, they cannot be considered as reliable indicators of market performance.

An alternative source of private returns information is to create synthetic returns from published rent and capitalization rate (or yield) data. In the UK, CB Hillier Parker produce a regular (quarterly) series of market rents and yields for hypothetical, beacon properties in a number of towns. These are then aggregated to produce regional and national indices. Calculated on a quarterly or annual basis, such returns will overstate achievable investment performance, since they ignore the impact of the contractual terms of leases. However, they will be more responsive to market conditions than portfolio-based indices and are, thus, useful as barometers of change. In the USA, the American Council of Life Insurers publish capitalization rates which can be combined with NCREIF rent data to produce a similar barometer (see, e.g. Ling and Naranjõ, 1999).

Price and return indices for public market real estate can be obtained readily from standard sources: the FTSE in the UK, CRSP in the USA, Datastream, for example. Care must be taken with these series; researchers must be mindful of composition changes and survivorship bias. For US real estate investment trusts, the NAREIT index is commonly used. The explosive growth of REITs in the 1990s (increasing from \$9 billion in 1990 to \$44 billion in 1994 and peaking in 1997 at \$140 billion) and the changing nature of the REIT market once again requires a health warning to be placed on the data. Furthermore, the overall REIT index includes mortgage REITs, hybrid REITs and healthcare REITs as well as commercial property equity REITs. For international markets, Global Property Research, based in the Netherlands, publish country and regional–continental indices of property company performance.

In comparing public and private real estate markets, analysts and researchers must be aware of many issues: the different nature of index construction; uncertainty relating to appraisal-based private returns;

appraisal-induced smoothing and serial correlation; the impact of gearing (leverage) on public-market returns, for example. Furthermore, international comparisons must be mindful of differences in the nature of the investment vehicle. For example, REITs are a passthrough, income distribution vehicle while UK property companies pay dividends and may retain earnings for investment. This will alter the relationship between the public property stock, other equities and the underlying real estate asset.

We have dwelt at some length on these definitional and measurement issues to emphasize that real estate is 'different' and that caution must be exercised in utilizing published performance indices. Analysis and research must be mindful of the institutional structure of the market in order to avoid misuse of statistics and misleading interpretations of data. Next we examine the structure of returns, turning first to the direct, private, market, before considering patterns and distributions in the public market and the linkage between the two markets.

3.3 THE PRIVATE, DIRECT REAL ESTATE MARKET

As the previous section implied, analysis of return distributions in the direct real estate market is hampered by the low frequency of data and uncertainty concerning the validity of appraisal-based returns. Nonetheless, concern has been expressed about the distributional characteristics of real estate returns and the possible impact of non-normality. In addition to attempts to 'desmooth' property returns (that is, to attempt to remove serial correlation and aggregation effects to extract the 'true' market signal), a number of authors have tested for normality. The results point both to peaked, fat-tailed distributions and, more tentatively, to skewness.

Young and Graff (1995) examine returns distributions for US institutional private real estate as captured in the NCREIF database. They decompose annual returns data for individual properties (grouped by type of property) over the period 1980–1992 into two components – the mean return for a property type in any one year and a residual return for the individual property in that year. The residual series is taken as representing the asset-specific risk for that year. They then use the methodology suggested by McCulloch to fit stable distributions to the residual series and estimate the parameters of the characteristic function. The α parameter for the whole sample, at 1.48 is significantly below the value of 2.0 that characterizes a normal distribution. This result held for the great majority of years and property types. The β parameters, as a measure of skewness, were typically negative: for the whole sample, β was -0.47, significantly different from zero at the 99% confidence level. Tentatively, they point to time variance in the skewness parameter.

These findings broadly confirm those of Miles and McCue (1984) and Hartzell *et al.* (1986) who find evidence of non-normality in terms of skewness and kurtosis, and Myer and Webb (1994) who provide evidence of non-normal kurtosis and autocorrelation in private real estate returns. In similar vein, Byrne and Lee (1997) test quarterly returns for sector/region disaggregations of the NCREIF index between 1983 and 1994. Although the number of observations is comparatively small, normality is rejected using the Jarque–Bera test for ten of the sixteen sub-sectors. Consistent with earlier findings, they detect positive kurtosis and, typically, negative skewness. They suggest that if returns are best characterized by stable Paretian distributions with infinite variance, portfolio-optimization strategies using the variance as a measure of risk are inappropriate. Instead, they propose use of the mean absolute deviation.

Graff *et al.* (1997) examine the distributional characteristics of Australian real estate based on the Property Council of Australia's Performance Index. This index illustrates many of the problems of working with direct real estate data, in that there is only a short time series (1984–1996), low-frequency (annual) data, just over 500 properties in the sample (and hence the likelihood of market tracking error) and the capital component of the returns is based on valuations rather than transactions. As with Young and Graff (1995), McCulloch's method is used to test distributional parameters of individual property return residuals after removal of the time-specific property-type return. The mean alpha parameter, at 1.59 is significantly below the value of 2.0 characteristic of a normal distribution. The betas do not give any clear indication of skewness (nor, in contrast to Young and Graff's US results do they appear to be time varying). The *C* parameter, as a proxy for risk, suggests both heteroscedasticity and time variance.

3.4 THE PUBLIC, INDIRECT REAL ESTATE MARKET

The public, or indirect, real estate market consists largely of shares in listed property vehicles. A distinction must be drawn between distributed earnings vehicles such as Real Estate Investment Trusts (REITs) and more conventional real estate companies. The former are vehicles whereby all income after deduction of management charges is distributed to shareholders. They are frequently tax transparent and, hence, subject to restrictions on investment policy and behaviour – for example, there may be strict limitations on debt to equity ratios. Property companies, by contrast, are able to retain earnings: return thus comes from dividend payments and any share price appreciation. Real estate companies may be further sub-divided into property investment companies and developer-traders. The latter are typically valued on a price–

earnings ratio basis, have higher gearing ratios and generally exhibit higher betas than property investment companies whose share price is based on discounted net asset value.

The behaviour of exchange traded real estate securities is, in many ways, more similar to that of other equities (particularly small capitalization stocks) than of the underlying private real estate. Certainly, reported contemporaneous correlations between traded real estate and stock indices are far higher than those between the direct property market and either stocks or traded real estate. This has led some to question whether there is a separate real estate factor at all, or whether traded property stocks represent a pure property play. This is explored further in the next section. More recent evidence suggests closer links between REITs and the underlying property market. It is thus reasonable to treat their returns as representative of some form of property market performance. Nonetheless, research on the distribution of indirect real estate returns produces results that are consistent with stock market research: that is, with non-normality, peaked distributions and fat tails.

Lizieri and Satchell (1997a,b) examined the distribution of monthly property company returns in the UK between 1972 and 1992. They found strong evidence of non-normality, with Jarque–Bera tests rejecting the null hypothesis at 0.001 and beyond. Returns exhibited positive skewness and kurtosis and were fat-tailed. Equity market returns in general (proxied by the FT All Share index) were similarly non-normal. The residual stock series resulting from an orthogonalization based on regressing stock returns on property returns ($FTAS_t = \alpha + \beta FTPROP_t + \upsilon_t$) appeared much closer to (log) normality.

Seiler *et al.* (1999) examine the return distributions of equity real estate investment trusts (EREITs) for quarterly data from 1986 to 1996. The Kolmogorov–Smirnov, Shapiro–Wilks and Lilliefors tests generally reject normality, despite the small number of observations. By sector, Office REIT returns appear the least normal, while the tests do not reject normality for Industrial REITs. The office returns are characterized by very high volatility, a low mean return and positive skewness. Comparative figures for the direct market show office property returns exhibiting negative skewness, a disturbing contradiction. Myer and Webb (1993) analyse quarterly returns from a small sample of REITs over the period 1978-1990. While a composite index of REITs shows no evidence of non-normality, individual REITs have significant skewness and kurtosis and are non-normal by at least one of the normality tests employed. As with Seiler *et al.*, comparative direct market returns are shown to be non-normal.

Lu and Mei (1999) provide comparative evidence of return distributions for property sector share indices in ten emerging markets. Hampered by short time-series, they apply Anderson–Darling normality tests which weakly reject normality in four of the ten markets. As with the common stocks in those markets, the real estate returns are fat-tailed and positively kurtotic. Kurtosis is greater in monthly than in quarterly data which they take as implying that there are abnormal jumps in the return series that are not persistent and are masked in higher-frequency data. Interestingly, for portfolio strategy purposes, they find that cross-market correlations are increasingly positive when US market conditions are poor – that is '*you get diversification when you don't need it*'.

Almost all the studies of REIT and property company returns report very low autocorrelation coefficients. Typically, in monthly data, the first-order coefficient is significant and negative (see, for example, Nelling and Gyourko, 1998), possibly indicating some sort form of mean reversion, but others are non-significant. This contrasts sharply with evidence from the private market where positive serial correlation is marked in sub-annual data and persistent. As previously noted, this pattern is generally attributed to measurement issues or to appraiser behaviour (but see Lai and Wang, 1998 for a contrary view).

3.5 A PROPERTY FACTOR? REAL ESTATE AND CAPITAL MARKET INTEGRATION

A key question to be confronted in considering indirect real estate returns is are they stock or property? This has been the subject of considerable research. This question is embedded within a broader issue: is there a separate real estate factor? If so, is that property factor priced? As with the distributional issues covered above, analysis is made complex by the nature of real estate data.

Many researchers have noted that REIT and property company share returns have much closer contemporaneous correlations with the stock market than with the underlying real estate market. Typical coefficients range between 0.65 and 0.85. Correlations between the listed real estate securities and the underlying market are generally much lower and are frequently indistinguishable from zero. These results hold even where researchers have attempted to correct for appraisal smoothing in the direct property market and for gearing (leverage) in the indirect, public market series (see, for example, Barkham and Geltner, 1995). Gordon and Canter (1999) suggest (on the basis of rolling correlations) that there is international evidence that real estate stocks are behaving less like stocks and more like property: particularly where the firm is a distributed earnings vehicle, like a REIT. In the USA, they show rolling 36-month correlations between REITs and the stock market falling from over 0.75 in 1990 to under 0.30 in 1998.

Barkham and Geltner (1995) suggest that there is price discovery between the direct and indirect markets in both the USA and the UK. They suggest, on the basis of Granger causality tests, that the public market leads the private market, implying that information is impounded into prices more efficiently in exchange-traded markets. Wang *et al.* (1997) demonstrate cointegration between public and private markets with, again, price discovery from the indirect to the direct market. Monthly private property returns are predictable using lagged values of public and private returns. Whether such predictability could be used profitably given transaction costs and illiquidity on the direct market is moot. Long-run cointegration between real estate and stock markets is demonstrated by Okunev and Wilson (1997) and Wilson *et al.* (1998). However, portfolio diversification and arbitrage opportunities rest, critically, on short-term differences and adjustment processes.

Other research has addressed the issue of the integration of real estate markets with other capital markets. Such research typically tests whether there is a separately priced property factor or whether risk factors are similarly priced in real estate and other markets. As such, they are joint tests of market integration and the asset pricing model employed. Thus, for example, Liu *et al.* (1990) orthogonalize property returns and find that they are priced in the stock market. However, the result is dependent on the validity of the single index, CAPM framework employed. A range of studies are reviewed in Corgel *et al.* (1995) and in Ling and Naranjõ (1999). The consensus seem to be that indirect real estate markets are integrated with other capital markets but direct property markets are segmented.

Ling and Naranjõ (1999) employ a multi-factor risk model to test whether risk premia are priced in the same way across US asset markets. They test a variety of private and public market real estate indices. With constant risk premia, they are unable to reject the null hypothesis that real estate stocks and non-property stocks are priced in the same way. However, direct real estate returns appear to be priced differently. With time-varying premia, these results broadly hold. Integration is accepted in 80% of quarters for the exchange-listed real estate returns but rejected for the vast majority of direct market returns.

Such results are somewhat troubling. The performance of the listed real estate securities is ultimately dependent upon the underlying private market in that the asset values of the firms depend upon the capital value of the real estate owned, the ability to pay dividends depends upon the net operating income from the property and the ability to trade profitably depends on increases in capital values which, in turn, depend on rental change and expectations of future growth. As a result, a close link between markets might be expected. Yet differences persist even after correction for serial correlation in the direct market and gearing effects in the public market. The standard explanation is that appraisals are failing to respond to market changes and, as a result, returns from valuation-based indices are an inadequate proxy of market performance. However intuitively appealing, this remains an assertion. It is also possible that misunderstanding of the nature of the property market has led to mispricing in the public markets. The evidence of price discovery from public to private markets gives some support for the former thesis but is not conclusive.

3.6 NON-LINEARITY IN REAL ESTATE RETURNS

The bulk of published real estate research on return distributions has been confined to testing for normality or fitting single distributions. However, there is a small body of work that has examined non-linearity in returns. These studies point tentatively to non-linear forms, with implications both for further research and for portfolio strategies.

Lizieri *et al.* (1998) examine the monthly returns on UK property company shares and US equity REITs using a Threshold Autoregressive (TAR) model. A two-regime solution is proposed, with the regimes separated by the level of real interest rates. The results are similar for the two markets. The regime-switching model outperforms a linear, autoregressive model. In the USA, in the lower interest rate environment, returns are characterized by mean-reverting behaviour about a positive trend. In the higher interest rate environment, returns exhibit a random walk around a falling trend, with values falling with little volatility. UK returns follow the same pattern. The steepness of the trend slope and a negative intercept mean that prices fall more sharply in the second regime than they rise in the first, consistent with the Black leverage effect.

Maitland-Smith and Brooks (1999) investigate non-linearity in the UK and US markets, research hampered by the lack of high-frequency data. For US markets, they use NCREIF quarterly returns from 1978 to 1995; in the UK, they use the Jones Lang Wootton quarterly series from 1977 to 1995 and the IPD Monthly Index, 1987–1995. In all cases, Jarque–Bera, Lilliefors and Shapiro–Wilks tests overwhelmingly reject normality. They argue, in contrast to prevailing views, that this results as much from skewness as kurtosis. Threshold autoregression (again conditioned on real interest rates) indicates two regimes. They then apply a Hamilton-style Markov switching model to the data which, effectively, tests the hypothesis that the returns are generated by a mixture of two (or more) normal distributions. Tests for normality on the returns sorted into regimes are less likely to be rejected although the authors caution against over-interpretation given small sub-sample size.

Ambrose *et al.* (1992) test for deterministic non-linearity in daily US real estate (REIT) and stock market returns, using a fractal structure approach. For stock market returns, they are unable to find evidence that would reject a hypothesis that returns follow a random walk, although they suggest that returns are non-normal. The REIT series, by contrast, does exhibit significant persistence. However, this was found to be attributable to short-term bias, rather than long-run effects. Similar results are found for other stock market industry groups.

Newell *et al.* (1996) test Australian property unit trust returns for chaotic behaviour but find little evidence of chaos. They suggest that non-linear stochastic models are more appropriate. Newell and Matysiak (1997) conduct a battery of tests on daily and weekly UK property company returns and conclude that there is little evidence to support any hypothesis of chaotic behaviour, but that there is evidence that the series are non-random and non-linear in nature. Ward and Wu (1994) find evidence of property market 'memory' and smoothing in UK property market returns and suggest that returns series may exhibit fractal integration. In similar vein, Okunev and Wilson (1997) examine the relationship between REIT and stock market series. While conventional (linear) cointegration tests imply that the series are segmented, further tests indicate the presence of a non-linear adjustment process between the series, implying fractional integration. However, they note that the adjustment process is protracted, implying diversification potential.

Research into non-linearity, deterministic/chaotic behaviour, fractional integration and other more complex returns behaviour is hampered by data inadequacy. Exchange listed real estate securities are less problematic – although composition changes, alteration to tax and legal structures and survivorship bias must be considered. However, the low-frequency, short time series available in the direct market make interpretation of such tests unreliable and require bootstrapping to generate confidence intervals. Nonetheless, the preliminary evidence does suggest that the possibility of non-linear returns structures must be considered in modelling behaviour and defining investment strategies.

3.7 THE UK REAL ESTATE MARKET: MODELS OF RETURN DISTRIBUTIONS

Comparatively little work has been published on fitting theoretical distributions to observed frequency distributions although, as discussed above, several authors have argued against normal distributions. There are, however, several programs including BestFit and Crystal Ball available that will fit alternative distributions to frequency distributions. In this section we report the results from applying BestFit for Windows[3] to the sample data.

The data comprised monthly total returns for the series shown in Table 3.1 for the period from 31 December 1986 to 31 December 1998. The data consist of direct (valuation-based) institutional property returns reported by the

[3]Palisade Corporation 1993–1996 Copyright.

Table 3.1 Description of dataset used in the distribution-fitting exercise

FTALL	FT-All Share Return Index, End Month Value, Log Difference
Gilts	Medium Dated Gilts, Return Index, Log Difference
RPI	Retail Price Index (Headline), Log Difference
FT-RealEstate	FT-Real Estate Sector Return Index (Spliced), Log Difference
FT-Construct	FT-Construction Sector Index, Log Difference
IPDMI	IPD Monthly Returns Index, Log Difference
IPDCityOff	IPD City Offices Return Index, Log Difference
IPDSEInd	IPD South East Industrial Return Index, Log Difference
IPDSERet	IPD South East Retail Return Index, Log Difference
IPDMWInd	IPD Midland & Wales Industrial Return Index, Log Difference
IPDNScOff	IPD Northern & Scottish Office Index, Log Difference
Resid1	Residuals from FTProp = alpha + beta FTALL *R*-bar-sq = 0.605, beta = 1.013 (.068)
IPDMIUns	IPD Monthly Returns Unsmoothed (purged of first-order autocorrelation)
IPDCOUns	IPD City Offices Returns Unsmoothed (purged of first-order autocorrelation)
IPDSEIndUns	IPD South East Industrial Returns Unsmoothed (purged of first-order autocorrelation)
IPDSERetUns	IPD South East Retail Returns Unsmoothed (purged of first-order autocorrelation)
IPDMWIndUns	IPD Midland & Wales Industrial Returns Unsmoothed (purged of first-order autocorrelation)
IPDNScoOffUns	IPD Northern & Scottish Office Returns Unsmoothed (purged of first-order autocorrelation)

Note: Unsmoothing is achieved by regressing X_t on X_{t-1} and using the beta to remove the autocorrelation, that is, $X_t^* = (X_t - \beta X_{t-1})/(1 - \beta)$ This leaves the means (almost) unchanged but results in an increase in the standard deviation of around 4*x* for the whole index and somewhere between 1.7 and 2.9 for the sector/regions. Betas lie in the range 0.57–0.85. Other unsmoothing methods have been suggested in the literature: it is unlikely that their adoption would alter the results significantly.

Investment Property Databank (IPD) with series for all property and sub-indices for specified regional and sectoral groups of property; property company and construction firm share series; a residual series estimated by orthogonalizing property company share performance on the overall equity market; and, for comparison, All Share and Gilt series. The fitting exercise was performed on the whole period and then repeated on the sub-sample March 1988 to December 1998 to avoid the effect of the extreme observations around and immediately following October 1987. It is, of course, arguable that the returns in that short period October 1987 to February 1988 revealed relevant and even important information about the behaviour of the returns from investments in the long run. It is also plausible that the returns in that period would distort the curve-fitting process if used in the comparatively small sample of 132 returns.

The BestFit program offers 37 different distributions but many of these are inappropriate on *a priori* grounds. There are only five distributions that are

(1) continuous and (2) open-ended at both high and low ends.[4] These are Extreme Value, Error function, Logistic, Normal and Student's t distribution.

The Extreme Value distribution, often associated with Gumbel (1958), is found in three forms although the first is by far the most common. It has been used in a wide range of applications from earthquake magnitudes (Fahmi and Abbasi, 1991), horse racing (Henery, 1984) and the stock market (Wiggins, 1991). The Distribution function is given by:

$$F(x) = e^{-e^{\frac{-x-a}{b}}} \qquad -\infty < x < \infty,\ b > 0 \tag{3.1}$$

where $a = mode$, the mean is given by $a - b\Gamma'(1)$ and the standard deviation is $b\pi/\sqrt{6}$

The Error function is also known as the exponential power distribution and is symmetric but can be leptokurtic or platykurtic depending on the shape parameter c. Its probability density function is given by

$$f(x) = \frac{e^{\frac{-|x-a|^{2/c}}{2b}}}{b^{0.5}2^{c/2}\Gamma(1+c/2)} \qquad -\infty < x < \infty,\ b > 0,\ c > 0 \tag{3.2}$$

where mean $= a$, variance $= [2^c b^2 \Gamma(3c/2)]/\Gamma(c/2)$. If $a = 0$ and $b = c = 1$, then the error function corresponds to a standard normal variate.

The Logistic distribution is not commonly used in modelling returns but may be appropriate for modelling the returns of indices because one possible use suggested in the program includes '... the approximation of the midrange of a set of variables with the same distribution. For example, the average of the minimum and maximum prices brought by identical items at auction.' (BestFit, 1998). The probability distribution is given by:

$$f(x) = \frac{e^{\frac{-(x-a)}{b}}}{b\left(1 + e^{\frac{-(x-a)}{b}}\right)^2} \tag{3.3}$$

where $a =$ mean and $k = \pi b/\sqrt{3} =$ standard deviation.

The t-distribution has been used in modelling returns and more specifically ratios (McLeay, 1986) and includes the Normal distribution as a member. The probability distribution is given by:

$$f(x; v) = \frac{\{\Gamma[(v+1)/2]\}}{\sqrt{\pi v}\Gamma(v/2)\left[1 + \left(\frac{x^2}{v}\right)\right]^{(v+1)/2}} \qquad -\infty < x < \infty, v = 1, 2, \ldots \tag{3.4}$$

[4]In principle, the lower bound should be -1, but the variability of the frequency distributions would not suggest any fixed lower bound.

Table 3.2 Distribution of FT-All Share Index

Test\full sample	Distributions (ranked by likelihood) Unrestricted fitting (including transformed distributions)			Open-ended distributions	Goodness of fit result
Chi-square	Weibull rejected	Logistic rejected	Beta rejected	Error function	Rejected
				Logistic	Rejected
				Normal	Rejected
				Student's *t*	Rejected
				Extreme Value	Rejected
Kolmogorov–Smirnov	Weibull rejected	Logistic >0.1	Beta rejected	Error function	Rejected
				Logistic	>0.1
				Normal	Rejected
				Student's *t*	Rejected
				Extreme Value	Rejected
Anderson–Darling	Logistic >0.15	Weibull rejected	Beta >0.05	Error function	Rejected
				Logistic	>0.15
				Normal	Rejected
				Student's *t*	Rejected
				Extreme Value	Rejected
Sub-sample					
Chi-square	Logistic >0.28	Normal >0.23	Weibull >0.14	Error function	Rejected
				Logistic	>0.28
				Normal	>0.23
				Student's *t*	Rejected
				Extreme Value	Rejected
Kolmogorov–Smirnov	Logistic >0.15	Extreme Value rejected	Normal rejected	Error function	Rejected
				Logistic	>0.15
				Normal	Rejected
				Student's *t*	Rejected
				Extreme Value	Rejected
Anderson–Darling	Logistic >0.15	Normal rejected	Weibull rejected	Error function	Rejected
				Logistic	>0.15
				Normal	Rejected
				Student's *t*	Rejected
				Extreme Value	Rejected

Note: In this and subsequent tables, the figures in the body of the table approximate to the probability that the empirical distribution may be described by the theoretical distribution. Where that probability is below 0.05, the distributional form is rejected. The appearance of the Weibull and Beta distributions may seem odd since both are restricted to positive values. In fitting the distributions, however, the software transforms the values by adding to or multiplying by constants. While the distributions may have some empirical descriptive power, they cannot be inferred to have economic plausibility.

where v is a positive integer. The t-distribution is symmetrical and the kurtosis is given by $3(v-2)/(v-4)$ for $v > 4$.

There are fourteen other distributions that have specific lower end boundaries. One can justify using these distributions since the lower bound of a returns distribution is -1 or -100% in any one period. However, the program will also fit any distribution to a sample by appropriate

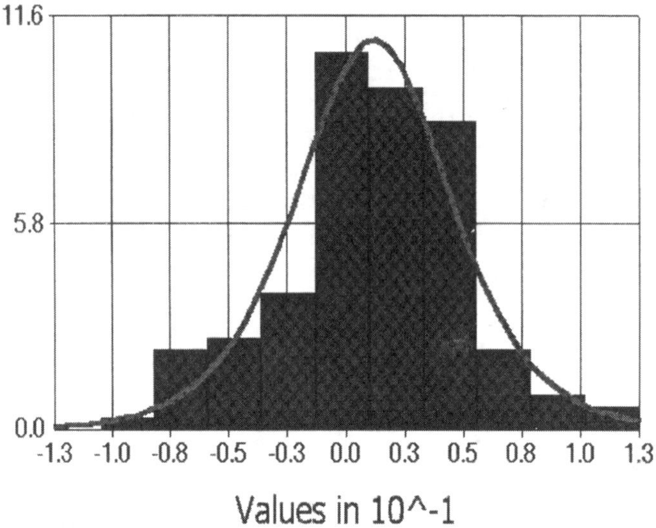

Figure 3.1 Fitted and observed returns for FT-All Share Index (March 1988 to December 1998)

transformation. For example, the Chi-squared distribution has a lower bound of zero but can be fitted to data that includes the minimum value of −0.5 by adding 0.5 to every observation and then subtracting 0.5 from the fitted Chi-squared value. In the following analysis we report the three distributions highest in the list ranked by the goodness of fit to the empirical data.

There are three tests used to test the goodness of fit of the theoretical distributions: the Chi-square test, the Kolmogorov–Smirnov and the Anderson–Darling test. The ranking is carried out using each test in turn and the goodness-of-fit tests are carried out for every distribution.

The results of this analysis of the FT-All Share index show first how sensitive is the fitting process to outlying observations (Table 3.2). When the full sample is used, all tests for normality reject the hypothesis that the normal distribution is an adequate fit of the observed returns. Instead we find that the suggested distributions are Beta and Logistic, with the Weibull being narrowly rejected at the 0.05 level. Of these three, only the Logistic remains untransformed. The transformation of the Weibull involves the addition of 1.22 to the returns: the fit may be almost acceptable using the Kolmogorov–Smirnov test but it has no rationale. Similarly the Beta distribution fitting involves a transformation of dividing the returns by 2.26 and then adding 1.22 to the result. For the sub-sample, the normal is not rejected by the chi-square test and is narrowly rejected by the Anderson–Darling test.

In both the full sample and the sub-sample, the Logistic distribution appears the most plausible using all the tests. Figure 3.1 shows the fitted and observed returns for the FT-All Share Index from March 1988 to December 1998. Table 3A.1 provides comparable analysis for a long-term Government bond index while Table 3A.2 summarizes the results for the two FT-A sector indices (Construction and Property). In all cases, the diagnostic tests provide similar support for the Logistic and Normal distributions: particularly in the case of the construction sector.

3.7.1 Direct property indices

Table 3.3 presents the results for the IPD monthly index. The index consists of properties held by funds which all have valuations at monthly intervals. Because the distribution of properties in this index differs sharply from the IPD Annual index (having too few City Offices, for example), it can be argued that it is not representative of the institutional property market but, by definition, the portfolios consist of properties that are of 'institutional quality'. The results are reasonably consistent with those for the other assets, the logistic and normal distributions adequately describe the returns distributions of property. The Beta and Gamma distributions are revealed to fit the distributions only after adding 0.0209 to the monthly returns (to both the returns in the full sample and the sub-sample).

To counter the smoothing problem, discussed above, the analysis is repeated using returns unsmoothed using a simple regression procedure. These results are presented in Table 3.4. Unfortunately, the results are not supportive of the process of unsmoothing. One of the reasons for unsmoothing the returns from the property indices is the wish to create an indicator that will be more responsive to market information than the appraisal-based valuations. One would therefore suppose that the unsmoothed series would be closer than the unadjusted series to a Normal Distribution; a result that would be consistent with the Weak Form of the Efficient Market Hypothesis. However, in comparing Table 3.3 and Table 3.4, we find that the unsmoothed series appear to be less easily modelled than the raw (smoothed) series.

In examining Figure 3.2, which presents the differences between a Normal distribution and the unsmoothed returns from the IPD Monthly Index, we find that the actual returns, even after adjustment, contain too many returns about zero and too few larger negative and positive returns. This might be expected in a thinly traded market in which prices move only in response to new company-specific (here, property-specific) information and in which that information arrives only infrequently. This corresponds to behavioural studies of valuer behaviour. In other words, the unsmoothing procedure does not correct for the thinness of the trading in the property market.

Table 3.3 Distribution of returns from IPD Monthly Property Index

Test\full sample	Distributions (ranked by likelihood) Unrestricted fitting (including transformed distributions)			Open-ended distributions	Goodness of fit result
Chi-square	Logistic >0.59	Normal >0.47	Weibull >0.47	Error function	Rejected
				Logistic	>0.59
				Normal	>0.47
				Student's *t*	Rejected
				Extreme Value	Rejected
Kolmogorov–Smirnov	Normal >0.15	Beta >0.15	Weibull >0.1	Error function	Rejected
				Logistic	>0.15
				Normal	>0.15
				Student's *t*	Rejected
				Extreme Value	Rejected
Anderson–Darling	Beta >0.15	Gamma >0.15	Erlang >0.15	Error function	Rejected
				Logistic	>0.15
				Normal	Rejected
				Student's *t*	Rejected
				Extreme Value	Rejected
Sub-sample					
Chi-square	Logistic >0.25	Gamma >0.23	Weibull >0.17	Error function	Rejected
				Logistic	>0.25
				Normal	>0.13
				Student's *t*	Rejected
				Extreme Value	Rejected
Kolmogorov–Smirnov	Beta >0.15	Weibull >0.05	Erlang >0.15	Error function	Rejected
				Logistic	>0.1
				Normal	Rejected
				Student's *t*	Rejected
				Extreme Value	Rejected
Anderson–Darling	Beta >0.15	Erlang >0.15	Gamma >0.15	Error function	Rejected
				Logistic	>0.1
				Normal	Rejected
				Student's *t*	Rejected
				Extreme Value	Rejected

3.7.2 The Sub-Sector Direct Property indices

The analysis for various sub-sectors of the IPD Monthly Index (for geographical and sector groupings of properties) are summarized in Tables 3.5–3.7. Because the direct property indices do not exhibit the structural break in October 1987 that was so obvious in the equity markets, the analysis is carried out on the full samples only. It can be seen from Tables 3.5 and 3.6 that, as with the IPD Monthly Index, the unsmoothing procedure makes very little difference to the fit of plausible distributions. Overall, the most appropriate distribution appears to the Logistic distribution – but even here it is rejected in most cases (generally having a probability of around 0.025). As before, the main reason for the inappropriate fit is the excess of returns around

Table 3.4 Distribution of returns from IPD Monthly Property Index (unsmoothed)

Test\full sample	Distributions (ranked by likelihood) Unrestricted fitting (including transformed distributions)			Open-ended distributions	Goodness of fit result
Chi-square	Logistic rejected	Error function rejected	Triangular rejected	Error function	Rejected
				Logistic	Rejected
				Normal	Rejected
				Student's t	Rejected
				Extreme Value	Rejected
Kolmogorov–Smirnov	Logistic >0.15	Extreme Value rejected	Normal rejected	Error function	Rejected
				Logistic	>0.15
				Normal	Rejected
				Student's t	Rejected
				Extreme Value	Rejected
Anderson–Darling	Logistic >0.15	Normal rejected	Beta rejected	Error function	Rejected
				Logistic	>0.15
				Normal	Rejected
				Student's t	Rejected
				Extreme Value	Rejected
Sub-sample					
Chi-square	Logistic rejected	Error function rejected	Triangular rejected	Error function	Rejected
				Logistic	Rejected
				Normal	Rejected
				Student's t	Rejected
				Extreme Value	Rejected
Kolmogorov–Smirnov	Logistic >0.15	Extreme Value rejected	Normal rejected	Error function	Rejected
				Logistic	>0.15
				Normal	Rejected
				Student's t	Rejected
				Extreme Value	Rejected
Anderson–Darling	Logistic >0.1	Normal rejected	Beta rejected	Error function	Rejected
				Logistic	>0.1
				Normal	Rejected
				Student's t	Rejected
				Extreme Value	Rejected

zero. In descriptive diagnostics, this is revealed in the measurement of kurtosis. This is sharply revealed in Table 3.8, which summarizes the kurtosis of the property sector indices and compares the measures to their theoretical counterparts. In all cases, the kurtosis of the empirical distribution is substantially higher than implied by the respective distribution. By contrast to the direct property indices, the residual series from regression of property company share returns on the all share index (shown in Table 3.5) appears easier to model, with the normal shown as the favoured distribution.

3.7.3 Quarterly returns

If the atypical behaviour of property returns can be explained by the thinness of the market and the lack of liquidity and trading, we should expect to see the

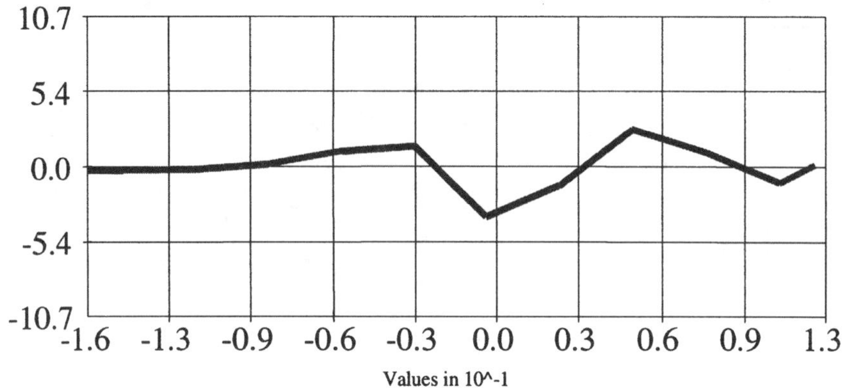

Figure 3.2 Differences between normal distribution and actual distribution of IPD monthly returns (unsmoothed) – negative values imply actual > normal

distributions to conform more closely with other market returns over longer trading intervals. We therefore converted the returns of the direct property indices (unsmoothed) to quarterly returns and re-estimated the distributions. The results are summarized in Table 3.7 and are consistent with this interpretation. In comparing Tables 3.5 and 3.7 we find that normality is rejected for all five selected sub-sectors of the IPD (Unadjusted) Monthly Property indices but accepted for two of the five sub-sectors of the Quarterly index with a third being narrowly rejected. The logistic distribution is not

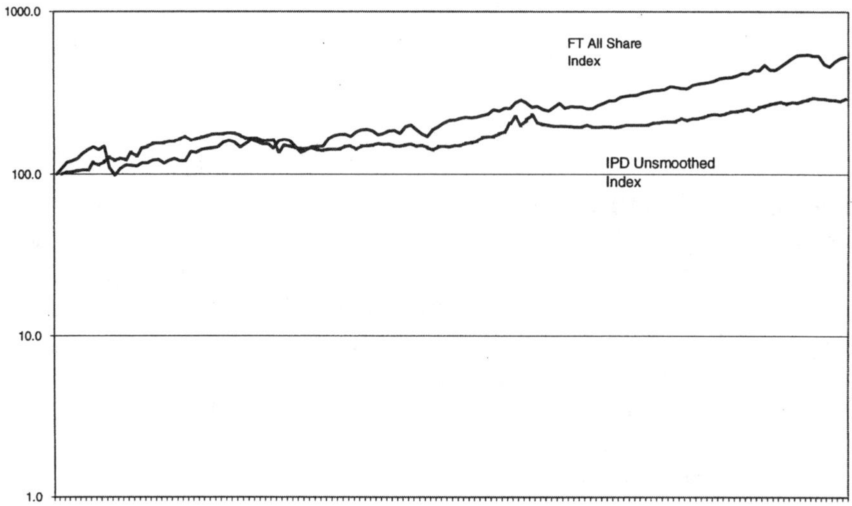

Figure 3.3 Time series (log-scale) of FT-All Share and IPD Property Index

Table 3.5 Distribution of returns from IPD Monthly Sub-Sector Indices (unadjusted)

		Goodness of fit results		
	Open-ended distributions	*IPDCityOff*	*IPDSERet*	*IPDNScOff*
Chi-square	Error function	Rejected	Rejected	Rejected
	Logistic	Rejected	Rejected	Rejected
	Normal	Rejected	Rejected	Rejected
	Student's *t*	Rejected	Rejected	Rejected
	Extreme Value	Rejected	Rejected	Rejected
Kolmogorov–Smirnov	Error function	Rejected	Rejected	Rejected
	Logistic	>0.1	Rejected	Rejected
	Normal	Rejected	Rejected	Rejected
	Student's *t*	Rejected	Rejected	Rejected
	Extreme Value	Rejected	Rejected	Rejected
Anderson–Darling	Error function	Rejected	Rejected	Rejected
	Logistic	Rejected	Rejected	Rejected
	Normal	Rejected	Rejected	Rejected
	Student's *t*	Rejected	Rejected	Rejected
	Extreme Value	Rejected	Rejected	Rejected
		IPDSEInd	*IPDMWInd*	*Residl*
Chi-square	Error function	Rejected	Rejected	>0.07
	Logistic	Rejected	Rejected	>0.08
	Normal	Rejected	Rejected	>0.09
	Student's *t*	Rejected	Rejected	Rejected
	Extreme Value	Rejected	Rejected	Rejected
Kolmogorov–Smirnov	Error function	Rejected	Rejected	>0.15
	Logistic	Rejected	Rejected	>0.1
	Normal	Rejected	Rejected	>0.05
	Student's *t*	Rejected	Rejected	Rejected
	Extreme Value	Rejected	Rejected	Rejected
Anderson–Darling	Error function	Rejected	Rejected	>0.15
	Logistic	Rejected	Rejected	>0.1
	Normal	Rejected	Rejected	>0.05
	Student's *t*	Rejected	Rejected	Rejected
	Extreme Value	>0.05	Rejected	Rejected

rejected in two of the monthly indices and is not rejected in any of the quarterly indices although the results of the different significance tests do not always agree. Specifically, the Chi-squared test differs most from the Kolmogorov–Smirnov and the Anderson–Darling tests, albeit not in any systematic way.

It was not appropriate to estimate returns over any longer interval because the small-sample properties of the tests would lead to inconclusive results. However, we infer that as the trading interval is increased, the behaviour of the property indices would conform more closely to the returns from other capital markets.

Table 3.6 Distribution of returns from IPD Monthly Sub-Sector Indices (unsmoothed)

	Open-ended distributions	Goodness of fit result *IPDCOUns*	*IPDSERetUns*	*PDNScoOffUns*
Chi-square	Error function	Rejected	Rejected	Rejected
	Logistic	Rejected	Rejected	Rejected
	Normal	Rejected	Rejected	Rejected
	Student's *t*	Rejected	Rejected	Rejected
	Extreme Value	Rejected	>0.05	Rejected
Kolmogorov–Smirnov	Error function	Rejected	Rejected	Rejected
	Logistic	Rejected	Rejected	Rejected
	Normal	Rejected	Rejected	Rejected
	Student's *t*	Rejected	Rejected	Rejected
	Extreme Value	Rejected	>0.05	Rejected
Anderson–Darling	Error function	Rejected	Rejected	Rejected
	Logistic	Rejected	Rejected	Rejected
	Normal	Rejected	Rejected	Rejected
	Student's *t*	Rejected	Rejected	Rejected
	Extreme Value	Rejected	>0.05	Rejected
		IPDSEIndUns	*IPDMWIndUns*	
Chi-square	Error function	Rejected	Rejected	
	Logistic	Rejected	Rejected	
	Normal	Rejected	Rejected	
	Student's *t*	Rejected	Rejected	
	Extreme Value	Rejected	Rejected	
Kolmogorov–Smirnov	Error function	Rejected	Rejected	
	Logistic	>0.15	>0.15	
	Normal	Rejected	Rejected	
	Student's *t*	Rejected	Rejected	
	Extreme Value	Rejected	Rejected	
Anderson–Darling	Error function	Rejected	Rejected	
	Logistic	>0.15	>0.1	
	Normal	Rejected	Rejected	
	Student's *t*	Rejected	Rejected	
	Extreme Value	Rejected	Rejected	

3.8 CONCLUSIONS

The empirical results presented above support the existing real estate literature in emphasizing that it is unsafe to assume normality of property returns. For the unadjusted IPD monthly data, normality was rejected by a number of test procedures while other distributions – notably the logistic – were favoured. When sub-sector returns were analysed, normality was rejected in almost all cases. This, allied to the fact that the distribution of property returns appears to behave in a different way from those of equities and bonds (and, indeed, of securitized real estate), has implications for asset allocation. The inclusion of

Table 3.7 Distribution of quarterly returns from IPD Sub-Sector Indices (unadjusted)

	Open-ended distributions	Goodness of fit result *IPDCityOff*	*IPDSERet*	*IPDNScOff*
Chi-square	Error function	>0.20	Rejected	Rejected
	Logistic	>0.50	>0.09	Rejected
	Normal	>0.44	>0.09	Rejected
	Student's *t*	Rejected	Rejected	Rejected
	Extreme Value	Rejected	Rejected	>0.07
Kolmogorov–Smirnov	Error function	Rejected	Rejected	Rejected
	Logistic	>0.15	>0.15	>0.15
	Normal	Rejected	>0.15	Rejected
	Student's *t*	Rejected	Rejected	Rejected
	Extreme Value	Rejected	Rejected	>0.05
Anderson–Darling	Error function	Rejected	Rejected	Rejected
	Logistic	>0.15	>0.15	>0.10
	Normal	Rejected	>0.10	Rejected
	Student's *t*	Rejected	Rejected	Rejected
	Extreme Value	Rejected	>0.05	Rejected
		IPDSEInd	*IPDMWInd*	*IPDMI*
Chi-square	Error function	Rejected	Rejected	Rejected
	Logistic	Rejected	>0.05	>0.07
	Normal	Rejected	Rejected	>0.13
	Student's *t*	Rejected	Rejected	Rejected
	Extreme Value	>0.30	>0.50	Rejected
Kolmogorov–Smirnov	Error function	Rejected	Rejected	Rejected
	Logistic	>0.15	>0.15	>0.15
	Normal	Rejected	Rejected	>0.15
	Student's *t*	Rejected	Rejected	Rejected
	Extreme Value	Rejected	>0.15	>0.10
Anderson–Darling	Error function	Rejected	Rejected	Rejected
	Logistic	>0.15	>0.15	>0.15
	Normal	Rejected	Rejected	>0.15
	Student's *t*	Rejected	Rejected	Rejected
	Extreme Value	>0.05	>0.10	>0.15

real estate returns, especially when measured over small intervals, alongside other asset classes in optimizing procedures may produce misleading results.

The aberrant behaviour of real estate returns has often been attributed to the appraisal-based nature of capital returns and the problem of valuation smoothing. It has been asserted that unsmoothing the data will result in a returns series that impounds data more rapidly and, hence, produce returns distributions closer to those that would be expected in an informationally efficient market. The evidence here does not support that contention. Unsmoothing the returns does not result in returns distributions that are easier to model or that conform to normality. It appears that this results from the high proportion of returns that are close to zero. We argue that this is a

Table 3.8 Kurtosis of actual property returns, compared with model distributions

Returns	Actual	Error function	Logistic	Normal	Student's t	Extreme Value
IPD monthly	3.34	3.0	4.2	3.0	3.0	5.4
IPD monthly unsmoothed	6.24	3.0	4.2	3.0	3.0	5.4
City Offices unsmoothed	8.72	3.0	4.2	3.0	3.0	5.4
SE Offices unsmoothed	8.49	3.0	4.2	3.0	3.0	5.4
SE Retail unsmoothed	15.0	3.0	4.2	3.0	3.0	5.4
MW Industrials unsmoothed	7.34	3.0	4.2	3.0	3.0	5.4
N Scot Offices unsmoothed	4.62	3.0	4.2	3.0	3.0	5.4

result of the thinly traded market and slow arrival of information, resulting in static individual valuations.

If our inference were correct, real estate markets should produce returns that are more similar to those in other asset markets over longer trading and analysis periods. The analysis of quarterly data is consistent with this view. Returns are easier to model and the normal distribution is favoured on a number of tests both for the aggregate index and at sub-sector level. We suspect that, were there longer time series, still better results could be achieved with annual data. This is consistent with the longer holding periods that characterize investment property (themselves a response to the different structure of the property market, in particular greater specific risk and uncertainty and higher transaction costs). Again, this may cause problems for a formal quantitative mixed asset-allocation procedure where the model demands higher-frequency data.

Finally, we emphasize that risk and return characteristics of real estate differ from other asset classes. The heterogeneity, indivisibility and large lot size of the assets, the thinly traded market, the importance of valuations rather than transactions in determining returns and the high transaction costs that drive longer holding periods all have an impact on the return structure. As a result, great care must be taken in analysing and interpreting real estate returns and in using these returns in optimized allocations for mixed-asset portfolios.

REFERENCES

Adair, A., Hutchinson, N., MacGregor, B., McGreal, S. and Nanthakumaran, N. (1996) 'An Analysis of Valuation Variation in the UK Commercial Property Market', *Journal of Property Valuation and Investment*, **14**, 34–47.

Ambrose, B., Ancel, E and Griffiths, M. (1992) 'The Fractal Structure of Real Estate Investment Trust Returns', *Journal of the American Real Estate and Urban Economics Association*, **20**, 25–54.

Ball, M., Lizieri, C. and MacGregor, B. (1998) *The Economics of Commercial Property Markets*, Routledge, London.

Barkham, R. and Geltner, D. (1994) 'Unsmoothing British Valuation-Based Returns Without Assuming an Efficient Market', *Journal of Property Research*, **11**, 810-95.

Barkham, R. and Geltner. D. (1995) 'Price Discovery in American and British Property Markets', *Journal of the American Real Estate and Urban Economics Association*, **23**, 21–44.

BestFit (1998) *BestFit Manual*, Palisade Corporation, Newfield, New York.

Blundell, G. and Ward, C. (1987) 'Property Portfolio Allocation: A Multifactor Model', *Land Development Studies*, **4**, 145–156.

Brooks, C. and Tsolacos, S. (1999) 'The Impact of Economic and Financial Factors on UK Property Performance', *Journal of Property Research*, **16**, 139–152.

Brown, G. (1991) *Property Investment and the Capital Markets*, E and FN Spon, London.

Brown, G. (1992) 'Valuation Accuracy: Developing the Economic Issues', *Journal of Property Research*, **9**, 199–207.

Byrne, P. and Lee, S. (1997) 'Real Estate Portfolio Analysis Under Conditions of Non-Normality: The Case of NCREIF', *Journal of Real Estate Portfolio Management*, **3**, 37–46.

Corgel, J., McIntosh, W. and Ott. S. (1995) 'Real Estate Investment Trusts: A Review of the Financial Economics Literature', *Journal of Real Estate Literature*, **3**, 13–43.

Evans, M., Hastings, N. and Peacock, B. (1993) *Statistical Distributions* 2nd edn, John Wiley, New York.

Fahmi, K. and Al Abbasi, J. (1991) 'Application of a Mix Distribution of Extreme Values to Earthquake Magnitudes in Iraq and Conterminous Regions', *Geophysical Journal of the Royal Astronomical Society*, **107**, 209–217.

Fisher, J., Geltner, D. and Webb, B. (1994) 'Value Indices of Commercial Real Estate: A Comparison of Index Construction Methods', *Journal of Real Estate Finance and Economics*, **9**, 137–164.

Geltner, D. (1991) 'Smoothing in Appraisal Based Returns', *Journal of the American Real Estate and Urban Economics Association*, **13**, 15–31.

Geltner, D. (1993) 'Estimating Market Values from Appraised Values Without Assuming an Efficient Market', *Journal of Real Estate Research*, **8**, 325–345.

Gordon, J. and Canter, T. (1999) 'International Real Estate Securities: A Test of Capital Market Integration', *Journal of Real Estate Portfolio Management*, **5**, 161–170.

Graff R., Harrington, A. and Young, M. (1997) 'The Shape of Australian Real Estate Returns', *Journal of Real Estate Research*, **14**, 291–308.

Gumbel E. (1958) *Statistics of Extreme Distributions*, Columbia University Press, New York.

Gyourko, J. and Keim, D. (1992) 'What Does the Stock Market Tell Us About Real Estate Returns?' *Journal of the American Real Estate and Urban Economics Association*, **20**, 457–486.

Hartzell, D., Hekman, J. and Miles, M. (1986) 'Diversification Categories in Investment Real Estate', *Journal of the American Real Estate and Urban Economics Association*, **14**, 230–254.

Henery, R. (1984) 'An Extreme-Value Model for Predicting the Results of Horse Races', *Applied Statistics*, **33**, 125–133.

Johnson, N., Kotz, S. and Balakrishnan (1995) *Continuous Univariate Distributions*, Volumes 1 & 2, John Wiley, New York.

Lai, T.-Y. and Wang, K. (1998) 'Appraisal Smoothing: The Other Side of the Story', *Real Estate Economics*, **26**, 511–535.

Ling, D. and Naranjõ, A. (1999) 'The Integration of Commercial Real Estate Markets and Stock Markets', *Real Estate Economics*, **27**, 483–516.

Liu, C., Hartzell, D. and Grissom, T. (1990) 'The Integration of the Real Estate Market and the Stock Market, Some Preliminary Evidence', *Journal of Real Estate Finance and Economics*, **3**, 261–282.

Lizieri, C. and Satchell, S. (1997a) 'Interactions Between Property and Equity Markets: An Investigation of the Linkages in the United Kingdom 1972–1992', *Journal of Real Estate Finance and Economics*, **15**, 11–26.

Lizieri, C. and Satchell, S. (1997b) 'Property Company Performance and Real Interest Rates: A Regime Switching Approach', *Journal of Property Research*, **14**, 85–97.

Lizieri, C., Satchell, S., Worzala, E. and Daccó, R. (1998) 'Real Interest Regimes and Real Estate Performance: A Comparison of US and UK Markets', *Journal of Real Estate Research*, **16**, 339–356.

Lizieri, C. and Venmore-Rowland, P. (1993) 'Valuations, Prices and the Market: A Rejoinder', *Journal of Property Research*, **10**, 77–84.

Lu, K. and Mei, J. (1999) 'The Return Distribution of Property Shares in Emerging Markets', *Journal of Real Estate Portfolio Management*, **5**, 145–160.

Maitland-Smith, J. and Brooks, C. (1999) 'Threshold Autoregressive and Markov Switching Models: An Application to Commercial Real Estate', *Journal of Property Research*, **16**, 1–20.

Matysiak, G. and Wang, P. (1995) 'Commercial Property Market Prices and Valuations: Analysing the Correspondence', *Journal of Property Research*, **12**, 181–202.

McCue, T. and Kling, J. (1994) 'Real Estate Returns and the Macro-Economy: Some Empirical Evidence', *Journal of Real Estate Research*, **9**, 277–287.

McLeay, S. (1986) 'Student's *t* and the Distribution of Financial Ratios', *Journal of Business, Finance and Accounting*, **13/2**, 209–222.

Miles, M. and McCue, T. (1984) 'Commercial Real Estate Returns', *Journal of the American Real Estate and Urban Economics Association*, **12**, 335–277.

Myer, N. and Webb, J. (1993) 'Return Properties of Equity REITs, Common Stocks and Commercial Real Estate', *Journal of Real Estate Research*, **8**, 87–106.

Myer, N. and Webb, J. (1994) 'Statistical Properties of Returns: Financial Assets versus Commercial Real Estate', *Journal of Real Estate Finance and Economics*, **8**, 267–282.

Nelling, E. and Gyourko, J. (1998) 'The Predictability of Equity REIT Returns,' *Journal of Real Estate Research*, **16**, 251–268.

Newell, G. and Matysiak, G. (1997) *An Empirical Investigation into the Presence of Chaotic Behaviour in UK Property Markets*, Royal Institution of Chartered Surveyors Research Report, RICS Books, London.

Newell, G., Peat, M. and Stevenson, M. (1996) 'Testing for Evidence of Non-Linear Structure in Australian Real Estate Market Returns', Working Paper #61, University of Technology, Sydney, Australia.

Okunev, J. and Wilson, P. (1997) 'Using Non-Linear Tests to Examine Integration Between Real Estate and Stock Markets', *Real Estate Economics*, **25**, 487–503.

Quan, D. and Quigley, J. (1989) 'Inferring an Investment Return Series for Real Estate from Observations on Sales', *Journal of the American Real Estate and Urban Economics Association*, **17**, 218–230.

Quan, D. and Quigley, J. (1991) 'Price Formation and the Appraisal Function in Real Estate Markets', *Journal of Real Estate Finance and Economics*, **4**, 127–146.

Quan, D. and Titman, S. (1999) 'Do Real Estate Markets and Stock Prices Move Together? An International Analysis', *Real Estate Economics*, **27**, 183–207.

Ross, S. and Zisler, R. (1991) 'Risk and Return in Real Estate', *Journal of Real Estate Finance and Economics*, **4**, 175–190.

Seiler, M., Webb, J. and Myer, N. (1999) 'Are EREITs Real Estate?' *Journal of Real Estate Portfolio Management*, **5**, 171–181.

Wang, P., Lizieri, C. and Matysiak, G. (1997) 'Information Asymmetry, Long Run Relationship and Price Discovery in Property Markets', *European Journal of Finance*, **3**, 261–275.

Ward, C. and Wu, W. (1994) 'The Valuation Smoothing Effects on Property Returns: Does the Market Have a Memory?' *Proceedings, The Cutting Edge Property Research Conference*, pp. 45–68, London, RICS.

Wiggins J. (1991) 'Empirical Tests of the Bias and Efficiency of the Extreme Variance Estimator for Common Stocks', *Journal of Business of the University of Chicago*, **64**, 417–432.

Wilson, P. and Okunev, J. (1999) 'Spectral Analysis of Real Estate and Financial Asset Markets', *Journal of Property Investment and Finance*, **17**, 61–74.

Young, M. and Graff, R. (1995) 'Real Estate is Not Normal: A Fresh Look at Real Estate Return Distributions', *Journal of Real Estate Finance and Economics*, **10**, 223–259.

APPENDIX

Table A.1 Distribution of UK Government Bond (medium-term) returns.

Gilts	Ranked by likelihood				
Test\full sample	Unrestricted fitting (including transformed distributions)			Open-ended distributions	Goodness of fit result
Chi-square	Normal >0.73	Logistic >0.71	Triang. >0.61	Error function	Rejected
				Logistic	>0.71
				Normal	>0.73
				Student's t	Rejected
Kolmogorov–Smirnov	Weibull >0.1	Normal >0.15	Logistic >0.15	Error function	Rejected
				Logistic	>0.15
				Normal	>0.15
				Student's t	Rejected
Anderson–Darling	Normal >0.15	Logistic >0.15	Weibull rejected	Error function	Rejected
				Logistic	>0.15
				Normal	>0.15
				Student's t	Rejected
Sub-sample					
Chi-square	Logistic >0.87	Normal >0.85	Triang. >0.59	Error function	Rejected
				Logistic	>0.87
				Normal	>0.85
				Student's t	Rejected
Kolmogorov–Smirnov	Weibull >0.1	Normal >0.15	Logistic >0.15	Error function	Rejected
				Logistic	>0.15
				Normal	>0.15
				Student's t	Rejected
Anderson–Darling	Logistic >0.15	Normal >0.15	Weibull Rejected	Error function	Rejected
				Logistic	>0.15
				Normal	>0.15
				Student's t	Rejected

Table A.2 Distribution of FT Sector Indices return

	FT-Real Estate			FT-Construct	
Test\full sample	Open-ended distributions	Goodness of fit result	*Test\full sample*	Open-ended distributions	Goodness of fit result
Chi-Square	Error function	Rejected	Chi-square	Error function	Rejected
	Logistic	>0.14		Logistic	>0.71
	Normal	Rejected		Normal	>0.73
	Student's t	Rejected		Student's t	Rejected
Kolmogorov–Smirnov	Error function	Rejected	Kolmogorov–Smirnov	Error function	Rejected
	Logistic	>0.15		Logistic	>0.15
	Normal	>0.05		Normal	>0.15
	Student's t	Rejected		Student's t	Rejected
Anderson–Darling	Error function	Rejected	Anderson–Darling	Error function	Rejected
	Logistic	>0.15		Logistic	>0.15
	Normal	Rejected		Normal	>0.15
	Student's t	Rejected		Student's t	Rejected
Sub-sample			*Sub-sample*		
Chi-square	Error function	Rejected	Chi-square	Error function	Rejected
	Logistic	>0.87		Logistic	>0.87
	Normal	>0.85		Normal	>0.85
	Student's t	Rejected		Student's t	Rejected
Kolmogorov–Smirnov	Error function	Rejected	Kolmogorov–Smirnov	Error function	Rejected
	Logistic	>0.15		Logistic	>0.15
	Normal	>0.15		Normal	>0.15
	Student's t	Rejected		Student's t	Rejected
Anderson–Darling	Error function	Rejected	Anderson–Darling	Error function	Rejected
	Logistic	>0.15		Logistic	>0.15
	Normal	>0.15		Normal	>0.15
	Student's t	Rejected		Student's t	Rejected

Chapter 4

Modelling emerging market risk premia using higher moments

SOOSUNG HWANG AND STEPHEN E. SATCHELL

Reprinted with permission from the *International Journal of Finance and Economics* 4 (1999).

ABSTRACT

The purpose of this chapter is to assess the incremental value of higher moments in modelling CAPMs of emerging markets. While it is recognized that emerging markets are unlikely to yield sensible results in a mean-variance world, the high skewness and kurtosis present in emerging markets returns make our assessment potentially interesting. Generalized method of moments (GMM) is used for the estimation. We also present new versions of higher-moment market models of the data-generating process of the individual emerging markets and use these to identify model parameters. We find some evidence that emerging markets are better explained with additional systematic risks such as co-skewness and co-kurtosis than the conventional mean-variance CAPM.

4.1 INTRODUCTION

Many empirical studies on emerging markets suggest that methods of conventional finance such as the mean-variance CAPM are highly misleading when applied to pricing assets. There are many explanations given: non-stationarity due to evolving degrees of market integration, the importance of non-economic factors such as political risk, the presence of survivorship and re-emerging bias in emerging markets data; country selection bias, and the evolution from an emerging market to a mature one.

In this study, we focus on the highly significant skewness and kurtosis prevalent in emerging markets data. The question we explore in this study is whether emerging markets may be better explained with additional risk factors such as higher moments, e.g. skewness and kurtosis. We develop higher-moment CAPMs, and test them using generalized method of moments since the distribution function of emerging markets return is not known. Our empirical results show that emerging markets are better explained with higher-moments CAPMs. In addition, co-kurtosis has at least as much explanatory power as co-skewness for the countries used in this study.

In addition, we also use an alternative approach using data-generating processes conditioning on the market as in Sharpe's market model. This is because the high multicollinearity in sample co-moments seems to make it hard to jointly estimate co-skewness and co-kurtosis. To reduce these difficulties, specific models are introduced as candidate data-generating processes; these are the quadratic and cubic market models. We show that higher-moment data-generating processes are consistent with higher-moment CAPMs, and empirical tests reveal that the collinearity in the parameters appears to be reduced.

We note that while the use of higher moments seems to explain emerging markets better than conventional CAPMs, the higher-moment CAPMs are based on an assumption of stationarity in emerging market returns. Since there is clear evolution in these markets, our basic assumption is probably inappropriate. In future research, we hope to investigate this problem further by combining the ideas of this chapter with the evolving models of Bekaert and Harvey (1995).

Research on emerging markets investment has identified the following features: high returns, high volatility, low correlation between emerging and mature markets and low correlation between emerging markets which has increased through time. Much of the research has concentrated on the question of the usefulness of conventional finance to price assets in emerging markets. The results suggest that the mean-variance CAPM is highly misleading and that a capitalization-weighted portfolio seriously under-performs such simple constructs as an equally weighted portfolio, for example.

Explanations for the theoretical shortcomings involve non-stationarity due to, for example, evolving degrees of market integration, the importance of non-economic factors, such as political risk, and the inadequacy of two-fund separation and representative agent based arguments. Bekaert *et al.* (1997) discuss the above and also present other explanations concerned with the nature of data; the presence of survivorship bias, the data are chosen over a short period, the data miss the longer period of earlier failure (re-emerging bias); there is also the presence of country selection bias. Other references for the above discussion are numerous. Results on portfolio evaluation can be found in Masters (1998).

It is probably unlikely that any version of the CAPM will work in these markets. One reason may be due to liberalization within the sample period such that a local CAPM was valid before the structural break and a world CAPM was valid after the break: see Bekaert and Harvey (1995, 1997). More recently some markets, i.e. Malaysia, have been trying to engineer a reverse process, referred to as submerging markets. All in all, a conventional model will face difficulties.

It is likely that one cannot model risk premia in those markets without including political/social variables. However, we are not aware of much modelling work that uses the highly significant skewness and kurtosis prevalent in emerging markets data; see, for example, Bekaert *et al.* (1998) for the evidence of significant skewness and kurtosis in these markets. Since there exists a literature on the incorporation of higher moments into risk premia, see Arditti (1967), Jean (1971, 1973), Ingersoll (1975), Kraus and Litzenberger (1976), Friend and Westerfield (1980), Sears and Wei (1985, 1988), Homaifar and Graddy (1988), and Lim (1989), it seems worth while to explore this modelling strategy, if only to eliminate it as a potential explanation. Therefore, throughout this study, we implicitly assume that higher moments of returns exist; for the three-moment CAPMs, the first three moments are assumed to exist and for the four-moment CAPMs, the first four moments are assumed to exist.

Although a theory of asset pricing using co-skewness is well-known, a theory involving co-skewness and co-kurtosis is not. Homaifar and Graddy (1988) derive a higher-moment CAPM with Sharpe's (1964) methodology and test the higher-moment CAPM using principal component regression, latent root regression, and ordinary least square regression. In this chapter we develop higher-moment CAPMs in a different way (see Section 4.2) and test them using Hansen's (1982) generalized method of moments (GMM). To implement and estimate these models, certain marginal rates of substitution between different moments need to be identified. We achieve this by considering (a) quartic approximations to utility functions, (b) logarithmic utility; these calculations extend existing results in the non-normal CAPM literature.

In Section 4.3 we describe our data and estimation technique. Following Lim (1989), we use a multivariate approach with generalized method of moments (GMM). This procedure is known to be consistent but inefficient relative to maximum likelihood. However, it has the important property of being implementable without having to specify the data-generating process (DGP) for returns. It also avoids the measurement error problem present in traditional cross-sectional asset pricing model such as Kraus and

Litzenberger (1976), Friend and Westerfield (1980), Sears and Wei (1988) and Homaifar and Graddy (1988).

There is enormous difficulty in assessing the correct data-generating process for emerging market returns. Our results reflect the difficulty of modelling returns in these markets; skewness and kurtosis move in a collinear manner with the market. To reduce these difficulties, specific models are introduced as candidate DGPs in Section 4.4 these are the quadratic and cubic market models. Assuming that the data are generated by these processes implies specific restrictions for the higher moment CAPMs which are presented in Theorem 4; these results are new to the literature. The relationship between the higher-moment CAPMs and the higher-moment market models is investigated and the higher-moment market models are estimated for the emerging markets. We present conclusions in Section 4.5.

4.2 HIGHER-MOMENT CAPMs

In this section, we present various versions of the higher-moment CAPM. It is assumed that there is a representative (mature-market) investor, and that all returns are in units of period 1 consumption. We suppose that there is a riskless asset whose return is r_f and N risky assets whose ith return is represented as r_i. Investment proportions on the riskless asset and the N risky assets are x_0 and x_i ($i = 1, 2, 3, \ldots, N$), where $x_0 + \sum_{i=1}^{N} x_i = 1$. We assume that for the investor, the initial investment is 1 and the end-of-period wealth is represented as w. Then the end-of-period wealth is

$$w = x_0(1 + r_f) + \sum_{i=1}^{N} x_i(1 + r_i) \tag{4.1}$$

Note that the portfolio return for the investor is $r_p = x_0 r_f + \sum_{i=1}^{N} x_i r_i$.

The first four moments of the end-of-period wealth and their relationship with systematic risk measures (i.e. beta, systematic skewness, and systematic kurtosis) can be derived as in Kraus and Litzenberger (1976) (see Appendix 1). That is, if we define the systematic risk measures, β_{ip}, γ_{ip}, and θ_{ip} as

$$\beta_{ip} = \frac{E[\{r_i - E(r_i)\}\{r_p - E(r_p)\}]}{E[\{r_p - E(r_p)\}^2]} \tag{4.2}$$

$$\gamma_{ip} = \frac{E[\{r_i - E(r_i)\}\{r_p - E(r_p)\}^2]}{E[\{r_p - E(r_p)\}^3]} \tag{4.3}$$

$$\theta_{ip} = \frac{E[\{r_i - E(r_i)\}\{r_p - E(r_p)\}^3]}{E[\{r_p - E(r_p)\}^4]} \tag{4.4}$$

then it follows that

$$\sigma(w) = \sum_{i=1}^{N} x_i \beta_{ip} \sigma(r_p) \tag{4.5}$$

where $\sigma(z) = E[\{z - E(z)\}^2]^{1/2}$,

$$\gamma(w) = \sum_{i=1}^{N} x_i \gamma_{ip} \gamma(r_p) \tag{4.6}$$

where $\gamma(z) = E[\{z - E(z)\}^3]^{1/3}$, and

$$\theta(w) = \sum_{i=1}^{N} x_i \theta_{ip} \theta(r_p) \tag{4.7}$$

where $\theta(z) = E[\{z - E(z)\}^4]^{1/4}$ and z is a random variable (we note that the above parameters all have the property that they are homogeneous of degree 1 in x). The measures, β_{ip}, γ_{ip}, and θ_{ip}, are known as beta, systematic skewness and systematic kurtosis and, as we shall see, are natural measures of systematic risk, or exposure, of an asset to market variance, skewness and kurtosis. Here we use the subscript p to refer to the portfolio of interest. Throughout this study, $\sigma(z)$, $\gamma(z)$, and $\theta(z)$ are called standard deviation, skewness, and kurtosis. Note that skewness and kurtosis are generally defined as $E[\{z - E(z)\}^3]/\sigma(z)^3$ and $E[\{z - E(z)\}^4]/\sigma(z)^4$, respectively. In this study we call these expressions 'normalized skewness' and 'normalized kurtosis' to separate them from our definitions in equations (4.6) and (4.7) .

The investment problem is described next; the investor maximizes the expected utility of end-of-period wealth subject to a budget constraint as follows:

$$Max\ E[U(w)] = f(E(w), \sigma(w), \gamma(w), \theta(w)) \tag{4.8}$$

$$\textit{subject to} \qquad 1 = x_0 + \sum_{i=1}^{N} x_i$$

Taking the first-order conditions for the Lagrangian which is formed for the above maximization problem and solving for the investor's equilibrium condition, we obtain the following equation (see Appendix 2):

$$E(r_i) - r_f = \left[\frac{dE(w)}{d\sigma(w)}\right] \beta_{ip} \sigma(r_p) + \left[\frac{dE(w)}{d\gamma(w)}\right] \gamma_{ip} \gamma(r_p) + \left[\frac{dE(w)}{d\theta(w)}\right] \theta_{ip} \theta(r_p) \tag{4.9}$$

In order to move from the individual equilibrium model to a market equilibrium model, we need a portfolio separation theorem. Under this theorem, all individual investors maximize their utility with two funds; a riskless asset and the market portfolio. This is referred to as two-fund money separation (TFMS). Conditions which ensure TFMS are that all agents have a hyperbolic absolute risk aversion (HARA) utility with the same 'cautiousness' parameter. In this case, the individual investor's optimum portfolio composition is equivalent to that of the market portfolio. Therefore, equation (4.9) becomes

$$E(r_i) - r_f = \left[\frac{dE(w)}{d\sigma(w)}\right]\beta_{im}\sigma(r_m) + \left[\frac{dE(w)}{d\gamma(w)}\right]\gamma_{im}\gamma(r_m) + \left[\frac{dE(w)}{d\theta(w)}\right]\theta_{im}\theta(r_m) \tag{4.10}$$

where r_m is the rate of return on the market portfolio. We present the above result as theorem 1.

Theorem 1. *The four-moment CAPM can be represented as*

$$E(r_i) - r_f = \alpha_1\beta_{im} + \alpha_2\gamma_{im} + \alpha_3\theta_{im} \tag{4.11}$$

where $\alpha_1 = \frac{dE(w)}{d\sigma(w)}\sigma(r_m)$, $\alpha_2 = \frac{dE(w)}{d\gamma(w)}\gamma(r_m)$ *and* $\alpha_3 = \frac{dE(w)}{d\theta(w)}\theta(r_m)$.

Proof. See above.

Remark 1. *We expect the market price of beta reduction,* α_1*, to be positive as in the conventional CAPM. On the other hand, the market price of co-skewness,* α_2*, should be negative (positive) when* $\gamma(r_m) > 0$ $(\gamma(r_m) < 0)$*, since*

$$\frac{dE(w)}{d\gamma(w)} = -\frac{\partial E[U(w)]/\partial\gamma(w)}{\partial E[U(w)]/\partial E(w)} < 0$$

under non-increasing absolute risk aversion, see equations (4.15) and (4.17). Therefore, α_2 *is expected to have the opposite sign as* $\gamma(r_m)$*, see Kraus and Litzenberger (1976). Finally, the market price of co-kurtosis,* α_3*, is expected to be positive, since*

$$\frac{dE(w)}{d\theta(w)} = -\frac{\partial E[U(w)]/\partial\theta(w)}{\partial E[U(w)]/\partial E(w)} > 0$$

see equations (4.15) and (4.18). That is, the positive α_3 *is an additional measure of degree of dispersion in returns and thus should have the similar explanation to* α_1.

Remark 2. *If* $\alpha_3 = 0$*, we have the Kraus and Litzenberger (1976) (KL) three-moment CAPM. We refer to equation (4.11) as the KL four-moment CAPM.*

It is important to note that equation (4.11) has been derived without any assumptions abut the DGP generating returns. Indeed this section is written consciously trying to avoid specifying a model for emerging market returns. Authors, notably Kraus and Litzenberger (1976, 1983), have specified a DGP relating r_i to a quadratic conditional expectation function (CEF) in r_m. This can then be used to make inferences about co-skewness. Likewise, if we were to add a cubic CEF, we could model co-kurtosis. Such an approach will be left to Section 4.4.

Empirical results on the three-moment CAPM are not consistent: KL found significant coefficients on beta and co-skewness, while Friend and Westerfield (1980) did not. Sears and Wei (1985) argued that the empirical value of market risk premium, $E(r_m) - r_f$, can affect the estimation of asset pricing models, that is, coefficients on beta and co-skewness. When we apply equation (4.10) to the market portfolio, we obtain the following equation:

$$E(r_m) - r_f = \left[\frac{dE(w)}{d\sigma(w)}\right]\sigma(r_m) + \left[\frac{dE(w)}{d\gamma(w)}\right]\gamma(r_m) + \left[\frac{dE(w)}{d\theta(w)}\right]\theta(r_m) \qquad (4.12)$$

since $\beta_{im} = \gamma_{im} = \theta_{im} = 1$ when i is the market portfolio. Dividing equation (4.10) by equation (4.12), we present as a corollary to theorem 1 the Sears and Wei (1985) version of the four-moment CAPM.

Corollary 2. *The Sears and Wei (1985) (SW) four-moment CAPM is represented as*

$$E(r_i) - r_f = (b_1\beta_{im} + b_2\gamma_{im} + b_3\theta_{im})(E(r_m) - r_f) \qquad (4.13)$$

where

$$b_1 = \frac{\sigma(r_m)}{\sigma(r_m) + k_1\gamma(r_m) + k_2\theta(r_m)}, \quad b_2 = \frac{k_1\gamma(r_m)}{\sigma(r_m) + k_1\gamma(r_m) + k_2\theta(r_m)},$$

$$b_3 = \frac{k_2\theta(r_m)}{\sigma(r_m) + k_1\gamma(r_m) + k_2\theta(r_m)},$$

$$k_1 = \frac{dE(w)/d\gamma(w)}{dE(w)/d\sigma(w)}, \quad \text{and } k_2 = \frac{dE(w)/d\theta(w)}{dE(w)/d\sigma(w)}$$

Remark 3. *If $k_2 = 0$, we have the SW three-moment CAPM.*

Here, k_1 is interpreted as the market's marginal rate of substitution between skewness and risk and k_2 is the market's marginal rate of substitution between kurtosis and risk. Therefore, the coefficients of KL models have the following relationship with those of SW models: $\alpha_1 = b_1(E(r_m) - r_f)$ and $\alpha_2 = b_2(E(r_m) - r_f)$.

Theoretically, the market risk premium is always positive. However, in practice, there may be a period when the sample value of the market risk premium has a negative sign. SW argue that the tests of asset-pricing model may be affected by the sign of the market risk premium. These formulae depend upon the assumption that equation (4.11) holds for the market as well, which will be discussed later.

For the SW four-moment CAPM in equation (4.13), we further investigate the marginal rates of substitution. The investor's expected utility of end of period wealth function may be approximated as follows using a Taylor series about $E(w)$:

$$E[U(w)] \approx U(E(w)) + \frac{U''(E(w))}{2!}\sigma(w)^2 + \frac{U'''(E(w))}{3!}\gamma(w)^3 + \frac{U''''(E(w))}{4!}\theta(w)^4 \tag{4.14}$$

The non-satiation and decreasing marginal utility conditions require $U'(E(w)) > 0$ and $U''(E(w)) < 0$, respectively. In addition, the sufficient condition for the non-increasing absolute risk aversion is $U'''(E(w)) > 0$. Turning to preference for the fourth moment, Scott and Horvath (1980) show in Theorem 2 that $U''''(E(w)) < 0$.[1] Therefore, using these conditions, when we differentiate equation (4.14) with respect to $E(w)$, $\sigma(w)$, $\gamma(w)$, $\theta(w)$, we obtain[2]

$$\frac{\partial E[U(w)]}{\partial E(w)} \approx U'(E(w)) > 0 \tag{4.15}$$

$$\frac{\partial E[U(w)]}{\partial \sigma(w)} \approx U''(E(w))\sigma(w) < 0 \tag{4.16}$$

$$\frac{\partial E[U(w)]}{\partial \gamma(w)} \approx \frac{U'''(E(w))}{2!}\gamma(w)^2 > 0 \tag{4.17}$$

$$\frac{\partial E[U(w)]}{\partial \theta(w)} \approx \frac{U''''(E(w))}{3!}\theta(w)^3 < 0 \tag{4.18}$$

[1]Scott and Horvath (1980, A3, p. 916) use the extra condition called strict consistency in preference direction. This is a strong condition. More generally, Kraus and Litzenberger (1983) show that in a Pareto-efficient allocation, the fourth derivative of the aggregated utility function of the representative agent does not exhibit a negative or positive sign, even if all the individuals have utility functions that have fourth derivatives with the same sign.

[2]Strict consistency in preference will imply that

$$\frac{\partial E[U(w)]}{\partial \gamma(w)} > 0$$

See Scott and Horvath, 1980, theorem 1. For the approximation given by equation (4.14), we only require that $U'''(E(w)) > 0$.

Note that the rates of the marginal substitution can be represented as

$$k_1 = \frac{\partial E[U(w)]/\partial\gamma(w)}{\partial E[U(w)]/\partial\sigma(w)}$$

and

$$k_2 = \frac{\partial E[U(w)]/\partial\theta(w)}{\partial E[U(w)]/\partial\sigma(w)}$$

using equations (A2.5), (A2.6), and (A2.7) in Appendix 2.

Remark 4. *The marginal rates of substitution will have the following signs;* $k_1 < 0$ *and* $k_2 > 0$.

Negative k_1 has the interpretation that rational investors prefer positive skewness and reduced risks. On the other hand, k_2 is positive, since investors dislike dispersion which both variance and kurtosis measure. As mentioned in Scott and Horvath (1980), $U''''(E(w)) < 0$ may be explained in the same way as $U''(E(w)) < 0$. That is, investors dislike, in the above sense, dispersion of wealth for a given expected wealth. It therefore follows that in some situations, kurtosis may become an additional risk measure for assets which variance alone fails to explain.

For the four-moment CAPM, it seems to be difficult to identify k_1 and k_2. One solution is to use a known utility function which is parameter-free. One obvious candidate is log-utility, $U(w) = ln(w)$. In this case, we can represent the CAPM with skewness and kurtosis as follows (see Appendix 3),

$$E(r_i) - r_f = (L_1\beta_{im} + L_2\gamma_{im} + L_3\theta_{im})(E(r_m) - r_f) \tag{4.19}$$

where

$$L_1 = \frac{E(w)^2\sigma(r_m)^2}{E(w)^2\sigma(r_m)^2 - E(w)\gamma(r_m)^3 + \theta(r_m)^4},$$

$$L_2 = -\frac{E(w)\gamma(r_m)^3}{E(w)^2\sigma(r_m)^2 - E(w)\gamma(r_m)^3 + \theta(r_m)^4},$$

and

$$L_3 = \frac{\theta(r_m)^4}{E(w)^2\sigma(r_m)^2 - E(w)\gamma(r_m)^3 + \theta(r_m)^4}$$

Table 4.1 Various versions of the CAPM

Names	Models	Equations	Subsections and tables
Model I	Mean-variance CAPM	(4.37)	'Mean-variance CAPM (Model I)', Table 4.5
Model II	KL three-moment CAPM	(4.38)	'KL Three-moment CAPM (Model II)', Table 4.6
Model III	KL four-moment CAPM	(4.11)	'KL Four-moment CAPM (Model III)', Table 4.8
Model IV	KL second- and fourth-moment CAPM	(4.40)	'KL Second and Fourth-moment CAPM (Model IV)', Table 4.9
Model V	SW three-moment CAPM	(4.39)	'SW Three-moment CAPM (Model V)', Table 4.7
Model VI	SW four-moment CAPM	(4.13)	*
Model VII	SW four-moment CAPM with log-utility	(4.19)	*

*Does not report results for these models because of convergence problem.

To summarize this section, we present seven models in Table 4.1. In the following section, the estimation method for each model is described and results follow.

4.3 EMPIRICAL TESTS

All empirical tests in this paper are presented from an American investors' point of view. Returns of emerging markets are represented in dollars. For the riskless rate of return, we use the 3-month US treasury bill. As a proxy of the market portfolio, Morgan Stanley Capital International (MSCI) world index total returns are used. Our emerging market return series from the International Finance Corporation (IFC) global data set consist of 17 countries from January 1985 to January 1997 for a total of 145 observations. All the above assumptions may involve difficulties, but they are standard.

Note that the rates of return on the riskless asset are not constant through time. As in KL, the observed excess rates of return on the individual countries deflated by unity plus the riskless interest rates, $R_{it} = (r_{it} - r_{ft})/(1 + r_{ft})$, are used and the observed excess rates of return on the market portfolio are also deflated in the same way. This is a method to make moments of the rate of returns intertemporal constants under a changing riskless interest rate (see Fama, 1970). Under certain circumstances, it allows us to use one period models for time-series data.

Table 4.2 reports the first four moments of the data used in this study. As pointed out in Bekaert *et al.* (1998), returns of the emerging markets are higher than the world market portfolio in 10 out of 17 emerging markets. In particular, all the unconditional volatilities of the emerging markets are higher

Table 4.2 Statistical properties of emerging markets returns

	Mean	S.D.	Normalized skewness	Normalized excess kurtosis	Jarque–Bera ($\chi^2(2)$)
(A) The first four moments of emerging markets monthly returns – October 1987 market crash included					
3-month Treasury Bill	0.4836	0.1391	−0.0582	−0.8356*	4.30
Market portfolio	0.7389	4.1172	−0.8400**	3.4145**	87.49**
Greece	1.0433	10.6924	0.8131**	3.6292**	95.55**
Argentina	1.7178	22.1976	0.3413*	7.9997**	389.45**
Brazil	0.7965	18.6065	−0.5772**	2.7326**	53.16**
Chile	2.3414	7.5944	−0.0525	−0.0902	0.12
Mexico	1.6373	14.1496	−2.5179**	13.6087**	1272.11**
India	0.4136	9.3931	0.2482	0.5015	3.01
Korea	0.5534	8.0101	0.3289	−0.0088	2.61
Thailand	1.0643	8.9447	−0.8012**	3.5682**	92.43**
Zimbabwe	1.7897	8.7361	0.1766	2.2272**	30.72**
Jordan	0.0796	4.6921	0.1068	1.1560**	8.35**
Colombia	1.9170	8.0836	1.1363**	2.6627**	74.04**
Venezuela	0.7336	14.1033	−1.3266**	6.1726**	272.72**
Taiwan	1.2000	13.5401	−0.1512	1.8391**	20.99**
Malaysia	0.5891	7.5910	−0.9332**	3.5182**	95.83**
Pakistan	0.5060	6.9609	0.7881**	3.6939**	97.45**
Philippines	2.2517	9.7324	0.0456	2.6773**	43.36**
Nigeria	0.0543	16.6513	−3.1868**	25.2309**	4091.56**
(B) The first four moments of emerging markets monthly returns – October 1987 market crash excluded					
3-month Treasury Bill	0.4840	0.1395	−0.0656	−0.8461**	4.43
Market portfolio	0.8756	3.7873	−0.2021	0.7578*	4.46
Greece	1.1423	10.6628	0.8144**	3.6977**	98.64*
Argentina	1.9019	22.1637	0.3321	8.1215**	401.17**
Brazil	0.9575	18.5698	−0.5973**	2.8237**	56.79**
Chile	2.5070	7.3535	0.1149	−0.4768	1.69
Mexico	2.0338	13.3659	−2.5457**	15.9036**	1684.69**
India	0.4105	9.4259	0.2484	0.4778	2.87
Korea	0.5688	8.0359	0.3223	−0.0290	2.52
Thailand	1.3602	8.2334	−0.1618	1.0315**	7.06*
Zimbabwe	1.7265	8.7334	0.1920	2.2689**	31.99**
Jordan	0.0860	4.7079	0.1025	1.1291**	7.96*
Colombia	1.9212	8.1117	1.1309**	2.6222**	72.45**
Venezuela	0.7072	14.1489	−1.3176**	6.1098**	267.49**
Taiwan	1.5148	13.0440	0.0538	1.5970**	15.48**
Malaysia	0.8487	6.9419	−0.2360	0.3158	1.95
Pakistan	0.5149	6.9843	0.7818**	3.6476**	95.16**
Philippines	2.3412	9.7063	0.0348	2.7566**	45.94**
Nigeria	0.0580	16.7093	−3.1768**	25.0455**	4033.68**

*Denotes significance at 5% level.

**Denotes significance at 1% level.

Morgan Stanley world index is used for the market portfolio. Deflated excess returns are used for the market portfolio and emerging markets.

than that of the market portfolio. Consideration of the third and fourth moments shows that 14 out of 17 emerging markets are not normally distributed. Panel B of Table 4.2 shows certain statistical properties of emerging markets when the market crash of October 1987 is excluded. The results are similar to those of panel A except for the market portfolio and Malaysia. This indirectly indicates that emerging market returns are not closely correlated with developed market returns. In addition, note that the number of significant coefficients of kurtosis is larger than the corresponding number of skewness coefficients. That is, the main source of non-normality in emerging markets is kurtosis rather than skewness.

For the SW higher-moment CAPM we need the marginal rates of substitution. In the next subsection, we first estimate the marginal rates of substitution between risk and skewness and kurtosis for the American investor. Then the higher-moment CAPMs will be estimated using emerging market data.

4.3.1 Estimation of the marginal rates of substitution

A potential difficulty with our estimation is that the marginal rates of substitution, k_1 and k_2, inferred from the emerging markets data are wildly inaccurate measures of k_1 and k_2. Emerging market returns have quite different statistical properties from US asset returns and the marginal rates of substitution calculated from emerging market returns may be different from those calculated from domestic US data. If k_1 and k_2 are inferred from emerging markets, the estimates of the marginal rates of substitution are sensitive to the countries selected, since the first four moments of emerging markets are quite different across countries (see Table 4.2). This means that the indirect utility function of the representative US investor inferred from our emerging market returns is likely to contaminate all our other results via the nonlinearity of the model. For these reasons, the marginal rates of substitution are estimated separately using a US database rather than emerging markets data. This procedure assumes that American investors have the same marginal rates of substitution over domestic and overseas investment. It is only the moments that matter in the indirect utility function, not the location of the asset.

To reduce measurement errors in beta, co-skewness, and co-kurtosis, risk asset portfolios are formed with a grouping procedure similar to the procedures used by Kraus and Litzenberger (1976) and Sears and Wei (1988). We use monthly deflated excess returns on 273 US stocks in the MSCI world universe from January 1985 to January 1997. The S&P 500 index total returns are used as a proxy of the market portfolio and the 3-month US treasury bill is used for the riskless rate of return.

First, we calculate systematic risks using 5 years' monthly deflated excess returns. Then stocks are ranked into N-tiles (N groups) on the basis of beta estimates, and then for each group, stocks are ranked again into N-tiles on the basis of co-skewness estimates; therefore, the number of the risk asset portfolios for beta and co-skewness is N^2. In addition, for risk asset portfolios for beta, co-skewness, and co-kurtosis, stocks are ranked again into N-tiles on the basis of co-kurtosis estimates for each groups obtained for the risk asset portfolios of beta and co-skewness.. Therefore, the number of risk asset portfolios for beta, co-skewness, and co-kurtosis is N^3. The subsequent 12-month deflated excess returns for the risk portfolios are calculated for each group. This procedure is repeated for the entire sample period beginning each January. The final subsequent portfolio returns consist of 13-month returns from January 1996 to January 1997. This provides 85 monthly deflated excess returns from January 1990 to January 1997 for each of the N^2 (or N^3) portfolios.

To avoid a risk of spurious correlation between the systematic risks of the portfolios obtained above, the sample estimates of the systematic risks for the portfolios are calculated as follows, see Kraus and Litzenberger (1976);

$$\widehat{\beta}_{imt} = \frac{\sum_{s=1,s\neq t}^{T}(R_{is} - \overline{R}_i)(R_{ms} - \overline{R}_m)}{\sum_{s=1}^{T}(R_{ms} - \overline{R}_m)^2} \tag{4.20}$$

$$\widehat{\gamma}_{imt} = \frac{\sum_{s=1,s\neq t}^{T}(R_{is} - \overline{R}_i)(R_{ms} - \overline{R}_m)^2}{\sum_{s=1}^{T}(R_{ms} - \overline{R}_m)^3} \tag{4.21}$$

$$\widehat{\theta}_{imt} = \frac{\sum_{s=1,s\neq t}^{T}(R_{is} - \overline{R}_i)(R_{ms} - \overline{R}_m)^3}{\sum_{s=1}^{T}(R_{ms} - \overline{R}_m)^4} \tag{4.22}$$

The marginal rates of substitution are calculated using the GMM method. The orthogonality conditions are derived as follows. We obtain the following relationships from the SW four-moment CAPM in equation (4.13);

$$k_1 = \frac{b_2\sigma(r_m)}{b_1\gamma(r_m)} \quad \text{and} \quad k_2 = \frac{b_3\sigma(r_m)}{b_1\theta(r_m)}.$$

These relationships can also be represented as

$$b_2 = \frac{k_1 b_1\gamma(r_m)}{\sigma(r_m)} \quad \text{and} \quad b_3 = \frac{k_2 b_1\theta(r_m)}{\sigma(r_m)}.$$

Replacing b_2 and b_3 with these relationships, the SW four-moment CAPM can be rewritten as

$$E(r_i) - r_f = (b_1\beta_{im} + \frac{k_1 b_1 \gamma(r_m)}{\sigma(r_m)}\gamma_{im} + \frac{k_2 b_1 \theta(r_m)}{\sigma(r_m)}\theta_{im})(E(r_m) - r_f) \quad (4.23)$$

and therefore, our orthogonality condition, $h_t(\mathbf{\Theta})$, for the estimation of k_1 and k_2 is

$$E[R_{it} - b_0 - b_1\{\widehat{\beta}_{imt} + \widehat{\gamma}(R_m)\widehat{\gamma}_{imt}\widehat{\sigma}(R_m)^{-1}k_1 + \widehat{\theta}(R_m)\widehat{\theta}_{imt}\widehat{\sigma}(R_m)^{-1}k_2\}R_{mt}] = 0 \quad (4.24)$$

where R_{it} and R_{mt} are deflated excess returns of portfolio i and the market portfolio at time t, $\widehat{\sigma}(R_m)$, $\widehat{\gamma}(R_m)$, $\widehat{\theta}(R_m)$, $\widehat{\beta}_{imt}$, $\widehat{\gamma}_{imt}$, and $\widehat{\theta}_{imt}$ are sample estimates, and $\mathbf{\Theta}' = (\alpha_0, \alpha_1, k_1, k_2)$ is a vector of parameters to be estimated. Therefore, for the estimation of k_1 and k_2, we have four parameters to estimate and N^3 orthogonal conditions ($N^3 - 4$ degrees of freedom). On the other hand, for the estimation of k_1, we have three parameters, $\mathbf{\Theta}' = (\alpha_0, \alpha_1, k_1)$, and N^2 orthogonal conditions ($N^2 - 3$ degrees of freedom). The parameters are estimated until convergence by iterating on the weighting matrix.

In this study, for the estimation of k_1, N is set to 5 and 25 risky asset portfolios are formed. For the estimation of k_1 and k_2, N is set to 3 and 27 portfolios are constructed. This should give us sensible estimates of the marginal rates of substitution: results are reported in Table 4.3.

Panel A of Table 4.3 reports the estimates of the market's marginal rate of substitution between skewness and risk, $\widehat{k_1}$, for the SW three-moment CAPM. The model is not rejected both when the market crash of October 1987 is included and when it is excluded. Note that negative k_1 is expected. This implies that the representative investor likes positive skewness. We have negative k_1 (−0.1266) when the market crash of October 1987 is included but positive k_1 (0.1693) when it is excluded. However, these estimates are not significantly different from zero and we do not find evidence of a significant relation between risk and skewness. Lim (1989) and Sears and Wei (1988) find a significant negative relationship between skewness and risk when the SW three-moment CAPM is not rejected. However, their results are sensitive to the sample period used.

Panel B of Table 4.3 reports the estimates of k_1 and k_2 for the SW four-moment CAPM in equation (4.13). Note that in this four-moment CAPM, $\widehat{k_1}$ has the correct sign (negative) both when the market crash of October 1987 is included (−3.7964) and when it is excluded (−0.3047). However, none of them are significantly different from zero. On the other hand, although we expect positive $\widehat{k_2}$ (the representative investor is averse to kurtosis), the estimates

Table 4.3 GMM estimates of the marginal rates of substitution

			Estimates	Normalized
(A) Three-moment CAPM				
Market crash of October 1987 included	Sample estimates	Mean of market portfolio	0.8475	
		S.D. of market portfolio	4.2001	
		Skewness of market portfolio	−4.8976	−1.5855
		Kurtosis of market portfolio	7.7044	8.3215
	GMM estimates	Marginal rate of substitution between skewness and risk (k_1)	−0.1266 (1.4736)	
	Lagrange multiplier statistics – χ^2 (22)		16.9016	
Market crash of October 1987 excluded	Sample estimates	Mean of market portfolio	1.0239	
		S.D. of market portfolio	3.6406	
		Skewness of market portfolio	−2.2615	−0.2397
		Kurtosis of market portfolio	5.0779	0.7849
	GMM estimates	Marginal rate of substitution between skewness and risk (k_1)	0.1693 (0.2574)	
	Lagrange multiplier statistics – χ^2 (22)		24.2233	
(B) Four-moment CAPM				
Market crash of October 1987 included	GMM estimates	Marginal rate of substitution between skewness and risk (k_1)	−3.7964 (5.9402)	
		Marginal rate of substitution between kurtosis and risk (k_2)	−2.7887 (4.0337)	
	Lagrange multiplier statistics – χ^2 (23)		20.1909	
Market crash of October 1987 excluded	GMM estimates	Marginal rate of substitution between skewness and risk (k_1)	−0.3047 (2.0027)	
		Marginal rate of substitution between kurtosis and risk (k_2)	−1.6856 (7.3457)	
	Lagrange multiplier statistics – χ^2 (23)		25.8026	

For panel (A) the three-moment CAPM in equation (4.24) by setting $k_2 = 0$ is used for the GMM estimate of k_1. Chi-square (22) statistics at 10% is 30.8. Values in parentheses are the standard errors of the estimates. Values in the 'normalized' column are sample estimated normalized skewness and normalized excess kurtosis. For panel (B) the four-moment CAPM in equation (4.24) is used for the GMM estimates of k_1 and k_2. Chi-square (23) statistics at 10% is 32.0.

when the market crash of October 1987 is included and when it is excluded are negative (−2.7887 and −1.6856, respectively). Again all estimates are not significantly different from zero, suggesting that the expected relationship between skewness and risk is not strong.

We do not find positive evidence on a relationship between risk and skewness or kurtosis for US investors for the given sample period. We believe that it is difficult to find significant estimates of k_1 and k_2 in mature markets, since the returns in these markets are close to normal and do not have significantly large skewness or kurtosis. In our example, this argument is supported by the fact that the estimates of the normalized skewness and normalized excess kurtosis of the S&P 500 index return in Table 4.3 are not significantly different from zero when the 1987 market crash is excluded. When the 1987 market crash is included, we have significant estimates both for normalized skewness and normalized excess kurtosis. However, the 1987 market crash, one observation, does not seem enough to give us significant estimates of k_1 and k_2.

Another reason why we fail to have significant estimates of k_1 and k_2 may be the time-varying properties of risks. The studies of Friend and Westerfield (1980), Lim (1989), and Sears and Wei (1988) suggest that estimates of k_1 change in different sample periods. Time-varying systematic risks may be an appropriate tool for the analysis. In addition, estimates of higher moments are more sensitive to a small number of extreme returns. In this case, although we construct portfolios in an appropriate way to reduce measurement errors, *ex post* returns may have quite different properties from *ex ante* returns especially in higher moments.

4.3.2 Estimation procedure of higher-moment CAPM

The four-moment CAPM is tested using Hansen's (1982) generalized method of moments (GMM); this procedure is distribution free and is used when the assumption of normality is not appropriate. The evidence presented in panel B of Table 4.2 strongly suggests that it would be inappropriate to assume normality for emerging market returns. We explain the GMM estimation for the SW four-moment CAPM of equation (4.13). Detailed explanations for the other models follow later. Note that all the other models use the same procedure, differing only in the orthogonality conditions imposed.

Following the three-moment CAPM of Lim (1989), the orthogonality conditions, $h_t(\Theta)$, for estimating the SW four-moment CAPM are

$$E\begin{bmatrix} \{\sigma(R_m) + k_1\gamma(R_m) + k_2\theta(R_m)\}R_{it} \\ -\{\sigma(R_m)\beta_{im} + k_1\gamma(R_m)\gamma_{im} + k_2\theta(R_m)\theta_{im}\}R_{mt} \end{bmatrix} = 0 \tag{4.25}$$

$$E\left[R_{it}R_{mt} - \mu(R_m)R_{it} - \beta_{im}\{R_{mt} - \mu(R_m)\}^2\right] = 0 \tag{4.26}$$

$$E\begin{bmatrix} R_{it}R_{mt}^2 - 2\mu(R_m)R_{it}R_{mt} + \mu(R_m)^2R_{it} - \sigma(R_m)^2R_{it} \\ -\gamma_{im}\{R_{mt} - \mu(R_m)\}^3 \end{bmatrix} = 0 \tag{4.27}$$

$$E\begin{bmatrix} R_{it}R_{mt}^3 - 3\mu(R_m)R_{it}R_{mt}^3 + 3\mu(R_m)^2R_{it}R_{mt} \\ -\mu(R_m)^3R_{it} - \gamma(R_m)^3R_{it} - \theta_{im}\{R_{mt} - \mu(R_m)\}^4 \end{bmatrix} = 0 \tag{4.28}$$

$$E[R_{mt} - \mu(R_m)] = 0 \tag{4.29}$$

$$E\left[\{R_{mt} - \mu(R_m)\}^2 - \sigma(R_m)^2\right] = 0 \tag{4.30}$$

$$E\left[\{R_{mt} - \mu(R_m)\}^3 - \gamma(R_m)^3\right] = 0 \tag{4.31}$$

$$E\left[\{R_{mt} - \mu(R_m)\}^4 - \theta(R_m)^4\right] = 0 \tag{4.32}$$

where $i = 1, ..., N$ and N is the number of emerging markets. The first N orthogonality conditions come from the four-moment CAPM of equation (4.13). The next $3N$ orthogonality conditions are N conditions for beta, N conditions for co-skewness, and N conditions for co-kurtosis. The last four orthogonality conditions are for mean, variance, skewness, and kurtosis of the market returns. Therefore, we have $4N + 4$ orthogonality conditions and $3N + 6$ parameters, $\boldsymbol{\Theta} \equiv (\beta_{1m}, \beta_{2m}, ..., \beta_{Nm}, \gamma_{1m}, \gamma_{2m}, ..., \gamma_{Nm}, \theta_{1m}, \theta_{2m}, ..., \theta_{Nm}, \mu(R_m), \sigma(R_m), \gamma(R_m), \theta(R_m), k_1, k_2)'$, to be estimated. There are $N - 2$ overidentifying restrictions in the system. The numbers of the overidentifying restrictions for the other models are explained later.

Without losing asymptotic efficiency, we apply a linear Taylor series approximation about our sample estimators to deal with the nonlinearity of the orthogonality conditions.[3] For the one-step Gauss–Newton procedure, the GMM estimate, $\widehat{\boldsymbol{\Theta}}_T$, is the value of $\boldsymbol{\Theta}$ that minimizes

$$[g_T(\boldsymbol{\Theta})]' \overline{\mathbf{S}}_T^{-1} [g_T(\boldsymbol{\Theta})]$$

where

$$g_T(\boldsymbol{\Theta}) \equiv T^{-1} \sum_{t=1}^{T} h_t(\boldsymbol{\Theta})$$

and

$$\overline{\mathbf{S}}_T \equiv T^{-1} \sum_{t=1}^{T} [h_t(\overline{\boldsymbol{\Theta}})] [h_t(\overline{\boldsymbol{\Theta}})]' \tag{4.33}$$

and sample estimators of the parameter vector, $\overline{\boldsymbol{\Theta}}$, are calculated from the definition of each parameter.

---

[3]The estimators obtained using this method are asymptotically the same as the unmodified estimators; see Lim (1989).

Table 4.4 Correlation matrix between $\bar{\beta}_{im}$, $\bar{\gamma}_{im}$ and $\bar{\theta}_{im}$

	$\bar{\beta}_{im}$	$\bar{\gamma}_{im}$	$\bar{\theta}_{im}$
Market crash of October 1987 included			
$\bar{\beta}_{im}$	1		
$\bar{\gamma}_{im}$	0.6673	1	
$\bar{\theta}_{im}$	0.8873	0.8826	1
Market crash of October 1987 excluded			
$\bar{\beta}_{im}$	1		
$\bar{\gamma}_{im}$	0.2612	1	
$\bar{\theta}_{im}$	0.9386	0.3712	1

The GMM estimate can be treated as if

$$\widehat{\mathbf{\Theta}}_T \approx N(\mathbf{\Theta}_0, (T\widehat{\mathbf{D}}_T\overline{\mathbf{S}}_T^{-1}\widehat{\mathbf{D}}_T')^{-1}) \tag{4.34}$$

where

$$\widehat{\mathbf{D}}_T = \frac{\partial g_T(\mathbf{\Theta})}{\partial \mathbf{\Theta}'}|_{\mathbf{\Theta}=\widehat{\mathbf{\Theta}}_T} \tag{4.35}$$

The Lagrange Multiplier (LM) test statistic for the validity of the restricted four-moment CAPM is

$$T\left[g_T(\widehat{\mathbf{\Theta}})\right]'\overline{\mathbf{S}}_T^{-1}\left[g_T(\widehat{\mathbf{\Theta}})\right] \rightarrow \chi^2(N-2) \tag{4.36}$$

since we have $N-2$ degrees of freedom. Note that this test statistic is equivalent to that of the overidentifying restrictions; see Hansen (1982).

There is a statistical problem in estimating higher-moment CAPMs; the systematic risk measures, β_{im}, γ_{im}, and θ_{im}, are collinear. The correlation matrix obtained from sample estimators, $\overline{\beta}_{im}$, $\overline{\gamma}_{im}$, and $\overline{\theta}_{im}$ is reported in Table 4.4. It is apparent that the data are quite collinear which may well lead to identification problems.

A referee has commented that when all 17 emerging markets are considered jointly, the GMM system becomes too large. For example, for our SW four-moment CAPM, we have 72 $(17 \times 4 + 4)$ orthogonality conditions. In this case, the estimation results may become unreliable: see Ferson and Foerster (1994) and Bekaert and Uris (1996) for further discussion on this point. The referee also suggests grouping emerging markets sensibly to avoid collinearity problem in the GMM system.

Accordingly we have divided our emerging markets into groups to reduce the orthogonality conditions and possible multicollinearity. In previous work Hwang and Satchell (1998a,b) analyse both currency and equity return in emerging markets, and suggest that there are different regional factors in these markets. They find that emerging markets factors can be related to Asia, Southern Asia, Latin America, Central America, and Middle East groupings. In this study, we divide the 17 emerging markets into three groups and estimate a GMM system for each of the three groups. The three groups are the Asian group which includes India, Korea, Thailand, Taiwan, Malaysia, Pakistan, and Philippines (seven countries), the Latin American Group which includes Argentina, Brazil, Chile, Mexico, Colombia, and Venezuela (six countries), and the Other Country group which includes Greece, Zimbabwe, Jordan, and Nigeria (four countries). This reduces the number of orthogonality conditions to 32 ($7 \times 4 + 4$) for the Asian group with the SW four-moment CAPM and less for the other two groups.

Mean-variance CAPM (Model I)

Table 4.5 reports the results of the GMM estimates of the mean-variance CAPM for the emerging markets. That is,

$$E(R_i) = \alpha_1 \beta_{im} \tag{4.37}$$

where $\alpha_1 = E(R_m)$. For the mean-variance CAPM, the orthogonality conditions consist of equations (4.37), (4.36), and (4.29) and the number of the overidentifying restrictions is N.

Table 4.5 shows that the LM statistics do not reject the mean-variance CAPM except for the Latin American group. Note that Asian markets are relatively well explained with the traditional mean-variance CAPM. The value of the adjusted R^2 is relatively high. India and Pakistan are not explained by the mean-variance CAPM. The results are consistent with Hwang and Satchell (1998a,b) who show that Eastern Asia has different factors from those of Southern Asia such as India, Pakistan, and Sri Lanka.

On the other hand, the mean-variance CAPM is rejected for the Latin American markets both when the market crash of October 1987 is included and when it is excluded. Only Mexico which has a strong relation with the USA is explained by the mean-variance CAPM. Also note that Greece has a significant beta. Greece is often considered one of the European markets which has a significant contribution to the world index. The values of the adjusted R^2 are small for the Latin America and Other Country groups, suggesting that the mean-variance CAPM is not an appropriate model for these markets.

The results in Table 4.5 suggest that the mean-variance CAPM can be used for Eastern Asian countries and countries which have a close relationship with mature markets. One of the main reasons why the Latin American markets are not explained with the mean-variance CAPM may be the highly volatile Latin American currency returns, see Hwang and Satchell (1998a,b).

Table 4.5 GMM estimates of mean-variance CAPM

Group	Country	Beta		Lagrange multiplier test chi-square	Adjusted R^2
(A) Market crash of October 1987 included					
Latin America	Argentina	−0.1661	(0.5596)	19.2529**	0.0899
	Brazil	0.6249	(0.4223)	(df: 6)	
	Chile	0.4009	(0.1865)*		
	Mexico	1.3657	(0.3066)**		
	Colombia	0.1485	(0.1481)		
	Venezuela	−0.3096	(0.2746)		
Asia	India	−0.2277	(0.1776)	5.8164	0.2149
	Korea	0.6023	(0.1558)**	(df: 7)	
	Thailand	0.8235	(0.2392)**		
	Taiwan	0.8252	(0.3287)**		
	Malaysia	0.8107	(0.1910)**		
	Pakistan	0.0799	(0.1266)		
	Philippines	0.9535	(0.2261)**		
Other Countries	Greece	0.4482	(0.2126)*	5.9612	0.0464
	Zimbabwe	0.1971	(0.1842)	(df: 4)	
	Jordan	0.1385	(0.1049)		
	Nigeria	0.3122	(0.3102)		
(B) Market crash of October 1987 excluded					
Latin America	Argentina	−0.4721	(0.6014)	23.3978**	0.0591
	Brazil	0.5455	(0.4838)	(df: 6)	
	Chile	0.1895	(0.1647)		
	Mexico	0.8529	(0.2221)**		
	Colombia	0.2254	(0.1711)		
	Venezuela	−0.4059	(0.3150)		
Asia	India	−0.2345	(0.2036)	5.0968	0.2163
	Korea	0.6753	(0.1574)**	(df: 7)	
	Thailand	0.7052	(0.1922)**		
	Taiwan	0.7349	(0.3318)*		
	Malaysia	0.6934	(0.1541)**		
	Pakistan	0.0970	(0.1475)		
	Philippines	1.0701	(0.2538)**		
Other Countries	Greece	0.4365	(0.2444)*	4.9969	0.0750
	Zimbabwe	0.3149	(0.1907)*	(df: 4)	
	Jordan	0.1490	(0.1197)		
	Nigeria	0.3395	(0.3677)		

*Denotes significance at 5% level.
**Denotes significance at 1% level.
Numbers in parentheses are standard errors. The CAPM estimated is $E(R_i) - r_f = (E(R_m) - r_f)\beta_i$.

KL three-moment CAPM (Model II)

Table 4.6 shows the results of the GMM estimates for the following KL three-moment CAPM;

$$E(R_i) = \alpha_1\beta_{im} + \alpha_2\gamma_{im} \tag{4.38}$$

Table 4.6 GMM estimates of KL three-moment CAPM

Group	Country	Beta		Co-skewness		Kraus and Litzenberger (1976)		Lagrange multiplier test chi-square	Adjusted R^2
						α_1	α_2		
(A) Market crash of October 1987 included									
Latin America	Argentina	−0.3605	(0.5655)	4.3880	(1.5129)**	0.6526	0.2851	14.0651**	0.3089
	Brazil	0.4892	(0.4292)	3.2379	(1.2170)**	(1.3011)	(0.3292)	(df: 4)	
	Chile	0.3032	(0.1974)	1.9471	(0.9131)*				
	Mexico	1.1198	(0.3616)**	4.1734	(2.0827)*				
	Colombia	0.1571	(0.1512)	0.0408	(0.1745)				
	Venezuela	−0.2132	(0.2752)	−1.4043	(0.5494)**				
Asia	India	−0.1986	(0.1722)	−0.1989	(0.3136)	1.3524	−0.1615	4.9826	0.2558
	Korea	0.5713	(0.1577)**	0.0161	(0.2633)	(0.9992)	(0.3805)	(df: 5)	
	Thailand	0.8287	(0.2788)**	2.6818	(2.4250)				
	Taiwan	0.8684	(0.3680)**	2.9329	(2.6610)				
	Malaysia	0.8065	(0.2127)**	2.1808	(2.0532)				
	Pakistan	0.0829	(0.1226)	−0.0928	(0.1590)				
	Philippines	0.9897	(0.2244)**	1.6814	(1.2023)				
Other Countries	Greece	0.4510	(0.2069)*	0.6977	(0.7244)	4.8183	−1.9001	0.9416	0.7319
	Zimbabwe	0.1390	(0.1861)	−0.4539	(0.4749)		(3.7150)	(1.9751)	(df: 2)
	Jordan	0.1247	(0.0949)	0.2337	(0.2271)				
	Nigeria	0.0810	(0.2645)	−0.1446	(0.2484)				

Table 4.6 Continued

Group	Country	Beta		Co-skewness		Kraus and Litzenberger (1976)		Lagrange multiplier test chi-square	Adjusted R^2
						α_1	α_2		
(B) Market crash of October 1987 excluded									
Latin	Argentina	−0.2776	(0.6024)	10.7892	(12.1322)	2.2005	0.1534	15.7981**	0.3696
America	Brazil	0.3154	(0.4508)	6.7817	(8.0795)	(1.5568)	(0.2531)	(df: 3)	
	Chile	0.2973	(0.1630)*	1.4210	(1.8135)				
	Mexico	0.6910	(0.2371)**	1.4933	(2.2841)				
	Colombia	0.3046	(0.1567)*	0.1381	(1.2004)				
	Venezuela	−0.1054	(0.2892)	−5.3016	(6.5286)				
Asia	India	−0.2273	(0.2006)	−0.1251	(1.1785)	1.0084	0.1327	2.8400	0.5609
	Korea	0.6553	(0.1588)**	−0.4719	(1.0729)	(0.8485)	(0.2458)	(df: 5)	
	Thailand	0.6048	(0.2112)**	4.3329	(5.3127)				
	Taiwan	0.5482	(0.3441)	5.1181	(6.4922)				
	Malaysia	0.6569	(0.1602)**	2.9922	(3.7053)				
	Pakistan	0.0966	(0.1465)	−0.3278	(0.6964)				
	Philippines	0.9045	(0.2766)**	5.2197	(6.5957)				
Other	Greece	0.3322	(0.2205)	−0.1184	(2.8129)	3.0577	0.0562	2.1532	0.4252
Countries	Zimbabwe	0.3521	(0.1787)*	0.4599	(1.4982)	(2.2279)	(0.5678)	(df: 2)	
	Jordan	0.0835	(0.1141)	0.9390	(2.2144)				
	Nigeria	0.2069	(0.3502)	−1.1654	(2.4932)				

*Denotes significance at 5%.
**Denotes significance at 1%.
Numbers in parentheses are standard errors. The three-moment CAPM estimated is $E(R_i) - r_f = \alpha_1\beta_i + \alpha_2\gamma_i$.

The orthogonality conditions are equations (4.38), (4.26), (4.27), (4.29), (4.30), and (4.31). For the KL three-moment CAPM, the number of the over-identifying restrictions is $N - 2$.

Here, we do not reject the model for the Asian and Other Country groups, but reject the model for the Latin American group at the 1% level as we did in the mean-variance CAPM. Although the coefficients, α_1 and α_2, are not significant as in Friend and Westfield (1980), Lim (1989), and Sears and Wei (1988), the market price of beta, α_1, and the market price of co-skewness, α_2, have correct signs when the 1987 crash is excluded; α_1 and α_2 are positive, since $\gamma(r_m) < 0$. Investors need more return for the negative skewness of the market portfolio over the test period and thus, expected returns should increase to the co-skewness. These results do not apply with the case when the 1987 crash is included, since Asian and Other Country groups have negative α_2. However, the coefficients are insignificant.

Another interesting point is that none of the estimates of γ_{im} is significant when the 1987 crash is excluded, while we can find significant $\widehat{\gamma}_{im}$ in the Latin American group when it is included. In particular, the adjusted R^2 increases dramatically for the Latin America and other countries groups, especially when the 1987 crash is included. Here, the adjusted R^2 for these two groups are now larger than that of Asia. For the Asian countries the adjusted R^2 is not increased with the inclusion of co-skewness and none of the co-skewness estimates are significant in the presence of the 1987 market crash. This suggests that for these countries co-skewness may not be an appropriate risk measure. It is by no means clear, however, that it is correct to regard the 1987 crash as a one-off bizarre event to be ignored or downscaled.

The addition of co-skewness as a risk measure increases the explanatory power of the KL three-moment CAPM for some emerging markets. Our results suggest that Latin America and Other Country groups can be explained better with co-skewness.

SW three-moment CAPM (Model V)

Table 4.7 shows the results of the GMM estimates for the SW three-moment CAPM;

$$E(R_i) = \left[\frac{\sigma(R_m)\beta_{im}}{\sigma(R_m) + k_1\gamma(R_m)} + \frac{k_1\gamma(R_m)\gamma_{im}}{\sigma(R_m) + k_1\gamma(R_m)}\right] E(R_m) \tag{4.39}$$

In this case, the orthogonality conditions consist of equations (4.39), (4.26), (4.27), (4.29), (4.30), and (4.31), and the number of the overidentifying restrictions is N. This differs from the KL model by using the restrictions of the marginal rate of substitution between skewness and risk (k_1).

Table 4.7 GMM estimates of the SW three-moment CAPM

Group	Country	Beta		Co-skewness		Marginal rate of substitution, k_1	Lagrange multiplier test chi-square
(A) Market crash of October 1987 included							
Latin America	Argentina	−0.2352	(0.5592)	3.0413	(1.5962)*	−0.0762	18.3257**
	Brazil	0.5810	(0.4223)	2.4827	(1.3035)*		(df: 6)
	Chile	0.2997	(0.1848)	1.2873	(0.9725)		
	Mexico	1.2170	(0.2890)**	2.6217	(2.2558)		
	Colombia	0.0838	(0.1491)	−0.0162	(0.2215)		
	Venezuela	−0.3093	(0.2731)	−1.1109	(0.6244)*		
Asia	India	−0.2113	(0.1528)	0.3623	(27.1801)	−0.0762	33.2984**
	Korea	0.8426	(0.1231)**	−1.4376	(33.1106)		(df: 7)
	Thailand	0.3098	(0.1252)**	3.0454	(35.9829)		
	Taiwan	0.3307	(0.2147)	3.6698	(49.8408)		
	Malaysia	0.3918	(0.1090)**	1.9604	(29.3719)		
	Pakistan	0.1498	(0.1028)	−0.6788	(21.5858)		
	Philippines	0.7566	(0.2057)**	6.2330	(65.7401)		
Other Countries	Greece	0.4248	(0.2122)*	0.5103	(1.1966)	−0.0762	5.9314
	Zimbabwe	0.2131	(0.1836)	−0.2746	(0.7604)		(df: 4)
	Jordan	0.1317	(0.1048)	0.2565	(0.4019)		
	Nigeria	0.3066	(0.3075)	−0.0837	(0.4896)		

Table 4.7 Continued

Group	Country	Beta		Co-skewness		Marginal rate of substitution, k_1	Lagrange multiplier test chi-square
(B) Market crash of October 1987 excluded							
Latin America	Argentina	0.3179	(0.5586)	1.5638	(6.9722)	0.1552	29.8616**
	Brazil	0.5087	(0.4986)	1.9612	(6.7243)		(df: 6)
	Chile	0.5029	(0.1678)**	0.2635	(1.7795)		
	Mexico	0.8861	(0.2266)**	0.5793	(2.8248)		
	Colombia	0.2329	(0.1763)	−0.3747	(2.0441)		
	Venezuela	−0.2515	(0.3578)	−1.3355	(5.4844)		
Asia	India	−0.1348	(0.2219)	0.2302	(32.0763)	0.1552	18.0976*
	Korea	0.7458	(0.1637)**	−0.4047	(27.9801)		(df: 7)
	Thailand	0.3980	(0.1683)**	−0.0483	(35.4312)		
	Taiwan	0.3008	(0.2826)	−0.9132	(52.8443)		
	Malaysia	0.4484	(0.1484)**	0.6586	(23.5707)		
	Pakistan	0.1579	(0.1625)	−0.5712	(26.2289)		
	Philippines	0.6525	(0.2120)**	−0.9978	(58.3052)		
Other Countries	Greece	0.4449	(0.2366)*	−0.0250	(2.3713)	0.1552	5.9529
	Zimbabwe	0.2901	(0.1900)	0.4824	(1.2224)		(df: 4)
	Jordan	0.1367	(0.1213)	0.8921	(1.8387)		
	Nigeria	0.3127	(0.3695)	−1.2667	(2.1351)		

*Denotes significance at 5% level.
**Denotes significance at 1%.
Numbers in parentheses are standard errors. The three-moment CAPM estimated is

$$E(R)_i - r_j = \left(\frac{\sigma(R_m)}{\sigma(R_m) + k_i\gamma(R_m)}\beta_i + \frac{k_i\gamma(R_m)}{\sigma(R_m) + k_i\gamma(R_m)}\gamma_i\right)(E(R_m) - r_f).$$

As explained above, the marginal rates of substitution reported in Table 4.3 are used for the estimation of the SW three-moment CAPM model in the emerging markets. This is known as a sequential GMM technique.. That is, consistent estimates $\widehat{k}_1$ of k_1 will be used as given values for the estimation of the SW three-moment CAPM. The sampling errors in the estimation of k_1 should be considered when other parameters in the SW three-moment CAPM are estimated for the fixed $\widehat{k}_1$; see Bekaert (1994), Burnside (1994), and Heaton (1995) for further details. We use the Newey and West (1987) method to construct a consistent estimate of the variance–covariance matrix as in Bekaert (1994). In addition, we use a multi-step Gauss–Newton procedure: using the previous estimators of $\mathbf{S}_T$ and $\mathbf{\Theta}_T$, the calculation was repeated until there is no change in the estimates of $\mathbf{\Theta}_T$.

Table 4.7 reports the results of the multi-step Gauss–Newton procedure. The LM statistics show that we reject the SW three-moment CAPM at 1% level for Latin America and Asia (four out of six cases). As in the KL three-moment CAPM, none of the estimates of γ_{im} except some Latin American countries is significant. We do not calculate adjusted R^2 values for the SW three-moment CAPM, since the SW three-moment CAPM is a non-linear model.

The SW three-moment CAPM does not seem to explain emerging markets well. The LM statistics of the SW three-moment CAPM are much larger than those of the KL three-moment CAPM. In addition, the number of significant beta and co-skewness in the SW three-moment CAPM is smaller than that in the KL three-moment CAPM.

Although the SW three-moment CAPM allows us to divide coefficients of the KL three-moment CAPM into the market risk premium and the marginal rates of substitution, the results in Table 4.7 do not seem to be encouraging. The KL higher-moment CAPMs are an *ex ante* model as is the conventional mean-variance CAPM and thus, theoretically we do not expect a negative market premium. In addition, the actual average value of our deflated excess market returns used in this study (deflated excess MSCI world index total returns) is always positive. These theoretical and empirical explanations suggest that we may not get a great deal of insight from the SW higher-moment CAPM. Moreover, as explained above, we have some difficulties in estimating the marginal substitution rates.

We tried to estimate the SW four-moment CAPM as described by equations (4.25) to (4.32). However, this failed to converge.

KL four-moment CAPM (Model III)

In Table 4.8 we represent the results of the GMM estimates for the KL four-moment CAPM given by equation (4.11). Here, the orthogonality conditions

Table 4.8 GMM estimates of KL four-moment CAPM

Group	Country	Beta		Co-skewness		Co-kurtosis		Kraus and Litzenberger (1976)			Lagrange multiplier test chi-square	Adjusted R^2
								α_1	α_2	α_3		
(A) Market crash of October 1987 included												
Latin	Argentina	−0.2735	(0.5445)	2.4148	(1.9374)	0.3097	(0.6350)	−6.8755*	−0.9120	6.1857*	4.0432	0.8680
America	Brazil	0.3982	(0.3912)	2.2398	(1.6816)	0.8111	(0.3510)*	(3.8163)	(1.0850)	(2.9170)	(df: 3)	
	Chile	0.1105	(0.1661)	0.8044	(1.0366)	0.5503	(0.3220)*					
	Mexico	1.0021	(0.2962)**	1.4360	(2.2327)	1.7245	(0.6178)**					
	Colombia	−0.0212	(0.1537)	−0.0325	(0.3551)	0.1882	(0.1326)					
	Venezuela	−0.2681	(0.2604)	−0.9959	(0.9525)	−0.3833	(0.2704)					
Asia	India	−0.2122	(0.1747)	−0.0521	(0.2335)	−0.1913	(0.1187)	6.2822	3.9333	−9.1157	0.9240	0.7403
	Korea	0.6037	(0.1514)**	−0.0255	(0.2409)	0.3438	(0.1221)**	(7.0614)	(6.0249)	(12.3959)	(df: 4)	
	Thailand	0.8216	(0.2777)**	2.7040	(2.3255)	1.6346	(0.4367)**					
	Taiwan	0.8749	(0.3594)**	2.9871	(2.5386)	1.7828	(0.4721)**					
	Malaysia	0.8391	(0.2161)**	2.2161	(1.9793)	1.4644	(0.3629)**					
	Pakistan	0.1055	(0.1116)	−0.0292	(0.1367)	0.0332	(0.0456)					
	Philippines	0.8401	(0.2273)**	1.4389	(1.0576)	0.9744	(0.2433)**					
Other	Greece	0.4672	(0.2131)*	0.5608	(0.8149)	0.7609	(0.1299)**	5.8229	−0.7827	−1.9953	0.8560	0.7343
Countries	Zimbabwe	0.1448	(0.1868)	−0.3589	(0.5195)	−0.2637	(0.1623)	(4.1364)	(4.0986)	(4.6666)	(df: 1)	
	Jordan	0.1057	(0.1023)	0.2110	(0.2537)	0.1265	(0.0928)					
	Nigeria	0.1033	(0.2904)	−0.1922	(0.3040)	0.1556	(0.1296)					

Table 4.8 Continued

Group	Country	Beta		Co-skewness		Co-kurtosis		Kraus and Litzenberger (1976)			Lagrange multiplier test chi-square	Adjusted R^2
								α_1	α_2	α_3		
(B) Market crash of October 1987 excluded												
Latin	Argentina	−0.2555	(0.6016)	10.4321	(10.5650)	−0.2615	(0.7698)	2.8003	0.1568	−0.4775	15.7894**	0.3712
America	Brazil	0.3209	(0.4523)	6.9989	(7.5721)	0.5785	(0.5610)	(3.1288)	(0.2529)	(2.4001)	(df: 3)	
	Chile	0.2974	(0.1629)*	1.4744	(1.7013)	0.2433	(0.1706)					
	Mexico	0.6860	(0.2319)**	1.6703	(2.2681)	0.7722	(0.2069)**					
	Colombia	0.3247	(0.1765)*	0.2655	(1.2198)	0.5857	(0.1585)**					
	Venezuela	−0.1280	(0.3188)	−5.5679	(6.2577)	−0.6739	(0.4655)					
Asia	India	−0.2651	(0.2151)	−0.9959	(1.7098)	−0.3551	(0.1980)*	−2.8462	−0.2449	3.7297	2.1662	0.7352
	Korea	0.6339	(0.1614)**	−0.5464	(1.1604)	0.5723	(0.1661)**	(3.7133)	(0.4895)	(3.5975)	(df: 4)	
	Thailand	0.5170	(0.2172)**	4.6942	(5.8607)	0.9967	(0.3814)**					
	Taiwan	0.5873	(0.3620)	4.6307	(6.3161)	1.1686	(0.5624)*					
	Malaysia	0.6254	(0.1580)**	3.5637	(4.3531)	0.9215	(0.2216)**					
	Pakistan	0.0303	(0.1525)	−0.9247	(1.1897)	−0.0222	(0.0900)					
	Philippines	0.8676	(0.2804)**	4.6934	(6.3668)	1.5131	(0.4887)**					
Other	Greece	0.4214	(0.2446)*	−0.0998	(2.1106)	0.8279	(0.2674)**	7.3458	−0.1767	−2.6033	0.4189	0.8257
Countries	Zimbabwe	0.2470	(0.1885)	0.5034	(1.1200)	0.0182	(0.1619)	(5.7803)	(0.7813)	(3.0823)	(df: 1)	
	Jordan	0.1375	(0.1269)	0.9783	(1.7754)	0.2699	(0.2024)					
	Nigeria	0.0990	(0.2789)	−1.2669	(1.9591)	0.2834	(0.2153)					

*Denotes significance at 5% level.
**Denotes significance at 1% level.
Numbers in parentheses are standard errors. The four-moment CAPM estimated is $E(R_i) - r_f = \alpha_1\beta_i + \alpha_2\gamma_i + \alpha_3\theta_i$.

consist of equations (4.11), (4.26), (4.27), (4.28), (4.29), (4.30), (4.31), and (4.32), and the number of the overidentifying restrictions is $N - 3$. The sample estimators of α_1, α_2, and α_3 are obtained from the GMM estimation described in Section 4.3.2. The LM statistics in Table 4.8 shows that we do not reject the model at the 5% level except Latin America when the 1987 market crash is excluded. The adjusted R^2 values are larger than those in Tables 4.6 and 4.5. The LM statistics and R^2 indicate that the KL four-moment CAPM explains emerging markets better than other models we reported in the previous subsections.

As explained in Section 4.2, we expect $\alpha_1 > 0, \alpha_2 > 0$, and $\alpha_3 > 0$, since $\widehat{\gamma}(r_m) < 0$. None of the coefficients are significant except α_1 and α_3 of Latin American group in the presence of the market crash.

When we compare the results to those of the KL three-moment CAPM in Table 4.6, the numbers of significant co-kurtosis terms are nine when the market crash is included and also nine when it is excluded, respectively, without changes in the significance of the estimated β_{im}. Interestingly, the significance of co-skewness in Latin America for the KL three-moment CAPM disappears and none of the co-skewness estimates in the KL four-moment CAPM is significant. This suggests that Latin American countries can be better explained with co-kurtosis than co-skewness when the 1987 market crash is included.

The adjusted R^2 values of the four-moment CAPM are all higher than those of the KL three-moment CAPM. In particular, Latin American and Asian groups when the 1987 market crash is included and Asian and Other Country groups when it is excluded show significant benefits from the inclusion of the co-kurtosis. However, the Other Country group in the presence of the market crash and the Latin American group when the 1987 market crash is excluded do not have larger adjusted R^2 by adding co-kurtosis; see the adjusted R^2 in Tables 4.5 and 4.6.

KL second- and fourth-moment CAPM (Model IV)

The different explanatory power of systematic risks in Tables 4.5, 4.6, and 4.8 is further investigated by estimating the mean-variance CAPM with co-kurtosis. In Table 4.9 we report the estimation results of the model. The CAPM with co-kurtosis is represented as

$$E(R_i) = \alpha_1 \beta_{im} + \alpha_3 \theta_{im} \tag{4.40}$$

When the skewness of the market portfolio is negligible, that is, $\gamma(r_m) \approx 0$, the second term of the right-hand side of equation (4.11) may be disregarded ($\alpha_2 = (dE(w)/d\gamma(w))\gamma(r_m) \approx 0$). The orthogonality conditions for the CAPM

Table 4.9 GMM estimates of KL second- and fourth-moment CAPM

Group	Country	Beta		Co-kurtosis		Kraus and Litzenberger (1976) α_1	Kraus and Litzenberger (1976) α_3	Lagrange multiplier test chi-square	Adjusted R^2
(A) Market crash of October 1987 included									
Latin	Argentina	−0.1266	(0.4831)	0.3770	(0.6129)	−5.3487	4.2478	6.1082	0.8593
America	Brazil	0.5943	(0.3460)*	0.9074	(0.3443)**	(2.9863)	(2.2005)	(df: 4)	
	Chile	0.1127	(0.1569)	0.5460	(0.2926)*				
	Mexico	0.9465	(0.2635)**	1.6870	(0.5457)**				
	Colombia	−0.0414	(0.1523)	0.1997	(0.1251)				
	Venezuela	−0.3756	(0.2658)	−0.4609	(0.2736)*				
Asia	India	−0.1948	(0.1705)	−0.2247	(0.1361)*	1.6804	−0.4713	4.5508	0.2538
	Korea	0.5705	(0.1561)**	0.3602	(0.1384)**	(1.3350)	(0.8838)	(df: 5)	
	Thailand	0.8473	(0.2768)**	1.6423	(0.4618)**				
	Taiwan	0.8874	(0.3676)**	1.8050	(0.4953)**				
	Malaysia	0.8184	(0.2152)**	1.4395	(0.3957)**				
	Pakistan	0.0874	(0.1209)	0.0281	(0.0494)				
	Philippines	0.9869	(0.2249)**	1.1077	(0.2836)**				
Other	Greece	0.4739	(0.2130)*	0.7564	(0.1304)**	5.8727	−2.7068	0.9239	0.6650
Countries	Zimbabwe	0.1568	(0.1839)	−0.2581	(0.1643)	(3.7425)	(2.2894)	(df: 2)	
	Jordan	0.0966	(0.0839)	0.1209	(0.0868)				
	Nigeria	0.1321	(0.2516)	0.1599	(0.1281)				

Table 4.9 Continued

Group	Country	Beta		Co-kurtosis		Kraus and Litzenberger (1976)		Lagrange multiplier test chi-square	Adjusted R^2
						α_1	α_3		
(B) Market crash of October 1987 excluded									
Latin	Argentina	0.1666	(0.4949)	0.2133	(0.7550)	1.7905	0.4485	16.6484**	0.1577
America	Brazil	0.5162	(0.4163)	0.7534	(0.5199)	(2.8412)	(1.8993)	(df: 4)	
	Chile	0.3528	(0.1619)*	0.3237	(0.1736)*				
	Mexico	0.7016	(0.2279)**	0.8043	(0.2082)**				
	Colombia	0.2918	(0.1760)*	0.6116	(0.1610)**				
	Venezuela	−0.2442	(0.3084)	−0.8147	(0.4456)*				
Asia	India	−0.2515	(0.2085)	−0.3811	(0.1980)*	−1.1257	1.7968	2.9034	0.6427
	Korea	0.6272	(0.1547)**	0.5860	(0.1692)**	(2.2127)	(1.7209)	(df: 5)	
	Thailand	0.5644	(0.2134)**	1.0384	(0.3858)**				
	Taiwan	0.5603	(0.3545)	1.1592	(0.5767)*				
	Malaysia	0.6575	(0.1553)**	0.9467	(0.2227)**				
	Pakistan	0.0634	(0.1543)	−0.0103	(0.0918)				
	Philippines	0.8921	(0.2762)**	1.5166	(0.4910)**				
Other	Greece	0.4298	(0.2383)*	0.8158	(0.2673)**	6.8025	−2.4800	0.5460	0.7676
Countries	Zimbabwe	0.2545	(0.1885)	0.0290	(0.1611)	(4.9611)	(2.8957)	(df: 2)	
	Jordan	0.1184	(0.1089)	0.2471	(0.1943)				
	Nigeria	0.1370	(0.2486)	0.3049	(0.2023)				

*Denotes significance at 5% level.
**Denotes significance at 1%level.
Numbers in parentheses are standard errors. The three-moment CAPM estimated is $E(R_i) - r_f = \alpha_1\beta_i + \alpha_3\theta_i$.

with kurtosis are equations (4.40), (4.26), (4.28), (4.29), (4.30), (4.31), and (4.32) and the number of overidentifying restrictions is $N - 2$.

As in Table 4.8, the signs on the coefficients (α_1 and α_3) are not always positive and the estimates are not significant. The LM statistics show that we reject only one case, the Latin American group when the 1987 market crash is excluded. This is the same as the KL four-moment CAPM. However, the number of significant beta and co-kurtosis terms is larger than those of the KL four-moment and three-moment CAPMs.

The adjusted R^2 values in Table 4.9 together with those in Tables 4.5, 4.6, and 4.8 suggest the following. When the 1987 market crash is included, the Latin American group is explained with beta and co-kurtosis, the Asian group is explained by beta, co-skewness, and co-kurtosis, and the Other Country group is explained by beta and co-skewness or beta and co-kurtosis. On the other hand, when the 1987 market crash is excluded, the Latin American group is explained with beta and co-skewness, and the Asian and the Other Country groups are explained by beta, co-skewness, and co-kurtosis.

The KL second- and fourth-moment CAPM does not seem to be inferior to the Kraus and Litzenberger three-moment CAPM for emerging markets. The number of significant risks and the LM statistics support the KL second- and fourth-moment CAPM rather than the KL three-moment CAPM. The individual emerging markets may be better explained with co-kurtosis rather than co-skewness. Concluding from Table 4.9, co-kurtosis rather than co-skewness may be a more appropriate additional risk measure for the emerging markets.

4.3.3 Summary of GMM results

The adjusted R^2, LM statistics, and number of significant systematic risks support the modelling of higher moments for emerging markets. Our ancillary assumptions about the α_is and k_is and their signs are not contradictory to the empirical findings.

Attempts to utilize log-utility, which obviates the need to estimate k_1 and k_2, did not do any better, indeed our iterations failed to converge. This is the reason why we do not report results for the SW four-moment CAPM with log-utility. Another assumption, that of a simple representative agent, seems too strong as well. It may be better to consider a multiple-agent equilibrium so that risk premia are generated by more than two funds. However, pricing assets in this situation tends to be much more complicated.

Turning to the role of the market crash, all estimations were re-calculated without October 1987. The effect of this was actually minimal except that co-skewness was dramatically increased without the crash. This seemingly paradoxical result follows from the fact that the numerator of co-skewness did not change much with the exclusion of the crash while the denominator was substantially reduced.

4.4 HIGHER-MOMENT DGPs

The previous sections avoid a specification of the DGP and use the GMM to estimate the higher-moment CAPMs. However, as mentioned earlier, the estimated versions of the higher-moment CAPMs have a statistical problem, non-identifiability between risk measures. Barone-Adesi (1985) suggests the quadratic market model can be used to reduce the collinearity problem in the KL three-moment CAPM.

In this section, we specify the DGPs; the linear market model, the quadratic market model, and the cubic market model. The DGPs are shown to be consistent with their equivalent higher-moment CAPMs as well as reducing the multicollinearity of the systematic risk measures.

We first consider the linear market model. That is, the DGP of an asset i is presented as a linear function of the excess rate of return on the market portfolio,

$$r_{i,t} - r_f = \alpha_{0,i} + \alpha_{1,i}(r_{m,t} - r_f) + \varepsilon_{i,t} \tag{4.41}$$

Subtracting the expected value of equation (4.41) from equation (4.41), and using the definition of the systematic risk measures, β_{im}, γ_{im}, and θ_{im}, in equations (4.2), (4.3), and (4.4), we obtain $\beta_{im} = \gamma_{im} = \theta_{im} = \alpha_{1,i}$. That is, when individual asset's excess rate of return is simply represented as a linear function of excess rate of return on the market portfolio, the mean-variance CAPM rather than higher-moment CAPMs should be used. Otherwise, the systematic risk measures in the higher-moment CAPMs are perfectly collinear.

For the following quadratic market model,

$$r_{i,t} - r_f = \alpha_{0,i} + \alpha_{1,i}(r_{m,t} - r_f) + \alpha_{2,i}(r_{m,t} - E(r_m))^2 + \varepsilon_{i,t} \tag{4.42}$$

using the same method as in the linear market model, we obtain

$$\beta_{im} = \alpha_{1,i} + \alpha_{2,i}\frac{\gamma(r_m)^3}{\sigma(r_m)^2} \tag{4.43}$$

$$\gamma_{im} = \alpha_{1,i} + \alpha_{2,i}\frac{\theta(r_m)^4 - \sigma(r_m)^4}{\gamma(r_m)^3} \tag{4.44}$$

We suggest only beta and co-skewness, since for the two parameters, $\alpha_{1,i}$ and $\alpha_{2,i}$, of the quadratic market model, only the first two systematic risk measures can be derived, unless other information on the relation between co-kurtosis and beta and co-skewness is available; Kraus and Litzenberger (1976) and Barone-Adesi (1985) provide further discussion on the quadratic market model. Equations (4.43) and (4.44) give us some insight into the nature of the multicollinearity between β_{im} and γ_{im}. For example, if the weights on $\alpha_{2,i}$ in equations (4.43) and (4.44) are equal, $\beta_{im} = \gamma_{im}$. If either $\alpha_{1,i}$ or $\alpha_{2,i}$ is constant for all i, then β_{im} and γ_{im} will be collinear.

A generalization of equation (4.42) is the cubic market model given below

$$r_{i,t} - r_f = \alpha_{0,i} + \alpha_{1,i}(r_{m,t} - r_f) + \alpha_{2,i}(r_{m,t} - E(r_m))^2 + \alpha_{3,i}(r_{m,t} - E(r_m))^3 + \varepsilon_{i,t} \tag{4.45}$$

We can use equation (4.45) to evaluate the relationships given in equation (4.11). We present this as a theorem.

Theorem 3. *If we assume the validity of the KL four-moment CAPM as given by equation (4.11) and a DGP as in equation (4.45), then the systematic risk measures, β_{im}, γ_{im}, and θ_{im}, are*

$$\beta_{im} = \alpha_{1,i} + \frac{\alpha_{2,i}\gamma(r_m)^3 + \alpha_{3,i}\theta(r_m)^4}{\sigma(r_m)^2} \tag{4.46}$$

$$\gamma_{im} = \alpha_{1,i} + \frac{\alpha_{2,i}\left\{\theta(r_m)^4 - \sigma(r_m)^4\right\} + \alpha_{3,i}\left\{\phi(r_m)^5 - \gamma(r_m)^3\sigma(r_m)^2\right\}}{\gamma(r_m)^3} \tag{4.47}$$

$$\theta_{im} = \alpha_{1,i} + \frac{\alpha_{2,i}\left\{\phi(r_m)^5 - \sigma(r_m)^2\gamma(r_m)^3\right\} + \alpha_{3,i}\left\{\varphi(r_m)^6 - \gamma(r_m)^6\right\}}{\theta(r_m)^4} \tag{4.48}$$

where $\phi(r_m) = E[\{r_m - E(r_m)\}^5]^{1/5}$, $\varphi(r_m) = E[\{r_m - E(r_m)\}^6]^{1/6}$, *and the other parameters are defined the same as in the previous sections.*

Proof. See the explanation of the above linear market model. We omit details.

The higher-moment CAPMs depend on the highest moment of the DGP; if the DGP is quadratic, we cannot use the four-moment CAPM but the three-moment CAPM. Only when the DGP is cubic, can we use the four-moment CAPM. Therefore, if the unknown DGP is a quadratic and the four-moment CAPM is estimated, the four-moment CAPM is not identifiable, and the multicollinearity problem in the systematic risk measures creates estimation problems.

Tables 4.10 and 4.11 report the GLS estimates for the quadratic and cubic market models. Here we do not divide the 17 emerging markets into groups,

Table 4.10 GLS estimates based on quadratic market DGP

Country	$\alpha_{0,i}$	S.D.	$\alpha_{1,i}$	S.D.	$\alpha_{2,i}$	S.D.
(A) Market crash of October 1987 included						
Greece	0.8756	1.0062	0.4070	0.2289*	−0.0079	0.0243
Argentina	4.4622	2.0655*	−0.5873	0.4698	−0.1372	0.0499**
Brazil	1.8761	1.7309	0.4292	0.3937	−0.0830	0.0419*
Chile	2.9395	0.6984**	0.1738	0.1589	−0.0432	0.0169**
Mexico	2.3858	1.2652*	0.7375	0.2878**	−0.0768	0.0306**
India	0.6787	0.8924	−0.2418	0.2030	−0.0051	0.0216
Korea	−0.4141	0.7225	0.6848	0.1643**	0.0274	0.0175
Thailand	2.1843	0.7407**	0.4689	0.1685**	−0.0871	0.0179**
Zimbabwe	1.3116	0.8298	0.1954	0.1887	0.0198	0.0201
Jordan	0.0273	0.4447	0.1274	0.1012	−0.0025	0.0108
Colombia	1.6706	0.7696*	0.1602	0.1750	0.0076	0.0186
Venezuela	0.2366	1.3374	−0.1325	0.3042	0.0353	0.0323
Taiwan	2.3212	1.2062*	0.5610	0.2744*	−0.0912	0.0292**
Malaysia	1.2512	0.6091*	0.5949	0.1386**	−0.0654	0.0147**
Pakistan	0.3395	0.6639	0.0800	0.1510	0.0064	0.0161
Philippines	2.1227	0.8707**	0.7180	0.1980**	−0.0239	0.0211
Nigeria	−0.4712	1.5865	0.2663	0.3609	0.0195	0.0384
R^2		0.0732				
(B) Market crash of October 1987 excluded						
Greece	0.6960	1.0663	0.3845	0.2350	0.0077	0.0380
Argentina	5.1883	2.1833**	−0.5468	0.4812	−0.1971	0.0777**
Brazil	2.7666	1.8216	0.5044	0.4015	−0.1580	0.0649**
Chile	2.7069	0.7381**	0.1349	0.1627	−0.0223	0.0263
Mexico	1.6316	1.3266	0.6300	0.2924*	−0.0105	0.0472
India	0.5478	0.9459	−0.2580	0.2085	0.0062	0.0337
Korea	−0.3603	0.7662	0.6990	0.1689**	0.0223	0.0273
Thailand	2.1431	0.7855**	0.4383	0.1731**	−0.0819	0.0280**
Zimbabwe	1.6125	0.8766*	0.2351	0.1932	−0.0064	0.0312
Jordan	0.1652	0.4704	0.1422	0.1037	−0.0143	0.0167
Colombia	1.6537	0.8163*	0.1606	0.1799	0.0089	0.0291
Venezuela	−0.4197	1.4083	−0.1956	0.3104	0.0911	0.0501*
Taiwan	2.3138	1.2795*	0.5330	0.2820*	−0.0889	0.0456*
Malaysia	1.1875	0.6458*	0.5682	0.1423**	−0.0587	0.0230**
Pakistan	0.2249	0.7036	0.0690	0.1551	0.0161	0.0251
Philippines	2.6773	0.9121**	0.7731	0.2010**	−0.0711	0.0325**
Nigeria	−0.6133	1.6825	0.2562	0.3708	0.0314	0.0599
R^2		0.0565				

*Denotes significance at 5% level.

**Denotes significance at 1% level.

The quadratic market DGP estimated is

$R_{i,t} - r_f = \alpha_{0,i} + \alpha_{1,i}(R_{m,t} - r_f) + \alpha_{2,i}(R_{m,t} - E(R_m))^2 + \varepsilon_{i,t}$.

Table 4.11 GLS estimates based on cubic market DGP

Country	$\alpha_{0,i}$	S.D.	$\alpha_{1,i}$	S.D.	$\alpha_{2,i}$	S.D.	$\alpha_{3,i}$	S.D.
(A) Market crash of October 1987 included								
Greece	0.4772	1.0249	0.1095	0.2884	0.0442	0.0395	0.0045	0.0027*
Argentina	5.2017	2.1075**	−0.0352	0.5931	−0.2340	0.0811**	−0.0084	0.0056
Brazil	2.4631	1.7675	0.8676	0.4975*	−0.1598	0.0681*	−0.0066	0.0047
Chile	2.8332	0.7172**	0.0944	0.2018	−0.0293	0.0276	0.0012	0.0019
Mexico	1.8950	1.2892	0.3711	0.3628	−0.0126	0.0496	0.0056	0.0034
India	0.6731	0.9176	−0.2460	0.2583	−0.0044	0.0353	0.0001	0.0024
Korea	−0.3786	0.7429	0.7113	0.2091**	0.0228	0.0286	−0.0004	0.0020
Thailand	1.9739	0.7579**	0.3118	0.2133	−0.0596	0.0292*	0.0024	0.0020
Zimbabwe	1.6516	0.8446*	0.4492	0.2377*	−0.0246	0.0325	−0.0039	0.0022*
Jordan	0.0526	0.4572	0.1463	0.1287	−0.0058	0.0176	−0.0003	0.0012
Colombia	1.4588	0.7878*	0.0021	0.2217	0.0353	0.0303	0.0024	0.0021
Venezuela	−0.0436	1.3716	−0.3417	0.3860	0.0720	0.0528	0.0032	0.0036
Taiwan	2.0629	1.2370*	0.3682	0.3481	−0.0574	0.0476	0.0029	0.0033
Malaysia	1.1021	0.6241*	0.4836	0.1757**	−0.0459	0.0240*	0.0017	0.0016
Pakistan	0.2952	0.6825	0.0469	0.1921	0.0122	0.0263	0.0005	0.0018
Philippines	2.1892	0.8950**	0.7677	0.2519**	−0.0325	0.0345	−0.0008	0.0024
Nigeria	−0.6575	1.6301	0.1273	0.4588	0.0439	0.0628	0.0021	0.0043
R^2		0.0807						
(B) Market crash of October 1987 excluded								
Greece	0.9391	1.0482	−0.3218	0.3640	0.0446	0.0400	0.0140	0.0056**
Argentina	4.9295	2.1802*	0.2052	0.7571	−0.2364	0.0831**	−0.0149	0.0116
Brazil	2.7323	1.8292	0.6039	0.6352	−0.1632	0.0698*	−0.0020	0.0097
Chile	2.6681	0.7404**	0.2477	0.2571	−0.0282	0.0282	−0.0022	0.0039
Mexico	1.6378	1.3323	0.6122	0.4626	−0.0096	0.0508	0.0004	0.0071
India	0.4818	0.9482	−0.0665	0.3293	−0.0038	0.0362	−0.0038	0.0050
Korea	−0.3585	0.7695	0.6940	0.2672**	0.0225	0.0293	0.0001	0.0041
Thailand	2.2904	0.7776**	0.0104	0.2700	−0.0596	0.0297*	0.0085	0.0041*
Zimbabwe	1.4856	0.8729*	0.6036	0.3031*	−0.0257	0.0333	−0.0073	0.0046
Jordan	0.2172	0.4701	−0.0088	0.1632	−0.0064	0.0179	0.0030	0.0025
Colombia	1.8264	0.8049**	−0.3412	0.2795	0.0351	0.0307	0.0099	0.0043*
Venezuela	−0.5277	1.4110	0.1182	0.4900	0.0747	0.0538	−0.0062	0.0075
Taiwan	2.5197	1.2715*	−0.0650	0.4415	−0.0576	0.0485	0.0118	0.0068*
Malaysia	1.2730	0.6440*	0.3199	0.2236	−0.0458	0.0246*	0.0049	0.0034
Pakistan	0.2021	0.7063	0.1353	0.2453	0.0127	0.0269	−0.0013	0.0038
Philippines	2.9147	0.8906**	0.0835	0.3093	−0.0351	0.0340	0.0136	0.0047**
Nigeria	−0.5281	1.6881	0.0085	0.5862	0.0443	0.0644	0.0049	0.0090
R^2		0.0727						

*Denotes significance at 5% level.
**Denotes significance at 1% level.
The cubic market DGP estimated is
$R_{i,t} - r_f = \alpha_{0,i} + \alpha_{1,i}(R_{m,t} - r_f) + \alpha_{1,i}(R_{m,t} - E(R_m))^2 + \alpha_{3,i}(R_{m,t} - E(R_m))^3 + \varepsilon_{i,t}$.

since the problems that arise in a large system in GMM estimation is not expected in the GLS estimation that we carry out. Table 4.10 shows that the significant estimates of $\alpha_{1,i}$ are all positive and the significant estimates of $\alpha_{2,i}$ are all negative except one. This implies that individual emerging market returns increase (decrease) as the market portfolio increases (decreases), but decrease as the world market returns become more volatile. In addition, Table 4.11 reports that the significant estimates of $\alpha_{3,i}$ are all positive except one. This has the implication that the emerging market returns increase (decrease) as the positive (negative) skewness of the market portfolio becomes larger. However, the total number of significant estimates in the cubic market model is less than that in the quadratic market model. The R^2 values also suggest that there is not much gain from using the cubic market model.

The R^2 values are relatively small, when they are compared with other R^2 values in the previous tables. The difference comes from the fact that the R^2 values in Tables 4.5–4.9 are obtained from the cross-sectional calculation, while the R^2 values in Tables 4.10 and 4.11 are obtained from the seemingly unrelated regressions model. The beta, co-skewness, and co-kurtosis calculated from the GLS estimates of the DGP parameters (see the relationship between systematic risk measures and $\alpha_{1,i}$, $\alpha_{2,i}$, and $\alpha_{3,i}$) are not significantly different from the sample estimators, $\overline{\beta}_{im}$, $\overline{\gamma}_{im}$, and $\overline{\theta}_{im}$.

4.5 CONCLUSION

This study proposes the four-moment CAPM that explicitly involves skewness and kurtosis as additional risk measures. We use a multivariate approach and estimate the models with GMM. Like studies for mature markets such as Friend and Westerfield (1980), Sears and Wei (1988), Homaifar and Graddy (1988), and Lim (1989), our study shows that there is no significant relationship between expected return and risk (α_1), skewness (α_2), and kurtosis (α_3). However, we also find insignificant marginal rates of substitution between risk and skewness (k_1) and kurtosis (k_2). This is due to the lack of normalized skewness and normalized kurtosis in US returns.

Despite the poor estimates of the coefficients and marginal rates of substitution, however, higher-moment CAPMs seem to be preferred to the conventional mean-variance CAPM. Some test statistics such as the adjusted R^2 and the LM statistics reported in this study suggest that emerging markets are better explained with higher-moments CAPMs. Interestingly, co-kurtosis has at least as much explanatory power as co-skewness. This is consistent with the result in Table 4.2 that the main source of non-normality in emerging markets is kurtosis rather than skewness.

Our initial approach explicitly imposes the condition that the market is efficient, $\beta_{mm} = \gamma_{mm} = \theta_{mm} = 1$ as in Sears and Wei (1985, 1988) and Lim (1989). When we use an alternative approach using DGPs, we can condition on the market, as in Sharpe's market model. In addition, the high multicollinearity in sample co-moments seems to make it hard to jointly estimate co-skewness and co-kurtosis. Therefore, we specified higher-moment DGPs such as the quadratic market model as in Kraus and Litzenberger (1976) and Barone-Adesi (1985). We showed that higher-moment DGPs are consistent with higher-moment CAPMs, while reducing the collinearity in the parameters.

Adding a note of realism to our study, we acknowledge that we are applying a stationary analysis to an evolutionary problem. Our reason for doing so is to assess the degree of explanation possible using higher-moment CAPMs with emerging markets data. Our predictable conclusion is that while the use of higher moments seems to improve matters, it cannot compensate for the fundamental non-stationarity of emerging market returns. The non-normality of emerging market returns is not enough in itself to build models that fail to take account of the evolutionary nature of emerging markets. Nevertheless, we do not regard the construction of these models as having no practical relevance. In Hwang and Satchell (1998a,b) we have used models similar to the ones in this chapter to assess risk adjusted performance of emerging market funds. We found there that outperformance in emerging markets is eliminated once risk adjustment for higher moments is carried out.

APPENDIX 1

Since the initial investment is set to 1, the moments of end-of-period wealth are equivalent to those of the rate of return on the portfolio. That is, $\sigma(w) = \sigma(r_p)$, $\gamma(w) = \gamma(r_p)$ and $\theta(w) = \theta(r_p)$. The equation, $\sum_{i=1}^{N} x_i\beta_{ip} = 1$, can be shown as

$$\sum_{i=1}^{N} x_i\beta_{ip} = \sum_{i=1}^{N} x_i \frac{E[\{r_i - E(r_i)\}\{r_p - E(r_p)\}]}{E[\{r_p - E(r_p)\}^2]} \tag{A1.1}$$

$$= \frac{E[\{\sum_{i=1}^{N} x_i r_i - \sum_{i=1}^{N} x_i E(r_i)\}\{r_p - E(r_p)\}]}{E[\{r_p - E(r_p)\}^2]}$$

$$= 1$$

using $\sum_{i=1}^{N} x_i r_i = r_p - x_0 r_f$ and $\sum_{i=1}^{N} x_i E(r_i) = E(r_p) - x_0 r_f$. Therefore, $\sigma(w) = \sum_{i=1}^{N} x_i \beta_{ip}\sigma(r_p)$. With the same method, $\sum_{i=1}^{N} x_i\gamma_{ip} = 1$ and $\sum_{i=1}^{N} x_i\theta_{ip} = 1$ can be easily shown and the results follow.

APPENDIX 2

A Lagrangian for the given maximization problem is

$$L = E[U(w)] - \lambda(x_0 + \sum\nolimits_{i=1}^{N} x_i - 1) \tag{A2.1}$$

The first derivatives of the Lagrangrian with respect to x_0 and x_i are

$$\frac{\partial L}{\partial x_0} = \frac{\partial E[U(w)]}{\partial E(w)}(1 + r_f) - \lambda = 0 \tag{A2.2}$$

$$\frac{\partial L}{\partial x_i} = \frac{\partial E[U(w)]}{\partial E(w)}(1 + E(r_i)) + \frac{\partial E[U(w)]}{\partial \sigma(w)}\beta_{ip}\sigma(r_p) \tag{A2.3}$$

$$+ \frac{\partial E[U(w)]}{\partial \gamma(w)}\gamma_{ip}\gamma(r_p) + \frac{\partial E[U(w)]}{\partial \theta(w)}\theta_{ip}\theta(r_p) - \lambda = 0$$

using

$$\frac{\partial E(w)}{\partial x_i} = 1 + E(r_i), \quad \frac{\partial \sigma(w)}{\partial x_i} = \beta_{ip}\sigma(r_p), \quad \frac{\partial \gamma(w)}{\partial x_i} = \gamma_{ip}\gamma(r_p), \text{ and } \frac{\partial \theta(w)}{\partial x_i} = \theta_{ip}\theta(r_p)$$

Rearranging equations (A2.2) and (A2.3), we obtain the following equation:

$$E(r_i) - r_f = -\frac{\frac{\partial E[U(w)]}{\partial \sigma(w)}}{\frac{\partial E[U(w)]}{\partial E(w)}}\beta_{ip}\sigma(r_p) - \frac{\frac{\partial E[U(w)]}{\partial \gamma(w)}}{\frac{\partial E[U(w)]}{\partial E(w)}}\gamma_{ip}\gamma(r_p) - \frac{\frac{\partial E[U(w)]}{\partial \theta(w)}}{\frac{\partial E[U(w)]}{\partial E(w)}}\theta_{ip}\theta(r_p) \tag{A2.4}$$

In addition, since the expected utility curve of the investor is constant at the maximum, the changes in expected return and variance are zero for the given skewness and kurtosis. Using this property, the total differential of $E[U(w)]$ is set to zero, and we obtain the following equations:

$$dE[U(w)] = \frac{\partial E[U(w)]}{\partial E(w)}dE(w) + \frac{\partial E[U(w)]}{\partial \sigma(w)}d\sigma(w) = 0 \tag{A2.5}$$

$$dE[U(w)] = \frac{\partial E[U(w)]}{\partial E(w)}dE(w) + \frac{\partial E[U(w)]}{\partial \gamma(w)}d\gamma(w) = 0 \tag{A2.6}$$

$$dE[U(w)] = \frac{\partial E[U(w)]}{\partial E(w)}dE(w) + \frac{\partial E[U(w)]}{\partial \theta(w)}d\theta(w) = 0 \tag{A2.7}$$

When these three equations are used for the marginal rate of substitutions in equation (A2.4), the results follow.

APPENDIX 3

For the logarithmic utility function, a Taylor approximation of the investor's expected utility of end-of-period wealth yields

$$E[U(w)] = \log(E(w)) - \frac{\sigma(w)^2}{2E(w)^2} + \frac{\gamma(w)^3}{3E(w)^3} - \frac{\theta(w)^4}{4E(w)^4} \quad \text{(A3.1)}$$

Therefore,

$$\frac{\partial E[U(w)]}{\partial E(w)} = \frac{1}{E(w)} + \frac{\sigma(w)^2}{E(w)^3} - \frac{\gamma(w)^3}{E(w)^4} + \frac{\theta(w)^4}{E(w)^5} \quad \text{(A3.2)}$$

$$\frac{\partial E[U(w)]}{\partial \sigma(w)} = -\frac{\sigma(w)}{E(w)^2} \quad \text{(A3.3)}$$

$$\frac{\partial E[U(w)]}{\partial \gamma(w)} = \frac{\gamma(w)^2}{E(w)^3} \quad \text{(A3.4)}$$

$$\frac{\partial E[U(w)]}{\partial \theta(w)} = -\frac{\theta(w)^3}{E(w)^4} \quad \text{(A3.5)}$$

When these equations are put into equation (A2.4), we obtain the following equation:

$$E(r_i) - r_f = \frac{\frac{\sigma(w)}{E(w)^2}\beta_{ip}\sigma(r_p) - \frac{\gamma(w)^2}{E(w)^3}\gamma_{ip}\gamma(r_p) + \frac{\theta(w)^3}{E(w)^4}\theta_{ip}\theta(r_p)}{\frac{1}{E(w)} + \frac{\sigma(w)^2}{E(w)^3} - \frac{\gamma(w)^3}{E(w)^4} + \frac{\theta(w)^4}{E(w)^5}} \quad \text{(A3.6)}$$

Under the TFMS assumption used in this study, the above equation is

$$E(r_i) - r_f = \frac{E(1+r_m)^3\sigma(r_m)^2\beta_{im} - E(1+r_m)^2\gamma(r_m)^3\gamma_{im} + E(1+r_m)\theta(r_m)^4\theta_{im}}{E(1+r_m)^4 + E(1+r_m)^2\sigma(r_m)^2 - E(1+r_m)\gamma(r_m)^3 + \theta(r_m)^4} \quad \text{(A3.7)}$$

since $w = w_0(1+r_m)$ and thus, $\sigma(w) = w_0\sigma(r_m)$, $\gamma(w) = w_0\gamma(r_m)$, and $\theta(w) = w_0\theta(r_m)$. For the market portfolio, equation (A3.7) is

$$E(r_m) - r_f = \frac{E(1+r_m)^3\sigma(r_m)^2 - E(1+r_m)^2\gamma(r_m)^3 + E(1+r_m)\theta(r_m)^4}{E(1+r_m)^4 + E(1+r_m)^2\sigma(r_m)^2 - E(1+r_m)\gamma(r_m)^3 + \theta(r_m)^4} \quad \text{(A3.8)}$$

Dividing equation (A3.7) by (A3.8), the following equation is obtained:

$$E(r_i) - r_f = \frac{E(1 + r_m)^2\sigma(r_m)^2\beta_{im} - E(1 + r_m)\gamma(r_m)^3\gamma_{im} + \theta(r_m)^4\theta_{im}}{E(1 + r_m)^2\sigma(r_m)^2 - E(1 + r_m)\gamma(r_m)^3 + \theta(r_m)^4}(E(r_m) - r_f) \tag{A3.9}$$

By defining

$$L_1 = \frac{E(1 + r_m)^2\sigma(r_m)^2}{E(1 + r_m)^2\sigma(r_m)^2 - E(1 + r_m)\gamma(r_m)^3 + \theta(r_m)^4},$$

$$L_2 = -\frac{E(1 + r_m)\gamma(r_m)^3}{E(1 + r_m)^2\sigma(r_m)^2 - E(1 + r_m)\gamma(r_m)^3 + \theta(r_m)^4}$$

and

$$L_3 = \frac{\theta(r_m)^4}{E(1 + r_m)^2\sigma(r_m)^2 - E(1 + r_m)\gamma(r_m)^3 + \theta(r_m)^4}$$

we obtain the following four-moment CAPM for the investor who has log-utility function:

$$E(r_i) - r_f = (L_1\beta_{im} + L_2\gamma_{im} + L_3\theta_{im})(E(r_m) - r_f) \tag{A3.10}$$

ACKNOWLEDGEMENTS

The authors thank anonymous referees for very helpful remarks. The first author would like to thank the Newton Trust and Dresdner Kleinwort Benson for financial support. The second author would like to thank Inquire for financial support.

REFERENCES

Arditti, F.D. (1967) 'Risk and the Required Return on Equity', *Journal of Finance*, **22**, 19–36.

Barone-Adesi, G. (1985) 'Arbitrage Equilibrium with Skewed Asset Returns', *Journal of Financial and Quantitative Analysis*, **20**, 299–313.

Bekaert, G. (1994) 'Exchange Rate Volatility and Deviations from Unbiasedness in a Cash-in-advance Model', *Journal of International Economics*, **36**, 29–52.

Bekaert, G. and Harvey, C.R. (1995) 'Time-Varying World Market Integration', *Journal of Finance*, **50**, 403–444.

Bekaert, G. and Harvey, C.R. (1997) 'Emerging Equity Market Volatility', *Journal of Financial Economics*, **43**, 29–77.

Bekaert, G., Erb, C.B., Harvey, C.R. and Viskanta, T.E. (1997) 'What Matters for Emerging Equity Market Investments', *Emerging Markets Quarterly*, September, 17–46.

Bekaert, G., Erb, C.B., Harvey, C.R. and Viskanta, T.E. (1998) 'Distributional Characteristics of Emerging Market Returns and Asset Allocation', *Journal of Portfolio Management*, Winter, 102–116.

Bekaert, G. and Uris, M.S. (1996) 'Diversification, Integration and Emerging Market Closed-End Funds, *Journal of Finance*, **51**, 835–869.

Burnside, C. (1994) 'Hansen–Jagannathan Bounds as Classical Tests of Asset-Pricing Models, *Journal of Business and Economic Statistics*, **12**, 57–79

Fama, E. (1970) 'Multiperiod Consumption-Investment Decisions', *American Economic Review*, **60**, 163–174.

Ferson, W.E. and Foerster, S.R. (1994) 'Finite Sample Properties of the Generalized Method of Moments in Tests of Conditional Asset Pricing Models, *Journal of Financial Economics*, **36**, 29–55.

Friend, I. and Westerfield, R. (1980) 'Co-Skewness and Capital Asset Pricing', *Journal of Finance*, **35**, 897–919.

Hansen, L.P. (1982) 'Large Sample Properties of Generalized Method of Moments Estimators', *Econometrica*, **50**, 1029–54.

Heaton, J. (1995) 'An Empirical Investigation of Asset Pricing with Temporally Dependent Preference Specifications', *Econometrica*, **63**, 681–717.

Homaifar, G. and Graddy, D.B. (1988) 'Equity Yields in Models Considering Higher Moments of the Return Distribution', *Applied Economics*, **20**, 325–334.

Hwang, S. and Satchell, S.E. (1998a) 'Evaluation of Mutual Fund Performance in Emerging Markets', *Emerging Markets Quarterly*, **2**, 39–50.

Hwang, S. and Satchell, S.E. (1998b) 'Empirical Identification of Common Factors in Emerging Markets Returns', Unpublished manuscript, Department of Applied Economics, Cambridge University.

Ingersoll, J. (1975) 'Multidimensional Security Pricing', *Journal of Financial and Quantitative Analysis*, **10**, 785–798.

Jean, W.H. (1971) 'The Extension of Portfolio Analysis to Three or More Parameters', *Journal of Financial and Quantitative Analysis*, **6**, 505–515.

Jean, W.H. (1973) 'More on Multidimensional Portfolio Analysis', *Journal of Financial and Quantitative Analysis*, **8**, 475–490.

Kraus, A. and Litzenberger, R.H. (1975) 'Market Equilibrium in a Multiperiod State Preference Model with Logarithmic Utility', *Journal of Finance*, **30**, 1213–1227.

Kraus, A. and Litzenberger, R.H. (1976) 'Skewness Preference and the Valuation of Risk Assets', *Journal of Finance*, **31**, 1085–1100.

Kraus, A. and Litzenberger, R.H. (1983) 'On the Distributional Conditions for a Consumption-oriented Three Moment CAPM', *Journal of Finance*, **38**, 1381–1391.

Lim, K. (1989) 'A New Test of the Three-Moment Capital Asset Pricing Model', *Journal of Financial and Quantitative Analysis*, **24**, 205–216.

Masters, S. (1998) 'The Problem with Emerging-Markets Indexes', *Journal of Portfolio Management*, Winter, 93–100.

Newey, W. and West, K. (1987) 'A Simple, Positive Semi-Definite, Heteroskedasticity and Autocorrelation Consistent Covariance Matrix, *Econometrica*, **55**, 703–708.

Scott, R. C. and Horvath, P.A. (1980) 'On the Direction of Preference for Moments of Higher Order Than the Variance', *Journal of Finance*, **35**, 915–919.

Sears, R. S. and Wei, K.C.J. (1985) 'Asset Pricing, Higher Moments, and the Market Risk Premium: A Note', *Journal of Finance*, **40**, 1251–1253.

Sears, R. S. and Wei, K.C.J. (1988) 'The Structure of Skewness Preferences in Asset Pricing Models with Higher Moments: An Empirical Test', *Financial Review*, **23**, 25–38.

Sharpe, W. (1964) 'Capitalist Asset Prices: A Theory of Market Equilibrium under Conditions of Risk', *Journal of Finance*, **19**, 425–442.

Chapter 5

Are stock prices driven by the volume of trade? Empirical analysis of the FT30, FT100 and certain British shares over 1988–1990

L.C.G. ROGERS, STEPHEN E. SATCHELL, AND YOUNGJUN YOON

ABSTRACT

This chapter explains how volume of trade appears to influence the log-return distribution of assets. To compensate for this is rather difficult. One strategy if you wish to predict prices is to consider the joint distribution of price and volume and derive the marginal distribution of price. This will be typically more fat-tailed than the normal. One can base confidence intervals on the predicted price based on the marginal distribution which will be smaller than under normality. The point estimate of price should be the same. A simpler alternative is to work with the conditional distribution of price given volume. To predict prices you can derive a confidence internal, but this will depend upon predictions of tomorrow's volume which may prove rather troublesome.

5.1 INTRODUCTION

For many years both financial economists and statisticians have been concerned with describing the behaviour of stock prices. The price changes in a stock market can be regarded as a result of the influx of new information into the market and of the re-evaluation of existing information. At any point in time there will be many items of information available. Thus, price changes between transactions will reflect the interactions of many different items of information. For example, in the prediction of price changes the difficulty comes from the uncertain arrival of new information as well as the random quantity of information at each point of the time series under study. Even though there is a remarkable discrepancy between the concepts of behaviour of stock prices held by professional stock market analysts, on the one hand, and by academics on the other, the form of the distribution of stock returns is important to both groups because it is a crucial assumption for mean-variance portfolio theory, theoretical models of capital asset prices, and the prices of contingent claims. In this chapter we examine the distribution of daily and weekly logarithmic returns of the FT100, FT30 and the firms that make up the FT30 over the period of 1988 to 1990. We uncover the usual results found by authors working with American data, namely that logarithmic returns measured either daily or weekly do not look normally distributed.

We then briefly discuss the literature that relates the price distribution to the volume of shares traded, a topic which has been examined in great detail by financial economists. The contribution of this chapter is to use volume, rather than time, as the forcing variable in our stochastic process for prices. Based on this assumption that business activity (volume) is driving the price and not time, we 'change the clock' of our process and re-evaluate the distribution of logarithmic returns when a certain volume of trade has elapsed, equal to the average weekly volume. This brings about a significant change in the distribution. It now appears much more normal and adds evidence to the hypothesis that share prices follow a subordinated log-normal process where the conditioning variable is volume. In Section 5.2 we present a review of the existing literature and the mathematical framework. In Section 5.3 we discuss normality testing, stock price indices and the price-volume relationship. In Section 5.4 we present our conclusions. We include definitions of the different normality tests in an appendix.

5.2 EARLY RESEARCH

Past studies of time series of prices at short intervals on a speculative market such as that for corporation shares, indices or futures on commodities are usually compatible with the log-normal random walk model which we shall describe next. We shall present this model in its continuous time version, the form in which it is currently most popular in financial economics. We assume that $s(t)$, the price of the asset at time t, is generated by

$$ds(t) = \alpha(t, s)s(t)dt + \sigma(t, s)s(t)dW(t) \tag{1}$$

where α and σ represent instantaneous mean and volatility, respectively, and

$W(t)$ is standard Brownian motion (BM). The use of equation (5.1) is based on the hypothesis that the continuous Brownian motion is followed during periods between transactions and during periods of exchange closure, even though prices cannot be observed in such intervals. It is well known that, if $\alpha(t, s) = \alpha$ and $\sigma(t, s) = \sigma$ where α and σ are constant, equation (5.1) has the solution

$$s(t) = s(0)\exp[(\alpha - \tfrac{1}{2}\sigma^2)t + \sigma(W(t) - W(0))] \tag{5.2}$$

and that in the logarithmic form,

$$\ln\left(\frac{s(t)}{s(t-1)}\right) = (\alpha - \tfrac{1}{2}\sigma^2) + \sigma(W(t) - W(t-1)) \tag{5.3}$$

We see from equation (5.3) that $\ln(s(t))$ follows a random walk with drift and that errors are *i.i.d.* $N(0, \sigma^2)$, i.e.

$$\ln s(t) = \ln s(t-1) + (\alpha - \tfrac{1}{2}\sigma^2) + \xi(t) \tag{5.4}$$

where

$$\xi(t) = \sigma(W(t) - W(t-1)) \sim N(0, \sigma^2)$$

The increments in the price process are stationary in the mean and independent. If the mean is zero, this is exactly the random walk model. Here, the price changes are not absolute price changes but changes in the logarithmic prices which are independent of one another because stock market investors are interested in proportionate changes in the value of stocks.[1] Henceforth we will use the notation $S(t) = \ln(s(t))$ and $\Delta S(t) = \ln(s(t)) - \ln(s(t-1))$.

Besides empirical realism, the random walk model has a theoretical basis. If price changes are predictable, then alert speculators can make money until these opportunities are removed. Based on this argument, the efficient markets hypothesis implies that security prices reflect all publicly available information. This was first shown by Bachelier in 1900, when he derived the diffusion equation of a random walk model for security from a condition that speculators should receive no information from past prices. Later, Kendall (1953) confirmed that each period's price change was not significantly

[1]The reasons for using changes in logarithmic price is well explained in *E*. Fama (1965): the change in logarithmic price is the yield, with continuous compounding, from holding the security for that day; taking logarithms neutralizes most of the price level effect since the variability of simple price changes is an increasing function of the price level; for changes less than ±15% the change in logarithmic price is very close to the percentage price change.

correlated with the preceding period's price change nor with the price change of any earlier period. While Kendall worked with serial correlations for each series separately, Osborne (1959) worked with ensembles of price changes, which appeared to be approximately normally distributed with a standard deviation proportional to the square root of the length of the period. This proportionality of the standard deviation of price differences to the square root of the differencing period is a characteristic of a random walk and had been pointed out much earlier by Bachelier (1900). In Bachelier's case, however, the differences were arithmetic, while in Osborne's they were logarithmic.

Normality of asset returns was a popular assumption in investigations of investors' behaviour. For this reason in the early stage of stock market study, the normal distribution was considered as a good description of stock market returns. The normal distribution arises in many stochastic processes involving large numbers of independent variables. The traditional justification of log-normality is based on a multiplicative version of the Central Limit Theorem because the change of returns within a certain interval is a product of each individual transaction change of returns. The normal distribution has special virtues; it is linked with the classical Central Limit Theorem; it is stable, meaning any linear combination of independent normals is itself normal; and it is analytically tractable.

In the general theory of random walks the form or shape of the distribution need not be specified. Previous authors (Clark, 1973; Epps and Epps, 1976; Fama, 1963; Mandelbrot, 1963; Tauchen and Pitts, 1983) have found that the price changes $\Delta S_t = \ln(s(t)) - \ln(s(t-1))$, however independent, are not normally distributed. Instead of having the normal shape, which would be the case if the components in ΔS_t were almost independent and almost identically distributed, ΔS_t is consistently more leptokurtic (is more peaked and has fatter tails) than normality indicates. Also, several authors have noted that the nature of the return distribution may change as the period length changes. Assuming that the distribution is stationary with finite mean and variance, this would imply that the leptokurtosis observed in the distribution of daily returns will become less severe as we increase the interval of measurement. This is because we are adding together independent increments with a finite variance which allows an application of the Central Limit Theorem. However, conditions sufficient for the Central Limit Theorem are not met by the influences which make up ΔS_t. The standard Central Limit Theorem holds only when the number of random variables being added is at least non-stochastic; in the case of speculative markets, this restriction may be violated. The number of individual effects added together to give the price change during a certain interval is random, making the standard Central Limit Theorem inapplicable. Although this does not exclude the possibility of normal distributions from our consideration, it gives an insight into why non-normality may arise in practice.

Two responses to these empirical findings have evolved. The first centred on the use of stable Paretian distributions (see Fama, 1963, and Mandelbrot, 1963). We shall not discuss the stable distribution in this chapter but look directly at the second approach, the use of subordinated stochastic processes. The hypothesis is that the distribution of price changes is subordinate to a stochastic process generated from a mixture or combination of distributions. The price series evolves at different rates during identical intervals of time where the variance of the distribution is itself a random variable. The different evolution of price series on different days is due to the fact that information is available to traders at a varying rate. Therefore, the distribution of price changes should be defined conditional on the information-generating process, so that the limit distribution of price changes is subordinate to some distribution. For example, if $P(t)$ is normal with stationary independent increments, and $T(t)$ has stationary independent positive increments with finite second moments which are independent of P, then the subordinated stochastic process $P(T(t))$ has stationary independent increments and the kurtosis of the increments of $P(T(t))$ is an increasing function of the variance of the increments of $T(t)$. Therefore, the introduction of any directing process makes the distribution of the increments of $P(T(t))$ only more leptokurtic. The limit distribution of a random sum of random variables which obey the Central Limit Theorem is asymptotically normal with random variance, or new terminology, subordinate to the normal distribution. Upton and Shannon (1979) found that the asymptotic tendencies of the return distribution are in agreement with the implications of the subordinated stochastic process approach rather than the stable Paretian distribution. Kon (1984) proposed a discrete mixture of normal distributions rather than a continuous mixture to explain the observed significant kurtosis (fat tail) and significant positive skewness[2] in the distribution of daily rate of returns for a sample of common stocks and indices. He found that the data could be well described by a mixture of normals, the actual number of normal distributions involved may vary across firms. Stationarity tests on the parameter estimates of the discrete mixture of normal distributions model revealed significant differences in the mean estimates that can explain the observed skewness in security returns. Significant differences in the variance estimates also can explain the observed kurtosis.

[2]There is some evidence indicating that the assumption of symmetric empirical distributions may be violated for certain phenomena, see Fielitz and Smith (1972) and Leitch and Paulson (1975).

5.3 TESTING NORMALITY IN THE INDIVIDUAL STOCKS

We next describe our data. We collected the data for two Financial Times indices and 30 individual British companies for the period of 1/1/88-31/12/90. We chose this period to avoid any difficulty due to distributional shifts pre and post the October 1987 crash. We started at 1/1/88 to allow some of the short-run perturbations of the crash to settle down. It is an interesting question as to whether there has been a distributional shift before and after the crash, but we shall not address it in this chapter. Two indices, FT-SE100 and FT30, were chosen since they have distinct features, which will be explained later in this section. The 30 companies[3] chosen are the constituents of the FT30 index. Three different time intervals, daily, weekly and fortnightly, were used for the normality tests. For the weekly and fortnightly data, Friday was chosen as the day to measure returns from.

The goodness-of-fit tests of normality[4] are based on the skewness statistic $\sqrt{b_1}$, the kurtosis statistic b_2, a joint test using $\sqrt{b_1}$, and b_2 (Bera–Jarque Test), and definitions are given in the Appendix. Where these tests are used, some care should be taken; they are asymptotic tests and can only be justified by a relatively large sample size, also the tests are sensitive to outliers (e.g. unusually large deviations perhaps caused by stock crashes) (see Spanos, 1986). To cover this weakness, Klein's method is added, which is based on the comparison of observed frequencies with theoretical frequency within quantile limits. Also, we reported the results from the Kolmogorov-Smirnov test.[5] Detailed descriptions of these tests are in the Appendix.

We apply these test procedures to the 30 constituent companies of the FT30. The results are generated in Table 5.1 for daily, Table 5.2 for weekly, and Table 5.3 for fortnightly. Only 12 companies out of 30 satisfied the five test statistics used for normality based on the fortnightly data at $\alpha = 0.05$, 11 for the weekly data. None of the daily data satisfy all test statistics. This leads us to reject the normal distribution of the stock returns traded in the London Stock Exchange. Most of them failed to satisfy the kurtosis statistic b_2, especially in the daily

[3]The weekly result for Beecham is omitted because of insufficient data since it was merged into SmithKline Beecham during the period.

[4]Tests for departures from normality can be divided into parametric and non-parametric tests depending on whether the alternative is given a parametric form or not. Several works on the power of tests for normality reported that b_2 and $\sqrt{b_1}$ are generally preferred, see (see D'Agostino and Pearson, 1973; Gastwirth and Owens, 1977; Saniga and Miles, 1979; Shapiro and Wilk, 1965; Shapiro, Wilk and Chen, 1968).

[5]Since the Kolmogorov–Smirnov test requires the complete specification of the null distribution, the mean and variance of the specified simple normal hypothesis were taken as the (known) mean and variance of the actual alternative distribution. This will cause a slight mismeasurement akin to using normal tables for the t test. Our smallest sample is 156 observations, which renders this effects quite negligible.

Table 5.1 $(S_2 - S_1)$, $(S_3 - S_2)$, $(S_4 - S_3)$, ... (daily price)

	B–J	$\sqrt{b_1}$	b_2	Klein's χ^2 (27)	K–S
Allied-Lyons	331.2	0.505	6.089	110.7	0.057
Asda-MFI	1026.3	−0.391	8.650	148.8	0.079
BICC	197.2	−0.196	5.470	82.74	0.048
BOC	109.1	0.048	4.857	150.4	0.051
BTR	1108.8	−0.649	8.485	90.70	0.055
Beecham	14.39	0.161	3.878	44.28	0.038
Blue Circle	64.31	0.224	4.356	96.56	0.058
Boots	156.1	−0.042	5.223	58.79	0.058
British Airways	117.1	−0.071	4.921	199.6	0.067
British Gas	19.79	0.058	3.784	77.19	0.068
British Petrol	120.4	0.392	4.790	64.71	0.062
British Telecom	48.61	0.202	4.174	78.98	0.059
Cadbury	1224.8	1.064	8.857	142.2	0.092
Courtaulds	353.8	0.414	6.245	92.00	0.062
Gen. Electric	136.4	0.222	5.032	168.4	0.083
Glaxo	27.05	0.037	3.923	40.13	0.038
Grand Metro.	40.68	−0.123	4.109	43.98	0.050
GKN	134.7	−0.482	4.828	105.9	0.064
Guinness	319.8	0.601	5.948	129.8	0.065
Hanson Trust	76.68	−0.042	4.557	90.85	0.060
Hawker Siddeley	1782.9	−1.052	10.22	102.2	0.060
ICI	312.7	−0.696	5.824	55.07	0.045
Lucas	781.1	−0.356	7.925	113.8	0.067
M & S	130.8	0.059	5.033	122.2	0.072
Nat. West. Bank	371.3	0.095	6.426	108.2	0.063
P & O	178.5	−0.024	5.378	75.62	0.044
Royal Ins.	81.80	−0.086	4.601	129.5	0.061
Tate & Lyle	43.30	0.087	4.159	134.7	0.077
Thorn-EMI	85.96	0.027	4.650	54.58	0.050
Trusthouse	6.945	0.063	3.452	79.61	0.063

$\chi^2(2) = 5.99$	at $\alpha = 0.05$	and	$\chi^2(2) = 9.21$	at $\alpha = 0.01$
$-0.23 \leq \sqrt{b_1} \leq 0.28$	at $\alpha = 0.05$	and	$-0.403 \leq \sqrt{b_1} \leq 0.403$	at $\alpha = 0.01$
$2.51 \leq b_2 \leq 3.57$	at $\alpha = 0.05$	and	$2.37 \leq b_2 \leq 3.98$	at $\alpha = 0.01$
$KS \leq 1.36/\sqrt{N}$	at $\alpha = 0.05$	and	$KS \leq 1.63/\sqrt{N}$	at $\alpha = 0.01$
$\chi^2(27) = 40.1$	at $\alpha = 0.05$	and	$\chi^2(27) = 47.0$	at $\alpha = 0.01$

data, while the symmetry looked quite reasonable. The tables suggest that the length of interval is closely related to the kurtosis of stock returns. Weekly versus daily of not rejecting the null hypothesis is 14 versus 1. This indicates that daily information arrivals fluctuate relatively more than weekly ones. This phenomenon becomes more apparent in our fortnightly data of Table 5.3. Only nine companies failed to satisfy the kurtosis statistic, and in general normality is improved. However, there exists a difficulty in symmetry due to the insufficient data since the fortnightly data reduced the sample size. This evidence is consistent with the findings of other authors.

Table 5.2 $(S_2 - S_1), (S_3 - S_2), (S_4 - S_3)$, ... (weekly price)

	B–J	$\sqrt{b_1}$	b_2	Klein's χ^2 (12)	K–S
Allied-Lyons	30.28	0.664	4.702	41.04	0.090
Asda-MFI	28.29	−0.519	3.416	11.29	0.051
BICC	1.632	−0.140	3.416	9.803	0.053
BOC	1.701	0.091	3.478	15.01	0.067
BTR	8.118	−0.339	3.889	9.311	0.041
Beecham	–	–	–	–	–
Blue Circle	5.572	0.431	3.337	9.783	0.057
Boots	0.853	0.091	2.687	11.83	0.042
British Airways	3.720	0.110	3.724	16.19	0.049
British Gas	12.88	0.231	4.330	17.69	0.053
British Petrol	7.801	0.421	3.702	21.96	0.063
British Telecom	7.816	0.271	3.953	10.93	0.057
Cadbury	388.3	1.838	9.799	27.93	0.107
Courtaulds	0.777	−0.162	3.119	8.831	0.030
Gen. Electric	0.313	−0.087	3.133	4.739	0.042
Glaxo	3.354	0.242	3.531	9.253	0.040
Grand Metro.	1.284	−0.122	3.372	9.937	0.046
GKN	1.225	−0.203	3.152	20.08	0.041
Guinness	3.990	0.244	3.612	14.62	0.049
Hanson Trust	0.897	−0.185	2.980	10.12	0.050
Hawker Siddeley	44.45	−0.792	5.080	25.87	0.050
ICI	10.94	−0.254	4.194	12.27	0.065
Lucas	49.08	−0.424	5.614	19.70	0.062
M & S	0.452	0.125	2.913	8.444	0.045
Nat. West. Bank	31.67	0.543	4.922	8.595	0.064
P & O	1.048	−0.115	3.329	7.529	0.038
Royal Ins.	6.284	0.322	3.743	9.471	0.044
Tate & Lyle	6.696	0.353	3.730	38.93	0.050
Thorn-EMI	2.266	−0.293	2.928	9.243	0.047
Trusthouse	2.809	0.302	3.258	8.897	0.061

$\chi^2(2) = 5.99$	at $\alpha = 0.05$	and	$\chi^2(2) = 9.21$	at $\alpha = 0.01$
$-0.23 \leq \sqrt{b_1} \leq 0.28$	at $\alpha = 0.05$	and	$-0.403 \leq \sqrt{b_1} \leq 0.403$	at $\alpha = 0.01$
$2.51 \leq b_2 \leq 3.57$	at $\alpha = 0.05$	and	$2.37 \leq b_2 \leq 3.98$	at $\alpha = 0.01$
$KS \leq 1.36/\sqrt{N}$	at $\alpha = 0.05$	and	$KS \leq 1.63/\sqrt{N}$	at $\alpha = 0.01$
$\chi^2(12) = 21.0$	at $\alpha = 0.05$	and	$\chi^2(12) = 26.2$	at $\alpha = 0.01$

5.3.1 Indices and their distributions

There has always been the need for a summary statistic to measure stock market performance, since the aggregate performance of the stock market is an indicator of the state of the overall economy and monitoring the performance of the market provides a powerful source of information for investment decisions. As a summary of the direction and extent of average changes of stock prices, stock price averages[6] or indices provide a convenient way to summarize general market movements. They are constructed by

Table 5.3 $(S_2 - S_1)$, $(S_3 - S_2)$, $(S_4 - S_3)$, ... (fortnightly price)

	B–J	$\sqrt{b_1}$	b_2	Klein's χ^2 (3)	K–S
FT30 Index	0.215	−0.104	2.849	0.697	0.034
FT100 Index	0.310	−0.047	2.705	1.973	0.034
Allied-Lyons	3.779	0.382	3.760	4.391	0.066
Asda-MFI	56.55	−1.179	6.439	8.004	0.085
BICC	1.463	−0.244	2.540	4.654	0.065
BOC	0.035	0.020	3.096	1.635	0.062
BTR	1.637	−0.325	3.282	3.762	0.083
Blue Circle	1.475	0.299	2.690	3.171	0.072
Boots	0.600	−0.150	2.692	1.106	0.046
British Airways	0.788	−0.245	3.026	2.620	0.067
British Gas	0.093	0.066	2.489	2.040	0.064
British Petrol	1.552	0.203	3.558	2.007	0.071
British Telecom	0.690	−0.198	2.765	3.093	0.046
Cadbury	63.33	1.453	6.322	15.90	0.133
Courtaulds	3.023	−0.435	2.586	5.477	0.064
Gen. Electric	0.023	−0.037	2.962	3.438	0.073
Glaxo	0.263	−0.034	2.723	2.331	0.051
Grand Metro.	0.593	−0.115	2.640	3.439	0.040
GKN	0.553	−0.201	3.086	0.557	0.036
Guinness	16.39	−0.541	4.967	2.343	0.051
Hanson Trust	1.455	0.174	2.428	1.160	0.069
Hawker Siddeley	24.75	−1.110	4.638	14.67	0.1169
ICI	4.045	−0.537	3.299	2.025	0.048
Lucas	8.645	−0.117	4.614	3.521	0.082
M & S	1.590	0.341	3.154	4.609	0.070
Nat. West. Bank	7.491	0.137	4.493	7.115	0.088
P & O	2.644	−0.341	2.411	5.513	0.070
Royal Ins.	1.453	0.248	3.447	3.745	0.081
Tate & Lyle	0.241	0.010	3.271	1.586	0.062
Thorn-EMI	2.069	−0.265	2.404	8.086	0.098
Trusthouse	2.508	0.409	3.316	1.994	0.072

$\chi^2(2) = 5.99$	at $\alpha = 0.05$	and	$\chi^2(2) = 9.21$	at $\alpha = 0.01$
$-0.23 \leq \sqrt{b_1} \leq 0.28$	at $\alpha = 0.05$	and	$-0.403 \leq \sqrt{b_1} \leq 0.403$	at $\alpha = 0.01$
$2.51 \leq b_2 \leq 3.57$	at $\alpha = 0.05$	and	$2.37 \leq b_2 \leq 3.98$	at $\alpha = 0.01$
$KS \leq 1.36/\sqrt{N}$	at $\alpha = 0.05$	and	$KS \leq 1.63/\sqrt{N}$	at $\alpha = 0.01$
$\chi^2(3) = 7.81$	at $\alpha = 0.05$	and	$\chi^2(3) = 11.3$	at $\alpha = 0.01$

[6]Even though the price average such as the Dow Jones Average has been widely quoted, it is criticized for the following reasons; splitting bias in which the divisor for the average has to be adjusted regularly to accommodate splits and it implicitly puts more weight to the stocks that remain unsplit, anti-growth bias since growth stocks split more than non-growth stocks, arithmetic mean bias which gives equal weight to equal absolute rather than the percentage changes in stock prices, etc.

sampling; selecting some manageable number of stocks to act as a proxy for the universe of all stocks. The sample is then weighted in some way, assigning different levels of importance to various component stocks. Next, the weighted sample is averaged, arithmetically or geometrically, to produce a single summary number. If it is a price index, the weighted average of the sample is further divided by a constant to relate it to an arbitrary but intuitively meaningful base value.

Indices are usually weighted by the number of shares outstanding for each stock multiplied by the price of the stock. These capitalization weights reflect relative weights based on each company's capitalization. FT-SE 100, S&P 500 and NYSE indices belong to this category. The value weight indicates changes in the aggregate market value of stocks. Thus, changes in general market value are more reflected in these indices for studies of relationships between stock prices and other things in the national economy with more importance to a relatively few large companies.

The FT-Actuaries Share Indices are weighted arithmetic averages of the price relative; the weights used being the initial capitalization, subsequently modified to maintain the continuity when capital and constituent changes occur. They are derived to show the longer-term changes associated with the value of a portfolio over time, although still reflecting day-to-day movements. The Financial Times–Stock Exchange 100 Share Index generally represents the 100 largest companies by market capitalization. The choice of 100 shares was to hit the balance between the practical difficulty of collecting around 750 shares on a real-time basis needed to turn the All Share Index into a real-time index, and yet having sufficient cover of the market to closely follow the movement of the All Share Index. It mirrors the movement of a typical institutional portfolio. A base figure of 1000 was chosen to make the index more tradeable on the futures or options markets as a high base contract figure usually produces whole number changes every day. As a preliminary, we carried out the same tests reported in Tables 5.1 and 5.2 for the FT100 from 1/1/88 to 31/12/90. The results are presented in Table 5.3. We delay the discussions of results until after an analysis of the FT30.

The Financial Times Ordinary Share Index (FT30) is the geometric average of 30 securities on an unweighted or unit-weighted basis and aims to show short-term movements in the market. The geometric average[7] involves the product of *n* numbers of component stocks and the *n*th root of that product which preserves the integrity of successive upward and downward percentage changes in stock prices. The Index is calculated on a 'real-time' basis from the

[7]It has an unavoidable downward bias; the geometric mean is always less than the arithmetic mean of the same numbers.

start of trading at 9 a.m. A closing Index is produced soon after 5 p.m. on the basis of prices collected at the close down of the Stock Exchange SEQA system. Since the Index is unweighted the calculation is simple. Also, it is sensitive because it is based on heavily traded blue chip shares which are the first to respond to any changes in stock market sentiment. The equal-weight indices may be more appropriate for indicating movements in the prices of typical or average stocks and are better indicators of the expected change in the prices of stocks selected at random since relatively small companies are more sensitive to economic trends. Thus it has been widely followed up to the advent of the FT100.[8] The 30 constituents are carefully selected so as to form a representative spread across British industry and commerce. The number 30 was originally chosen as the best compromise between ease and spread of calculation, on the one hand, and, on the other, the need to avoid too large an influence by freak movements in one or two individual share prices. Its constituents are heavy industry (6), textiles (4), motor and aviations (3), electrical manufacturer and radio (3), building materials (3), food, drink and tobacco (6), retail stores (2), financial institutions (2), miscellaneous (1).

Since the FT30 is a geometric average index, it is easier to make allowances for capital changes, and to replace constituents, without the need for rebasing. Moreover, it damps down the impact of large rises in individual constituents. Despite its advantages it tends to bias the Index downwards over the longer term. This is partly a purely mathematical effect,[9] but it also reflects the way that poorly performing constituents enter into the Index. Therefore, the FT30 Index should not be used as a long-term measure of market levels or as a yardstick for portfolio performance. It should be used for the purpose for which it was precisely designed, as a sensitive indicator of the mood of the market, originally from day-to-day and now from hour-to-hour.

We present the results of our normality tests on the indices in Table 5.4 and Table 5.5. The normality tests of the FT100 and the FT30 show similar conclusions to the individual stocks as before. Each day of the trading days from Monday to Friday was tested. Only Monday and Friday for the FT30 and Wednesday for the FT100 follow a normal distribution at the 5% level. There is no striking improvement in the FT30 compared with individual shares while the FT100 looks reasonably normal. In fact, the FT100 index satisfies all the tests at the 1% level.

A possible problem with these datasets is the presence of serial correlation. We investigated the FT30 and FT100 daily and weekly data. The only

---

[8]The Index has been used since 1935. About a quarter of its constituents have remained in the 30 throughout the period.

[9]This is by Jensen's Inequality, $E[g(X))] \leq g(E[X])$ where h is convex.

Table 5.4 Tests for normality of FT100

	Monday	Tuesday	Wednesday	Thursday	Friday
Observations	157	157	156	156	157
Bera–Jarque χ^2 (2)	**3.3529**	**1.0450**	**2.2581**	6.6615	**4.3629**
$\sqrt{b_1} = m_3/m_2^{3/2}$	**0.0610**	**−0.1771**	**−0.2545**	**−0.2496**	**0.2709**
$b_2 = m_4/m_2^2$	3.7078	**3.1877**	**3.3010**	3.8845	3.6146
Klein's χ^2 (12)	**15.8752**	21.9950	**6.6425**	**7.6476**	**10.3683**

Notes: Details and definitions of the notation are given in the Appendix.
Here and in Table 5.6 the bold numbers indicate not rejecting the null hypothesis of normality.

Table 5.5 Tests for normality of FT30

	Monday	Tuesday	Wednesday	Thursday	Friday
Observations	157	157	156	156	157
Bera–Jarque χ^2 (2)	**1.8002**	6.6907	6.3208	9.9176	**2.8183**
$\sqrt{b_1} = m_3/m_2^{3/2}$	**−0.0247**	0.3476	**−0.2507**	−0.2845	**0.2448**
$b_2 = m_4/m_2^2$	**3.5239**	3.7390	3.8528	4.1008	**3.4403**
Klein's χ^2 (12)	**6.7854**	**11.0823**	**7.1537**	**11.6313**	**18.1187**

$\chi^2(2) = 5.99$	at $\alpha = 0.05$	and	$\chi^2(2) = 9.21$	at $\alpha = 0.01$
$-0.23 \leq \sqrt{b_1} \leq 0.28$	at $\alpha = 0.05$	and	$-0.403 \leq \sqrt{b_1} \leq 0.403$	at $\alpha = 0.01$
$2.51 \leq b_2 \leq 3.57$	at $\alpha = 0.05$	and	$2.37 \leq b_2 \leq 3.98$	at $\alpha = 0.01$
$\chi^2(12) = 21.0$	at $\alpha = 0.05$	and	$\chi^2(12) = 26.2$	at $\alpha = 0.01$

significant autocorrelations found were the first lagged variables for daily data in both cases, in fact the coefficient for the FT30 was estimated at 0.083 with a *t*-level of 2.226 and for the FT100 0.084 with a level of 2.257. For stationary processes, the behaviour of test statistics based on functions of the first four moments will not be influenced by autocorrelation under the null at least asymptotically. However, the power of the tests may well be affected. Since the alternative to normality is not specified, this seems a problem for further research. One could fit an Edgeworth-type family under the alternative and calculate the power function as a function of the autocorrelation coefficient, but we have not done this. If the autocorrelation processes were non-stationary this would influence our test statistics, but then the question of testing for normality becomes meaningless.

Log-normal and log-stable distributions have multiplicative stability but not additive stability. Strictly speaking, if individual asset returns are log-normally (or log-stably) distributed, FT100 returns must have some other distribution while FT30 has a log-normal distribution. Thus if we believe the process has each share generated by equation (5.1), we might expect better results for normality for the FT30 than for the FT100. Against this, there is a possibility that adding more shares together, in the case of the FT100, will induce normality via central limit theorem results. The results in Tables 5.4 and 5.5 indicate that instability under addition, and the problem of changing weights, are not a practical concern under the conditions studied because there is little evidence that FT30 is better suited to a normal distribution than FT100.[10] The practical importance of these complications is an empirical question.

5.3.2 The price–volume relationship

The price–volume relation is critical to the debate over the empirical distribution of stock prices. According to Karpoff (1987), the variance of the daily price change and the mean daily trading volume depend upon three factors: (1) the average daily rate at which new information flows to the market, (2) the extent to which traders disagree when they respond to new information, and (3) the number of active traders in the market. In general, volume is positively related to the magnitude of the price change and, in equity markets, to the price change *per se*. Clark (1973) derives the positive relationship through randomness in the number of within-period transactions. The daily price change is the sum of a random number of within-day price changes. The variance of the daily price change is thus a random variable with a mean proportional to the mean number of daily transaction. Since the trading volume is related positively to the number of within-day transactions, so the trading volume is related positively to the variability of the price change. Another possibility, suggested by Tauchen and Pitts (1983), comes from the fact that the change in the market price on each within-day transaction or market clearing is the average of the changes in all of the traders' reservation prices. Assuming that there is a positive relationship between the extent to which traders disagree when they revise their reservation prices and the absolute value of the change in the market price, the price variability–volume relationship arises because the volume of trading is positively related to the extent to which traders disagree when they revise their reservation prices.

When sampled over fixed calendar intervals (e.g. days), rates of return turned to appear kurtotic compared to the normal distribution in the previous tests. Here, we can develop the explanation of price behaviour by incorporating volume into our consideration. Price–volume tests generally support the mixture of distributions hypothesis which implies that price data are generated by a conditional stochastic process with a changing variance parameter that can be proxied by volume. Osborne (1959) attempted to model

[10] In fact, there are 12 for FT30 versus 14 for FT100 significant entries in the tables.

the stock price change as a diffusion process with variance dependent on the number of transactions. This could imply a positive correlation between V and $|\Delta S|$, as later developed by Clark (1973), Tauchen and Pitts (1983), and Harris and Gurel (1986). In statistical terms, we are postulating a conditional distribution of ΔS, given V. If we assume a marginal distribution of V we know the joint distribution of ΔS and V, and if we integrate out V we have the marginal distribution of ΔS. This marginal distribution may well exhibit the characteristics discussed earlier.

Clark (1973) used trading volume as a measure of the speed of evolution from new information. The distribution of the increments of the price process would then have a distribution subordinate to that of the price changes on individual trades, and directed by the distribution of trading volume. Trading volume is taken as an instrument for the true operational time, or an imperfect clock measuring the speed of evolution of the price-change process. Clark showed that the kurtosis has been very much reduced when price changes with similar volumes were considered. His method is to group by similar volume classes, treating each observation independently, not as time-series data. As long as there is no autocorrelation, his regrouping works. However, if there is any serial correlation, this method will be misleading. Epps and Epps (1976) have suggested that volume moves with measures of within-day price variability because the distribution of the transaction price change is a function of volume. The change in the logarithm of price can therefore be viewed as following a mixture of distributions, with transaction volume as a mixing variable. Tauchen and Pitts (1983) derived a bivariate normal mixture model of price and volume with a likelihood function based on the variance-components scheme. They also considered growth in the size of speculative markets; as the number of traders grows secularly over days, the variance of price changes declines monotonically while the mean volume of trading grows linearly with traders.

First, following Clark's (1973) method, the normalities of weekly FT30 and FT100 changes were tested conditional on the traded volume. Instead of grouping the samples within the same range of volume, the prices were

Table 5.6 Tests for normality conditional on volume

	FT-SE100 Index	FT-30 Index
Observations	157	157
Bera–Jarque χ^2 (2)	**1.6505**	**0.2492**
$\sqrt{b_1} = m_3/m_2^{3/2}$	**0.2270**	**0.2477**
$b_2 = m_4/m_2^2$	**2.5869**	**3.0129**
Klein's χ^2 (12)	**12.8490**	**11.0454**

Table 5.7 Price change at every equal amount of traded volume based on weekly averages

	B–J	$\sqrt{b_1}$	b_2	Klein's χ^2 (12)	K–S
FT30 Index	0.249	0.247	3.012	11.05	0.054
Allied-Lyons	9.573	0.203	4.187	15.06	0.059
Asda-MFI	0.310	−0.074	2.834	4.427	0.053
BICC	4.034	−0.400	3.073	19.26	0.037
BOC	0.958	−0.190	3.060	11.88	0.065
BTR	16.80	−0.513	4.258	15.73	0.061
Blue Circle	7.147	0.225	3.947	16.59	0.054
Boots	0.480	−0.121	2.872	5.296	0.044
British Airways	2.120	−0.286	2.958	8.973	0.045
British Gas	0.573	0.052	3.281	8.381	0.056
British Petrol	1.155	0.190	2.804	5.674	0.055
British Telecom	0.159	0.066	3.084	8.378	0.034
Cadbury	5.429	0.498	3.024	18.82	0.060
Courtaulds	16.75	−0.331	4.474	22.62	0.063
Gen. Electric	4.769	0.304	3.608	21.60	0.059
Glaxo	3.115	−0.317	2.721	10.53	0.051
Grand Metro.	2.130	−0.269	3.198	11.73	0.061
GKN	14.66	−0.688	3.659	23.09	0.068
Guinness	21.97	0.007	4.907	15.80	0.072
Hanson Trust	0.182	0.082	2.970	13.86	0.044
Hawker Siddeley	2.807	−0.329	3.022	6.110	0.043
ICI	0.663	−0.030	3.314	6.726	0.039
Lucas	39.75	−0.066	5.494	29.17	0.054
M & S	8.721	0.382	3.870	10.23	0.040
Nat. West. Bank	21.59	0.264	4.744	8.464	0.052
P & O	53.59	0.653	5.621	14.09	0.058
Royal Ins.	1.415	0.152	3.360	8.354	0.044
Tate & Lyle	2.661	−0.143	3.572	15.61	0.038
Thorn-EMI	0.179	0.081	2.960	9.308	0.044
Trusthouse	4.245	−0.098	3.789	10.66	0.041

$\chi^2(2) = 5.99$	at $\alpha = 0.05$	and	$\chi^2(2) = 9.21$	at $\alpha = 0.01$
$-0.23 \leq \sqrt{b_1} \leq 0.28$	at $\alpha = 0.05$	and	$-0.403 \leq \sqrt{b_1} \leq 0.403$	at $\alpha = 0.01$
$2.51 \leq b_2 \leq 3.57$	at $\alpha = 0.05$	and	$2.37 \leq b_2 \leq 3.98$	at $\alpha = 0.01$
$KS \leq 1.36/\sqrt{N}$	at $\alpha = 0.05$	and	$KS \leq 1.63/\sqrt{N}$	at $\alpha = 0.01$
$\chi^2(3) = 21.0$	at $\alpha = 0.05$	and	$\chi^2(3) = 26.2$	at $\alpha = 0.01$

collected at every 4010 million volume of trade based on the London Stock Exchange as an approximation since FT30 and FT100 are not real instruments for trading. The reason for 4010 million is a convenience to compare the result with those from Tables 5.3 and 5.4 since 4010 million is an average weekly trading volume during the period.

While this is a very crude approximation to market activity, the results are very encouraging. Table 5.6 shows strong support for the subordinated stochastic process hypothesis with a volume-normalization. Both indices are not significant under the normal distribution hypothesis at $\alpha = 0.05$. The total

Table 5.8 Price change at every equal amount of traded volume based on fortnightly averages

	B–J	$\sqrt{b_1}$	b_2	Klein's χ^2 (3)	K–S
FT30 Index	0.957	−0.096	2.485	0.314	0.045
FT100 Index	1.604	−0.130	2.337	3.988	0.063
Allied-Lyons	1.593	−0.321	3.300	5.509	0.073
Asda-MFI	0.615	−0.180	2.748	3.013	0.071
BICC	4.137	−0.567	3.132	4.699	0.080
BOC	3.396	−0.508	2.803	4.334	0.046
BTR	0.491	−0.161	2.774	1.228	0.050
Blue Circle	2.417	0.415	2.730	7.915	0.062
Boots	0.827	−0.124	2.553	4.799	0.074
British Airways	3.201	−0.472	3.341	4.548	0.090
British Gas	2.436	0.275	2.318	3.839	0.063
British Petrol	1.132	0.076	2.422	0.810	0.051
British Telecom	1.633	−0.317	2.664	7.829	0.087
Cadbury	2.276	0.188	3.759	5.967	0.117
Courtaulds	1.891	−0.171	2.307	2.885	0.060
Gen. Electric	2.177	0.367	3.383	2.172	0.054
Glaxo	1.090	−0.252	3.299	2.137	0.053
Grand Metro.	3.226	−0.491	3.231	4.227	0.051
GKN	1.304	−0.221	2.536	2.279	0.047
Guinness	8.824	−0.440	4.417	2.205	0.048
Hanson Trust	0.856	−0.194	2.655	2.842	0.055
Hawker Siddeley	8.218	−0.718	3.727	7.689	0.114
ICI	3.397	−0.409	2.365	6.110	0.077
Lucas	2.768	−0.467	3.016	2.885	0.069
M & S	15.47	0.817	4.488	6.764	0.078
Nat. West. Bank	52.34	0.527	6.926	5.602	0.077
P & O	4.036	0.002	4.128	0.704	0.070
Royal Ins.	0.200	−0.118	2.914	2.444	0.047
Tate & Lyle	4.549	−0.449	3.793	1.093	0.053
Thorn-EMI	0.343	0.087	3.279	0.482	0.059
Trusthouse	2.089	−0.347	2.580	0.412	0.090

$\chi^2(2) = 5.99$	at $\alpha = 0.05$	and	$\chi^2(2) = 9.21$	at $\alpha = 0.01$
$-0.23 \leq \sqrt{b_1} \leq 0.28$	at $\alpha = 0.05$	and	$-0.403 \leq \sqrt{b_1} \leq 0.403$	at $\alpha = 0.01$
$2.51 \leq b_2 \leq 3.57$	at $\alpha = 0.05$	and	$2.37 \leq b_2 \leq 3.98$	at $\alpha = 0.01$
$KS \leq 1.36/\sqrt{N}$	at $\alpha = 0.05$	and	$KS \leq 1.63/\sqrt{N}$	at $\alpha = 0.01$
$\chi^2(3) = 7.81$	at $\alpha = 0.05$	and	$\chi^2(3) = 11.3$	at $\alpha = 0.01$

trade-volume of the London Exchange was used for indices measured in millions since the indices are not traded, and the trade-volume for individual companies is measured in thousands. When applied to individual companies, the normality was also improved by a 20% increase in the numbers of companies that satisfy all tests (see Table 5.7).

Finally, relating to footnote 5, we attempted to improve our $K - S$ test by eliminating the mean and variance. This can be chosen by the following argument. The rates of return normalized by volume $(S_t - S_t{-}_1)/\ V_t$ and

Table 5.9 $(S_2 - S_1)/V_2$, $(S_3 - S_2)/V_3$, $(S_4 - S_3)/V_4$, ... (daily price)

	B–J	$\sqrt{b_1}$	b_2	Klein's χ^2 (12)	K–S
FT30 Index	22.70	−0.191	3.758	46.68	0.034
Allied-Lyons	50.36	0.273	4.140	25.28	0.073
Asda-MFI	10.68	−0.028	3.579	73.07	0.072
BICC	226206	−4.566	87.19	133.3	0.212
BOC	35.60	−0.049	4.058	58.73	0.052
BTR	36.33	−0.238	3.962	43.34	0.064
Beecham	1.714	−0.129	2.807	25.99	0.057
Blue Circle	166.3	−0.232	5.249	56.53	0.070
Boots	12.37	0.113	3.584	20.42	0.063
British Airways	172.8	−0.084	5.334	60.98	0.067
British Gas	9.164	0.179	3.402	29.51	0.052
British Petrol	64.50	−0.052	4.426	36.15	0.045
British Telecom	0.070	0.011	3.042	49.68	0.054
Cadbury	11.40	0.124	3.548	47.49	0.046
Courtaulds	135.7	−0.084	5.067	51.94	0.053
Gen. Electric	15.40	−0.075	3.682	58.30	0.067
Glaxo	8.491	0.052	3.508	30.55	0.020
Grand Metro.	3.285	0.078	2.717	31.16	0.031
GKN	113.5	−0.104	4.886	63.84	0.050
Guinness	7.453	0.010	3.486	40.74	0.044
Hanson Trust	38.45	−0.169	4.051	59.29	0.081
Hawker Siddeley	1215.4	−0.055	9.206	72.26	0.079
ICI	10.60	−0.215	3.389	33.16	0.044
Lucas	1060.2	−0.041	8.797	116.2	0.070
M & S	3.929	−0.039	3.344	90.39	0.080
Nat. West. Bank	302.6	0.265	6.051	55.90	0.069
P & O	4.680	−0.099	3.331	46.10	0.038
Royal Ins.	45.25	−0.227	4.108	95.98	0.059
Tate & Lyle	210.5	−0.182	5.557	122.2	0.104
Thorn-EMI	11.44	−0.246	3.348	41.28	0.036
Trusthouse	275.0	0.422	5.829	21.27	0.051

$\chi^2(2) = 5.99$	at $\alpha = 0.05$	and	$\chi^2(2) = 9.21$	at $\alpha = 0.01$
$-0.23 \leq \sqrt{b_1} \leq 0.28$	at $\alpha = 0.05$	and	$-0.403 \leq \sqrt{b_1} \leq 0.403$	at $\alpha = 0.01$
$2.51 \leq b_2 \leq 3.57$	at $\alpha = 0.05$	and	$2.37 \leq b_2 \leq 3.98$	at $\alpha = 0.01$
$KS \leq 1.36/\sqrt{N}$	at $\alpha = 0.05$	and	$KS \leq 1.63/\sqrt{N}$	at $\alpha = 0.01$
$\chi^2(27) = 40.1$	at $\alpha = 0.05$	and	$\chi^2(27) = 47.0$	at $\alpha = 0.01$

$(S_{t+2} - S_{t+1})/\ V_{t+2} - (S_{t+1} - S_t)/\ V_{t+1}$ where S is the logarithmic price, were tested for the daily and weekly data. The latter one is motivated for the Kolmogorov–Smirnov test because it doesn't require specifying any parameter except the variance. Of course, since the variance is unknown, we have to estimate it and the discrepancy from the 'true' variable is quite minimal – see footnote 5. The reason of normalization by volume is that traded volume reflects the market activities, upon which the behaviour of prices depends. Then, the result is quite close to the normal distribution. Tables 5.7–5.10

Table 5.10 $(S_2 - S_1)/V_2$, $(S_3 - S_2)/V_3$, $(S_4 - S_3)/V_4$, ... (weekly price)

	B–J	$\sqrt{b_1}$	b_2	Klein's χ^2 (12)	K–S
FT30 Index	6.753	0.294	3.832	21.92	0.054
Allied-Lyons	13.44	0.298	4.309	11.11	0.061
Asda-MFI	2.147	−0.198	2.583	10.15	0.050
BICC	1.197	0.042	2.579	9.926	0.051
BOC	2.339	0.264	3.283	11.39	0.059
BTR	1.330	−0.134	2.636	8.070	0.044
Beecham	–	–	–	–	–
Blue Circle	10.74	0.459	3.899	9.616	0.050
Boots	1.000	0.047	2.619	14.58	0.045
British Airways	0.366	0.101	2.877	16.97	0.060
British Gas	35.00	0.294	5.245	16.28	0.055
British Petrol	0.855	0.151	2.800	9.522	0.046
British Telecom	0.205	−0.007	2.823	4.047	0.049
Cadbury	7.519	0.534	2.875	20.86	0.056
Courtaulds	0.128	−0.070	2.986	12.43	0.035
Gen. Electric	1.823	0.032	2.474	19.53	0.056
Glaxo	1.520	0.183	3.315	21.54	0.057
Grand Metro.	0.561	−0.108	2.801	8.944	0.039
GKN	1.633	−0.240	3.146	10.38	0.044
Guinness	1.322	0.222	3.077	6.755	0.029
Hanson Trust	1.935	−0.272	2.958	18.03	0.058
Hawker Siddeley	4.149	−0.396	3.108	15.97	0.068
ICI	0.378	0.040	3.228	6.476	0.030
Lucas	20.33	−0.163	4.738	29.72	0.057
M & S	1.290	0.170	2.713	7.605	0.053
Nat. West. Bank	12.33	0.456	4.033	17.23	0.063
P & O	2.634	−0.188	3.513	6.908	0.050
Royal Ins.	5.126	0.330	3.595	17.27	0.041
Tate & Lyle	2.550	0.211	3.462	19.52	0.062
Thorn-EMI	1.390	−0.190	2.737	20.31	0.061
Trusthouse	0.912	0.187	3.001	7.984	0.048

$\chi^2(2) = 5.99$	at $\alpha = 0.05$	and	$\chi^2(2) = 9.21$	at $\alpha = 0.01$
$-0.23 \leq \sqrt{b_1} \leq 0.28$	at $\alpha = 0.05$	and	$-0.403 \leq \sqrt{b_1} \leq 0.403$	at $\alpha = 0.01$
$2.51 \leq b_2 \leq 3.57$	at $\alpha = 0.05$	and	$2.37 \leq b_2 \leq 3.98$	at $\alpha = 0.01$
$KS \leq 1.36/\sqrt{N}$	at $\alpha = 0.05$	and	$KS \leq 1.63/\sqrt{N}$	at $\alpha = 0.01$
$\chi^2(12) = 21.0$	at $\alpha = 0.05$	and	$\chi^2(12) = 26.2$	at $\alpha = 0.01$

clearly show the improvement upon the normalization by volume, but the effect on the *K–S* test is minimal.

To summarize the results of our transformations, we shall use the Bera–Jarque statistic, which could be thought of as a quadratic loss function in skewness and kurtosis. For the 29 companies in the FT30, excluding Beecham because of merger within the data period, the average value of the Bera–Jarque for weekly data is 22.91 (Table 5.2), for the equal volume case it is 8.549 (Table 5.7) and for the volume weighted case it is 4.694 (Table 5.10). If we

Table 5.11 $(S_3 - S_2)/V_3$, $(S_2 - S_1)/V_3$, $(S_5 - S_4)/V_3$, $(S_4 - S_3)/V_4$ ... (daily price)

	B–J	$\sqrt{b_1}$	b_2	Klein's χ^2 (27)	K–S
FT30 Index	0.929	−0.095	2.849	21.17	0.027
Allied-Lyons	35.08	−0.125	4.472	22.59	0.056
Asda-MFI	10.68	−0.028	3.579	73.07	0.072
BICC	130828	−6.929	93.08	123.6	0.149
BOC	39.46	0.099	4.570	29.73	0.053
BTR	33.19	0.098	4.438	39.98	0.058
Beecham	0.458	0.038	3.224	2.118	0.041
Blue Circle	202.4	−0.125	6.576	39.48	0.051
Boots	34.50	0.183	4.434	36.13	0.052
British Airways	285.6	−0.307	7.214	32.00	0.043
British Gas	3.674	0.172	3.339	18.80	0.038
British Petrol	23.89	−0.223	4.148	60.07	0.050
British Telecom	3.364	−0.048	3.452	31.24	0.062
Cadbury	9.237	0.335	3.370	47.44	0.093
Courtaulds	144.1	0.016	6.024	38.94	0.059
Gen. Electric	5.820	−0.066	3.594	31.35	0.045
Glaxo	13.62	−0.051	3.924	26.65	0.060
Grand Metro.	0.014	0.012	2.982	33.34	0.031
GKN	105.8	0.649	5.244	94.64	0.091
Guinness	36.57	0.032	4.522	24.74	0.030
Hanson Trust	13.34	0.162	3.861	25.56	0.047
Hawker Siddeley	1211.9	0. 974	11.55	39.46	0.074
ICI	12.83	−0.450	8.345	84.28	0.096
Lucas	462.8	−0.450	8.345	84.28	0.096
M & S	8.824	0.135	3.698	33.56	0.043
Nat. West. Bank	319.8	0.174	7.493	55.78	0.102
P & O	3.829	−0.002	3.493	39.94	0.053
Royal Ins.	27.43	0.147	4.287	42.86	0.062
Tate & Lyle	47.97	−0.090	4.736	46.82	0.073
Thorn-EMI	2.172	0.108	3.302	26.47	0.058
Trusthouse	240.7	0.285	6.867	32.38	0.068

$\chi^2(2) = 5.99$	at $\alpha = 0.05$	and	$\chi^2(2) = 9.21$	at $\alpha = 0.01$
$-0.23 \leq \sqrt{b_1} \leq 0.28$	at $\alpha = 0.05$	and	$-0.403 \leq \sqrt{b_1} \leq 0.403$	at $\alpha = 0.01$
$2.51 \leq b_2 \leq 3.57$	at $\alpha = 0.05$	and	$2.37 \leq b_2 \leq 3.98$	at $\alpha = 0.01$
$KS \leq 1.36/\sqrt{N}$	at $\alpha = 0.05$	and	$KS \leq 1.63/\sqrt{N}$	at $\alpha = 0.01$
$\chi^2(27) = 40.1$	at $\alpha = 0.05$	and	$\chi^2(27) = 47.0$	at $\alpha = 0.01$

throw out the largest in each case and divide by 28, we get 9.86, 6.94 and 3.61 respectively. Further, when we used a volume amount equivalent to the average of two weeks' trade, only three out of 31 time series rejected the Bera–Jarque statistic (Table 5.8), which is also consistent with the fact that the nature of the return distribution becomes normal as the period length increases. We might hope that these adjustments to normalize each firm, indeed using our, admittedly crude, adjustment brings about a substantial improvement. For the FT30 the corresponding Bera–Jarque values are 30.28,

Table 5.12 $(S_3 - S_2)/V_3$, $(S_2 - S_1)/V_2$, $(S_5 - S_4)/V_5$, $(S_4 - S_3)/V_4$ ... (weekly price)

	B–J	$\sqrt{b_1}$	b_2	Klein's χ^2 (12)	K–S
FT30 Index	7.371	0.031	4.505	1.219	0.089
Allied-Lyons	12.69	−0.078	4.970	7.715	0.104
Asda-MFI	0.270	0.131	2.880	3.767	0.069
BICC	0.309	−0.090	2.750	2.123	0.083
BOC	0.437	0.180	3.073	2.160	0.070
BTR	3.806	−0.012	4.082	2.474	0.054
Beecham	–	–	–	–	–
Blue Circle	21.56	−0.305	5.502	9.549	0.101
Boots	0.873	−0.199	3.331	0.558	0.068
British Airways	2.590	−0.311	3.639	6.538	0.103
British Gas	72.68	1.140	7.143	4.219	0.134
British Petrol	1.164	0.286	2.823	1.105	0.087
British Telecom	0.100	−0.004	2.825	0.408	0.056
Cadbury	0.493	−0.148	2.747	0.729	0.054
Courtaulds	1.673	−0.109	2.316	5.131	0.096
Gen. Electric	0.137	0.010	2.796	3.237	0.071
Glaxo	0.380	−0.027	3.338	1.087	0.033
Grand Metro.	0.975	−0.250	3.224	4.534	0.073
GKN	0.323	−0.051	3.299	1.910	0.076
Guinness	0.268	−0.114	2.825	2.802	0.061
Hanson Trust	1.015	0.035	3.555	3.561	0.092
Hawker Siddeley	0.636	0.029	2.562	2.001	0.093
ICI	0.311	0.152	3.059	0.569	0.045
Lucas	1.716	0.031	3.724	4.377	0.131
M & S	1.136	0.240	3.346	2.381	0.072
Nat. West. Bank	8.706	0.676	3.922	7.570	0.062
P & O	4.441	−0.053	4.164	3.635	0.074
Royal Ins.	1.369	0.321	2.908	4.688	0.062
Tate & Lyle	1.961	−0.320	3.440	2.328	0.113
Thorn-EMI	2.735	−0.321	3.655	2.615	0.091
Trusthouse	0.563	−0.041	3.408	3.487	0.100

$\chi^2(2) = 5.99$	at $\alpha = 0.05$	and	$\chi^2(2) = 9.21$	at $\alpha = 0.01$
$-0.23 \leq \sqrt{b_1} \leq 0.28$	at $\alpha = 0.05$	and	$-0.403 \leq \sqrt{b_1} \leq 0.403$	at $\alpha = 0.01$
$2.51 \leq b_2 \leq 3.57$	at $\alpha = 0.05$	and	$2.37 \leq b_2 \leq 3.98$	at $\alpha = 0.01$
$KS \leq 1.36/\sqrt{N}$	at $\alpha = 0.05$	and	$KS \leq 1.63/\sqrt{N}$	at $\alpha = 0.01$
$\chi^2(12) = 21.0$	at $\alpha = 0.05$	and	$\chi^2(12) = 25.2$	at $\alpha = 0.01$

0.249, and 6.753. The improvement for the FT30 in the weekly equal volume case is quite remarkable. However, when we extended normality tests in the fortnightly data, the improvement is not so dramatic as in the weekly data. This is because a fortnight period is more normal and volume effects are averaged out in the fortnightly data (see Tables 5.3 and 5.8). We have not analysed our fortnightly observations any further as they appear normal in the first case and the number of observations is only 78.

5.4 CONCLUSION

We tested the normality of speculative asset returns and indices in the London Stock Exchange. Our results are consistent with previous studies. The difference between the FT30 and the FT100 was one of our interests. If individual asset returns were log-normally (or log-stably) distributed, FT30 is expected to be better suited to a normal distribution. However, we found that there was little evidence to support this assumption. When we normalized by volume, FT30 performed better under the normal hypothesis. This gives some support for the subordinated stochastic process hypothesis rather than the stable Paretian distribution or the normal distribution hypotheses. Still, this finding is limited to the specific time-period and specific market, further theoretical work and methods are required.

The length of period has an importance for the nature of the return distribution. In empirical observations, the minimum satisfactory period is called for because the possibility of significant non-stationarity of the return distribution increases as the time period lengthens. The problem of stationarity occurs both intra- and inter-period. For example, in order to observe log-normality in monthly returns it is necessary that the process remain stationary not only during the individual months but also over the collection of months observed. If the underlying process were slowly changing, it might be that log-normality might be observed over some short sampling interval, but over some longer sampling log-normality might be rejected due to significant cumulative changes in the process. The question of the appropriate length of individual periods, and appropriate length of sampling interval, is empirical.

Finally one can interpret our results in two ways. In the literature that regards prices following a logarithmic Brownian motion, we have shown that the clock of the process is volume, not time. In the literature that is concerned with the distribution of share prices, we have shown that the conditional distribution of logarithmic price changes given volume is normally distributed. These two ideas are not mutually exclusive. We have not considered how to model volume. If we were to do so, we could, in principle, derive the marginal distribution of prices and examine its properties directly.

APPENDIX

We encounter several distributions, related to the normal distribution, which play important parts in the theory of statistics precisely because they are the forms taken by the sampling distributions of various statistics in samples from normal populations. The special position which the normal distribution holds, mainly by virtue of the Central Limit Theorem in one or other of its forms, is reflected in the positions of central importance occupied by these related distributions. Tests for normality can be divided into parametric and nonparametric tests depending on whether the alternative is given a parametric form or not.

The Kolmogorov–Smirnov test is a test of goodness of fit. Goodness-of-fit tests are based on a comparison of the hypothesized cumulative distribution function $F(x)$ with the empirical distribution function $F_n(x)$ obtained from a random sample of n observations. That is, it is concerned with the degree of agreement between the distribution of a set of sample values (observed scores) and some specified theoretical distribution. It determines whether the scores in the sample can reasonably be thought to have come from a population having the theoretical distribution. The test involves specifying the cumulative frequency distribution which would occur under the theoretical distribution. The point at which these two distributions, theoretical and observed, show the greatest divergence is determined. Reference to the sampling distribution indicates whether such a large divergence is likely on the basis of chance. Define $F_0(X) = a$ completely specified cumulative frequency distribution function, the theoretical cumulative distribution under H_0 and $S_N(X) =$ the observed cumulative frequency distribution of a random sample of N observations $= k/N$ where k is the number of observations equal to or less than X. Then, the test statistic is $D = \max_x |F_0(X) - S_N(X)|$. The distribution of D is not known for the case when certain parameters of the population have been estimated from the sample. However, Massey (1951) gives some evidence which indicates that if the $K - S$ test is applied in such cases (e.g. for testing goodness of fit to a normal distribution with mean and standard deviation estimated from the sample), the use of the table will lead to a conservative test. Empirically the $K - S$ test exhibits surprisingly poor power (see D'Agostino, 1971; D'Agostino and Pearson, 1973; Pearson, D'Agostino and Bowman, 1977).

The most widely used parametric tests for normality are those based on the skewness-kurtosis. The parametric alternative in these tests comes in the form of the Pearson family of densities. The goodness-of-fit tests are based on the sample second, third and fourth moment of the empirical distributions. These are given, respectively, by

$$\sqrt{b_1} = \frac{m_3}{m_2^{3/2}} \text{ and } b_2 = \frac{m_4}{m_2^2} \tag{A.1}$$

where

$$m_r = \sum_{i=1}^{n}(X_i - \overline{X})^r/n \text{ and } \overline{X} = \sum_{i=1}^{n} X_i.$$

The second moment is measure of spread or dispersion, the third moment is measure of skewness or asymmetry, and the fourth moment is measure of excess or kurtosis, which is the degree of flatness of a density near its centre. The normal distribution has the property that its third and fourth cumulants are both zero. Then, $\sqrt{b_1}$ is a good measure of non-normality against highly skewed and long-tailed distribution since all odd moments of a random variable about its mean are zero if the density function of random variable is symmetrical about the mean, provided such moments exist. And b_2 is sensitive to continuous, symmetric alternatives with heavy tails.

Under the null hypothesis of population normality, $\sqrt{b_1}$and b_2 are independent and their standardized normal equivalent deviates are approximately $X(\sqrt{b_1})$ and $X(b_2)$, where $X(\cdot)$ denotes a standardized normal distribution, hence $X^2(\sqrt{b_1}) + X^2(b_2)$ is asymptotically $\chi^2(2)$, for details see equation (A2). Bera and Jarque (1981) using the Pearson family as the parametric alternative derived the following skewness-kurtosis test as a Lagrange multiplier test. Let BJ be the Bera–Jarque statistic, then

$$BJ_n = [\frac{n}{6}\hat{b}_1 + \frac{n}{24}(\hat{b}_2 - 3)^2 - \chi^2(2) \qquad \text{(A.2)}$$

where

$$\sqrt{\hat{b}_1} = [\frac{1}{n}\sum_{t=1}^{n} \hat{u}_t^3) \Big/ (\frac{1}{n}\sum_{t=1}^{n} \hat{u}_t^2)^{\frac{3}{2}}]$$

$$\hat{b}_2 = [\frac{1}{n}\sum_{t=1}^{n} \hat{u}_t^4) \Big/ (\frac{1}{n}\sum_{t=1}^{n} \hat{u}_t^2)^2]$$

where $\hat{u}_t$ is typically a regression residual in our case $\hat{u}_t = r_t - \bar{r} = r$. Notice that equation (A2) is the same as (A1) but that (A2) allows one to consider residuals from linear regressions with sets of regression variables other than just a constant.

ACKNOWLEDGEMENTS

Financial support from the Newton Trust and Inquire (UK) is gratefully acknowledged. The comments from David Damant (Paribas Asset Management) have been very helpful. This chapter was produced as a discussion paper for the Autumn 1991 Inquire Conference. Some of the contents are still rather preliminary.

REFERENCES

Affleck-Graves, J. and McDonald, W. (1989) 'Nonnormalities and Tests of Asset Pricing Theories', *Journal of Finance*, **XLIV**, 889–908.

Alexander, S.S. (1961) 'Price Movements in Speculative Markets: Trends or Random Walks', *Industrial Management Review*, **2**, 7–26.

Bachelier, L. (1990) *Theory of Speculation*. Reprinted in *The Random Character of Stock Market Prices* (1964), edited by P.H. Cootner.

Balvers, R., Cosimano, T. and McDonald, B. (1990) 'Predicting Stock Returns in an Efficient Market', *Journal of Finance*, **XLV**, 1109–1128.

Bera, A.K. and Jarque, C.M. (1981) 'An Efficient Large-Sample Test for Normality of Observations and Regression Residuals', Australian National University Working Papers in Econometrics No. 40, Canberra.

Bera, A.K., Jarque, C.M. and Lee, L.-F. (1984) 'Testing The Normality Assumption in Limited Dependent Variable Models', *International Economic Review*, **25**, 563–578.

Clark, P.K. (1973) 'A Subordinate Stochastic Process Model with Finite Variance for Speculative Prices', *Econometrica*, **41**, 135–155.

D'Agostino, R.B. (1971) 'An Omnibus Test of Normality for Moderate and Large Size Samples', *Biometrika*, **58**, 341–348.

D'Agostino, R.B. and Pearson, E.S. (1973) 'Tests for Departure From Normality: Empirical Results for the Distribution of b_2 and $\sqrt{b_1}$', *Biometrika*, **60**, 613–622.

Epps, T.W. and Epps, R.E. (1976) 'The Stochastic Dependence of Security Price Changes and Transaction Volumes: Implications for the Mixture-of-Distribution Hypothesis', *Econometrica*, **44**, 305–321.

Fama, E.F. (1963) 'Mandelbrot and the Stable Paretian Hypothesis', *Journal of Business*, **36**, 420–429.

Fama, E.F. (1965) 'The Behavior of Stock Market Prices', *Journal of Business*, **38**, 34–105.

Fielitz, B.D. and Smith, E.W. (1972) 'Asymmetric Stable Distributions of Stock Price Changes', *Journal of the American Statistical Association*, **67**, 813–814.

Gastwirth, J.L. and Owens, M.E.B. (1977) 'On Classical Tests of Normality', *Biometrika*, **64**, 135–139.

Harris, L. and Gurel, E. (1986) 'Price and Volume Effects Associated with Changes in the S&P 500 List: New Evidence for the Existence of Price Pressures', *Journal of Finance*, **XLI**, 815–829.

Karpoff, J.M. (1987) 'The Relation Between Price Changes and Trading Volume: A Survey', *Journal of Financial and Quantitative Analysis*, **22**, 109–126.

Kendall, M.G. (1953) 'The Analysis of Economic Time-Series-Part I: Prices', *Journal of the Royal Statistical Society*, Series A, **CXVI**, 11–25.

Klein, L. (1974), *Textbook of Econometrics*, Prentice-Hall, Englewood Cliffs, NJ.

Kon, S.J. (1984) 'Models of Stock Returns – A Comparison', *Journal of Finance*, **39**, 147–165.

Leitch, R.A. and Paulson, A.S. (1975) 'Estimation of Stable Law Parameters: Stock Price Behavior Application', *Journal of the American Statistical Association*, **70**, 690–697.

Luskin, D.L. (1987) *Index Options & Futures*, John Wiley, New York.

Mandelbrot, B. (1963) 'The Variation of Certain Speculative Prices', *Journal of Business*, **36**, 394–419.

Massey, F.J. Jr. (1951) 'The Kolmogorov-Smirnov Test for Goodness of Fit', *Journal of the American Statistical Association*, **46**, 68–78.

Osborne, M.F.M. (1959) 'Brownian Motion in the Stock Market', *Operations Research*, **7**, 145–173.

Pearson, E.S., D'Agostino, R.B. and Bowman, K.O. (1977) 'Tests for Departure from Normality: Comparison of Powers', *Biometrika*, **64**, 231–246.

Saniga, E.M. and Miles, J.A. (1979) 'Power of Some Standard Goodness-of-Fit Tests of Normality Against Asymmetric Stable Alternatives', *Journal of the American Statistical Association*, **74**, 861–865.

Shapiro, S.S. and Wilk, M.B. (1965) 'An Analysis of Variance Test for Normality (Complete Samples)', *Biometrika*, **52**, 591–611.

Shapiro, S.S., Wilk, M.B. and Chen, J. (1968) 'A Comparative Study of Various Tests for Normality', *Journal of the American Statistical Association*, **63**, 1343–1372.

Spanos, A. (1986) *Statistical Foundations of Econometric Modelling*, Cambridge University Press, Cambridge.

Tauchen, G.E. and Pitts, M. (1983) 'The Price Variability-Volume Relationship on Speculative Markets', *Econometrica*, **51**, 485–505.

Upton, D.E. and Shannon, D.S. (1979) 'The Stable Paretian Distribution, Subordinated Stochastic Processes, and Asymptotic Log-normality: An Empirical Investigation', *Journal of Finance*, **34**, 1031–1039.

Chapter 6

Testing for a finite variance in stock return distributions

JUN YU

ABSTRACT

In this chapter a test statistic is proposed to discriminate between finite variance distributions and infinite variance distributions for stock returns. The test statistic is the ratio of the sample interquartile range and the sample standard deviation. The asymptotic distribution of the test statistic is obtained. We show that the test is consistent against infinite variance distributions. The test is applied to Nikkei and CRSP indices. The results show that finite variance distributions except normality and lognormality cannot be rejected for Nikkei but all finite variance distributions considered have to be rejected at the 1% significance level for CRSP.

6.1 INTRODUCTION

Researchers have been interested in modelling stock return distributions for many years. One main reason for their interest is that the distribution form of return distributions has a direct bearing on the descriptive validity of theoretical models in finance. Such models include mean-variance portfolio theory, capital asset pricing models, and pricing models of derivative securities. In the search for satisfactory descriptive models of stock returns, many distributions have been attempted and some new distributions have been created over past decades. The distributions proposed include both unconditional and conditional distributions. Despite the recent bent toward using conditional distributions,[1] Tucker (1992) claims that the descriptive validity of unconditional distributions still remains unknown and it is not entirely clear which distribution one needs to use in practice.

All unconditional distributions or time-independent models can be divided by two families. One family has finite variance. Examples include the normal distribution, lognormal distribution, Student distribution, mixture of normals (MN), compound log-normal and normal distribution, mixed diffusion-jump (MDJ) process and more recent distributions, such as the generalized beta (GB) distribution, Weibull distribution, Variance Gamma (VG) distribution, hyperbolic distribution and generalized lambda distribution. The other family has infinite variance. A widely used infinite variance model is the stable distribution.

The stable distribution has been appreciated as a distribution to model stock returns for both statistical and economic reasons. Statistically speaking, the stable distribution has domains of attraction and belongs to its own domain of attraction. Economically, the stable distribution has unbounded variation, and hence is consistent with continuous-time equilibrium in competitive markets (see McCulloch, 1978).

Despite the above appealing properties, the stable distribution is less commonly used today. It has fallen out of favour for several reasons, First, it involves more difficulties in theoretical modelling. For example, standard financial theory, such as option theory, typically requires finite variance of returns. Second, some evidence has been documented against the stable distribution. For instance, by fitting both the Student and symmetric stable distributions into the same datasets, Blattberg and Gonedes (1974) find that likelihood from the Student distribution is larger than that from the symmetric stable distribution. Tucker (1992) finds, however, the asymmetric stable distribution outperforms the Student distribution in terms of the likelihood value when he fits both distributions into 200 randomly chosen stocks. Using the same datasets and the same criterion, he further reports that both the MDJ process and mixture of normals perform better than the asymmetric stable distribution. Using the Kolmogorov–Smirnov test, Mittnik and Rachev (1993) suggest that the Weibull distribution is the most suitable candidate to describe S&P500 daily index returns. Moreover, when investigating the tail behaviour, Akgiray and Booth (1987) find that the tails of the stable distribution are too thick to fit the empirical data. Relatedly, Lau, Lau and Wingender (1990) find that as the sample size gets larger the sample higher moments seem to converge

[1]The conditional distributions, sometimes called time-dependent models, include the autoregressive conditional heteroscedastic (ARCH) model (Engle, 1982), generalized autoregressive conditional heteroscedastic (GARCH) model (Bollerslev, 1982) and stochastic volatility (SV) model (Taylor, 1986).

while the stable distribution implies that the sample higher moments should increase rapidly with sample size. Finally, evidence provided by Blattberg and Gonedes (1974) indicates that the distribution of monthly returns conforms well to the normal distribution, while the stable distribution implies that long-horizon (for example, monthly) returns will be just as non-normal as short-horizon (for example, daily) returns.

The purpose of this chapter is to re-examine the descriptive power of finite variance distributions and infinite variance distributions as models of daily stock returns. Instead of examining overall goodness-of-fit of competing distributions or employing Bayesian model selection criteria, we concentrate on studying the variance behaviour of chosen distribution families. To be more specific, we propose a test statistic to distinguish between finite variance distributions and infinite variance distributions for modelling stock returns.

Particular attention is paid to variance for three principal reasons. First, as far as variance is concerned, an infinite variance model is fundamentally riskier than a finite variance model. Second, many financial models critically depend on the assumption on the second moment. Such models include the capital asset pricing models (CAPM),[2] the Black–Scholes option pricing model, and expected utility theory. As a result, finite variance and infinite variance could have very different implications for theoretical and empirical analysis. Finally, conventional asymptotic theories fail for some widely used statistics when the variance is not finite. For example, Rundle (1997) shows that the Box–Pierce Q-statistic does not tend to a conventional χ^2 in distribution if the random variable follows a stable distribution. Unfortunately, testing for finite variance or infinite variance based on a sample without choosing a specific distributional family will probably never be possible since such a test could have no power. Instead of directing the test on variance itself, we test a specific finite variance distribution against a specific infinite variance distribution.

The chapter is organized as follows. The next section introduces the test statistic, motivates the intuition behind it, and obtains the statistical properties of it. Section 6.3 summarizes the candidate models of stock returns. Section 6.4 applies the proposed test statistic to two actual series, the Nikkei Stock Average 225 daily index and the value-weighted CRSP daily index. Section 6.5 concludes. All the proofs are collected in the Appendix.

6.2 PROPOSED STATISTIC AND ITS PROPERTIES

Let P_t denote the nominal price of a financial instrument on trading day t.

[2]Examples include Lintner (1965), Mossin (1966) and Sharpe (1964).

Usually two definitions of returns are used:

$$Z_t = P_t / P_{t-1} \tag{6.1}$$

and

$$X_t = \ln(P_t) - \ln(P_{t-1}) \tag{6.2}$$

where Z_t is the simple return and is always positive,[3] and X_t is the compound return and can be positive or negative. Some statistical models are proposed to describe the simple return while many others describe the compound return. These two forms are, however, related to each other. For example, if the random variable Z is lognormally distributed, then $X = \ln(Z)$ is normally distributed. In this chapter, we will use X or x to represent a distribution of compound returns and Z or z to represent a distribution of simple returns. The proposed statistic is based on the compound return, X.

Suppose $\{X_i\}_{i=1}^n$ is a sequence of observations with a common distribution function $F(x)$, a common density function $f(x)$, a mean μ and variance σ^2. Let

$$s_n^2 = \frac{1}{n-1} \sum_{i=1}^{n} (X_i - \hat{\mu})^2$$

be the sample variance, where $\hat{\mu}$ is the sample mean. Denote the quantile process by $Q_n(t)$ (see Csörgő and Horváth, 1993, Chapter 6). The proposed test statistic is then defined as

$$T_n(\theta_0) = \frac{Q_n(1-\theta_0) - Q_n(\theta_0)}{s_n} \tag{6.3}$$

where $0 < \theta_0 < 0.5$. Hence the numerator is the θ_0-quartile range and is indeed the interquartile range when $\theta_0 = 0.25$. As an important special case $T_n(0.25)$ is the ratio of the sample interquartile range and the sample standard deviation. The statistic is the reciprocal to the statistic proposed by Shao, Yu and Yu (1999) (hereafter SYY). The advantages of using our statistic over the one in SYY will be discussed below.

The statistic (6.3) bears some resemblance with the 'Studentized' test $(x_{max} - x_{min})/s_n$, which has been proposed by David, Hartley and Pearson (1954) to test for normality and to detect heterogeneity of data. There are two important differences between our proposed test and the 'Studentized' test, however. First, our test includes the 'Studentized' test as a special case and hence can be used for more general purposes. Second, only the finite sample

[3]In the literature, $Z_t - 1$ is sometimes referred to as the simple return. It differs from the compound returns by a small amount according to Taylor series expansion.

distributions of the 'Studentized' test from a single normal population have been obtained. Not surprisingly, it cannot be used to test for finite variance distributions except for normality.

It seems natural to use sample variance or sample standard deviation to discriminate between finite variance distributions and infinite variance distributions. Unfortunately, the power based on the sample variance or sample standard deviation may not be good since a finite variance distribution can generate a larger sample variance than an infinite variance distribution, even when the sample size is large. By taking the ratio of two dispersion parameters, however, we standardize or reduce the dispersion in the proposed test for any finite variance distribution.

The rationale for the proposed test may work as follows. When the true data-generating process (DGP) has a finite variance, fewer observations come from the tails and hence $s_n \to \sigma$ as $n \to \infty$. Since both $Q_n(0.75)$ and $Q_n(0.25)$ are finite for any n, T_n converges to a positive number as $n \to \infty$. On the other hand, if the true DGP has infinite variance, more observations come from the tails compared with a finite variance DGP. Hence, s_n will increase with sample size while both $Q_n(0.75)$ and $Q_n(0.25)$ are still bounded away from zero. This implies that T_n will converge to 0 as $n \to \infty$. Consequently, it is reasonable to believe that a small T_n comes from a DGP with infinite variance rather than a DGP with finite variance. Thus we set up the hypothesis as

$$\begin{cases} H_0: & \text{DGP is a certain finite variance distribution,} \\ H_1: & \text{DGP is a certain infinite variance distribution.} \end{cases} \tag{6.4}$$

If H_0 is rejected, the distribution in H_0 should not be used as a candidate to model the returns.

In this chapter we assume $X_1, X_2, ..., X_n$ to be iid random variables. The properties of T_n are established below. Their proofs are found in the Appendix.

Proposition 1. *T_n is invariant for a scale-location family.*

This is an appealing property. For a scale-location family, no matter where the density locates and how large the scale is, the expectation of the statistic always takes the same value. In other words, if we think of T_n as a measure of risk, the risk associated with a scale-location family is a constant. Because of this property, any scale-location family can be treated as one model. Two statistics which have the feature of scale and location invariance are sample kurtosis and sample skewness. They have been widely used to detect departures from normality in practice.

Proposition 2. *If $\sigma^2 < +\infty$, and $Q(t)$ is continuous at θ_0 and $1-\theta_0$, then, under H_0*

$$T_n \overset{a.s.}{\rightarrow} T = \frac{q_1 - q_0}{\sigma} > 0, \tag{6.5}$$

where $q_1 = Q(1-\theta_0)$, $q_0 = Q(\theta_0)$ with $Q(t) = \inf\{x : F(x) \geq t\}$.

This result is very intuitive since it says that T_n converges almost surely to its population counterpart. According to this proposition, if the distribution in H_0 has good descriptive power, it must yield a value of T close enough to the empirical T_n.

Proposition 3. *Assume that*
(i) $f(q_1) > 0, f(q_0) > 0$.
(ii) $f(x)$ is continuous in a neighbourhood of q_1 and q_0.
(iii) $\sigma^2 < \infty$.
Under the above three assumptions, and under H_0 we have

$$\sqrt{n}(T_n - T) \overset{d}{\rightarrow} N(0, \Sigma^2) \tag{6.6}$$

that is,

$$T_n \overset{a}{\sim} N(T, \frac{\Sigma^2}{n}) \tag{6.7}$$

where

$$\Sigma^2 = \frac{1}{\sigma^2}\left\{\frac{\theta_0(1-\theta_0)}{f^2(q_0)} + \frac{\theta_0(1-\theta_0)}{f^2(q_1)} - \frac{2\theta_0^2}{f(q_0)f(q_1)}\right\} \tag{6.8}$$

The asymptotic distribution in Proposition 3 is the main result of the chapter since it provides the asymptotics to test the proposed hypothesis. Although T_n is invariant for a scale-location family, it is important to note that in general both T and Σ^2 depend on f and hence H_0. Generally, therefore, our statistic cannot be used to test the following hypotheses:

$$\begin{cases} H_0: & \text{DGP is any finite variance distribution,} \\ H_1: & \text{DGP is any infinite variance distribution.} \end{cases} \tag{6.9}$$

Instead T_n can be used as a non-nested test for a specific finite variance distribution against a specific infinite variance distribution. And the distribution form along with the parameters in H_0 has to be specified except for the scale and location parameters. In this sense the test is similar to a mis-specification test.

There are two advantages of using our proposed statistic over the test of SYY. One is that our test requires that only the second moment be finite while in the test of SYY the fourth absolute moment has to be finite. As we will see in Section 6.4, the fourth moment of some finite variance distributions may not be finite for actual series. The empirical evidence makes the test of SYY not applicable. The other advantage is that the asymptotic variance of our test has simpler expression and hence is easier to calculate.

Proposition 4. *Under assumptions of Proposition 3, if f is symmetric (that is, $f(q_1) = f(q_0)$) the asymptotic variance simplifies to*

$$\Sigma^2 = \frac{2\theta_0(1 - 2\theta_0)}{\sigma^2 f^2(q_0)} \tag{6.10}$$

Again the expression of the asymptotic variance is simpler than the corresponding one in SYY.

Proposition 5. *If $Q(t)$ is continuous at θ_0 and $1 - \theta_0$, the test 'Reject H_0 if $T_n < c$', for some $0 < c < +\infty$, is consistent against H_1.*

This is a valuable result because it guarantees a reasonable power of the proposed test in large samples, provided that the assumption in the proposition is satisfied.

6.3 CANDIDATE DISTRIBUTIONS FOR STOCK RETURNS

In this section we review the time-independent distributions for daily stock returns and briefly discuss the properties of competing distributions. In the finite variance family, we present the normal, lognormal, Student, mixture of normals, mixed diffusion-jump, compound lognormal and normal, generalized beta, Weibull, Variance Gamma, hyperbolic, and generalized lambda distributions. The stable distribution represents the infinite variance family. There are two common approaches to model return distributions. The first describes the underlying stochastic process that generates prices. Usually it claims that the security prices involve a mixture of distributions. Not surprisingly, most mixed distributions, such as the Student, mixture of normals, mixed diffusion-jump, compound lognormal and normal model and Variance Gamma distributions, take this approach. The second approach specifies a statistical distribution which provides a good fit to the actual observations and/or explains stylised facts observed in the empirical observations. A classical example which follows the second approach is the stable distribution.

6.3.1 Normal distribution

The first model used in the literature to describe daily stock returns is the normal distribution proposed by Bachelier (1900) and extended by Osborne (1959). The normal distribution is defined the probability density function (pdf)

$$f(x) = \frac{1}{\sqrt{2\pi\sigma^2}} \exp\left[\frac{(x-\mu)^2}{2\sigma^2}\right]. \tag{6.11}$$

The normal distribution is symmetric. The mean, variance and kurtosis are μ, σ^2, and 3 respectively. Black and Scholes (1973) provide a formula to price an option assuming the normality of underlying assets. Although the assumption of normality greatly simplifies the theoretical modelling, many empirical studies have shown evidence against it (see Blattberg and Gonedes, 1974; Clark, 1973; Kon, 1984; Niederhoffer and Osborne, 1966). For example, empirical daily stock returns usually exhibit fatter tails and higher kurtosis than the normal distribution. Despite evidence against normality, in this chapter we still choose it as a competing model because we want to check the validity of normality by using our test statistic. Note that all moments for the normal distribution exist. Furthermore, since the normal distribution belongs to a scale-location family, T_n is invariant to both μ and σ^2.

6.3.2 Lognormal distribution

The lognormal has been used widely for modelling stock return distributions (see, for example, Elton and Gruber, 1974). The pdf of the lognormal distribution is

$$f(z) = \frac{1}{z\sqrt{2\pi\sigma^2}} \exp\left[-\frac{(\ln z-\mu)^2}{2\sigma^2}\right], z > 0 \tag{6.12}$$

The mean and variance of the lognormal distribution are $\exp(\mu + \sigma^2/2)$, $(\exp(\sigma^2) - 1)(\exp(2\mu + \sigma^2))$. Obviously, if a simple return follows a lognormal distribution, the compound return should follow the corresponding normal distribution. Therefore, the lognormal distribution suffers the same problems as the normal distribution.

6.3.3 Student distribution

The Student distribution has been proposed to model the stock returns by Praetz (1972) and Blattberg and Gonedes (1974). Its pdf is

$$g(x) = \frac{\Gamma[(1+\nu)/2]\nu^{\nu/2}\sqrt{H}}{\Gamma(1/2)\Gamma(\nu/2)}[\nu + H(x-m)^2]^{-(\nu+1)/2} \tag{6.13}$$

where $\nu \geq 1$, and H, m, ν are the scale, location and degrees-of-freedom parameters. If $\nu \to \infty$, the Student distribution converges to the normal distribution. If $\nu = 1$, the Student distribution is the Cauchy distribution. When $\nu > 2$ the variance of the density is $\nu/(H(\nu - 2))$ and thus finite. If ν is finite, the Student distribution has thicker tails than the normal distribution. Hence, the degrees-of-freedom parameter ν determines the fatness of tails. Also, the Student distribution is symmetric around m. Therefore, T_n depends on ν but is invariant to both H and m. It is interesting to note that the Student distribution has a structural interpretation. According to Praetz (1972), if one believes returns follow a continuous mixture of normal distributions where the variance is an inverted gamma distribution, then the resulting distribution is the Student one.

6.3.4 Mixture of normals

Kon (1984) has proposed to use the mixture of discrete normals to model stock returns. Formally, the stock return X comes from $N(\mu_j, \sigma_j^2)$ with probability λ_j and $\lambda_1 + \cdots + \lambda_k = 1$. The mixture of normals has two advantages over the Student distribution. One is that it can capture the structural change not only in the variance but also in the mean. The other advantage is that it can be asymmetric. The pdf of the mixture of normals is given by

$$g(x) = \sum_{j=1}^{k} \lambda_j \frac{1}{\sqrt{2\pi\sigma_j^2}} \exp\left\{ -\frac{(x - \mu_j)^2}{2\sigma_j^2} \right\} \tag{6.14}$$

All moments exist for the density. In this chapter we will only use the mixture of two normals for two reasons. First, Tucker (1992) finds that among the family of mixture of normals the mixture of two normals has the greatest descriptive power. Second, as a rule of thumb, a model with too many parameters is avoided. The mixture of two normals has five parameters, $\lambda, \mu_1, \mu_2, \sigma_1^2$, and σ_2^2. T_n depends on all of them.

6.3.5 Mixed diffusion-jump (MDJ) process

Press (1967) and Merton (1976) have proposed a process which mixes Brownian motion and a compound Poisson process to model the movement of stock prices:

$$dP(t) = \alpha P(t)dt + \sigma_D P(t)dB(t) + P(t)(\exp(Q) - 1)dN(t) \tag{6.15}$$

where $B(t)$ is a standard Brownian motion (BM), $N(t)$ a homogeneous Poisson process with parameter λ, Q a normal variate with mean μ_Q and variance σ_Q^2. Merton (1976) provide a formula to price an option assuming the underlying asset follows the MDJ process.

Using Ito's Lemma, we can solve the stochastic differential equation (6.15) for the compound return $X(t)$:

$$X(t) = \mu_D + \sigma_D B(1) + \sum_{n=1}^{\Delta N(t)} Q_n, \tag{6.16}$$

where $\mu_D = \alpha - (\sigma_D^2/2)$. The density function for the process is,

$$g(x) = \sum_{n=0}^{\infty} \frac{e^{-\lambda}\lambda^n}{n!} \exp\left(- \frac{(x - \mu_D - n\mu_Q)^2}{2(\sigma_D^2 + n\sigma_Q^2)} \right) \frac{1}{\sqrt{2\pi(\sigma_D^2 + n\sigma_Q^2)}} \tag{6.17}$$

All moments are finite for the density. For example, $E(X) = \mu_D + \mu_Q\lambda$, $Var(x) = \sigma_D^2 + \sigma_Q^2\lambda + \mu_Q^2\lambda$. T_n depends on all five parameters $\mu_D, \sigma_D^2, \mu_Q, \sigma_Q^2$ and λ.

6.3.6 Compound lognormal and normal

The compound lognormal and normal model has been proposed by Clark (1973). Instead of assuming the variance of the normal distribution is an inverted gamma distribution as in the Student, Clark (1973) assumes that the returns are conditional normal, with the conditional variance parameter lognormally distributed. The rationale for lognormality of the conditional variance is that the variance is time variant and should be a function of trading volume or trading activities. This idea has motivated researchers to use the stochastic volatility model to describe financial time series; see Tauchen and Pitts (1983) and Taylor (1986, 1994). According to Clark (1973), the unobserved information flow, which is assumed to be independently distributed, produces a random volume of trade. Formally, $X|Y \sim N(\mu, Y\sigma_1^2)$ and $\log(Y) \sim N(0, \sigma_2^2)$. The pdf of the model is then

$$f(x) = \frac{1}{2\pi\sigma_1\sigma_2} \int_0^{\infty} y^{-3/2} \exp\left[- \frac{(x-\mu)^2}{2y\sigma_1^2} - \frac{\ln^2(y)}{2\sigma_2^2} \right] dy \tag{6.18}$$

All moments exist for this density. For example, $E(X) = \mu$, $Var(X) = \sigma_1^2 \exp(\sigma_2^2/2)$ and the kurtosis is $3\exp(\sigma_2^2)$ which is larger than 3 for any finite value of σ_2^2. Hence, σ_2^2 determines the tail behaviour of the density. The compound lognormal and normal distribution is symmetric around μ. T_n is invariant to μ and σ_1^2. A disadvantage of using the compound lognormal and normal distribution is that the pdf has no exact solution and hence the integration in equation (6.18) has to be done numerically.

6.3.7 Generalized beta distribution

The generalized beta distribution has been proposed by Bookstaber and McDonald (1987). Its pdf is defined by

$$f(z) = \frac{|a|z^{ap-1}}{b^{ap}B(p,q)(1+(z/b)^a)^{p+q}}, z \geq 0 \tag{6.19}$$

where the parameters b, p and q are positive and $B(p, q)$ is the beta function.[4] If $-p < k/a < q$, moments up to the kth order exist. For example, the kth order moments is[5]

$$E(Z^k) = \frac{b^k B(p + k/a, q - h/a)}{B(p,q)}. \tag{6.20}$$

From the above equation we note that the parameters a, b, p and q determine the shape and location of the density in a complex fashion. To be more specific, a and q determine the tail behaviour. The larger the value of a or q, the thinner the tails of the density. The skewness of the density is determined by p and q. Also both positive and negative skewness are permitted depending on the values of p and q. A great advantage of the generalized beta distribution is that it provides a great deal of flexibility with only four parameters. For example, it nests the lognormal, log-Student, log-Cauchy and Weibull distributions as special or limit cases. McDonald and Bookstaber (1991) provide a formula to price an option assuming the underlying asset follows the generalized beta distribution.

6.3.8 Weibull distribution

Mittnik and Rachev (1993) have proposed to use the Weibull distribution to model stock daily returns. The Weibull distribution is attractive since it is a type of min-stable distribution. More specifically, suppose $f_n = \min\{Z_1, \cdots, Z_n\}$, where $Z_1, \cdots, Z_n$ are iid random variates. For some real constants $c_n > 0$ and d_n, if $c_n f_n + d_n \xrightarrow{d} Z$, where Z is a random variable with non-degenerate distribution function f, then f could be the Weibull distribution.

The density function of the Weibull distribution is

$$f(z) = \frac{\alpha}{a}\left[\frac{z-b}{a}\right]^{\alpha-1} \exp\left[-(\frac{z-b}{a})^{\alpha}\right], z \geq b$$

---

[4]See Abramowitz and Stegun (1964) for further information about the beta function.

[5]Although in theory the generalized beta distribution will permit infinite variance when $-p < 2/a < q$ is not satisfied. In most empirical applications $-p < k/a < q$ holds for a large value of k and hence yields finite variance; see Bookstaber and McDonald (1987).

where α, b, and a are the index, location and scale parameters respectively. Thus, T_n depends on α but is invariant to a and b. The density can be asymmetric and has finite moments of all orders. For example, $E(Z) = a\Gamma(\frac{1}{\alpha}+1)+b$, $Var(Z) = a^2\{\Gamma(\frac{2}{\alpha}+1)-(\Gamma(\frac{1}{\alpha}+1))^2\}$.

6.3.9 Variance gamma distribution

The Variance Gamma (VG) distribution has been proposed by Madan and Seneta (1990). It is similar in spirit to the compound lognormal and normal distribution and Student distribution in the sense that the normal distribution is continuously mixed with another distribution of conditional variance. The VG distribution assumes that the conditional variance is distributed as a gamma variate. Formally, $X|V \sim N(\mu, V\sigma^2)$ and $V \sim \Gamma(c, \gamma)$. The density is then

$$f(x) = \int_0^\infty \frac{\exp(-(x-\mu)^2/(2v\sigma^2))c^\gamma v^{\gamma-1}\exp(-cv)}{\sigma\sqrt{2\pi v}\Gamma(\gamma)}\,dv \tag{6.21}$$

All moments exist for this density. For example, $E(X) = \mu$, $Var(X) = \sigma^2\frac{\gamma}{c}$ and the kurtosis is $3(1+\frac{1}{\gamma})$ which is larger than 3 for any positive value of γ. Hence, γ^{-1} can be regarded as a measure of the degree of long-tailedness. The VG distribution, however, is symmetric around μ. Hence, T_n is invariant to μ. Madan and Seneta (1990) show that the VG distribution can be approximated by a compound Poisson process with high jump frequency and low jump magnitudes. Also, they provide a formula to price an option assuming the underlying asset follows the VG distribution. However, a disadvantage of using the VG distribution is that the pdf has no analytic expression and hence the integration in equation (6.21) has to be done numerically.

6.3.10 Hyperbolic distribution

The hyperbolic distribution had been used in various scientific fields before it was applied to finance by Eberlein and Keller (1995). The hyperbolic distribution is characterized by its log-density being a hyperbola and hence permits heavier tails than the normal distribution.[6] Its pdf is

$$f(x) = \frac{\sqrt{\alpha^2-\beta^2}}{2\alpha\delta K_1(\delta\sqrt{\alpha^2-\beta^2})}\exp\left[-\alpha\sqrt{\delta^2+(x-\mu)^2}+\beta(x-\mu)\right] \tag{6.22}$$

[6]The log-density of the normal distribution is a parabola.

where α, β, δ, and μ are parameters, and K_1 the modified Bessel function of the third kind with index 1.[7] Parameters α and β determine the shape of the density while δ and μ determine the scale and location respectively. Therefore, T_n is invariant to both δ and μ.

6.3.11 Generalized lambda distribution

The generalized lambda distribution has been proposed by Corrado (1999). The two-parameter generalized lambda distribution has the pdf

$$f(x) = \frac{\lambda_2(\lambda_3, \lambda_4)}{\lambda_3 x^{\lambda_3 - 1} + \lambda_4(1 - x)^{\lambda_4 - 1}} \tag{6.23}$$

where $\lambda_2(\lambda_3, \lambda_4) = sign(\lambda_3)\sqrt{C_2 - C_1^2}$ with

$$C_1 = \frac{1}{\lambda_3 + 1} - \frac{1}{\lambda_4 + 1} \text{ and } C_2 = \frac{1}{2\lambda_3 + 1} + \frac{1}{2\lambda_4 + 1} - 2B(\lambda_3 + 1, \lambda_4 + 1).$$

The skewness and kurtosis are determined by the shape parameters λ_3 and λ_4. An advantage of using the generalized lambda distribution is that it has a closed-form expression for the percentile function which is given by

$$s(p) = \frac{1}{\lambda_2(\lambda_3, \lambda_4)}\left[p^{\lambda_3} - (1 - p)^{\lambda_3} + \frac{1}{\lambda_4 + 1} - \frac{1}{\lambda_3 + 1}\right] \tag{6.24}$$

Hence it is well suited to Monte Carlo simulation procedures, such as Monte Carlo Value-at-Risk analyses. The four-parameter generalized lambda distribution allows both the mean and variance to differ from 1 and its percentile function is given by

$$s(p) = a\left[1 + \frac{b}{\lambda_2(\lambda_3, \lambda_4)}(p^{\lambda_3} - (1 - p)^{\lambda_3} + \frac{1}{\lambda_4 + 1} - \frac{1}{\lambda_3 + 1})\right] \tag{6.25}$$

Corrado (1999) provides a formula to price an option assuming the underlying asset follows the generalized lambda distribution.

6.3.12 Stable distribution

Mandlebrot (1963) and Fama (1965) first proposed the stable distribution to model stock returns. The stable distribution is usually characterized by the characteristic function. The characteristic function of the general stable

[7]See Abramowitz and Stegun (1964) for further information about the Bessel function.

distribution is given by

$$c(t) = \begin{cases} \exp\{iat - |ct|^{\alpha}[1 - i\beta sign(t)\tan(\frac{\pi\alpha}{2})]\} & \text{if } \alpha \neq 1 \\ \exp\{iat - |ct|^{\alpha}[1 + i\beta \frac{2}{\pi} sign(t)\ln(|t|)]\} & \text{if } \alpha = 1 \end{cases} \tag{6.26}$$

where α, β, c, and a are index, skewness, scale, and location parameters respectively. The stable distribution can be skewed to the left or right, depending on the sign of β. If $\alpha = 1, \beta = 0$, the stable distribution is the Cauchy distribution. If $\alpha = 2, \beta = 0$, the stable distribution is the normal distribution. If $1 < \alpha < 2$, the most plausible case for actual financial series, the tails of the stable are fatter than those of the normal and the variance is infinite. Unfortunately, the density function has no closed form for $1 < \alpha < 2$. Hence, the density of the stable distribution has to be calculated numerically by inverting the characteristic function (3.26).

Despite the difficulty of evaluating the density function, the stable distribution has good statistical and economic properties. For example, it has domains of attraction (generalized central limit theorem) and it belongs to its own domain of attraction, i.e. the distribution of the sum of iid stable variates is in the stable family with the same index parameter; see Samorodnitsky and Taqqu (1994) for detailed statistical descriptions of the stable distribution. McCulloch (1978) demonstrates that no arbitrage can exploit the infinite speed of Brownian motion and that price processes exhibiting bounded variation generally are inconsistent with continuous-time equilibrium in competitive markets. The stable distribution has unbounded variation and is thus consistent with equilibrium.

6.4 APPLICATIONS

In the applications we apply the proposed test statistic to two data sets. The first series consists of 2017 daily observations of the spot index of Nikkei Stock Average 225 (NSA), covering the period from 1 January 1989 to 30 August 1997. The other series consists of 2529 daily observations of the spot index of value-weighted CRSP index, covering the period from 1 January 1986 to 1 December 1995. Figure 6.1 plots both simple and compound returns for these two series. Not surprisingly, the simple and corresponding compound returns have very similar patterns and approximately differ by 1. Also of note is that in CRSP the 1987 crash can be easily identified.

Table 6.1 reports T_n with $\theta_0 = 0.25$ for these two compound returns. Noticeably CRSP has a smaller value of $T_n(0.25)$. This is not surprising since CRSP includes the 1987 crash and hence has more outliers. The outliers increase the denominator in $T_n(0.25)$ and decrease the value of $T_n(0.25)$.

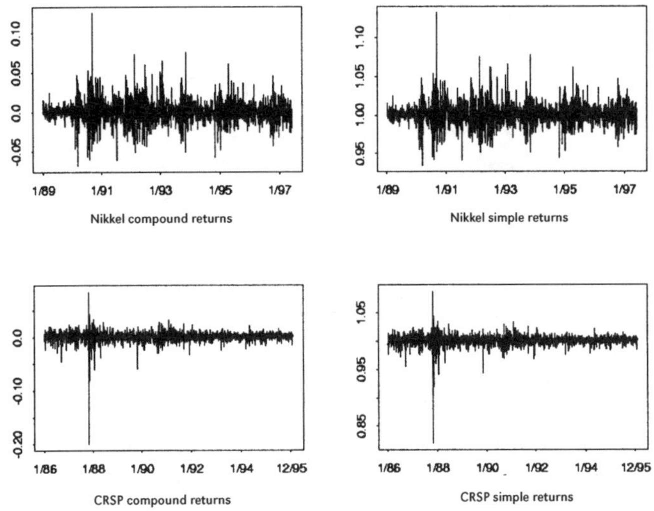

Figure 6.1 This graph plots the simple and compound returns of Nikkei and CRSP. Nikkei consists of 2017 daily observations of the spot index of Nikkei Stock Average 225 (NSA), covering the period from 1 January 1989 to 30 August 1997. CRSP consists of 2529 daily observations of the spot index of value-weighted CRSP index, covering the period from 1 January 1986 to 1 December 1995. The simple and compound returns are defined by P_t/P_{t-1} and $\ln P_t - \ln P_{t-1}$ respectively where P_t is the daily closing index at day t.

The hypothesis we are going to test is the one given by (6.4). Since all the competing distributions except the stable distribution have finite variance, we set H_0 to be one of the finite variance distributions and H_1 the stable distribution. For brevity we consider only those finite variance distributions which have attracted the most attention in the literature. Specifically, we use the normal, lognormal, Student, mixture of normals, mixed diffusion-jump, and generalized beta distributions as H_0 respectively. After setting up the hypothesis, we can obtain the asymptotic mean and asymptotic variance of $T_n(0.25)$ according to Proposition 2.3. The p-values are then calculatable.

Table 6.2 presents the maximum likelihood (ML) estimates of finite variance distributions for Nikkei.[8] In Table 6.2 we also present the log-likelihood of finite variance distributions. Of note is that the ML estimates guarantee the variance in every distribution to be finite. For example, the ML estimate of ν in the Student distribution is greater than 2 and the ML estimates of a, p, q in the generalized beta distribution satisfy $-p < k/a < q$ for $k = 2$. In terms of the likelihood value, the mixed diffusion-jump process provides the best fit to the

[8] To maximize the likelihood function of the MDJ process, we have to truncate the infinite sum in equation (6.17) after some value of N. In practice, we choose $N = 11$ which provides satisfactory accuracy; see Jorion (1988) for more detailed discussion.

Table 6.1 T_n of Nikkei and CRSP.

	Nikkei	CRSP
$T_n(0.25)$	1.0019	0.7861

Note: Nikkei consists of 2017 daily observations of the spot index of Nikkei Stock Average 225 (NSA), covering the period from 1 January 1989 to 30 August 1997. CRSP consists of 2529 daily observations of the spot index of value-weighted CRSP index, covering the period from 1 January 1986 to 1 December 1995. $T_n(0.25) = Q_n(0.75) - Q_n(0.25)/s_n$.

data, followed by the generalized beta and Student distributions with very small margin in between. However, the Student distribution has only three parameters, one parameter less than the generalized beta distribution and two less than the mixed diffusion-jump process. Hence, the Student distribution should be the choice among the finite variance distributions for Nikkei if the likelihood value and parsimony are one's concerns.

Table 6.3 presents the maximum likelihood estimates and the log-likelihood of the finite variance distributions for CRSP. Again the ML estimates imply that we cannot reject the hypothesis that the variance in every distribution is finite. In terms of the likelihood value, in spite of its parsimony the Student distribution surprisingly provides the best fit to the data, followed by the generalized beta and mixed diffusion-jump distributions with a substantial margin in between. As with Nikkei, the Student distribution should be the

Table 6.2 The ML estimates and log-likelihood of finite variance distributions for Nikkei

Distributions	ML Estimates	Log-likelihood
Normal	$\hat{\mu} = -0.00024, \hat{\sigma} = 0.01422$	5966
Lognormal	$\hat{\mu} = -0.00024, \hat{\sigma} = 0.01422$	5966
Student	$\hat{\nu} = 3.3774, \hat{H} = 10849.37$	6133
	$\hat{m} = -0.00024$	
MN	$\hat{\lambda} = 0.7122$	6128
	$\hat{\mu}_1 = -0.000019, \hat{\sigma}_1 = 0.0086$	
	$\hat{\mu}_2 = -0.00036, \hat{\sigma}_2 = 0.02279$	
MDJ	$\hat{\lambda} = 0.4969$	6134
	$\hat{\mu}_D = -0.000262, \hat{\sigma}_D^2 = 0.000061$	
	$\hat{\mu}_Q = -0.000288, \hat{\sigma}_Q^2 = 0.000275$	
GB	$\hat{a} = 453.67, \hat{b} = 0.9998$	6133
	$\hat{p} = 0.23197, \hat{q} = 0.23225$	

Note: Here and in Tables 6.3 and 6.4 MN represents the mixture of two normal distributions, MDJ the mixed diffusion-jump process and GB the generalized beta distribution.

Table 6.3 The ML estimates and log-likelihood of finite variance distributions for CRSP

Distributions	ML Estimates	Log-likelihood
Normal	$\hat{\mu} = 0.000514, \hat{\sigma} = 0.00906$	8305
Lognormal	$\hat{\mu} = 0.000514, \hat{\sigma} = 0.00906$	8305
Student	$\hat{\nu} = 2.8428, \hat{H} = 41465.89$	8905
	$\hat{m} = 0.000514$	
MN	$\hat{\lambda} = 0.9304$	8825
	$\hat{\mu}_1 = 0.0008488, \hat{\sigma}_1 = 0.0060$	
	$\hat{\mu}_2 = -0.00396, \hat{\sigma}_2 = 0.02599$	
MDJ	$\hat{\lambda} = 0.3512$	8860
	$\hat{\mu}_D = 0.001036, \hat{\sigma}_D^2 = 0.00002$	
	$\hat{\mu}_Q = -0.001487, \hat{\sigma}_Q^2 = 0.0001265$	
GB	$\hat{a} = 5691, \hat{b} = 1.001$	8878
	$\hat{p} = 0.0305, \hat{q} = 0.0338$	

choice among the finite variance distributions for CRSP if the likelihood value is the concern.

We then use the proposed statistic to test for validity of the finite variance distributions. Table 6.4 presents the asymptotic mean, asymptotic variance and p-value of T_n under the various finite variance distributions for Nikkei. By using the proposed test, as indicated by the p-values, both normality for compound returns and lognormality for simple returns have to be rejected at the 1% significance level. Note that other statistics, such as the sample kurtosis, may also reject normality and lognormality. In this respect our test provides a result consistent with the literature. Moreover, our test suggests that all the other finite variance distributions considered cannot be rejected, even at the 10% significance level. This finding is consistent with what has been normally found in the recent literature when other criteria have been used; see Tucker (1992) and Kon (1984).

Table 6.4 also presents the asymptotic mean, asymptotic variance and p-value of T_n under various finite variance distributions for CRSP. As with Nikkei, the normality and lognormality can be easily rejected for CRSP at the 1% significance level. However, our test indicates that all the other finite variance distributions considered have to be also rejected at the 1% significance level. The finding is very interesting and suggests that when the value of T_n becomes increasingly smaller, it is increasingly difficult to model the return by the existing finite variance distributions. The result is not surprising since a finite variance distribution tends to generate a value of T which is too large to match the empirical T_n. Intuitively speaking, therefore, finite variance distributions considered have difficulties in explaining the high risk that the CRSP series exhibits.

Of note is that the degrees-of-freedom estimates from the Student distribution for both Nikkei and CRSP are less than 4. This suggests that the fourth moment of the Student distribution is not finite for both series. This makes the test of SYY not applicable.

Table 6.4 The asymptotic distribution and p-value of $T_n(0.25)$ under various finite variance distributions for both Nikkei and CRSP

	Nikkei			CRSP		
	Mean	Variance	P-value	Mean	Variance	P-value
onumberormal	1.3490	0.001176	0	1.3490	0.00098	0
Lognormal	1.3490	0.001176	0	1.3490	0.00098	0
Student	0.9630	0.000696	0.930*	0.8389	0.000454	0.0066
MN	1.0220	0.000754	0.232*	1.0704	0.000638	0
MDJ	1.0163	0.000772	0.302*	0.9575	0.000565	0
GB	1.0374	0.000919	0.121*	1.0470	0.000899	0

*The corresponding finite variance distribution is significant at the 10% level.

6.5 CONCLUSIONS

This chapter has proposed a test to distinguish competing distributions for modelling daily stock returns with particular concern about variance behaviour. In the recent literature, the likelihood ratio test and Kolmogorov–Smirnov test have been used to compare the descriptive power of the competing distributions. Both tests suggest that distributions with finite variance outperform distributions with infinite variance. A common feature of these two tests is that all the observations receive the same weight. Model selection criteria, such as the Akaike Information Criterion (AIC) and the Bayesian Information Criterion (BIC), share the same spirit as the likelihood ratio test. Our test statistic, however, assigns different observations different weights. In fact in our test statistic outliers receive larger weight than inliers. Consequently, our test statistic prefers a distribution whose tail behaviour is closer to the empirical distribution to a distribution whose near-origin behaviour is closer to the empirical distribution. Although recent literature unanimously favours various finite variance distributions, our results suggest either direction, depending on the dataset used.

It is important to stress that the purpose of the proposed test is not to choose a distribution out of a fixed set of distributions as the 'best' one and hence different from that of model selection criteria. Our test could, however, serve as diagnostic checking in order to filter out a finite variance distribution which appears to be incompatible with the data in the sense that T is too far away from T_n.

APPENDIX

Proof of Proposition 1

Since the random variable X belongs to a scale-location family, we assume that

$$F(x) = G\left(\frac{x - \mu}{\sigma}\right),$$

where F is the distribution function of X, μ is the location of X, and σ is the scale of X. Define $Y = (X - \mu)/\sigma$, then $G(y)$ is the distribution function of Y. With the new notations, we have

$$\begin{aligned} s_n^2(X) &= \frac{1}{n-1}\sum_{i=1}^{n}(Y_i\sigma - \bar{Y}\sigma)^2 \\ &= \frac{\sigma^2}{n-1}\sum_{i=1}^{n}(Y_i - \bar{Y})^2 \\ &= \sigma^2 s_n^2(Y) \end{aligned}$$

and

$$\begin{aligned} F_n^{-1}(\theta_0) &= \inf\{x : F_n(x) \geq \theta_0\} \\ &= \inf\{x : G_n(\frac{x-\mu}{\sigma}) \geq \theta_0\} \\ &= \inf\{\sigma y : G_n(y) \geq \theta_0\} \\ &= \sigma G_n^{-1}(\theta_0) \end{aligned}$$

Therefore,

$$\begin{aligned} T_n(X, \theta_0) &= \frac{F_n^{-1}(1-\theta_0) - F_n^{-1}(\theta_0)}{s_n(X)} \\ &= \frac{\sigma G_n^{-1}(1-\theta_0) - \sigma G_n^{-1}(\theta_0)}{\sigma s_n(Y)} \\ &= T_n(Y, \theta_0) \end{aligned}$$

Proof of Proposition 2

The proposition follows immediately from the strong law of large numbers, since $s_n \stackrel{a.s.}{\rightarrow} \sigma$ and $Q_n(1-\theta_0) - Q_n(\theta_0) \stackrel{a.s.}{\rightarrow} q_1 - q_0$.

Proof of Proposition 3

Note that

$$\frac{s_n}{\sigma} \xrightarrow{a.s.} 1$$

under assumption (iii). Hence, we can consider the asymptotic behaviour of

$$\frac{Q_n(1-\theta_0) - Q_n(\theta_0)}{\sigma}$$

as opposed to

$$\frac{Q_n(1-\theta_0) - Q_n(\theta_0)}{s_n}$$

Note that

$$\frac{Q_n(1-\theta_0) - Q_n(\theta_0)}{\sigma} - \frac{q_1 - q_0}{\sigma} = \frac{Q_n(1-\theta_0) - q_1 - (Q_n(\theta_0) - q_0)}{\sigma} \tag{A.1}$$

According to the Bahadur representation (see Csörgő and Horváth, 1993, Chapter 3), we have

$$Q_n(1-\theta_0) - q_1 = -\frac{1}{nf(q_1)}\sum_{i-1}^{n}\{I\{X_i \le q_1\} - (1-\theta_0)\} + o_P(n^{-1/2})$$

and

$$Q_n(\theta_0) - q_0 = -\frac{1}{nf(q_0)}\sum_{i=1}^{n}\{I\{X_i \le q_0\} - \theta_0)\} + o_P(n^{-1/2})$$

The above two equations together yield

$$\sqrt{n}\Big(Q_n(1-\theta_0) - q_1 - (Q_n(\theta_0) - q_0)\Big)$$
$$= n^{-1/2}\left\{\frac{1}{f(q_1)}\sum_{i=1}^{n}\{I\{X_i \le q_1\} - (1-\theta_0)\} - \frac{1}{f(q_0)}\sum_{i=1}^{n}\{I\{X_i \le q_0\} - \theta_0)\}\right\}$$
$$+ o_P(1) \tag{A.2}$$

This proves equation (6.6). Equation (6.7) simply follows (6.6).

Proof of Proposition 5

Define $A_n = [T_n < c|H_1 \textit{ is true}]$ for some $0 < c < +\infty$. Provided H_1 is true, $T_n \stackrel{a.s.}{\rightarrow} 0$. Therefore,

$$A_n \stackrel{a.s.}{\rightarrow} \Omega$$

This implies

$$Pr[A_n] \rightarrow 1.$$

ACKNOWLEDGEMENTS

I would like to thank Professors John Knight, Cheng-Yen Lin, Qi-Man Shao and Hao Yu for helpful advice, and Professors Jun Cai, Y.K. Tse and Jian Yang for providing me with the datasets.

REFERENCES

Abramowitz, M. and Stegun, I.A. (1964) *Handbook of Mathematical Functions with Formulas, Graphs, and Mathematical Tables*, National Bureau of Standards, Washington, DC, Applied Mathematics Series No. 55.

Akgiray, V. and Booth, G. (1987) 'Compound Distribution of Models of Stock Returns: An Empirical Comparison', *Journal of Financial Research*, **10**, 269–280.

Bachelier, L. (1900) *Theorie de la Speculation*, Gauthier-Villars, Paris.

Black, F. and Scholes, M. (1973) 'The Pricing of Options and Corporate Liabilities', *Journal of Political Economics*, **81**, 637–653.

Blattberg, R. and Gonedes, N. (1974) 'A Comparison of Stable and Student Distribution', *Journal of Business*, **47**, 244–280.

Bollerslev, T. (1986) 'Generalized Autoregressive Conditional Heteroskedasticity', *Journal of Econometrics*, **31**, 307–327.

Bookstaber, R.M. and McDonald, J.B. (1987) 'A General Distribution for Describing Security Price Returns', *Journal of Business*, **60**, 401–424.

Clark, P.K. (1973) 'A Subordinated Stochastic Process Model with Finite Variance for Speculative Prices', *Econometrica*, **41**, 135–155.

Corrado, C.J. (1999) 'General Purpose, Semi-Parametric Option Pricing Formulas', University of Missouri.

Csörgő, M. and Horváth, L. (1993) *Weighted Approximations in Probability and Statistics*, John Wiley, New York.

David, H., Hartley, H., and Pearson, E. (1954) 'The Distribution of the Ratio, in a Single Normal Sample of Range of Standard Deviation', *Biometrika*, **41**, 482–493.

Eberlein, E. and Keller, U. (1995) 'Hyperbolic Distributions in Finance', *Bernoulli*, **1**, 281–299.

Elton E.J. and Gruber, M.J. (1974) 'Portfolio Theory When Investment Relatives are Lognormally Distributed', *Journal of Finance*, **29**, 1265–1274.

Engle, R.F. (1982) 'Autoregressive Conditional Heteroscedasticity with Estimates of the Variance of United Kingdom Inflation', *Econometrica*, **50**, 987–1007.

Fama, E. (1965) 'The Behavior of Stock Prices', *Journal of Business*, **47**, 244–280.

Jorion, P. (1988) 'On Jump Processes in the Foreign Exchange and Stock Markets', *Review of Financial Studies*, **1**, 427–445.

Kon, S. (1984) 'Model of Stock Returns – A Comparison', *Journal of Finance*, **39**, 147–165.

Lau, A., H. Lau, and Wingender, J. (1990) 'The Distribution of Stock Returns: New Evidence Against the Stable Model', *Journal of Business and Economic Statistics*, **8**, 217–223.

Lintner, J. (1965) 'The Valuation of Risk Assets and the Selection of Risky Investments in Stock Portfolios and Capital Budgets', *Review of Economics and Statistics*, **47**, 13–37.

Madan, D.B. and Seneta, E. (1990) 'The Variance Gamma (V.G.) Model from Share Market Returns', *Journal of Business*, **63**, 511–524.

Mandelbrot, B. (1963) 'The Variations of Certain Speculative Prices', *Journal of Business*, **36**, 394–419.

McCulloch, J. (1978) 'Continuous Time Processes with Stable Increments', *Journal of Business*, **51**, 601–619.

McDonald, J.B. and Bookstaber, R.M. (1991) 'Option Pricing for Generalized Distributions', *Communications in Statistics, Part A – Theory and Methods*, **20**, 4053–4068.

Merton, R. (1976) 'Option Pricing When Underlying Stock Returns are Discontinuous', *Journal of Financial Economics*, **3**, 125–144.

Mittnik, S. and Rachev, S.T. (1993) 'Modeling Asset Returns with Alternative Stable Distributions' (disc: P331-389), *Econometric Reviews*, **12**, 261–330.

Mossin, J. (1966) 'Equilibrium in a Capital Asset Market', *Econometrica*, **34**, 768–783.

Niederhoffer, V. and Osborne, M.F.M. (1966) "Market Making and Reversal on the Stock Exchange', *Journal of the American Statistical Association*, **61**, 897–916.

Osborne, M. (1959) 'Brownian Motions in the Stock Market', *Operation Research*, **7**, 145–173.

Praetz, P. (1972) 'The Distributions of Share Price Changes', *Journal of Business*, **45**, 49–55.

Press, S.J. (1967) 'A Compound Events Model of Security Prices', *Journal of Business*, **40**, 317–335.

Runde, R. (1997) 'The Asymptotic Null Distribution of the Box-Pierce Q-Statistic for Random Variables with Infinite Variance: An Application to German Stock Returns', *Journal of Econometrics*, **78**, 205–216.

Samorodnitsky, G. and Taqqu, M.S. (1994) *Stable Non-Gaussian Random Processes*, Chapman and Hall, New York.

Shao, Q., Yu, H., and Yu, J. (1999) 'A Test Statistic and its Application in Modelling Daily Stock Returns', The University of Auckland Working Paper No. 198.

Sharpe, W. (1964) 'Capital Asset Prices: A Theory of Market Equilibrium Under Conditions of Risk', *Journal of Finance*, **19**, 425–442.

Tauchen, G. and Pitts, M. (1983) 'The Price Variability – Volume Relationship on Speculative Markets', *Econometrica*, **51**, 485–505.

Taylor, S.J. (1986) *Modelling Financial Time Series*, John Wiley, New York.

Taylor, S.J. (1994) 'Modelling Stochastic Volatility', *Mathematical Finance*, **4**, 183–204.

Tucker, A. (1992): 'A Reexamination of Finite- and Infinite-Variance Distributions as Models of Daily Stock Returns', *Journal of Business and Economic Statistics*, **10**, 73–81.

Chapter 7

Implementing option pricing models when asset returns are predictable and discontinuous

GEORGE J. JIANG

ABSTRACT

The discontinuity and predictability of an asset's returns will affect the prices of options on that asset as shown respectively in Merton (1976a,b) and Lo and Wang (1995). In this chapter we investigate the joint effect of discontinuity and predictability of an asset's returns on the prices of options in a continuous-time jump-diffusion framework. We extend the Black–Scholes (1973) model through alternative specification of the drift term and the introduction of a jump component to incorporate predictability and discontinuity into the underlying asset price process. In addition, we model the conditional heteroscedasticity of asset returns through a predictable jump size process instead of the non-jump conditional volatility. From a model (mis-)specification point of view, we examine the basic properties of various competing models as well as their implications on European call option prices of the asset. We illustrate various patterns of mispricing of both the Black–Scholes model and the Merton model and demonstrate that the pricing errors can be significant when asset returns are discontinuous and to a certain extent predictable. In the case that the predictability is induced by a linear mean-reverting drift function as in Lo and Wang (1995), we propose adjustments to both the Black–Scholes (1973) and Merton (1976a) option pricing formulas. For models with conditional heteroscedasticity induced by the predictable jump size, the implications on option prices are investigated based on simulation results.

7.1 INTRODUCTION

When modelling financial asset returns, empirical stylized facts drawn from both static behaviour (unconditional distribution) and dynamic behaviour (conditional distribution) of state variables are the major factors in the consideration of model specification and selection. A model's ability to reproduce certain empirical stylized facts is often an important criterion to judge whether such a model represents the true underlying data-generating process (DGP). It is well documented in the literature that the Black–Scholes model which assumes asset returns follow continuous diffusion processes as random walk with drift and of constant conditional volatility is inconsistent with empirical findings on many traded assets. It is also well documented that the Black–Scholes option-pricing formula generates systematic biases of option prices. Since the early 1960s it has been observed, notably by Mandelbrot (1963) and Fama (1963, 1965), among others, that asset returns have leptokurtic distributions[1] and the volatilities of asset returns have strong intertemporal persistence. Extension of the underlying Black–Scholes model has been mainly along the following three directions in the literature.

One direction is to introduce time-varying conditional volatility or heteroscedasticity into the underlying asset price process through various volatility changing models, for instance the autoregressive conditional heteroscedasticity (ARCH) model introduced by Engle (1982), the generalized ARCH (GARCH) models extended by Bollerslev (1986) and Taylor (1986),[2] the continuous-time stochastic volatility (SV) model by Hull and White (1987) among others,[3] and the discrete-time SV model introduced by Taylor (1986).[4] It is undisputed that financial time series have time-varying and persistent conditional volatility or heteroscedasticity, i.e. financial time series exhibit different levels of volatility over time and are sometimes clustered with bunching of high- and low-volatility episodes. Such observations on volatility changes naturally lead to ARCH/GARCH models and stochastic volatility (SV) models. In fact, volatility varying or clustering and fat-tailed distributions of asset returns are believed to be intimately related. In the case of stochastic autoregressive volatility (SARV) models, it can be shown that the

[1]Such observation on the unconditional density has led people to propose modelling asset returns as iid draws from fat-tailed distributions, such as Student-t, Paretian or Lévy.

[2]For a survey of the ARCH/GARCH applications to financial time series, see Bollerslev, Chou and Kroner (1992). Duan (1995) considers the application of GARCH model in pricing options.

[3]Other examples include Johnson and Shanno (1987), Wiggins (1987), Scott (1987, 1991, 1997), Bailey and Stulz (1989), Chesney and Scott (1989), Melino and Turnbull (1990), Stein and Stein (1991), Heston (1993), Bates (1996), and Bakshi, Cao and Chen (1997).

[4]Other examples include Amin and Ng (1993), Andersen (1994), Taylor (1994), and Kim, Shephard and Chib (1996).

autoregressive behaviour of dynamic (conditional) volatility also implies (unconditional) fat-tailed distribution in the steady state.[5] Implications of changing volatility on option prices have been investigated in the literature. For instance, Hull and White (1987) show that when the conditional volatility is stochastic but uncorrelated with the stock price, the Black–Scholes model underprices the in-the-money and out-of-the-money options but overprices the at-the-money options. When the asset prices are also dependent on other factors, e.g. systematic volatility, stochastic interest rates, the joint effect of stochastic volatility and these factors can be complicated and the empirical investigation is far from being conclusive (e.g. Bailey and Stulz, 1989; Amin and Ng, 1993).

The second direction, pioneered by Merton (1976a), is to model the sampling path of underlying asset returns as a mixture of both a continuous diffusion process and a discontinuous jump process through the introduction of the jump component. Motivations of using the jump-diffusion process to model stock returns were clearly stated in Merton (1976a) in which he distinguishes two types of changes in the stock price: the 'normal' vibrations in price due to e.g. a temporary supply and demand imbalance, changes in capitalization rates or in the economic outlook, or other information that causes only marginal changes in the stock's value; and the 'abnormal' vibrations in price due to random arrivals of important new information about the stock that has more than a marginal effect on prices. The first type of price change can be modelled by a stochastic process with a continuous sampling path, e.g. a Wiener process, and the second type of price change can be modelled by a process which explicitly allows for jumps, e.g. a 'Poisson-driven' process.[6] In the case of foreign currency prices, shifts in interest rate differentials between two countries or monetary and fiscal policy changes are also believed to usually result in a revaluation of foreign currency. As Jorion (1988) points out, the foreign exchange market is characterized by active exchange rate management policies which do not exist in other securities' markets, e.g. the stock market. Therefore, stochastic processes which incorporate jumps might reflect the change of foreign currency prices better than the pure continuous-time Wiener process, and thus provide models which

[5]See Shephard (1996) and Ghysels, Harvey and Renault (1996) for statistical properties of SV models.

[6]Press (1967) first proposed a jump-diffusion model for stock price changes which is different from the 'random walk model' originally proposed by Bachelier in 1900 and its modified versions. Press assumes that the changes of logarithmic stock prices follow the distribution of a Poisson mixture of normal distributions, that is, the combination of a Wiener process and a compound Poisson process. The model resembles earlier random walk models in that it is a Markov process with discrete parameter space and continuous state space. But the presence of the compound Poisson process produces a non-Gaussian and essentially discontinuous process.

are more accurate in pricing currency options.[7] Apart from the formally justified motivations, any casual observation of the sampling paths of most financial asset returns can reveal discontinuity or jumps over time. Like the ARCH/GARCH or SV models, the jump-diffusion model can offer a formal link between the description of dynamic path behaviour and explanation of steady-state leptokurtic distributions. It can be shown that the analytical characteristics of such a distribution agree with what has been found empirically about most asset returns. That is, this distribution is in general skewed, leptokurtic, fatter-tailed, and more peaked around its mean compared to the distribution of a normal random variable. Moreover, if underlying asset prices are modelled in continuous-time diffusion processes, allowing for time-varying conditional volatility in the model would not be sufficient to reflect discontinuity of asset returns as the underlying processes are still continuous. Thus explicit inclusion of jump components, such as Bernoulli jump or Poisson jump, in the model seems to be essential to describe the dynamics of asset returns. The jump-diffusion option pricing model proposed by Merton (1976a) is an important alternative to and extension of the Black and Scholes (1973) model. Merton (1976a) suggested that distributions with fatter tails than the lognormal in Black and Scholes (1973) might explain the tendency for deep-in-the-money, deep-out-of-the-money, and short maturity options to sell for more than their Black–Scholes values, and the tendency of near-the-money and longer-maturity options to sell for less.

The third direction, initiated more recently by Lo and Wang (1995), is to extend the model to allow for certain predictability of asset returns as evidenced in empirical findings. As Lo and Wang (1995) point out, there is increasingly substantial evidence documenting that many financial asset returns are predictable to a certain degree.[8] Such an observation is a clear violation of one of the fundamental assumptions made in the Black and Scholes (1973) option pricing model in which they assume that asset returns are pure random walks, i.e. asset returns are perfectly unpredictable. Since predictability is often manifested through the specification of drift function, Lo and Wang (1995) proposed models with alternative drift functions to study the impact of predictability on option prices. It is a misconception in the

[7]Bodurtha and Courtadon (1987) claim that the systematic biases of the modified Black–Scholes American option pricing model for currency options are partly due to the jumps along the exchange rate processes.

[8]As Campbell, Lo and MacKinlay (1997) point out, modern financial economics teaches us that some perfectly rational factors may account for the predictability of asset returns. For example, the fine structure of securities markets and frictions in the trading process can generate predictability. Time-varying expected returns due to changing business conditions can generate predictability. A certain degree of predictability may be necessary to reward investors for bearing certain dynamic risks.

literature that the drift term of a diffusion model of asset returns does not affect option prices as it does not enter the option pricing formula. This misconception is due to the fact that a risk-neutral specification of an asset's return process is irrelevant to the functional form of the drift term specified in the objective measure since it is replaced by the risk-free rate of return with adjustments of risk factors. However, when fitting the model into the observed unconditional distribution of the underlying asset returns, specification of the drift term will have a direct impact on the value of the diffusion coefficient even though there is no alternative specification of the diffusion function. That leads to a different input of volatility in the option pricing formula and thus different option prices as output. Grundy (1991) also points out that strong mean reversion in the drift term could introduce a substantial disparity between the discrete-time sample volatility and the instantaneous conditional volatility of log-differenced asset prices. By comparing the polar cases of perfect predictability and perfect unpredictability, Lo and Wang (1995) successfully demonstrated that predictability of asset returns has a significant impact on the option prices of that asset, even though predictability is typically induced by the drift term which does not enter the option pricing formula.

In this chapter we investigate the joint implications of an asset return's predictability and discontinuity as well as conditional heteroscedasticity induced by predictable jump sizes on the option prices of an asset. We model the discontinuity of asset returns using a compound Poisson jump process as in Merton (1976a), and consider the most parsimonious form of predictability (autocorrelated asset returns) as in Lo and Wang (1995). However, unlike the current literature which introduces conditional heteroscedasticity through the non-jump instantaneous conditional volatility, we model conditional heteroscedasticity through the introduction of an uneven and yet correlated information flow process in the unobserved jump size process. We illustrate various patterns of mispricing of the Black–Scholes and Merton models and demonstrate that the pricing errors can be significant both statistically and economically. In the case that the predictability is induced by a linear mean-reverting drift function as in Lo and Wang (1995), we provide adjustments to both the Black–Scholes (1973) and Merton (1976a) option pricing formulas. For models with predictable jump sizes, we perform a comparison among alternative option pricing models based on simulation results.

In Section 7.2 we first review various option pricing models, namely the Black–Scholes (1973) and Merton (1973) model, the Merton (1976a) model, and the Lo–Wang (1995) model, then propose new option pricing models, namely the trending O-U jump-diffusion model and the jump-diffusion model with predictable jump size, to incorporate predictability and discontinuity as well as conditional heteroscedasticity; Section 7.3 investigates the implications of different model specifications on the prices of European call options using the Black–Scholes (1973) model as the benchmark model. The option pricing errors are measured in terms of the absolute difference and the relative percentage difference, as well as the Black–Scholes implied volatility; Section 7.4 contains discussion on related issues; and Section 7.5 concludes.

7.2 ALTERNATIVE MODEL SPECIFICATIONS AND OPTION PRICING

7.2.1 The Black–Scholes (1973) and Merton (1973) models

In the classic papers on the theory of option pricing by Black and Scholes (1973) and Merton (1973), the underlying asset's price $P(t)$ is assumed to follow an Itô diffusion process:

$$dP(t)/P(t) = \alpha(\cdot)dt + \sigma dW(t)$$

or

$$dp(t) = \mu(\cdot)dt + \sigma dW(t) \tag{7.1}$$

where $p(t) = lnP(t), \mu(\cdot) = \alpha(\cdot) - \frac{1}{2}\sigma^2$ is the drift coefficient, σ is the diffusion coefficient, and $W(t)$ is a Wiener process or a standard Brownian motion process. Under standard assumptions,[9] it can be shown that the no-arbitrage price at time t of an European call option $C(P(t), t; K, T, r, \sigma^2)$ on the stock with strike price K and expiration date T is given by:

$$C_{BS}(P(t), t; K, T, r, \sigma^2) = P(t)\Phi(d_1) - Ke^{-r(T-t)}\Phi(d_2) \tag{7.2}$$

where

$$d_1 \equiv \frac{ln(P(t)/K) + (r + \frac{1}{2}\sigma^2)(T-t)}{\sigma\sqrt{T-t}}, d_2 \equiv d_1 - \sigma\sqrt{T-t}$$

r is the instantaneous risk-free rate of return, and $\Phi(\cdot)$ is the cumulative distribution function (CDF) of a standard normal distribution. The most important and attractive feature of the above option pricing formula is that the diffusion coefficient σ^2 is the only unobserved element and the drift term in (7.1) can be any arbitrary function of $P(t)$ and even other economic variables. This is due to the fact that the drift term does not appear in the pricing partial differential equation (PDE) derived in the continuous-time no-arbitrage pricing framework of Black and Scholes (1973) and Merton (1973) or the more obvious fact that the risk-neutral specification of the price process is irrelevant to the drift function in the martingale pricing approach of Cox and Ross (1976) and Harrison and Kreps (1979).

[9] Namely, trading is continuous and 'frictionless', i.e. there is no transaction costs or differential taxes, and there is no restriction on borrowing or short-selling.

In particular, in Black and Scholes (1973) $\mu(\cdot)$ is assumed to be a constant, i.e. $\mu(\cdot) = \mu$. In other words, the underlying asset price $P(t)$ has a lognormal distribution and $p(t)$ follows a Brownian motion with a drift process or a random walk with drift. The major properties of the Brownian motion with a drift process include: (1) it is a non-stationary Gaussian process. (2) the first difference of $lnP(t)$ or $p(t)$ over $\tau(> 0)$ period, or the τ-period return of the asset $r_\tau(t) = ln(P(t)/P(t-\tau)) = \Delta_\tau p(t) = p(t) - p(t-\tau)$ is a stationary Gaussian process, with mean and variance given by

$$E[r_\tau(t)] = \mu\tau, \quad Var[r_\tau(t)] = \sigma^2\tau \tag{7.3}$$

In other words, the Brownian motion with drift process or the random walk with drift is a difference-stationary process. (3) It has independent increments, i.e. with $\delta \geq \tau$,

$$Cov[r_\tau(t), r_\tau(t-\delta)] = 0 \tag{7.4}$$

7.2.2 The Merton (1976a) jump-diffusion model

The jump-diffusion process proposed by Merton (1976a) to model asset returns, as a mixture of both a continuous diffusion path and a discontinuous jump path, can be written as:

$$dP(t)/P(t) = (\alpha(\cdot) - \lambda\alpha_0)dt + \sigma dW(t) + (Y(t) - 1)dQ_\lambda(t) \tag{7.5}$$

where
$\alpha(\cdot)$ is the instantaneous expected return on the asset;
σ^2 is the instantaneous volatility of the asset's return conditional on no arrivals of important new information (i.e. the Poisson jump event does not occur);
$Q_\lambda(t)$ is a Poisson counting process which is assumed to be iid over time, λ is the mean number of jumps per unit of time, i.e. the intensity parameter of the Poisson distribution with Prob$(dQ_\lambda(t) = 1) = \lambda dt$, Prob$(dQ_\lambda(t) = 0) = 1 - \lambda dt$;
$Y(t) - 1$ is the random jump size $(Y(t) \geq 0)$ representing the random variable percentage change in the underlying asset price if the Poisson event occurs, $\int_0^t (Y(\tau) - 1)dq_\lambda(\tau)$ is a compound Poisson process, and α_0 is the expectation of the relative jump size, i.e. $\alpha_0 = E[Y(t) - 1]$;
$dQ_\lambda(t)$, $dW(t)$ is assumed to be statistically independent.

If $\alpha(\cdot)$ is also a constant as assumed in Merton (1976a), following the Doléans–Dade exponential formula the random variable ratio of the asset price at time t to the asset price at time $t - \tau$ can be written as

$$P(t)/P(t-\tau) = exp[(\alpha - \sigma^2/2 - \lambda\alpha_0)\tau + \sigma(W(t) - W(t-\tau))]Y(n)$$

where $Y(n) = 1$ if $n = 0$; $Y(n) = \prod_{i=1}^{n} Y_i$ for $n \geq 1$ and $Y_i, i = 1, 2, ..., n$, are independently and identically distributed and n is Poisson-distributed with parameter $\lambda\tau$.

Due to the presence of 'jumps', it is impossible to construct a riskless portfolio of underlying asset and options, hence the Black–Scholes 'no arbitrage' technique can no longer be employed to price options. Under the assumption that the jump component represents only non-systematic risk, or the jump risk is diversifiable,[10] Merton (1976a) derives the call option pricing formula following the lines of the original Black–Scholes derivation which assumes that the CAPM is a valid description of equilibrium asset returns.[11] Let $C_M(P(t), t; K, T, r, \sigma^2)$ be the price of a European call option at time t for the jump-diffusion model with asset price $P(t)$, expiration date T, exercise price K, the instantaneous riskless rate r, and the constant non-jump instantaneous volatility σ^2, then $C_M(P(t), t; K, T, r, \sigma^2)$ solves the following integro-differential-difference equation

$$\begin{aligned}\frac{1}{2}\sigma^2 P(t)^2 \frac{\partial^2 C_M(P(t), t)}{\partial P^2(t)} + (r - \lambda\alpha_0)P(t)\frac{\partial C_M(P(t), t)}{\partial P(t)} + \frac{\partial C_M(P(t), t)}{\partial t} \\ + \lambda E_Y[C_M(P(t)Y(t), t) - C_M(P(t), t)] \\ = rC_M(P(t), t) \qquad (7.6)\end{aligned}$$

subject to the boundary conditions: $C_M(0, t) = 0, C_M(P(T), T) = Max[0, P(T) - K]$. If $\lambda = 0$, i.e. there is no jump, this pricing PDE reduces to the Black–Scholes equation and its solution for the option price formula is given by (7.2). Merton (1976a) showed that the solution of a call option price with jumps can be written as:

$$\begin{aligned}&C_M(P(t), t; K, T, r, \sigma^2) \\ &= \sum_{n=0}^{\infty} \frac{e^{-\lambda\tau}(\lambda\tau)^n}{n!} E_{Y(n)}[C_{BS}(P(t)Y(n)e^{-\lambda\alpha_0\tau}, t; K, T, r, \sigma^2)] \qquad (7.7)\end{aligned}$$

[10]Subsequent research by Jones (1984), Naik and Lee (1990) and Bates (1991) shows that Merton's option pricing formulas with modified parameters are still relevant under non-diversifiable jump risk or more general distributional assumptions.

[11]Alternatively, using the equivalent martingale measure approach of Cox and Ross (1976) and Harrison and Kreps (1979) as in Aase (1988) and Bardhan and Chao (1993) for general random, marked point process, or Jeanblanc-Picque and Pontier (1990) for non-homogeneous Poisson jumps, or using a general equilibrium argument as in Bates (1988), the same valuation PDE can also be derived.

where $Y(n) = 1$ for $n = 0$, $Y(n) = \prod_{i=1}^{n} Y_i$, for $n \geq 1$, $Y_i, i = 1, 2, ..., n$, are iid n jumps. Under the further condition that $Y(t)$ follows a log-normal distribution as assumed by Press (1967), i.e. $lnY(t) \sim i.i.d.N(ln(1+\alpha_0) - \frac{1}{2}\nu^2, \nu^2)$, thus $Y(n)$ has a log-normal distribution with the variance of logarithm of $Y(n)$, $Var[lnY(n)] = \nu^2 n$, and $E_{Y(n)}[Y(n)] = (1+\alpha_0)^n$, a closed-form solution is given by

$$C_M(P(t), t; K, T, r, \sigma^2) = \sum_{n=0}^{\infty} \frac{e^{-\lambda'\tau}(\lambda'\tau)^n}{n!} C_{BS}(P(t), t; K, T, \gamma_n, \nu_n^2) \tag{7.8}$$

where $\lambda' = \lambda(1+\alpha_0)$, $\nu_n^2 = \sigma^2 + n\nu^2/\tau$ and $\gamma_n = r - \lambda\alpha_0 + nln(1+\alpha_0)/\tau$. The option price is simply the weighted sum of the price conditional on knowing that exactly n Poisson jumps will occur during the life of the option with each weight being the probability that a Poisson random variable with intensity $\lambda'\tau$ will take on the value n.

The jump-diffusion process defined in equation (7.5) can be rewritten in terms of the logarithmic asset prices, i.e., $p(t) = lnP(t)$, as:

$$dp(t) = \mu(\cdot)dt + \sigma dW(t) + lnY(t)dQ_\lambda(t) \tag{7.9}$$

where $\mu(\cdot) = \alpha(\cdot) - \lambda\alpha_0 - \frac{1}{2}\sigma^2$. When $\mu(\cdot) = \mu$ and $Y(t)$ is assumed to be iid lognormal, i.e. $lnY(t) \sim i.i.d.N(\mu_0, \nu^2)$, the above process is a well-defined Markov process with discrete parameter space and continuous state space and the SDE (7.9) has an explicit solution.[12] The major properties of this process include: (1) it is a non-stationary compounding Poisson process. (2) similar to the Brownian motion with drift process, the first difference of $lnP(t)$ or $p(t)$ over $\tau(>0)$-period or the $\tau-$period return of asset $r_\tau(t)$ is a stationary process, with density given by

$$f(r_\tau(t) = r) = \sum_{n=0}^{\infty} \frac{e^{-\lambda\tau}(\lambda\tau)^n}{n!} \phi(r; \mu\tau + n\mu_0, \sigma^2\tau + n\nu^2) \tag{7.10}$$

which has an infinite series representation, where $\phi(x; \mu, \sigma)$ is the pdf of a standard normal distribution of $(x-\mu)/\sigma$. Let $\varphi_{r_\tau}(u)$ denote the characteristic function of the asset return r_τ, then $\ln\varphi_{r_\tau}(u) = \mu\tau ui - \frac{1}{2}\sigma^2\tau u^2 + \lambda\tau(\exp(\mu_0 ui - \frac{1}{2}\nu^2 u^2) - 1)$. It is easy to derive that

$$E[r_\tau] = (\mu + \lambda\mu_0)\tau, \quad Var[r_\tau] = (\sigma^2 + \lambda(\mu_0^2 + \nu^2))\tau$$
$$E[(r_\tau - E[r_\tau])^3] = \lambda\tau\mu_0(\mu_0^2 + 3\nu^2), \quad E[(r_\tau - E[r_\tau])^4] = 3Var[r_\tau]^2 + \phi_0 \tag{7.11}$$

[12] When $Y(t)$ is assumed to be lognormally distributed with $\alpha_0 = E[Y(t) - 1]$ and $\mu_0 = E[lnY(t)]$, the relation between α_0 and μ_0 is $\mu_0 = ln(1+\alpha_0) - \frac{1}{2}\nu^2$, where $\nu^2 = Var[lnY(t)]$.

where $\phi_0 = \lambda\tau\mu_o^4 + 6\lambda\tau\nu^2\mu_0^2 + 3\lambda\tau\nu^4$, and the distribution of r_τ is leptokurtic, more peaked in the vicinity of its mean than the distribution of a comparable normal random variable, asymmetric if $\mu_0 \neq 0$, and the skewness has the same sign as that of μ_0. These features are more consistent with the empirical findings on the unconditional distributions of asset returns. (3) Furthermore, $r_\tau(t)$ is a process with independent increments, i.e.

$$Cov[r_\tau(t), r_\tau(t-\delta)] = 0 \tag{7.12}$$

for $\delta \geq \tau$. Special cases of the above model include: Press (1967) with $\mu = 0$, Beckers (1981) and Ball and Torous (1985) with $\mu_0 = 0$, and Lo (1988) with $ln Y(t) = \kappa(p(t))$, i.e. the jump size is determined by the process itself.

7.2.3 The Lo–Wang (1995) model

As Lo and Wang (1995) point out, although it is well known that the Black–Scholes formula does not depend on the drift term $\mu(\cdot)$, it is rarely emphasized that the drift need not be a constant as in the case of geometric Brownian motion, but may be an arbitrary function of $P(t)$ and even other economic variables.[13] This remarkable fact implies that the Black–Scholes formula is applicable to a wide variety of price processes that exhibit complex patterns of predictability and dependence on other observed and unobserved economic factors. The fact that the drift term does not enter into the option pricing formula seems to imply that option prices are irrelevant to the functional form of the drift term. Since predictability of the stochastic process often manifests itself through the specification of drift function, this seems to imply that the predictability of the asset's return is irrelevant for option prices. Lo and Wang (1995) investigate the impact of asset return predictability on the prices of an asset's options by extending the drift function to incorporate various patterns of predictability.

The Lo and Wang (1995) model is an extension of the Black–Scholes (1973) model along another direction by assuming that the time-trended logarithmic price process $p(t)$ follows an Ornstein–Uhlenbeck process, i.e.,

$$dp(t) = (-\beta(p(t) - \mu t) + \mu)dt + \sigma dW(t) \tag{7.13}$$

or

$$p(t) = \mu t + q(t)$$

$$dq(t) = -\beta q(t)dt + \sigma dW(t)$$

---

[13]This was first observed by Merton (1973) and also explicitly acknowledged by Jagannathan (1984) and Grundy (1991).

where $\beta > 0$ ensures the stationarity of $q(t)$ which has the following explicit solution:

$$q(t) = e^{-\beta(t-t_0)}q_0 + \sigma \int_{t_0}^{t} e^{-\beta(t-s)}dW(s)$$

where $q_0 = q(t_0) = p(t_0) - \mu t_0$. The above model leads to the same European call option price formula as the Black–Scholes (1973) model given by equation (7.2).

The Ornstein–Uhlenbeck process $q(t)$ also has a normal transition density, and if the process does display the property of mean reversion ($\beta > 0$), then as $t_0 \to -\infty$ or $t - t_0 \to +\infty$, the marginal density of the stochastic process is invariant to time, i.e. the Ornstein–Uhlenbeck process is stationary with a Gaussian marginal density.[14] The major properties of the trending O-U process include: (1) unlike the Brownian motion with drift process which is 'difference-stationary', the O-U process is stationary and hence the trending O-U process is 'trend-stationary', i.e. $q(t)$, the detrending process of $p(t)$, is a stationary Gaussian process. (2) The first difference of $lnP(t)$ or $p(t)$ over $\tau(>0)$-period, or the τ-period return of the asset $r_\tau(t) = \Delta_\tau p(t) = \Delta_\tau q(t) + \mu\tau$ is also a stationary Gaussian process with mean and variance

$$E[r_\tau(t)] = \mu\tau, \quad Var[r_\tau(t)] = \frac{\sigma^2}{\beta}(1 - e^{-\beta\tau}) \tag{7.14}$$

which is different from the volatility for the increments of the Brownian motion with a drift process. Only if $\beta \to 0$ does $Var[r_\tau(t)] \to \sigma^2\tau$. An implication of trend-stationarity is that the unconditional variance of τ-period returns has a finite limit as τ increases without bound – in this case σ^2/β – in contrast to the case of a random walk in which the unconditional variance increases linearly with τ, i.e. $\sigma^2\tau$. (3) Increments of both $q(t)$ and $p(t)$ are no longer independent, i.e. for τ-period difference of the trending O-U process, $r_\tau(t) = \Delta_\tau p(t) = p(t) - p(t-\tau)$, we have for $\delta \geq \tau$,

$$Cov(r_\tau(t), r_\tau(t-\delta)) = -\frac{\sigma^2}{2\beta}e^{-\beta(\delta-\tau)}(1 - e^{-\beta\tau})^2$$

or

$$Corr(r_\tau(t), r_\tau(t-\delta)) = -\frac{1}{2}e^{-\beta(\delta-\tau)}(1 - e^{-\beta\tau}) \tag{7.15}$$

[14] To derive the stationary unconditional density function of the stochastic process, one can either assume $t_0 \to -\infty$ or $t - t_0 \to +\infty$ to obtain the steady-state marginal density function or assume the initial $p(t_0)$ at t_0 of the stochastic process follows the steady-state distribution.

Note that the first-order autocorrelation ($\delta = \tau$) of the trending O-U increments is always less than or equal to zero, bounded below by $-\frac{1}{2}$ and approaches $-\frac{1}{2}$ as τ goes to infinity, the second-order autocorrelation ($\delta = 2\tau$) is also always less than or equal to zero and bounded below by $-\frac{1}{8}$ and approaches $-\frac{1}{8}$ as τ goes to infinity, and so on. These, and other aspects of the trending O-U process, prove to be serious restrictions for many empirical applications.

7.2.4 The trending O-U jump-diffusion model

Like the Lo–Wang (1995) model in extending the Black–Scholes (1973) model, in this chapter we extend the Merton (1976a) jump-diffusion model by assuming that the time-trended logarithmic asset prices follow a jump-diffusion process with a linear mean-reverting drift function to incorporate certain pattern of asset return predictability, i.e.

$$dp(t) = (-\beta(p(t) - \mu t) + \mu)dt + \sigma dW(t) + ln Y(t) dQ_{\lambda}(t) \tag{7.16}$$

or

$$p(t) = \mu t + q(t)$$

$$dq(t) = -\beta q(t)dt + \sigma dW(t) + ln Y(t) dQ_{\lambda}(t)$$

where $\beta > 0$. For simplicity, we assume $\mu_0 = 0$. The model also represents a Markov process with discrete parameter and continuous state space, but it does not always have an explicit solution.

In a special case when $ln Y(t) \sim idN(0, e^{-2\beta(t-t_0)}\nu^2)$, i.e. the jump size is uncorrelated over time but decays exponentially, where t_0 is the initial time. The process is governed by the transition density given in the Appendix with conditional mean and variance $E[q(t)|q(t_0)] = e^{-\beta(t-t_0)}q(t_0)$, $Var[q(t)|q(t_0)] = \sigma^2/2\beta(1 - e^{-2\beta(t-t_0)}) + \lambda(t - t_0)e^{-2\beta(t-t_0)}\nu^2$. This process converges to the Ornstein–Uhlenbeck process since the jump component dies out as time goes to infinity. Suppose $q(t_0) \sim N(0, \sigma^2/2\beta)$, then $E[q(t)] = 0$, $Var[q(t)] = \sigma^2/2\beta + \lambda(t - t_0)e^{-2\beta(t-t_0)}\nu^2$. As $t_0 \to -\infty$, or $t - t_0 \to +\infty$, $q(t)$ converges to the Ornstein–Uhlenbeck process with a Gaussian marginal density $N(0, \sigma^2/2\beta)$. Further difference from the constant drift jump-diffusion model with iid lognormal jump is that the Ornstein–Uhlenbeck process with an exponentially decaying jump no longer has independent increments even though its driving processes, the Brownian motion and compound Poisson, both do. Let $r_\tau(t) = \Delta_\tau p(t) = p(t) - p(t - \tau) = \mu\tau + q(t) - q(t - \tau)$, we have $E[r_\tau] = \mu\tau$, $Var[r_\tau] = \frac{\sigma^2}{\beta}(1 - e^{-\beta\tau}) + \lambda(\tau + (1 - e^{\beta\tau})^2(t - \tau - t_0))e^{-2\beta(t-t_0)}\nu^2$,

$Cov[r_\tau(t), r_\tau(t-\delta)] = -\frac{\sigma^2}{2\beta}e^{-\beta(\delta-\tau)}(1-e^{-\beta\tau})^2 + \lambda(\tau + (1-e^{\beta\tau})(t-\tau-\delta-t_0)$ $(1-e^{\beta\tau})e^{-\beta(2t-\delta-2t_0)}\nu^2$ for $\delta \geq \tau$. Again as $t_0 \to -\infty$, or $t - t_0 \to +\infty$, we have $E[r_\tau] = \mu\tau$, $Var[r_\tau] \to \frac{\sigma^2}{\beta}(1-e^{-\beta\tau})$, $Cov[r_\tau(t), r_\tau(t-\delta)] \to -e^{-\beta(\delta-\tau)}$ $(1-e^{-\beta\tau})^2\frac{\sigma^2}{2\beta} < 0$ for $\delta \geq \tau$, or $Corr[r_\tau(t), r_\tau(t-\delta)] \to -\frac{1}{2}e^{-\beta(\delta-\tau)}$ $(1-e^{-\beta\tau}) < 0$ for $\delta \geq \tau$.

Since the only difference between (7.16) and (7.9) is the drift term, this model leads to the same European call option price formula as the Merton (1976a) model given by (7.7). In particular, if $\ln Y(t) \sim iid\ N(\mu_0, \nu^2)$, the option price formula is given by (7.8). In this case, the solution of $q(t)$ is represented by the following integral:

$$q(t) = e^{-\beta(t-t_0)}q(t_0) + \int_{t_0}^{t} e^{-\beta(t-u)}\sigma dW(u) + \int_{t_0}^{t} e^{-\beta(t-u)}\ln Y(u)dQ_\lambda(u) \quad (7.17)$$

It can be shown (see Appendix) that the second term follows a normal distribution with mean zero and variance

$$\frac{\sigma^2}{2\beta}(1-e^{-2\beta(t-t_0)})$$

The third term follows a compound Poisson distribution with mean

$$\frac{\lambda\mu_0}{\beta}(1-e^{-\beta(t-t_0)})$$

and variance

$$\frac{\mu_0^2+\nu^2}{2\beta}(1-e^{-2\beta(t-t_0)})$$

The distribution is asymmetric and skewed in the same direction as μ_0 and has fatter tails than the normal distributions. The first difference of $q(t)$ or $p(t)$ over the τ-period or the τ-period return of the asset $r_\tau(t) = \Delta_\tau p(t) = \Delta_\tau q(t) = \mu\tau$ is a co-variance stationary process, i.e. the covariance between $r_\tau(t)$ and $r_\tau(t-\delta)$ depends only on δ. When $\mu_0 = 0$, its mean and variance as well as skewness and kurtosis are given by

$$E[r_\tau(t)] = \mu\tau, Var[r_\tau(t)] = \frac{\sigma^2+\lambda\nu^2}{\beta}(1-e^{-\beta\tau})$$

$$E[(r_\tau(t) - E[r_\tau(t)])^3] = 0, E[(r_\tau(t) - E[r_\tau(t))^4] = 3Var[r_\tau(t)]^2 + \phi_0 \quad (7.18)$$

where

$$\phi_0 = \frac{3\lambda\nu^4}{2\beta}(1-e^{-\beta\tau})(1-e^{-\beta\tau}+2e^{-2\beta\tau})$$

As in the case of the Lo–Wang (1995) model, the return of asset is no longer uncorrelated, as seen from

$$Cov[r_\tau(t), r_\tau(t-\delta)] = -\frac{\sigma^2 + \lambda\nu^2}{2\beta} e^{-\beta(\delta-\tau)}(1 - e^{\beta\tau})^2$$

or

$$Corr[r_\tau(t), r_\tau(t-\delta)] = -\frac{1}{2} e^{-\beta(\delta-\tau)}(1 - e^{\beta\tau}) \tag{7.19}$$

where $\delta \geq \tau$. That is, as in the case of the trending O-U model, the trending O-U jump-diffusion model also assumes that the autocorrelations of stock returns are negative for all orders over a finite time period, with the first-order autocorrelation bounded between $(-\frac{1}{2}, 0]$ and the second autocorrelation bounded between $(-\frac{1}{8}, 0]$, and so on.

As Lo and Wang (1995) point out, an obvious deficiency in the trending O-U process as a general model of the asset return process is that its returns are negatively autocorrelated at all lags, which is inconsistent with the empirical findings for autocorrelations of many traded assets. For example, Lo and MacKinlay (1988, 1990) show that equity portfolios tend to be positively autocorrelated at shorter horizons, while Fama and French (1988) and Poterba and Summers (1988) find negative autocorrelation at longer horizons. The remedy for the above drawback proposed by Lo and Wang (1995) is to introduce other economic variables which are believed to play a role in determining the predictability of asset returns. The model proposed is the so-called 'multivariate trending O-U' process, with the 'bivariate trending O-U' process as a special case. In this chapter we can extend the trending O-U jump-diffusion process in the same direction, i.e. the following bivariate trending O-U jump-diffusion process:

$$dq(t) = -(\beta q(t) - \eta X(t))dt + \sigma dW_q(t) + ln Y(t) dQ_\lambda(t)$$

$$dX(t) = -\theta X(t)dt + \sigma_x dW_x(t) \tag{7.20}$$

where $\beta \geq 0, \eta \geq 0, q(t_0) = q_0, X(t_0) = X_0$, $W_x(t)$ and $W_q(t)$ are two standard Wiener processes such that $dW_q(t)dW_x(t) = \kappa dt$, $dW_x(t)dQ_\lambda(t) = 0$, and $X(t)$ is another stochastic process that may or may not be observable. The solution for the above system of linear SDE can be written as

$$q(t) = e^{-\beta(t-t_0)}q_0 + \frac{\eta}{\beta-\theta}(e^{-\theta(t-t_0)} - e^{-\beta(t-t_0)})X_0 + \int_{t_0}^{t} e^{-\beta(t-s)}\sigma dW_q(s)$$

$$+ \frac{\eta}{\beta-\theta}\int_{t_0}^{t}(e^{-\theta(t-s)} - e^{-\beta(t-s)})\sigma_x dW_x(s) + \int_{t_0}^{t} e^{-\beta(t-s)} ln Y(s) dQ_\lambda(s)$$

$$X(t) = e^{-\theta(t-t_0)}X_0 + \int_{t_0}^{t} e^{-\theta(t-s)}\sigma_x dW_x(s) \tag{7.21}$$

where $t \geq t_0$, $q(t)$ follows a mixture of normal distribution and compounding Poisson distribution and X follows a normal distribution given the initial values. The bivariate trending O-U jump-diffusion process can capture more complex patterns of autocorrelation than its univariate counterpart as seen from the first-order autocorrelation function (see Appendix). For a small holding period τ, the first-order autocorrelation function for the special case $\eta = \beta$ can be derived as

$$\rho_\tau(1) \approx -\frac{\tau}{2}(\beta - \frac{\theta COV_{qx}V_q}{1 - COV_{qx}V_q}) \tag{7.22}$$

where $COV_{qx} = Cov(q(t), x(t))$, $V_q = Var[q(t)]$. In this case, $\rho_\tau(1)$ can be either positive or negative, depending on whether $COV_{qx}V_q$ is greater or less than $\beta/(\beta+\theta)$. Since $\rho_\tau(1) \to -\frac{1}{2}$ as τ increases without bound for τ-period increments, or the continuously compound τ-period return, of any stationary process with linear mean-reverting drift function, when $1 > COV_{qx}V_x > \beta/(\beta+\theta)$, $\rho_\tau(1) > 0$, the bivariate trending O-U jump-diffusion process will display an autocorrelation pattern that matches the empirical findings of both Lo and MacKinlay (1988) and Fama and French (1988) simultaneously: positive autocorrelation for a short horizon and negative autocorrelation for a long horizon. Like the bivariate O-U process in Lo and Wang (1995), there is no longer a simple relationship between autocorrelation and the conditional volatility.

7.2.5 The jump-diffusion model with predictable jump size

In reality, predictability may not be reflected in the directly observed asset returns but in the not directly observed subordinated process, e.g. the information flow process. Earlier, several authors, including Mandelbrot and Taylor (1967) and Clark (1973), proposed to link asset returns *explicitly* to the flow of information arrivals which are non-uniform through time and quite often not directly observable. Conceptually, one can think of asset price movements as the realization of a process $P(t) = P(Z(t))$ where $Z(t)$ is a so-called directing process. This positive non-decreasing stochastic process $Z(t)$ can be thought of as being related to the arrival of information.[15] Suppose such an information flow has more than a marginal effect on asset prices,

[15] This idea of time deformation or subordinated stochastic process was also used by Mandelbrot and Taylor (1967) to explain fat-tailed returns, by Clark (1973) to explain volatility behaviour and was recently refined and further explored by Ghysels, Gourieroux and Jasiak (1995).

predictability of the information flow can be modelled by either assuming the jump intensity follows a temporarily correlated process or the jump size process follows a predictable process. For instance, in the currency exchange market, the value of a currency is subject to the changes of monetary policies or economic situations in both domestic and foreign economies. Major changes of such factors can be viewed as information shocks to the market, which are often followed by the release of important macroeconomic news. In the case that the market overreacts to information shock, it is not surprising to see that a negative (or respectively positive) jump could be followed by a positive (or respectively negative) jump. While in the case that the market underreacts to information shock, there might be a sequential positive or negative jumps associated with a major information shock. Similarly, in the stock market one often observes that the stock prices move in a cyclical pattern consisting of periods of upward movement and periods of downward movement mixed with periods of directionsless movements. In a upward trend a positive price change is followed by another positive price change, while in a downward trend a negative price change is followed by another positive price change on a daily basis, and the reversing point of such short-term trends is unpredictable. Such a phenomenon cannot be explained by a simple diffusion process driven by an increment-independent Gaussian Wiener process. A general specification of the jump process, however, could substantially reduce the tractability of the model and make it difficult to investigate its impact on option prices. In this section, we look at the simple case that the information arrival is still unpredictable, i.e. the Poisson counting process is still a temporarily independent process, but the jump size is predictable. That is,

$$dp(t) = \mu dt + \sigma dW(t) + ln Y(t) dQ_\lambda(t)$$

$$dln Y(t) = -\xi ln Y(t) dt + \sigma_Y dW_Y(t) \tag{7.23}$$

or

$$ln Y(t) = e^{-\xi(t-t_0)} ln Y(t_0) + \int_{t_0}^{t} e^{-\xi(t-s)} \sigma_Y dW_Y(s)$$

where $dW(t)dW_Y(t) = dW_Y(t)dQ_\lambda(t) = 0$, and $ln Y(t)$ is a stationary process when $\xi > 0$ with $E[ln Y(t)] = 0, Var[ln Y(t)] = \sigma_Y^2/2\xi$, and $Corr(ln Y(t), ln Y(t-\tau)) = e^{-\xi\tau}$ which approaches 1 as $\tau \to 0$ and 0 as $\tau \to \infty$. That is, the jump size follows a stationary process and has a short memory, the duration of the memory is determined by the value of parameter ξ – a larger value of ξ represents a shorter duration of memory and a smaller value of ξ represents a longer duration of memory. Since the sign of jump can be interpreted as the feature of information, say positive or negative news, such a specification implies that a positive (respectively negative) news is more likely to be followed by another positive (respectively negative) news, if it ever arrives. The model can explain the observed cyclical patterns of price movement for many traded assets.

This model is interesting in that the directly observed process is unpredictable while only the subordinated (hidden) process is partially predictable. It can be used to illustrate that such implicit predictability can also have significant impact on option prices. Let $r_\tau(t) = p(t) - p(t-\tau)$ be the τ-period return of the asset. It can be derived (see Appendix) that

$$E[r_\tau(t)] = \mu\tau, \quad Var[r_\tau(t)] = (\sigma^2 + \frac{\lambda\sigma_Y^2}{2\xi})\tau \tag{7.24}$$

and

$$Corr[r_\tau(t), r_\tau(t-\delta)] = 0 \tag{7.25}$$

for $\delta \geq \tau$. More interestingly, the conditional mean and volatility of the asset returns can be derived as

$$E[r_\tau(t)|\mathcal{F}_{t-\tau}] = \mu\tau + \frac{1-e^{-\xi\tau}}{\xi}\lambda ln Y(t-\tau)$$

$$Var[r_\tau(t)|\mathcal{F}_{t-\tau}] = Var[r_\tau(t)] - \frac{\lambda(1-e^{-2\xi\tau})}{4\xi^2}\sigma_Y^2 + \frac{\lambda(1-e^{-2\xi\tau})}{2\xi} ln^2 Y(t-\tau) \tag{7.26}$$

where $\mathcal{F}_{t-\tau}$ is a natural filtration which represents the information available at time $t-\tau$. Since $lnY(t)$, as an AR(1) process, is a temporarily correlated process, so is the conditional mean. In addition, the conditional volatility is time dependent and is driven by a predictable state variable, i.e. the conditional volatility is not only heteroscedastic but also correlated over time. This property is consistent with many empirical findings that the conditional volatility is intertemporally persistent, varying over time and sometimes clustered with bunching of high and low episodes. In the literature, the conditional heteroscedasticity in a jump-diffusion framework is typically introduced through the non-jump instantaneous conditional volatility. That is, the non-jump conditional volatility is changing and yet correlated over time; see e.g. Jorion (1988), Bates (1995, 1996), Ho, Perraudin and Søresen (1996), Bakshi, Cao and Chen (1997), and Scott (1997). From a model specification point of view, it is more reasonable to assume σ as a constant as it measures the 'normal' vibrations of asset returns and introduce time-varying and clustering volatility through the jump component which measures the 'abnormal' vibrations of asset returns.

7.3 IMPLICATIONS OF MODEL (MIS-)SPECIFICATION ON OPTION PRICES

Empirical evidence confirms systematic mispricing of the Black–Scholes call option pricing models. These biases have been documented with respect to the call option's exercise prices, its time to expiration, and the underlying common stock's volatility; see e.g. Black (1975), Gultekin, Rogalski and Tinic (1982), MacBeth and Merville (1979), Rubinstein (1985), and Bodurtha and Courtadon (1987). Various patterns of mispricing of the Black–Scholes model have been documented in the literature. Since there is a one-to-one relationship between volatility and the option's price through the Black–Scholes formula, an equivalent measure for the mispricing of Black–Scholes model is thus the implicit or implied Black–Scholes volatility, i.e. the volatility which generates the corresponding option price. The Black–Scholes model imposes a flat term structure of volatility, i.e. the volatility is constant across both maturity and moneyness of options. In reality this is not the case, and the Black–Scholes-implied volatility heavily depends on the calendar time, the time to maturity, and the moneyness of the options.[16] The price distortions, well known to practitioners, are usually documented in the empirical literature under the terminology of the *smile* effect, referring to the U-shaped pattern of implied volatilities across different strike prices. The use of implied volatility as a measure of mispricing has a few advantages. First, since volatility is an input factor in the Black–Scholes option pricing formula, the implied volatility can directly measure the magnitudes of input errors. Second, since the Black–Scholes implied volatility is assumed to be constant over time and to cross different degrees of moneyness and terms of expiration, the comparison base of the implied volatility is not sensitive to the calendar time, the moneyness, or the maturity as much as the absolute or relative errors of option prices. Third, empirical findings on the patterns of implied volatility are well documented and more agreeable for certain traded assets. The following stylized facts are extensively documented in the literature (see, for instance, Rubinstein, 1985; Clewlow and Xu, 1993; Taylor and Xu, 1994): (i) the U-shaped pattern of implied volatility as a function of moneyness has its minimum centred at near-the-money options; (ii) the volatility smile is often but not always symmetric as

[16]This may produce various biases in option pricing or hedging when Black–Scholes-implied volatilities are used to evaluate new options with different strike prices and maturities.

a function of moneyness; and (iii) the amplitude of the smile increases quickly when time to maturity decreases. Indeed, for short maturities the smile effect is very pronounced while it almost completely disappears for longer maturities.

In this chapter we use a slightly different definition of moneyness for options from the conventional one[17] following Ghysels, Harvey and Renault (1996). We define

$$x_t = ln(P(t)/Ke^{-r(T-t)})$$

If $x_t = 0$, the current stock price $P(t)$ coincides with the present value of the strike price K, the option is called at-the-money (ATM); if $x_t > 0$ (respectively $x_t < 0$), the option is called in-the-money (ITM) (respectively out-of-the-money (OTM)).

7.3.1 The Merton jump-diffusion price versus Black–Scholes price

The question raised in Merton (1976a) and answered in details in Merton (1976b) is as follows. Suppose an investor believes that the stock price dynamics follow a continuous sample-path process with a constant variance per unit time and therefore uses the standard Black–Scholes formula to evaluate the options when the true process for the underlying stock price is described by the jump-diffusion process (7.5) with constant drift. How will the investor's appraised value based on a misspecified process for the stock compare with the true value based on the correct process?

To make the comparison feasible and straightforward, Merton (1976b) assumed that $lnY \sim i.i.d.N(-\frac{1}{2}\nu^2, \nu^2)$, or $\alpha_0 = E[Y-1] = 0$. Let $V = \sigma^2\tau + N\nu^2$ be the random volatility of the true jump-diffusion process for the τ-period return, i.e. N is a Poisson-distributed random variable with intensity parameter $\lambda\tau$. So the true volatility observed over τ-period is

$$V_n = \sigma^2\tau + n\nu^2 \tag{7.27}$$

when $N = n$. From Merton's jump-diffusion option price formula, we have the true option price given by $C_M = E_n[C_{BS}(P(t), t; K, T, r, V_n/\tau)]$. Based on a sufficiently long time series of data, the investor can obtain a true unconditional volatility for a τ-period stock return, i.e.

$$V_{BS} = E[V] = (\sigma^2 + \lambda\nu^2)\tau \tag{7.28}$$

[17] In practice, it is more common to call an option as at-the-money, in-the-money, or out-of-the-money when $P(t) = K$, $P(t) > K$, or $P(t) < K$ respectively. For American-type options with the possibility of early exercise, it is more convenient to compare $P(t)$ with K, while for European-type options and from an economic point of view, it is more appealing to compare $P(t)$ with the present value of the strike price K.

and the incorrect price of the option based on the Black–Scholes model is given by $C_{BS} = C_{BS}(P(t), t; K, T, r, V_{BS}/\tau)$. In general, Merton (1976b) concluded as follows. First, due to the strict convexity in the stock price of the Black-Scholes option price formula (7.2), it is straightforward to show that *ceteris paribus*, $\partial C_M / \partial \lambda > 0$ at $\lambda = 0$, i.e. an option on a stock whose return tends to jump is more valuable than an option on a stock without a jump component. Second, for $x_t = 0$ or $P = Ke^{-r(T-t)}$, i.e. the option is at the money, $C_{BS} > C_M$, i.e. the Black–Scholes estimate will be larger than the true value and thus it overestimates the option. For either $x_t >> 0 (P >> Ke^{-r(T-t)})$ or $x_t << 0 (P << Ke^{-r(T-t)})$ i.e. the options are either deep ITM or deep OTM, $C_{BS} < C_M$, i.e. the Black–Scholes price will be smaller than the true value.

The exact magnitude of the difference depends very much on the values of parameters. For maximum effectiveness, Merton (1976b) used the following four parameters to gauge the specific patterns of Black–Scholes model biases: (i) $X_t = P/Ke^{-r(T-t)} = exp(x_t)$, i.e. the measure of moneyness; (ii) $V = (\sigma^2 + \lambda\nu^2)(T - t)$, the expected variance, or total volatility, of the logarithmic return on the stock over the life of the option which depends on both the stock volatility per unit period and the length of maturity; (iii) $\gamma = \lambda\nu^2/(\sigma^2 + \lambda\nu^2)$, the fraction of the total expected variance in the stock's return caused by the jump component which measures the significance of the jump factor in the process and therefore reflects the degree of misspecification of the Black–Scholes model; (iv) $\omega = \lambda(T - t)/V$, the ratio of the expected number of jumps over the life of the option to the expected variance of the stock's return. Like γ, ω is also a measure of the degree of misspecification. For given values of the above four parameters, Merton (1976b) showed that: (a) the Black–Scholes model tends to undervalue deep in- or out-of-the-money options, while it overvalues the near-the-money options; (b) in terms of percentage difference, there are two local extreme points: one is the largest percentage overvaluation of option price at-the-money, and the other is the largest percentage undervaluation for in-the-money options. There is no local maximum for the percentage undervaluation for out-of-the-money options, the error becomes increasingly larger as the option becomes more out-of-the-money; and (c) the magnitude of the percentage error increases as either γ increases or ω decreases. In particular, if the value of the total conditional volatility $\sigma^2 + \lambda\nu^2$ is fixed, an increase of $\lambda\nu^2$ will have a larger impact on the option prices. If $\lambda\nu^2$ is fixed, when λ is relatively small, but ν^2 is relatively large, then the difference between the Merton price and the Black–Scholes price will be relatively larger, especially for short-maturity and out-of-the money options. Otherwise, if the jump frequency is very high while the variance of the jump becomes very small, applying the Central Limit Theorem (see e.g. Cox and Ross, 1976 for this case), it can be shown that the compounding Poisson jump process approaches a continuous process with a corresponding normal distribution in the limit. Thus, the Merton jump-diffusion process and the Black–Scholes continuous sample process would not be distinguishable and hence the prices of options would not be very different.

Merton (1976b) focused his comparison on the relative percentage differences of option prices. In this chapter we compare the differences between the Merton (1976a) jump-diffusion prices and the Black–Scholes (1973) prices in terms of both absolute biases and relative percentage biases as well as implied Black–Scholes volatilities. In addition, we also look at the impact of asymmetric jump on the biases of option prices and the shapes of implied Black–Scholes volatilities. Setting the stock price $P = \$40.00$, the strike price K ranges from \$35.00 to \$50.00, maturities τ equal respectively $7, 14, 30, 91$ days, and the annualized compound risk-free rate $r = 5\%$, Figure 7.1(a), 7.1(b), 7.2(a), 7.2(b), 7.3(a) and 7.3(b) show the biases of the Black–Scholes model when stock returns follow a jump-diffusion for $\gamma = \lambda\nu^2/(\sigma^2 + \lambda\nu^2)$ changing from 1/2, to 3/4 while holding $\sigma^2 + \lambda\nu^2 = 0.4 \times (0.02)^2$ as constant. The Black–Scholes model tends to overprice near-the-money options and underprice both deep ITM and OTM options. The absolute differences are most pronounced for near-the-money options, while the percentage differences are most pronounced for deep OTM options. Overall, for both absolute and percentage differences, the biases increase as the time to expiration decreases and as the values of γ, i.e. the jump factor, increases. The implied Black–Scholes volatilities exhibit obvious U-shaped patterns (smiles) as the call option goes from deep OTM to ATM and then to deep ITM, with the deepest ITM call option implied volatilities taking the highest values. Furthermore, the volatility smiles are more pronounced and more sensitive to the time to expiration for short-term options than for medium-term and long-term options. Overall the implied Black–Scholes volatility smiles more as γ increases. Figures 7.1(c), 7.1(d), 7.2(c), 7.2(d), 7.3(c) and 7.3(d) show similar patterns of biases for the Black–Scholes model with λ decreasing or ν^2 increasing while holding both $\lambda\nu^2$ and $\sigma^2 + \lambda\nu^2$ (thus γ) as constants. When $\gamma = 1/4$ and λ decreases from 1/8 to 1/32 and the jump volatility increases from 0.00032 to 0.00128, both the absolute and percentage biases increase and the volatility smiles become more pronounced. Figures 7.4–7.6 further show the biases of the Black–Scholes model when the random jump is asymmetric. As expected, when $\alpha_0 > 0$, i.e. there is an expected positive jump, the Black–Scholes model tends to underprice OTM options and overprice ITM options. The absolute biases are more severe for near-the-money short-term options and for deep ITM or deep OTM long-term options. Similarly, the deep OTM options have the highest percentage errors. It is

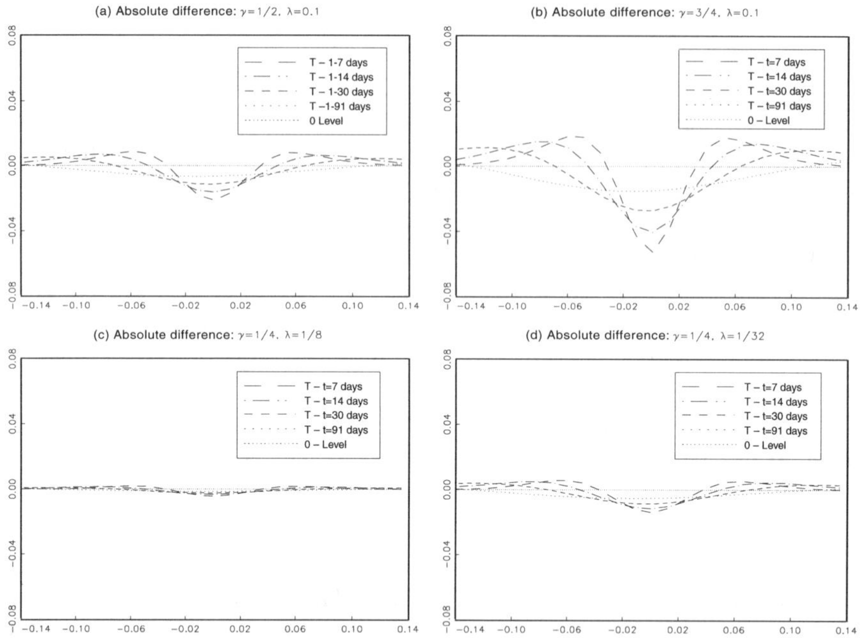

Figure 7.1 Merton (1976a) prices versus Black–Scholes (1973) prices – absolute differences (Merton price – Black–Scholes price). Setting stock price $P = \$40.00$, strike price $K = [\$35.00, \$50.00]$, time to maturity $\tau = 7$, 14, 30, 91 days, annualized compound risk-free rate $r = 5\%$. Parameter values $\gamma = \lambda\nu^2/(\sigma^2 + \lambda\nu^2)$. (a) $\lambda = 0.1$, $\sigma^2 = 0.2 \times (0.02)^2$, $\nu^2 = 2 \times (0.02)^2$, $\gamma = 1/2$; (b) $\lambda = 0.1$, $\sigma^2 = 0.1 \times (0.02)^2$, $\nu^2 = 3 \times (0.02)^2$, $\gamma = 3/4$; (c) $\lambda = 1/8$, $\sigma^2 = 0.3 \times (0.02)^2$, $\nu^2 = 0.00032$, $\gamma = 1/4$; and (d) $\lambda = 1/32$, $\nu^2 = 0.00128$, $\sigma^2 = 0.3 \times (0.02)^2$, $\gamma = 1/4$

obvious that a negative expected jump induces the implied volatility smile to be skewed to the right. This offers a potential explanation of the empirically often observed asymmetric volatility smiles as well as the reverse of slope from time to time for implied volatilities (see Taylor and Xu, 1994). Even though there is no clear conclusion on whether the asymmetric smile is a result of skewed underlying return distribution with excess kurtosis, the above evidence shows the other direction is true.

7.3.2 The Lo–Wang model price versus Black–Scholes price

Lo and Wang (1995) investigated the effect of predictability of asset returns on option prices by comparing polar cases of perfect unpredictability (random walk with drift), i.e. the Black–Scholes option prices and perfect predictability (certain with linear mean reverting drift), i.e. the option prices based on a trending O-U process. Let $r_\tau(t)$ be the continuously compounded returns of the asset, i.e. $r_\tau(t) = p(t) - p(t - \tau)$. The first-order autocorrelation of the arithmetic

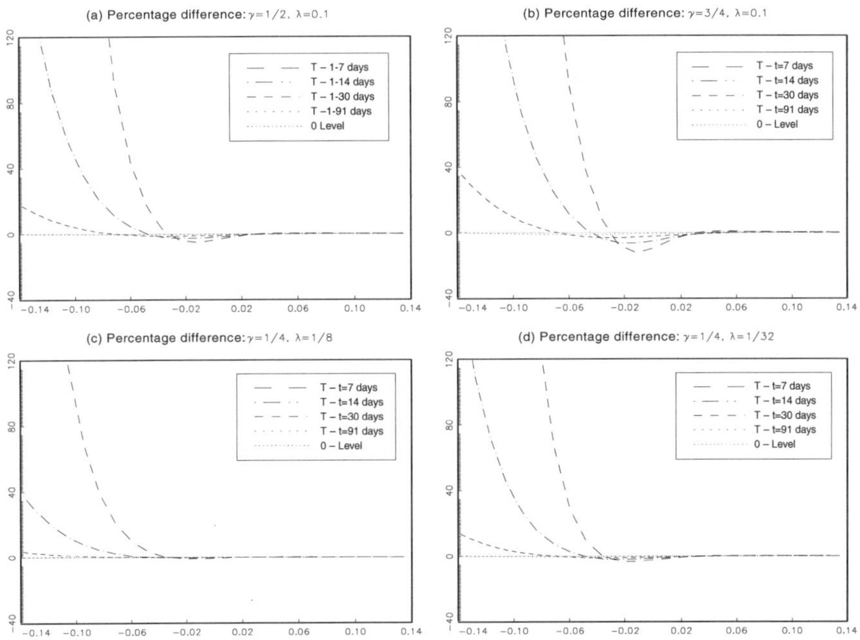

Figure 7.2 Merton (1976a) prices versus Black–Scholes (1973) prices – percentage differences ([Merton price – Black–Scholes price]/Black–Scholes prices). Setting stock price $P = \$40.00$, strike price $K = [\$35.00, \$50.00]$, time to maturity $\tau = 7$, 14, 30, 91 days, annualized compound risk-free rate $r = 5\%$. Parameter values $\gamma = \lambda\nu^2/(\sigma^2 + \lambda\nu^2)$. (a) $\lambda = 0.1$, $\sigma^2 = 0.2 \times (0.02)^2$, $\nu^2 = 2 \times (0.02)^2$, $\gamma = 1/2$; (b) $\lambda = 0.1$, $\sigma^2 = 0.1 \times (0.02)^2$, $\nu^2 = 3 \times (0.02)^2$, $\gamma = 3/4$; (c) $\lambda = 1/8$, $\sigma^2 = 0.3 \times (0.02)^2$, $\nu^2 = 0.00032$, $\gamma = 1/4$; and (d) $\lambda = 1/32$, $\nu^2 = 0.00128$, $\sigma^2 = 0.3 \times (0.02)^2$, $\gamma = 1/4$

Brownian motion increments is zero while that of the trending O-U process is always negative and bounded between $-\frac{1}{2}$ and 0. Therefore, as two competing models, the estimates of the diffusion function $\hat{\sigma}^2$ would be different (even though they are all constants) by matching the population moments of the marginal distribution of the τ-period asset returns of each process to the sample moments of the τ-period asset returns observations. Matching the mean, variance and the first-order autocorrelation, we have for the Brownian motion with drift process,

$$\bar{r}_\tau = \mu\tau, \quad s^2(r_\tau) = \sigma_{GB}^2\tau$$

$$\rho_\tau(1) = 0 \tag{7.29}$$

for the trending O-U process, we have

$$\bar{r}_\tau = \mu\tau, \quad s^2(r_\tau) = \frac{\sigma_{OU}^2}{\beta}(1 - e^{-\beta\tau})$$

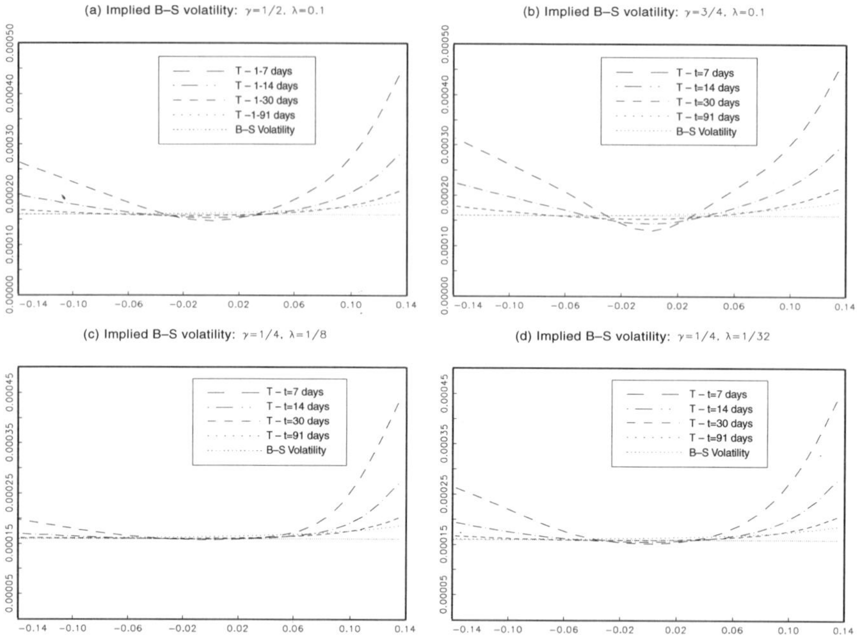

Figure 7.3 Merton (1976a) prices versus Black–Scholes (1973) prices – implied Black–Scholes volatility. Setting stock price $P = \$40.00$, strike price $K = [\$35.00, \$50.00]$, time to maturity $\tau = 7$, 14, 30, 91 days, annualized compound risk-free rate $r = 5\%$. Parameter values $\gamma = \lambda\nu^2/(\sigma^2 + \lambda\nu^2)$. (a) $\lambda = 0.1$, $\sigma^2 = 0.2 \times (0.02)^2$, $\nu^2 = 2 \times (0.02)^2$, $\gamma = 1/2$; (b) $\lambda = 0.1$, $\sigma^2 = 0.1 \times (0.02)^2$, $\nu^2 = 3 \times (0.02)^2$, $\gamma = 3/4$; (c) $\lambda = 1/8$, $\sigma^2 = 0.3 \times (0.02)^2$, $\nu^2 = 0.00032$, $\gamma = 1/4$; and (d) $\lambda = 1/32$, $\nu^2 = 0.00128$, $\sigma^2 = 0.3 \times (0.02)^2$, $\gamma = 1/4$

$$\rho_\tau(1) = -\frac{1}{2}(1 - e^{-\beta\tau}) \tag{7.30}$$

If returns of the asset over the holding period of the unit interval are used to obtain the unconditional variance $s^2(r_1)$ and returns over the holding period of the τ-unit interval are used to obtain the first-order autocorrelation coefficient $\rho_\tau(1)$, then the relationship between the diffusion function of the trending O-U model σ^2_{OU} and the diffusion function of the geometric Brownian motion model σ^2_{GB} is

$$\sigma^2_{OU} = \frac{ln(1 + 2\rho_\tau(1))}{\tau([1 + 2\rho_\tau(1)]^{1/\tau} - 1)}\sigma^2_{GB}, \quad \rho_\tau(1) \in (-\frac{1}{2}, 0] \tag{7.31}$$

Up to this point, the option pricing paradox is readily resolved by observing that the two data-generating processes, the Brownian motion with drift process and the trending O-U process, must fit the same price data – they are, after all, two

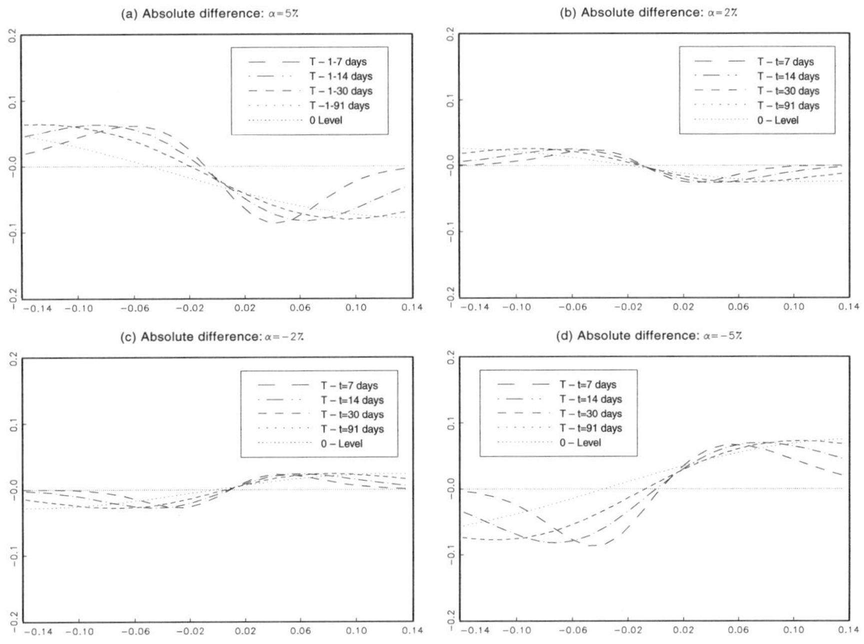

Figure 7.4 Merton (1976a) prices versus Black–Scholes (1973) prices – absolute differences (Merton price – Black–Scholes price). Setting stock price $P = \$40.00$, strike price $K = [\$35.00, \$50.00]$, time to maturity $\tau = 7$, 14, 30, 91 days, annualized compound risk-free rate $r = 5\%$. Parameter values $\lambda = 0.1$, $\sigma^2 = 0.3 \times (0.02)^2$, $\lambda\nu^2 = 0.1 \times (0.02)^2$, $\sigma^2_{BS} = \sigma^2 + \lambda(\mu_0^2 + \nu^2)$, $\mu_0 = ln(1 + \alpha_0) - \frac{1}{2}\nu^2$. (a) $\alpha_0 = 5\%$; (b) $\alpha_0 = 2\%$; (c) $\alpha_0 = -2\%$; and (d) $\alpha_0 = -5\%$

competing specifications of a single price process, the 'true' data-generating process. Therefore, in the presence of autocorrelation, the trending O-U process, the numerical value for the Black–Scholes input σ will be different from the case of no autocorrelation, as in the arithmetic Brownian motion. The above expression provides a simple adjustment for the input σ^2 of the Black–Scholes option price formula using the unconditional variance $s^2(r_1)$ of returns sampled at unit intervals, and the first-order autocorrelation $\rho_\tau(1)$ of returns sampled at τ-intervals.

Therefore when implementing the Black–Scholes model, the input value of σ^2 needs to be adjusted, i.e. not σ^2_{GB} but σ^2_{OU}. It can be verified that the adjustment factor $ln(1 + 2\rho_\tau(1))/(\tau([1 + 2\rho_\tau(1)]^{1/\tau} - 1)) \rightarrow 1$ as $\rho_\tau(1) \rightarrow 0$ and $\rightarrow +\infty$ as $\rho_\tau(1) \rightarrow -\frac{1}{2}$, and increasing in the absolute value of $\rho_\tau(1)$, hence the adjustment factor is greater than or equal to one. This implies that the option prices calculated from the trending O-U process are always higher than or equal to those calculated from the standard Black–Scholes model, and that the difference is an increasing function of the absolute value of the first-order autocorrelation coefficient. The impact of a specification error in the drift can

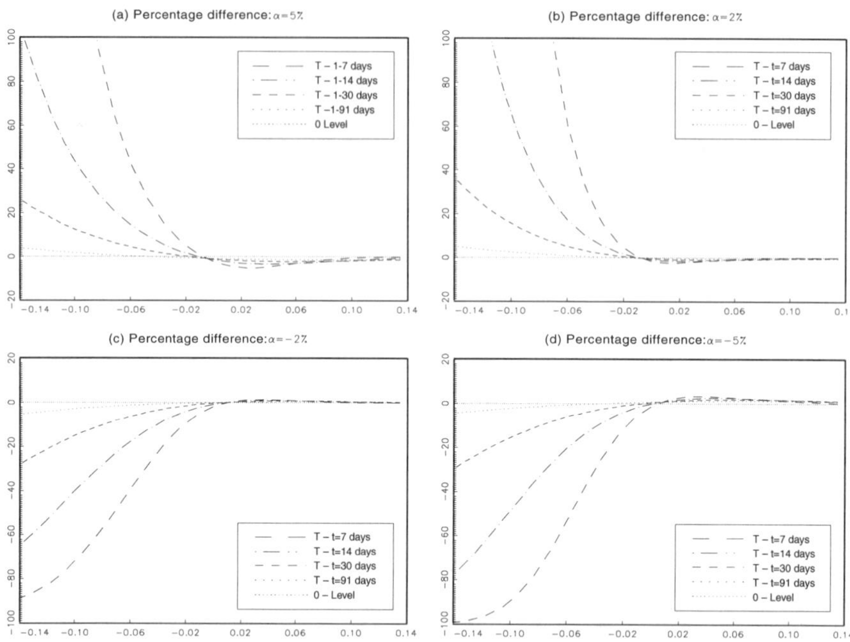

Figure 7.5 Merton (1976a) prices versus Black–Scholes (1973) prices – percentage differences ([Merton price – Black–Scholes price]/Black–Scholes price). Setting stock price $P = \$40.00$, strike price $K = [\$35.00, \$50.00]$, time to maturity $\tau = 7$, 14, 30, 91 days, annualized compound risk-free rate $r = 5\%$. Parameter values $\lambda = 0.1$, $\sigma^2 = 0.3 \times (0.02)^2$, $\lambda\nu^2 = 0.1 \times (0.02)^2$, $\sigma_{BS}^2 = \sigma^2 + \lambda(\mu_0^2 + \nu^2)$, $\mu_0 = ln(1 + \alpha_0) - \frac{1}{2}\nu^2$. (a) $\alpha_0 = 5\%$; (b) $\alpha_0 = 2\%$; (c) $\alpha_0 = -2\%$; and (d) $\alpha_0 = -5\%$

be related to the sensitivity of the Black–Scholes formula to changes in volatility σ. This sensitivity is measured by the derivative of the call price with respect to σ, and is often called the option's 'vega' $\partial C/\partial\sigma = P(t)\sqrt{T - t}\Phi'(d_1)$, where d_1 is defined in the Black–Scholes option pricing formula. From this expression, we can see that the prices of shorter-maturity options are less sensitive to changes in σ, while the prices of longer-maturity options are more sensitive. With given values of the parameters, Lo and Wang (1995) found that: (i) for fixed τ, the difference is more significant as the strike price increases even for short-term maturity options; (ii) as the maturity of options gets longer and the level of autocorrelation of the fixed interval returns (in terms of its absolute value as $\rho_\tau(1) \in (-\frac{1}{2}, 0]$ for O-U process) gets higher, the difference becomes more pronounced.[18]

[18]However, as the return horizon τ increases, the difference of option prices becomes increasingly less sensitive to predictability given the same level of autocorrelation. This is a symptom of all diffusion processes, since the increments of any diffusion process become less autocorrelated as the differencing interval declines.

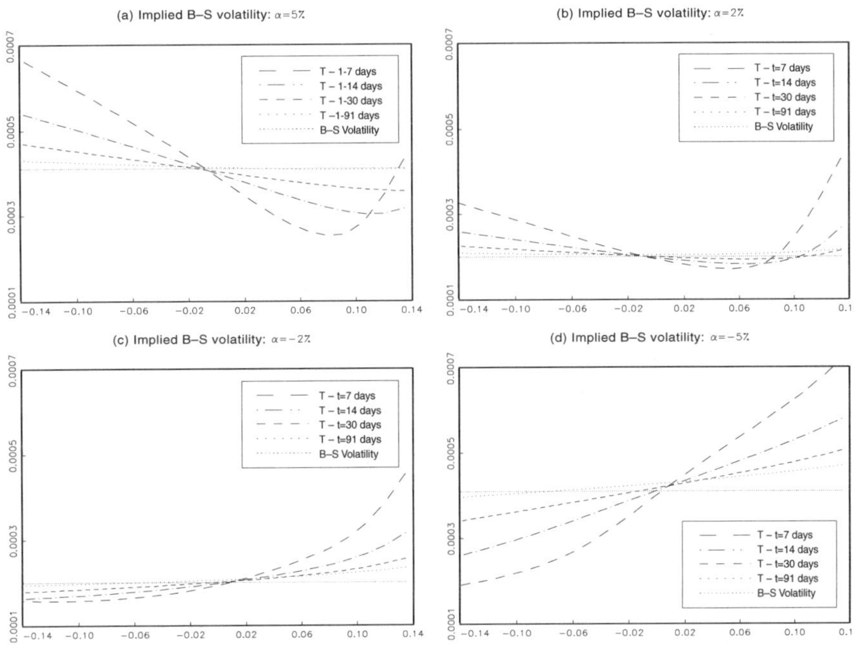

Figure 7.6 Merton (1976a) prices versus Black–Scholes (1973) prices – implied Black–Scholes volatility. Setting stock price $P = \$40.00$, strike price $K = [\$35.00, \$50.00]$, time to maturity $\tau = 7, 14, 30, 91$ days, annualized compound risk-free rate $r = 5\%$. Parameter values $\lambda = 0.1$, $\sigma^2 = 0.3 \times (0.02)^2$, $\lambda\nu^2 = 0.1 \times (0.02)^2$, $\sigma_{BS}^2 = \sigma^2 + \lambda(\mu_0^2 + \nu^2)$, $\mu_0 = ln(1 + \alpha_0) - \frac{1}{2}\nu^2$. (a) $\alpha_0 = 5\%$; (b) $\alpha_0 = 2\%$; (c) $\alpha_0 = -2\%$; and (d) $\alpha_0 = -5\%$

This is sufficient to say that not only the diffusion function but also the drift function matters for the option prices. And one of the important implications of the Black–Scholes option pricing model that investors only have to agree upon is the diffusion function σ^2, not the drift function, is under severe challenge. Figures 7.7–7.9 show the differences between the Black–Scholes option prices and the Lo–Wang prices when the underlying stock return's predictability is induced by linear mean-reverting drift. For the above reason, the Black–Scholes model underprices all options, most severely for long-term options in terms of absolute difference and deep OTM options in terms of percentage difference. As the absolute value of autocorrelation ρ increases, the difference increases. The implied Black–Scholes volatility is flat as both the trending O-U diffusion process and the arithmetic Brownian motion process assume constant conditional volatility. However the implied volatility is higher than the volatility calculated from the underlying arithmetic Brownian motion, i.e. the historical volatility. Interestingly, this observation is consistent with empirical findings on many traded assets that the implied Black–Scholes volatility from the observed

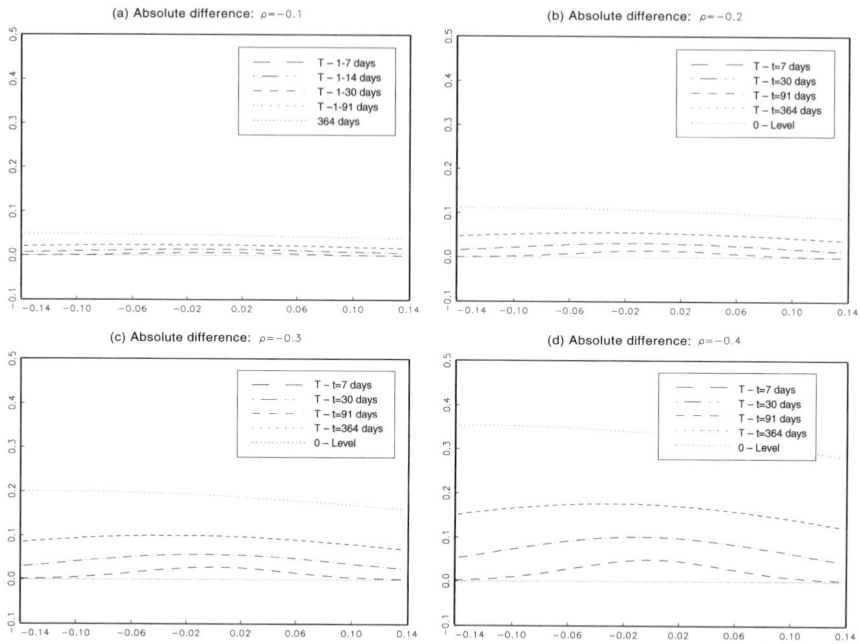

Figure 7.7 Lo–Wang (1995) prices versus Black–Scholes (1973) prices – absolute differences (Lo–Wang price – Black–Scholes price). Setting stock price $P = \$40.00$, strike price $K = [\$35.00, \$50.00]$, time to maturity $\tau = 7$, 14, 30, 91 days, annualized compound risk-free rate $r = 5\%$. Parameter values $\sigma^2 = (0.02)^2$, (a) $\rho = -0.1$; (b) $\rho = -0.2$; (c) $\rho = -0.3$; and (d) $\rho = -0.4$

option prices is often higher than the historical volatility of the underlying process.

To further understand the relationship between the unconditional moments of the data or the population, the predictability of the asset's return or the drift term, and the instantaneous volatility of the process, one can use the fact that a diffusion process is fully specified by its first two moments. Suppose $q(t)$ follows a well-defined diffusion process as

$$dq(t) = \mu(q(t))dt + \sigma(q(t))dW_t$$

with $q(t_0) = q_0$. Since the Brownian motion process W_t is a Gaussian process whose distribution is entirely characterized by its first two moments, it turns out that the distribution of the diffusion process which is driven by the Brownian motion is also entirely characterized by the first two moments of the process, i.e. the instantaneous mean

$$\mu(q(t)) = \lim_{h \to 0} E\{\frac{q(t+h) - q(t)}{h} | q(t)(\omega) = q(t)\}$$

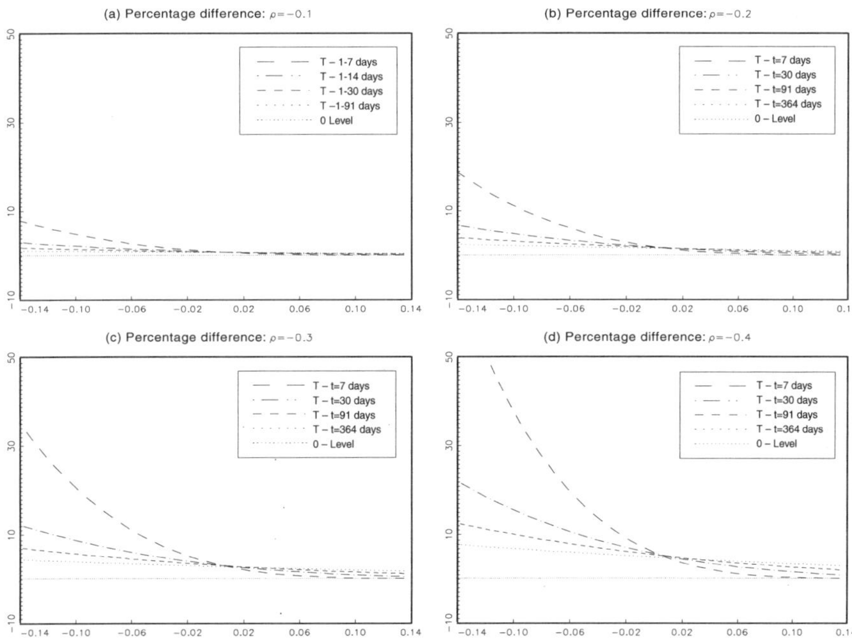

Figure 7.8 Lo–Wang (1995) prices versus Black–Scholes (1973) prices – percentage differences ([Lo–Wang price – Black–Scholes price]/Black–Scholes price). Setting stock price $P = \$40.00$, strike price $K = [\$35.00, \$50.00]$, time to maturity $\tau = 7$, 14, 30, 91 days, annualized compound risk-free rate $r = 5\%$. Parameter values $\sigma^2 = (0.02)^2$, (a) $\rho = -0.1$; (b) $\rho = -0.2$; (c) $\rho = -0.3$; and (d) $\rho = -0.4$

and the instantaneous variance

$$\sigma^2(q(t)) = \lim_{h \to 0} E\{\frac{[q(t+h) - q(t)]^2}{h} | q(t)(\omega) = q(t)\}$$

As a regular strong Markov process (see regularity conditions in e.g. Jiang and Knight, 1997), the underlying structure of the diffusion is entirely characterized by its transition density function which is related to the coefficients of the diffusion model through either the Kolmogorov backward equation or the Kolmogorov forward (or Fokker–Planck) equation (e.g. see Karlin and Taylor, 1981). This implies that specification of the drift and diffusion functions $\mu(\cdot)$ and $\sigma(\cdot)$ fully characterize the Markov structure, i.e. the dynamic properties, through the transition probability function.

Stronger relations between the coefficients of the diffusion process and its marginal density function can be derived if the stochastic process is stationary in the strict sense, or equivalently, there exists a stationary initial probability density $f(q_0)$ such that $f(q(t) = x) = \int f(q(t) = x | q_0 = u) f(q_0 = u) du = f(q_0 = x)$ for any x in the state space. Solving $f(q(t))$ from the Kolmogorov forward

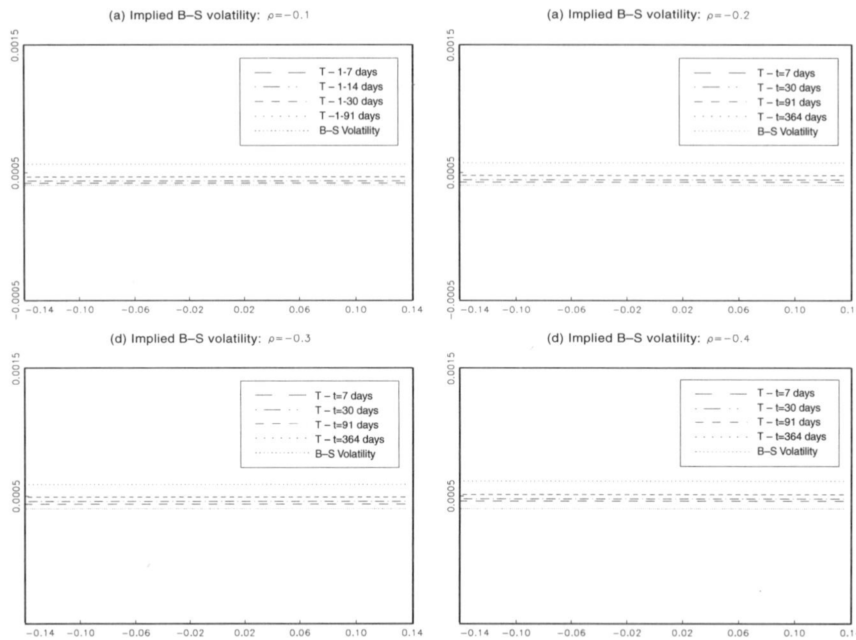

Figure 7.9 Lo–Wang (1995) prices versus Black–Scholes (1973) prices – implied Black–Scholes volatility. Setting stock price $P = \$40.00$, strike price $K = [\$35.00, \$50.00]$, time to maturity $\tau = 7$, 14, 30, 91 days, annualized compound risk-free rate $r = 5\%$. Parameter values $\sigma^2 = (0.02)^2$, (a) $\rho = -0.01$; (b) $\rho = -0.2$; (c) $\rho = -0.3$; and (d) $\rho = -0.4$

equation for $-\infty < q(t) < +\infty$ (e.g. log-stock prices are distributed over $(-\infty, +\infty)$), we have

$$f(q(t)) = \frac{A}{\sigma^2(q(t))} exp\{2 \int_{q^0}^{q_t} \frac{\mu(u)}{\sigma^2(u)} du\} \tag{7.32}$$

with the boundary conditions $f(+\infty) = f'(+\infty) = 0$, or $\sigma(+\infty) = \sigma'(+\infty) = 0$, where A is the normalizing constant, q^0 is an arbitrary interior point of the state space, i.e. $-\infty < q^0 < +\infty$. This implies further that the marginal density, i.e. the static properties, of the underlying Markov process is fully characterized by its coefficients under the regularity conditions. For example, from (7.32) we can derive that: (i) if $\mu(q(t)) = -\mu q(t)(\mu > 0)$, $\sigma(\cdot) = \sigma$, $f(q(t))$ turns out to be a Gaussian density over $(-\infty, +\infty)$; (ii) if $\mu(q(t)) = -\mu q(t)(\mu > 0), \sigma(q(t)) = \sigma q(t)^{1/2}, f(q(t))$ turns out to be a Gamma density over $(0, +\infty)$.

As with the boundary condition $f(+\infty) = f'(+\infty) = 0$, we have

$$\mu(q_t) = \frac{1}{2f(q_t)} \frac{d}{dq_t} [\sigma^2(q_t) f(q_t)]$$

or

$$\sigma^2(q_t) = \frac{2}{f(q_t)} \int_{-\infty}^{q_t} \mu(U) f(U) dU$$

That is, with any functional form specification for either the drift or the diffusion term, the other term will be specified through the above equations given the marginal density function of the diffusion process. For instance, (i) if we specify the drift term as a constant, i.e. $\mu(q(t)) = \mu$, it implies that

$$\sigma^2(q(t)) = 2\mu \frac{F(q(t))}{f(q(t))}$$

where $F(q(t))$ and $f(q(t))$ are respectively the marginal cumulative distribution and probability density functions; (ii) If we impose the linear specification of the drift term, i.e. $\mu(q_t) = a + bq_t$, it implies that

$$\sigma^2(q_t) = \frac{2F(q_t)}{f(q_t)} [a + bE_{Y_t}[y_t]]$$

where Y_t is a random variable with probability density function $f_{Y_t}(y_t) = f(y_t)/F(q_t)$, $0 \le y_t \le q_t$. Similarly, (i) if we specify the diffusion term as a constant, i.e. $\sigma(q_t) = \sigma$, it implies that

$$\mu(q_t) = \frac{\sigma^2}{2} \frac{f'(q_t)}{f(q_t)}$$

(ii) If we specify the diffusion term as the square-root of the level of the stochastic process, i.e. $\sigma(q_t) = \sigma q_t^{1/2}$, it implies that

$$\mu(q_t) = \frac{\sigma^2}{2}\left(1 + q_t \frac{f'(q_t)}{f(q_t)}\right)$$

It is obvious that the drift and diffusion functions are related to each other through fitting into the given conditional and/or unconditional distribution of underlying state variables.

7.3.3 Trending O-U jump-diffusion prices versus Black–Scholes, Merton jump-diffusion, and Lo–Wang model prices

In this section, we will investigate the joint effect of predictability and discontinuity in asset returns on option prices by comparing the option prices based on the Black–Scholes (1973) model, the Merton (1976a) model and the Lo–Wang (1995) model with those based on the trending O-U jump-diffusion model in Section 7.2.4. The question we raise and will be answered in this chapter is as follows. If the true process for the underlying asset price is described by the trending O-U jump-diffusion process in (7.16), but investor A believes that the asset price dynamics follow a continuous sample path process with a constant variance per unit time, therefore asset returns are perfectly unpredictable, so the investor uses the standard Black–Scholes option price formula (7.2) to evaluate the options on the asset. Investor B believes that the asset price dynamics also follow a continuous sample path process with a constant variance per unit time but a linear mean reverting drift, therefore asset returns are perfectly predictable, so the investor also uses the standard Black–Scholes option price formula (7.2) to evaluate options on the asset but with the input of an adjusted volatility based on the level of first-order autocorrelation. Investor C believes that the asset price dynamics follow a jump-diffusion process and the logarithmic asset price is a random walk, therefore asset returns are perfectly unpredictable, so the investor uses Merton's jump-diffusion option price formula (7.8) to evaluate the options on the asset. How will investors A, B and C's appraised values compare with the true values based on the correct process?

To make the comparison feasible and to clarify the nature of the misspecification, it is further assumed as in Merton (1976b) that $Y(t)$ is i.i.d. lognormal, i.e. $\ln Y(t) \sim N(-\frac{1}{2}\nu^2, \nu^2)$ or $\alpha_0 = E[Y(t) - 1] = 0$. In the next section we will relax this assumption and assume that $Y(t)$ is not i.i.d. but temporally correlated. For the true process, let $N\nu^2$ be the jump volatility over the τ-period, where N is a Poisson-distributed random variable with intensity parameter $\lambda\tau$. So the true jump volatility observed is $n\nu^2$ when $N = n$. The true option price is given by (7.8) with input of the conditional volatility $V_n = \sigma^2\tau + n\nu^2$ in the risk-neutral specification. Suppose there is one discretely sampled path of the process over τ-intervals with a sampling period long enough and a sample size large enough so that the sample moments are the same as the population moments. Let $\bar{r}_\tau$ be the mean of the sample and $s^2(r_\tau)$ the variance of the sample. We have

$$\bar{r}_\tau = \mu\tau, \quad s^2(r_\tau) = \frac{1 - e^{-\beta\tau}}{\beta}(\sigma^2 + \lambda\nu^2)$$

$$\rho_\tau(1) = -\frac{1}{2}(1 - e^{-\beta\tau}) \tag{7.33}$$

Trending O-U jump-diffusion price versus Black–Scholes price

For investor A, since it is believed that the underlying asset return process is a Brownian motion with a drift process or a random walk with drift, the distribution is totally determined by its first two moments, the constant drift and diffusion coefficients can be determined by matching the moments,

$$\bar{r}_\tau = \mu_A \tau, \ s^2(r_\tau) = \sigma_A^2 \tau$$

$$\rho_\tau(1) = 0 \tag{7.34}$$

The option price formula used by A is the Black–Scholes formula with input of the volatility σ_A^2.

The difference between investor A's price and the true price is due to the missing of both jump and predictability. Even though both processes are matched to the same data-generating process, the induced conditional volatility for the two models is different, i.e.

$$\sigma_A^2 \tau \neq E[V_n] = (\sigma^2 + \lambda \nu^2)\tau \tag{7.35}$$

unless $\beta = 0$. Since

$$\beta = -\frac{1}{\tau} ln(1 + 2\rho_\tau(1)) \tag{7.36}$$

The relationship between σ_A^2 and $E[V_n]$ can be derived as

$$\sigma_A^2 = \frac{2\rho_\tau(1)}{ln(1 + 2\rho_\tau(1))}(\sigma^2 + \lambda\nu^2), \rho_\tau \in (-\tfrac{1}{2}, 0] \tag{7.37}$$

It can be verified that $2\rho_\tau(1)/ln(1 + 2\rho_\tau(1)) \to 1$ as $\rho_\tau(1) \to 0$ and 0 as $\rho_\tau(1) \to -\frac{1}{2}$, and is a decreasing function of the absolute value of $\rho_\tau(1)$, therefore $2\rho_\tau(1)/ln(1 + 2\rho_\tau(1))$ will be less than or equal to one for $\rho_\tau(1) \in (-\frac{1}{2}, 0]$.

Figures 7.10–7.12 illustrate how the trending O-U jump-diffusion prices and Black–Scholes prices differ. Due to the presence of jump, Black–Scholes tends to overestimate near-the-money options and underestimate deep OTM and ITM options, while due to the presence of predictability induced by linear mean-reverting drift function, the Black–Scholes model tends to underestimate all options as $\sigma_A^2 \leq \sigma^2 + \lambda\nu^2$. While the jump factor has more impact on the short-term options, the presence of predictability has more impact on long-term options. When both factors are present, there is a trade-off for the valuation of near-the-money options. Figures 7.10(a), 7.10(b), 7.11(a) and 7.11(b) show that when the jump factor is relatively small ($\gamma = 1/4$), all options tend to be underpriced by the Black–Scholes model. As expected, the mispricing is most severe for long-term options in terms of the absolute

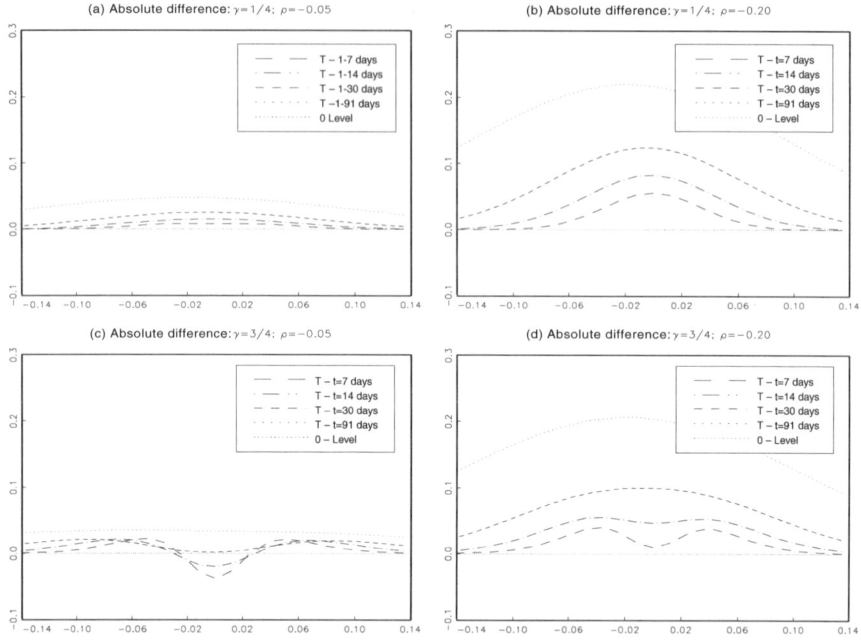

Figure 7.10 Trending O-U J-D prices versus Black–Scholes (1973) prices – absolute differences (trending O-U J-D price – B–S price). Setting stock price $P = \$40.00$, strike price $K = \$35.00$, \$50.00], time to maturity $\tau = 7$, 14, 30, 91 days, annualized compound risk-free rate $r = 5\%$. Parameter values $\lambda = 0.1$, (a) $\sigma^2 = 0.3 \times (0.02)^2$, $\lambda\nu^2 = 0.1 \times (0.02)^2$, $\gamma = 1/4$. $\rho = -0.05$; (b) $\sigma^2 = 0.3 \times (0.02)^2$, $\lambda\nu^2 = 0.1 \times (0.02)^2$, $\gamma = 1/4$, $\rho = -0.20$; (c) $\sigma^2 = 0.1 \times (0.02)^2$, $\lambda\nu^2 = 0.3 \times (0.02)^2$, $\gamma = 3/4$, $\rho = -0.05$; and (d) $\sigma^2 = 0.1 \times (0.02)^2$, $\lambda\nu^2 = 0.3 \times (0.02)^2$, $\gamma = 3/4$, $\rho = -0.20$

differences and for deep OTM options in terms of the percentage differences. Figures 7.10(c), 7.10(d), 7.11(c) and 7.11(d) show that as the jump factor increases to $\gamma = 3/4$, the Black–Scholes model tends to underprice short-term near-the-money options when the predictability is weak (low value of $|\rho|$). However, as $|\rho|$ increases, the near-the-money options are again undervalued by the Black–Scholes model when $|\rho|$ increases to 20%. In this case, the mispricing is most severe for both long-term options and near-the-money short-term options in terms of absolute differences. Also as expected, the implied volatility 'smile' is more pronounced for models with larger jump factors, as illustrated in Figures 7.12(c) and 7.12(d) compared to Figures 7.3(a) and 7.3(b). The differences between implied Black–Scholes volatilities are affected by both the jump factor and the predictability. Similarly, the implied Black–Scholes volatility is higher than the historical Black–Scholes volatility, especially for models with higher absolute values of autocorrelations or stronger predictability.

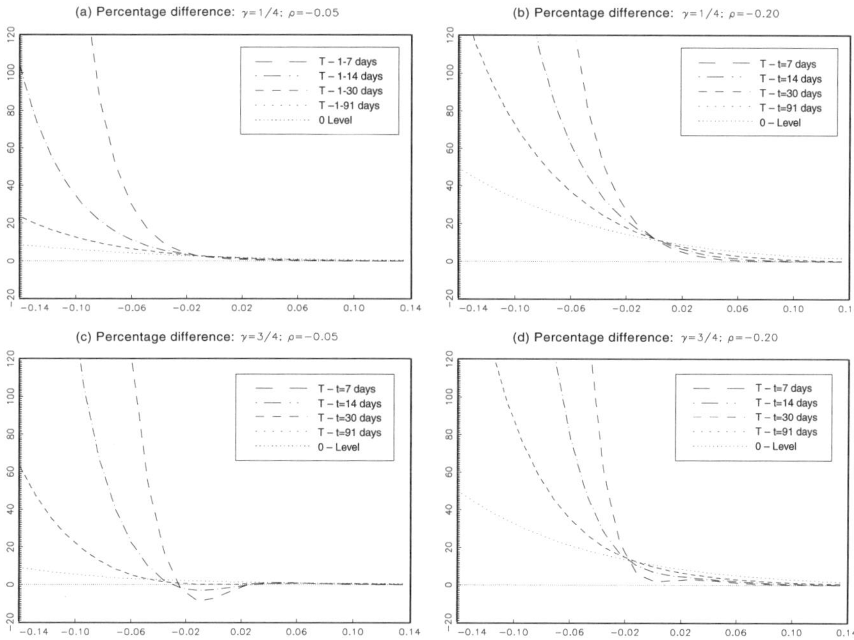

Figure 7.11 Trending O-U J-D prices versus Black–Scholes (1973) prices – percentage differences ([trending O-U J-D price – B–S price]/B–S price). Setting stock price $P = \$40.00$, strike price $K = [\$35.00, \$50.00]$, time to maturity $\tau = 7$, 14, 30, 91 days, annualized compound risk-free rate $r = 5\%$. Parameter values $\lambda = 0.1$, (a) $\sigma^2 = 0.3 \times (0.02)^2$, $\lambda\nu^2 = 0.1 \times (0.02)^2$, $\gamma = 1/4$. $\rho = -0.05$; (b) $\sigma^2 = 0.3 \times (0.02)^2$, $\lambda\nu^2 = 0.1 \times (0.02)^2$, $\gamma = 1/4$, $\rho = -0.20$; (c) $\sigma^2 = 0.1 \times (0.02)^2$, $\lambda\nu^2 = 0.3 \times (0.02)^2$, $\gamma = 3/4$, $\rho = -0.05$; and (d) $\sigma^2 = 0.1 \times (0.02)^2$, $\lambda\nu^2 = 0.3 \times (0.02)^2$, $\gamma = 3/4$, $\rho = -0.20$

Trending O-U jump-diffusion price versus Lo–Wang price

Investor B believes that the underlying asset price process also has constant volatility per unit time but the asset return has perfect predictability in terms of autocorrelation due to the linear mean reverting drift function. Investor B also uses the standard Black–Scholes option price formula (7.3) but the input of volatility is adjusted through matching the following unconditional moments:

$$\bar{r}_\tau = \mu_B \tau, \quad s^2(r_\tau) = \frac{1 - e^{-\beta\tau}}{\beta} \sigma_B^2$$

$$\rho_\tau(1) = -\frac{1}{2}(1 - e^{-\beta\tau})$$

In this case, $\sigma_B^2 = E[V_n]/\tau = \sigma^2 + \lambda\nu^2$, i.e. the conditional volatility, is the same as the true model. The only difference is that investor B misspecifies the

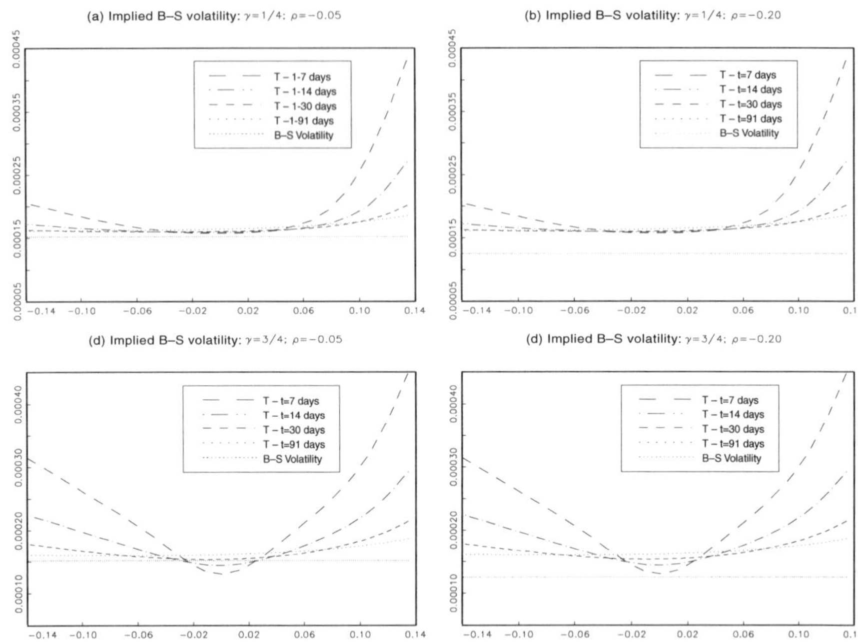

Figure 7.12 Trending O-U J-D prices versus Black–Scholes (1973) prices – implied Black–Scholes volatility. Setting stock price $P = \$40.00$, strike price $K = [\$35.00, \$50.00]$, time to maturity $\tau = 7$, 14, 30, 91 days, annualized compound risk-free rate $r = 5\%$. Parameter values $\lambda = 0.1$, (a) $\sigma^2 = 0.3 \times (0.02)^2$, $\lambda\nu^2 = 0.1 \times (0.02)^2$, $\gamma = 1/4$. $\rho = -0.05$; (b) $\sigma^2 = 0.3 \times (0.02)^2$, $\lambda\nu^2 = 0.1 \times (0.02)^2$, $\gamma = 1/4$, $\rho = -0.20$; (c) $\sigma^2 = 0.1 \times (0.02)^2$, $\lambda\nu^2 = 0.3 \times (0.02)^2$, $\gamma = 3/4$, $\rho = -0.05$; and (d) $\sigma^2 = 0.1 \times (0.02)^2$, $\lambda\nu^2 = 0.3 \times (0.02)^2$, $\gamma = 3/4$, $\rho = -0.20$

true jump-diffusion model as a continuous sample path process. The effect on option prices would be exactly as investigated in Merton (1976b) and Section 7.3.1.

Trending O-U jump-diffusion price versus Merton price

Investor C believes that the underlying asset price process follows a jump-diffusion and the asset returns are perfectly unpredictable and hence uses Merton's option pricing model (7.8). Let $V_C = \sigma_C^2\tau + N\nu_C^2$ be the conditional random volatility of the jump-diffusion process specified by investor C, where N is a Poisson distributed random variable with intensity parameter $\lambda_C\tau$. The parameters are to be estimated from the underlying sampling path and the option prices are to be calculated using the Merton's option pricing model (7.8) with the input of volatility $V_{Cn} = (\sigma_C^2 + n\nu_C)/\tau$ when $N = n$. The expected conditional volatility over the τ-period is $E[V_C] = (\sigma_C^2 + \lambda_C\nu_C^2)\tau$. To determine the parameters' value, one can match the following unconditional moments:

$$\bar{r}_\tau = \mu_C \tau, \;\; s^2(r_\tau) = (\sigma_C^2 + \lambda_C \nu_C^2)\tau$$

$$\rho_\tau(1) = 0 \tag{7.38}$$

from which we expect that the parameter values of σ_C^2, λ_C, and ν_C^2 are different from the true values σ^2, λ and ν^2 as

$$\mu_C = \mu$$

$$(\sigma_C^2 + \lambda_C \nu_C^2)\tau = \frac{1 - e^{-\beta\tau}}{\beta}(\sigma^2 + \lambda\nu^2) \tag{7.39}$$

Since option prices are determined not only by the total value of $(\sigma_C^2 + \lambda_C \nu_C^2)\tau$ but also by the value of $\lambda_C \nu_C^2$ given $(\sigma_C^2 + \lambda_C \nu_C^2)\tau$ and the value of λ_C given $\lambda_C \nu_C^2$, the value of each individual parameter matters. The above moment conditions are not sufficient to determine the values of σ_C^2, λ_C and ν_C^2 given the true parameter values σ^2, λ, and ν^2. We need at least two more moment conditions to determine the parameter values. One way to determine the relationship between the parameters in the misspecified model and the parameters in the true model is to solve for the ML estimators of the above parameters as functions of the parameter values of the true data-generating process. Unfortunately there are no explicit solutions. Here we use the method of cumulants matching, a variant of method of moments, to identify the parameter values.[19]

Let $K_i, i = 1, 2, ...,$ be the ith cumulant of the random variable. Based on the model specified by investor C, i.e. the model in Merton (1976b), one can derive that

$$K_1 = \mu_C \tau, \;\; K_2 = (\sigma_C^2 + \lambda_C \nu_C^2)\tau$$

$$K_3 = K_5 = 0, \;\; K_4 = 3\nu_C^4 \lambda_C \tau_C, \;\; K_6 = 15\nu_C^6 \lambda_C \tau_C \tag{7.40}$$

[19]The method of cumulants matching are often used in the finance literature to estimate jump-diffusion processes, see e.g. Press (1967), and Beckers (1981). As always, since the underlying model is misspecified, strictly speaking such an approach may involve both specification risk and estimation risk in pricing options as the choice of different cumulants may lead to different relationships between the misspecified parameters and the true parameters. However, investor C is not aware of the estimation risk as he believes that the specified process represents the true data-generating process (DGP) and the parameters are as if identified from the population instead of the sampling observations. In addition, the focus of this section is on misspecification errors instead of estimation errors which we will discuss in Section 7.4.

from which we can solve for

$$\mu_C = K_1/\tau, \;\; \lambda_C = 25K_4^3/3K_6^2\tau$$

$$\sigma_C^2 = K_2/\tau - 5K_4^2/3K_6\tau, \;\; \nu^2 = K_6/5K_4 \tag{7.41}$$

Based on the true O-U jump-diffusion process in (25), one can derive that (see Appendix)

$$K_1 = \mu\tau, \;\; K_2 = \frac{\sigma^2 + \lambda\nu^2}{\beta}(1 - e^{-\beta\tau}), \;\; K_3 = K_5 = 0$$

$$K_4 = \frac{3\lambda\nu^4}{4\beta}(1 - e^{-4\beta\tau} + (1 - e^{-\beta\tau})^4)$$

$$K_6 = \frac{15\lambda\nu^6}{6\beta}(1 - e^{-6\beta\tau} + (1 - e^{-\beta\tau})^6) \tag{7.42}$$

Matching the cumulants of the true data-generating process and those of the misspecified model, we have

$$\mu_C = \mu$$

$$\lambda_C = \frac{9(1 - e^{-4\beta\tau} + (1 - e^{-\beta\tau})^4)^3}{16\beta\tau(1 - e^{-6\beta\tau} + (1 - e^{-\beta\tau})^6)^2}\lambda$$

$$\sigma_C^2 = \frac{\sigma^2 + \lambda\nu^2}{\beta\tau}(1 - e^{-\beta\tau}) - \frac{3\lambda\nu^2}{8\beta\tau}\frac{(1 - e^{-4\beta\tau} + (1 - e^{-\beta\tau})^4)^2}{1 - e^{-6\beta\tau} + (1 - e^{-\beta\tau})^6}$$

$$\nu_C^2 = \frac{2\nu^2}{3}\frac{1 - e^{-6\beta\tau} + (1 - e^{-\beta\tau})^6}{1 - e^{-4\beta\tau} + (1 - e^{-\beta\tau})^4} \tag{7.43}$$

It can be verified that as $\rho_\tau(1) \to 0$ or $\beta \to 0$, $\lambda_C = \lambda, \sigma_C^2 = \sigma^2$, and $\nu_C^2 = \nu^2$. It can also be verified that, for $\rho_\tau(1) \in (-\frac{1}{2}, 1]$ or $\beta \in [0, +\infty)$, λ_C is increasing with λ, $\lambda_C \leq \lambda$ and λ_C is a decreasing function of the absolute value of $\rho_\tau(1)$ or β; ν_C^2 is also increasing with ν^2, $\nu_C^2 \leq \nu^2$ and ν_C^2 is an convex function of the absolute value of $\rho_\tau(1)$ or β; σ_C^2 is increasing with both σ^2 and ν^2, the relationship between σ_C^2 and β or $\rho_\tau(1)$ depends on the values of σ^2, λ, and ν^2. Further, $\gamma_C = \lambda_C\nu_C^2/(\sigma_C^2 + \lambda_C\nu_C^2) \leq \gamma = \lambda\nu^2/(\sigma^2 + \lambda\nu^2)$ and γ_C is a convex function of the absolute value of $\rho_\tau(1)$ or β; $\omega_C = \lambda_C/(\sigma_C^2 + \lambda_C\nu_C^2) \geq \omega = \lambda/(\sigma^2 + \lambda\nu^2)$ and ω_C is a concave function of $\rho_\tau(1)$ or β. The first relationship indicates that the misspecified model predicts a weaker jump factor in pricing options, while the second relationship indicates that the misspecified model predicts a stronger jump factor in pricing options. The exact effect is due to the dominance between these two effects.

Figures 7.13 and 7.14 illustrate the differences between trending O-U jump-diffusion prices and Merton (1976a) prices. In Figures 7.13(a), 7.13(b), 7.14(a) and 7.14(b) when the jump factor is relatively small, $\gamma = 1/4$, similar to the differences between the Lo–Wang (1995) model and the Black–Scholes (1973) model, all options are undervalued by the Merton model when the predictability induced by the linear mean-reverting function is present, with near-the-money and long-term options having the most severe absolute biases and deep OTM and long-term options the most severe relative percentage biases. However, when the jump factor increases to $\gamma = 1$, that is, the process is a pure jump process, the jump factor dominates for the short-term near-the-money options. As a result, the Merton model tends to overestimate short-term near-the-money options, while still significantly underestimating other options.

As noted, the above trending O-U jump-diffusion process permits only negative autocorrelations of all orders for the asset returns and restricts the patterns of predictability. A remedy of this drawback is an extension of the drift term to include more stochastic state variables, such as the bivariate trending O-U jump-diffusion process. However, like the bivariate O-U process in Lo and Wang (1995), there is no longer a simple relationship between autocorrelation and the conditional volatility. Thus there is no simple adjustment to the input of conditional volatility in the option pricing formula as we have seen. The bivariate O-U jump-diffusion model can serve as an example to show explicitly that increasing autocorrelation can affect option prices in either direction, depending on the particular specification of the drift function (see Lo and Wang, 1995). Unless predictability is defined in a specific manner as in Lo and Wang (1995) in which there is an unambiguous relation between predictability and option prices,[20] a simple relation between predictability and option prices is not available.

3.4 Option prices with predictable jump size versus Black–Scholes and Merton prices

Implications of the predictable jump sizes on option prices compared to the Black–Scholes option prices and Merton jump-diffusion option prices can be investigated similarly. If there is a large enough sample over a sufficiently long sampling period so that both the Black–Scholes volatility σ^2_{BS} and the

[20]The most common definition of predictability is the R^2 coefficient, i.e. the fraction of the unconditional variance of the dependent variable that is 'explained' by the conditional mean or predictor. This interpretation is appropriate with following three additional restrictions: (1) the unconditional variance of returns is fixed; (2) the drift is not a function of the log-price process (i.e. $\beta = 0$); (3) W_q and W_x are statistically independent. Under these restrictions, it may be shown that an increase in predictability, measured by R^2, always decreases σ and therefore decreases option prices.

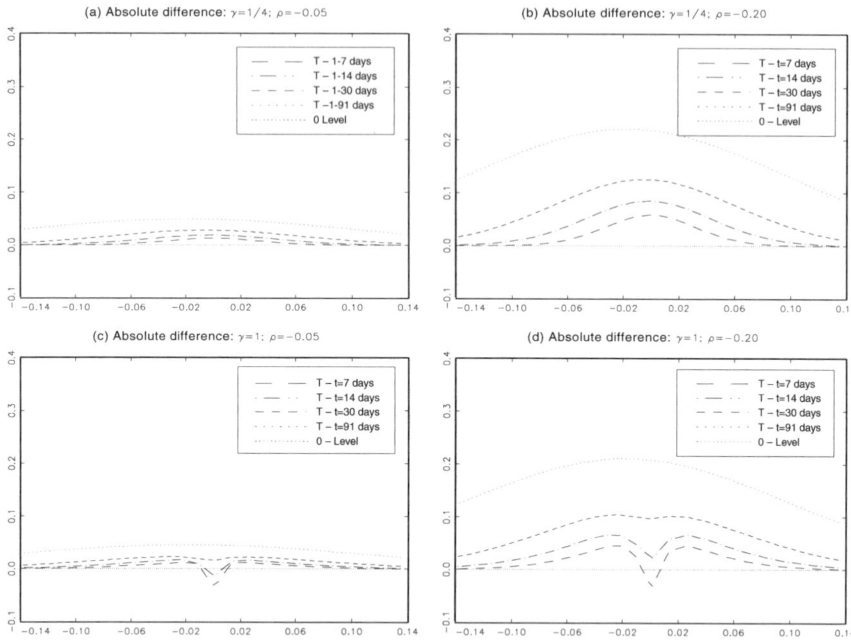

Figure 7.13 Trending O-U J-D prices versus Merton (1976a) prices – absolute differences (trending O-U J-D price – Merton price). Setting stock price $P = \$40.00$, strike price $K = [\$35.00, \$50.00]$, time to maturity $\tau = 7$, 14, 30, 91 days, annualized compound risk-free rate $r = 5\%$. Parameter values $\lambda = 0.1$, (a) $\sigma^2 = 0.3 \times (0.02)^2$, $\lambda\nu^2 = 0.1 \times (0.02)^2$, $\gamma = 1/4$, $\rho = -0.05$; (b) $\sigma^2 = 0.3 \times (0.02)^2$, $\lambda\nu^2 = 0.1 \times (0.02)^2$, $\gamma = 1/4$, $\rho = -0.20$; (c) $\sigma^2 = 0.00$, $\lambda\nu^2 = 0.4 \times (0.02)^2$, $\gamma = 1$, $\rho = -0.05$; and (d) $\sigma^2 = 0.00$, $\lambda\nu^2 = 0.4 \times (0.02)^2$, $\gamma = 1$, $\rho - -0.20$

parameters of Merton jump-diffusion volatility V_M can be identified by matching to the moments of true distribution (see Appendix), we have the volatility input of the Black–Scholes option pricing formula

$$\sigma_{BS}^2 = \sigma^2 + \frac{\lambda\sigma_Y^2}{2\xi} \tag{7.44}$$

and the input of the Merton jump-diffusion option pricing formula

$$V_M^n = \sigma^2 + n\frac{\sigma_Y^2}{2\xi} \tag{7.45}$$

where n is Poisson-distributed with intensity λ, i.e. $E[V_M^n] = \sigma^2 + \lambda\sigma_Y^2/2\xi$. The Black–Scholes option prices are given by (7.2) with σ_{BS}^2 as input of volatility, while the Merton jump-diffusion prices are given by (7.8) with V_M^n as input of volatility. Under the assumption that risk associated with the jump and jump size process is non-systematic and diversifiable, a similar PDE as (7.6) can be

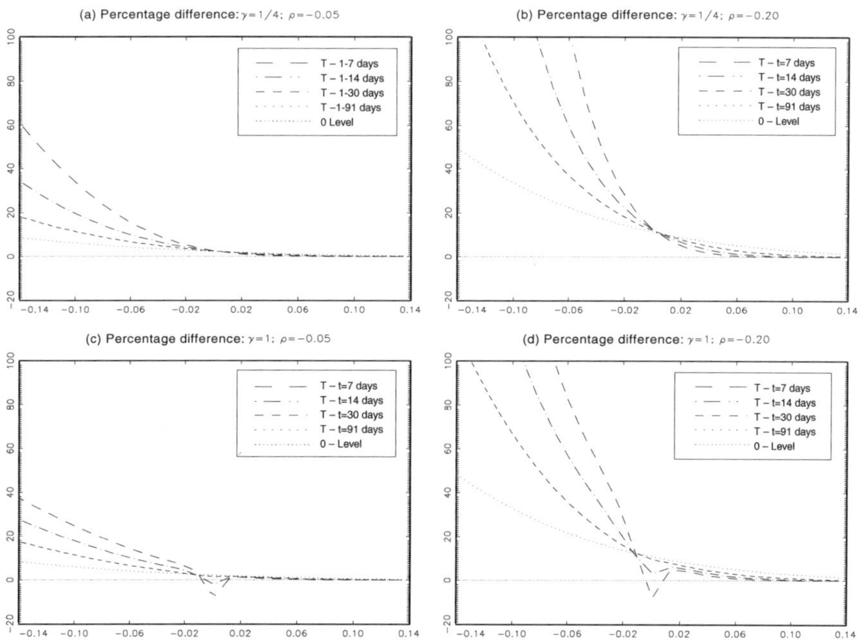

Figure 7.14 Trending O-U J-D prices versus Merton (1976a) prices – percentage differences ([trending OU JD – Merton price]/Merton price). Setting stock price $P = \$40.00$, strike price $K = [\$35.00, \$50.00]$, time to maturity $\tau = 7, 14, 30, 91$ days, annualized compound risk-free rate $r = 5\%$. Parameter values $\lambda = 0.1$, (a) $\sigma^2 = 0.3 \times (0.02)^2$, $\lambda\nu^2 = 0.1 \times (0.02)^2$, $\gamma = 1/4$, $\rho = -0.05$; (b) $\sigma^2 = 0.3 \times (0.02)^2$, $\lambda\nu^2 = 0.1 \times (0.02)^2$, $\gamma = 1/4$, $\rho = -0.20$; (c) $\sigma^2 = 0.00$, $\lambda\nu^2 = 0.4 \times (0.02)^2$, $\gamma = 1$, $\rho = -0.05$; and (d) $\sigma^2 = 0.00$, $\lambda\nu^2 = 0.4 \times (0.02)^2$, $\gamma = 1$, $\rho = -0.20$

derived for the call option prices except that the expectation of the jump component is conditional on initial time t. The true option prices, however, do not have a closed-form solution due to the dependence of jump size, but can be obtained through Monte Carlo simulation based on the risk-neutral specification of the asset price process where the instantaneous return of the asset is replaced by the risk-free rate of return.[21] The simulation of the jump component is based on the discrete approximation of Euler scheme, i.e. $\int_{t_0}^{t_0+\tau} lnY(t)dQ_\lambda(t) \approx \sum_{i=0}^{M} lnY(t_0 + i\Delta)(Q_\lambda(t_0 + (i+1)\Delta) - Q_\lambda(t_0 + i\Delta))$ where $\Delta = \tau/M$, $lnY(t_0 + i\Delta) = e^{-\xi\Delta} lnY(t_0 + (i-1)\Delta) + \int_{t_0+(i-1)\Delta}^{t_0+i\Delta} e^{-\xi(t_0+i\Delta-t)}\sigma_Y dW_Y(t)$ and $Q_\lambda(t_0 + (i+1)\Delta) - Q_\lambda(t_0 + i\Delta) \sim$ Poisson distribution with intensity parameter $\lambda\Delta$. The discretization error of the approximation goes to zero uniformly in probability over a finite time interval as the discretization interval goes to zero, i.e. $M \to \infty$ (see Protter and Talay,

[21]For the same reasons as the Merton (1976a) jump-diffusion model, the model specified here with modified parameters is also relevant in pricing options even under a non-diversifiable jump risk or more general distributional assumptions.

1996). In our simulation, the initial jump size is randomly drawn from its marginal distribution using the fact that $lnY(t_0) \sim N(0, \frac{\sigma_Y^2}{2\xi})$ and the dynamics of the jump size is simulated following the exact dynamic path using the fact that $\int_{t_0+(i-1)\Delta}^{t_0+i\Delta} e^{-\xi(t_0+i\Delta-t)}\sigma_Y dW_Y(t) \sim N(0, \frac{\sigma_Y^2}{2\xi}(1-e^{-2\xi\Delta}))$. Throughout the simulation, the antithetic variable technique is used to reduce the variation of the option prices (see Boyle, Broadie and Glasserman, 1996). The discretization interval is set as 10 intervals per day and the number of replication is set as 50, 000.

Figures 7.15–7.17 compare the option prices generated by jump-diffusion process with predictable jump sizes with Black–Scholes option prices, and Figures 7.18, and 7.19 compare the option prices generated by the jump-diffusion process with predictable jump sizes with Merton (1976a) option prices. As expected, the pricing errors for both the Black–Scholes model and the Merton model increase as the predictability of the jump size increases, i.e. the value of the memory duration parameter ξ decreases. Overall, the Merton (1976a) model tends to underprice options, and the absolute pricing errors are most severe for long-term options. This is similar to the case of predictable asset returns in which the first conditional moment of asset returns is predictable, while in this case when the jump size is predictable, both the first and second conditional moments of asset returns are predictable. The relative percentage errors of the Merton model are most severe for OTM options, more significantly for short-maturity options when ξ is high or the predictability of jump size is low but for all options including long-maturity options when ξ is low or the predictability of jump size is high. The pricing errors of the Black–Scholes model is mixed due to the misspecification of both jump and conditional heteroscedasticity induced by predictable jump sizes. Since the predictability of jump size has more impact on long-maturity options and the jump component has a greater effect on short-maturity options, the Black–Scholes model tends to underprice long-maturity options as well. For short-term options, it tends to overprice near-the-money options but underprice both deep ITM and OTM options. Similarly, the relative pricing errors are most severe for deep OTM options, more significantly for short-maturity options when ξ is high or the predictability of jump size is low but for all options including long-maturity options when ξ is low or the predictability of jump size is high. The implied volatility of the option prices generated from the jump-diffusion process with predictable jump size is obviously U-shaped, and the *smile* is more pronounced for short-maturity options. For long-maturity options, the implied volatility is almost flat across different degrees of moneyness. Still, in general the implied Black–Scholes volatility is higher than the underlying volatility, in particular for a lower value of ξ or a higher predictability of jump sizes.

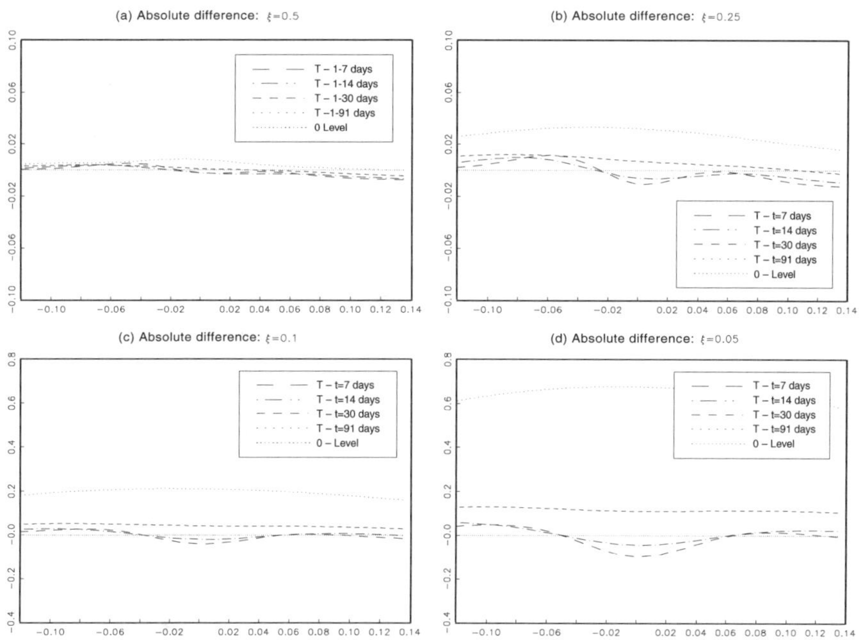

Figure 7.15 Prices with predictable jump size versus Black–Scholes (1973) prices – absolute differences (J-D price – Black–Scholes price). Setting stock price $P = \$40.00$, strike price $K = [\$35.00, \$50.00]$, time to maturity $\tau = 7$, 14, 30, 91 days, annualized compound risk-free rate $r = 5\%$. Parameter values $\lambda = 0.1$, $\sigma^2 = 0.3 \times (0.02)^2$, $\sigma_{BS}^2 = \sigma^2 + \lambda(\sigma_Y^2/2\xi)$. The conditional volatility of jump size process: $\sigma_Y^2 = (0.02)^2$, and the mean-reversion parameter: (a) $\xi = 0.5$; (b) $\xi = 0.25$; (c) $\xi = 0.1$; and (d) $\xi = 0.05$

7.4 DISCUSSION OF RELATED ISSUES

7.4.1 Information contained in historical asset prices and option prices

The dynamics of an asset's price movement are reflected in the historical price series, and such information is often referred as *primitive* information. When options on the asset are also traded on exchanges, the observed prices represent another source of information on the asset price dynamics, which is often referred as *derivative* information. While the primitive information consists of historical observations, the derivative information represents a market's forecast of the asset price movements in the future. As Melino (1994) also argues, since information about the stochastic properties of an asset price movements is contained in both the history of the price series as well as the prices of any options written on it, it is thus important and natural to combine two sources of information in model specification and selection as well as pricing options.

However, in practice the historical time series of asset prices are not always

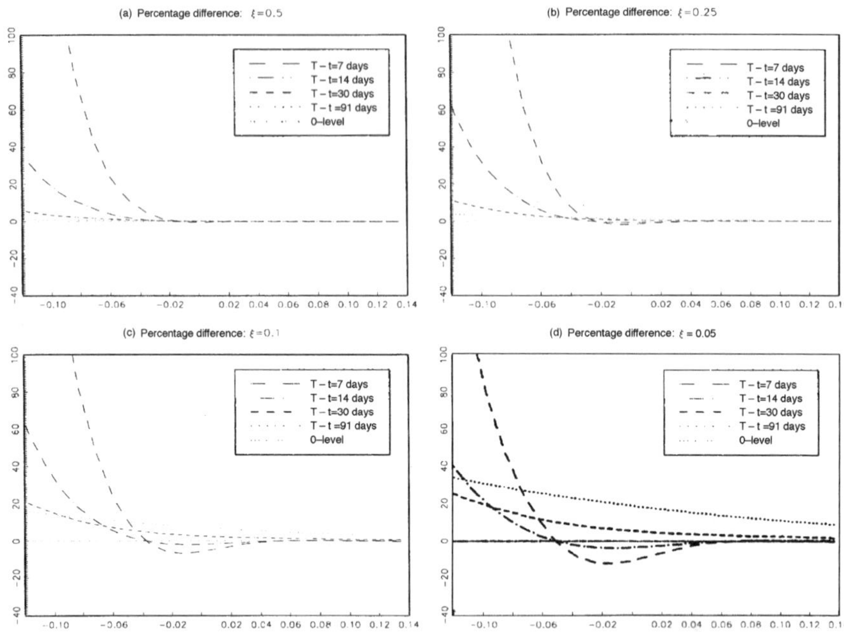

Figure 7.16 Prices with predictable jump size versus Black–Scholes (1973) prices – percentage differences ([J-D price – B-S price]/B-S price). Setting stock price $P = \$40.00$, strike price $K = [\$35.00, \$50.00]$, time to maturity $\tau = 7$, 14, 30, 91 days, annualized compound risk-free rate $r = 5\%$. Parameter values $\lambda = 0.1$, $\sigma^2 = 0.3 \times (0.02)^2$, $\sigma^2_{BS} = \sigma^2 + \lambda(\sigma^2_Y/2\xi)$. The conditional volatility of jump size process: $\sigma^2_Y = (0.02)^2$, and the mean-reversion parameter: (a) $\xi = 0.5$; (b) $\xi = 0.25$; (c) $\xi = 0.1$; and (d) $\xi = 0.05$

available. Even they are, it is not always easy to estimate the underlying model due to its complicated structure. Alternatively, a commonly used estimation method is to imply the underlying price process from observed market option prices. The problem with the use of the implied estimation method is that many applications often rely solely on the option prices observed at a single point of time to estimate (or back up) the underlying state variable dynamics and predict future (out-of-sample) option prices. From a statistical point of view, such a procedure has a few drawbacks. First, implied in the option prices is only the risk-neutral specification of underlying asset return dynamics in the equivalent martingale measure. Therefore the estimated model can only provide partial information for whether the underlying model specification in the objective measure is a reasonable representation of the true data-generating process. Second, in general the derivatives are less actively traded and less liquid than the underlying asset. Thus the options' trading is more subject to market microstructure-related spurious effects and thus the option prices tend to contain more noise. Apart from the fact that most option prices and underlying asset prices are not observed synchronously as they are often

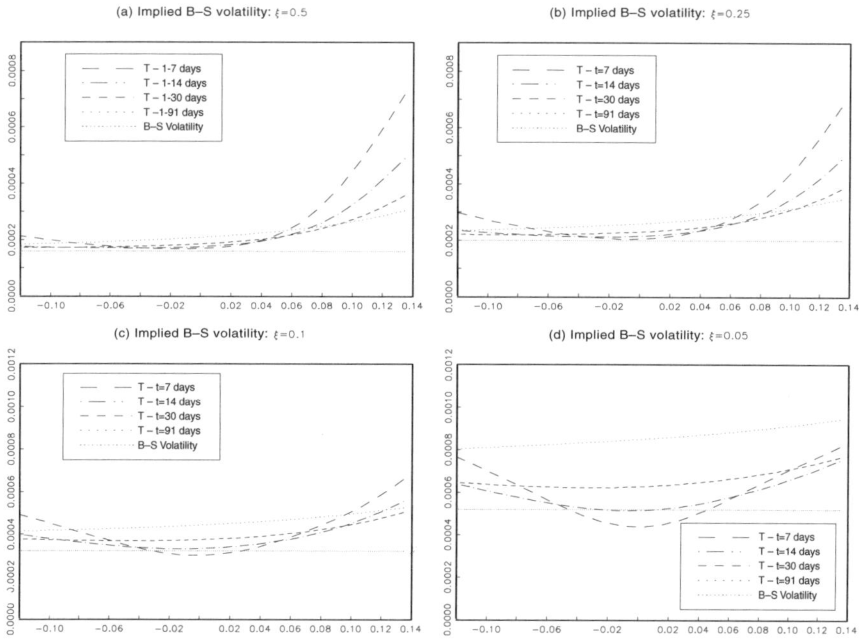

Figure 7.17 Prices with predictable jump size versus Black–Scholes (1973) prices – implied Black–Scholes volatility. Setting stock price $P = \$40.00$, strike price $K = [\$35.00, \$50.00]$, time to maturity $\tau = 7$, 14, 30, 91 days, annualized compound risk-free rate $r = 5\%$. Parameter values $\lambda = 0.1$, $\sigma^2 = 0.3 \times (0.02)^2$, $\sigma^2_{BS} = \sigma^2 + \lambda(\sigma^2_Y/2\xi)$. The conditional volatility of jump size process: $\sigma^2_Y = (0.02)^2$, and the mean-reversion parameter: (a) $\xi = 0.5$; (b) $\xi = 0.25$; (c) $\xi = 0.1$; and (d) $\xi = 0.05$.

traded in different markets, such noises can severely contaminate the estimation results and invalidate the statistical tests. Third, the option prices observed at a single point of time often fail to provide sufficient information to identify the dynamic properties of the underlying asset returns. This is evidenced in the dramatic day-to-day changes of the implied parameter values due to poor identification of the model. As Bates (1994) points out, one implication of the identification problem is that the parameter estimates of the model are uninformative. For instance, two sets of different parameter values can lead to similar sums of squared errors, which further invalidates any statistical tests of the model. Finally, the information contained in the sampling observations of underlying asset prices is neglected, which reduces the efficiency of the estimation procedure.

To combine both the primitive and derivative information the key is to identify the relationship between the specification of the price process of the underlying asset under the objective measure and the risk-neutral specification of the price process under the equivalent martingale measure. A general

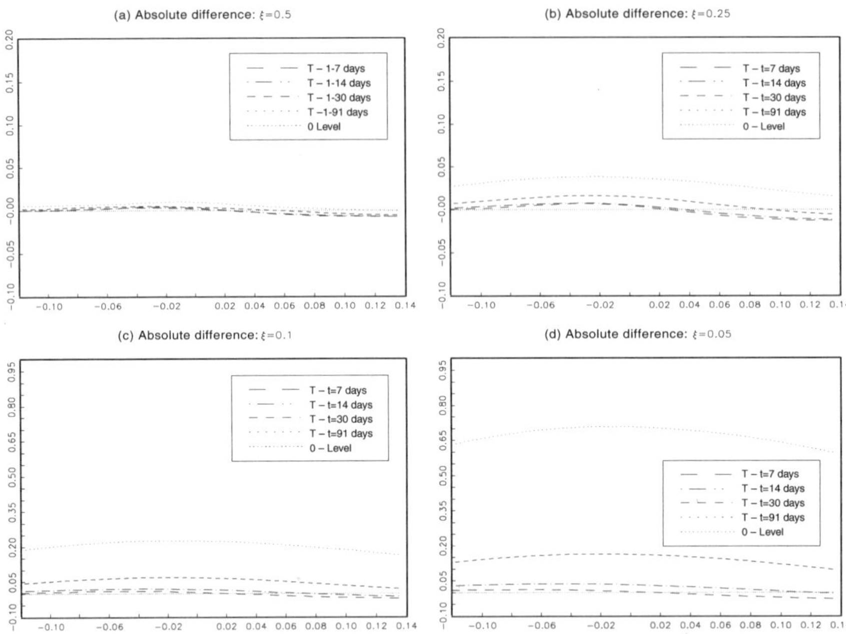

Figure 7.18 Prices with predictable jump size versus Merton (1976a) prices – absolute differences (J-D price – Merton price). Setting stock price $P = \$40.00$, strike price $K = [\$35.00, \$50.00]$, time to maturity $\tau = 7$, 14, 30, 91 days, annualized compound risk-free rate $r = 5\%$. Parameter values $\lambda = 0.1$, $\sigma^2 = 0.3 \times (0.02)^2$, $\nu^2 = \sigma_Y^2/2\xi$. The conditional volatility of jump size process: $\sigma_Y^2 = (0.02)^2$, and the mean-reversion parameter: (a) $\xi = 0.5$; (b) $\xi = 0.25$; (c) $\xi = 0.1$; and (d) $\xi = 0.05$

specification of an asset price process typically consists of the following terms: the conditionally non-stochastic time trend representing the asset's rate of return, and the conditionally stochastic components driven by random noises representing various risk factors. In the continuous-time framework, typically the components associated with risk factors, e.g. the conditional volatility, the jump volatility and the correlation between risk factors, are identical in both the objective model specification and risk-neutral specification, while the conditionally non-stochastic time trend, i.e. the drift term in the objective measure specification, is modified for the adjustment or compensation of risk factors in the risk-neutral specification (see e.g. Bates, 1988, 1991). While compensations for risk factors are determined by investors' preferences in the equilibrium and can be inferred from information of the market including the options market, the risk factors associated with an individual asset can in general be identified from the historical sampling path. From such a point of view, specification of the underlying asset price process is relevant in pricing options and thus the primitive information is also important. Furthermore,

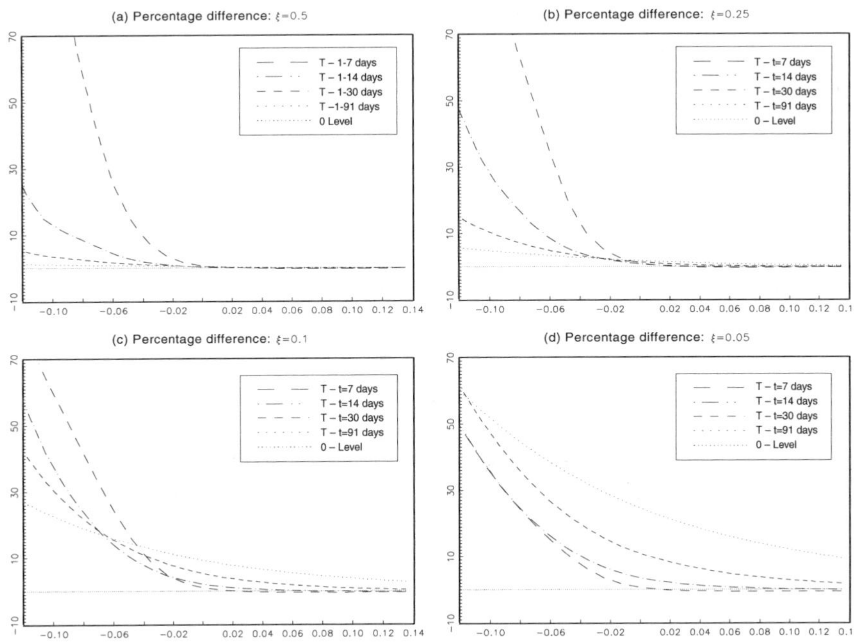

Figure 7.19 Prices with predictable jump size versus Merton (1976a) prices – percentage differences ([J-D price – Merton price]/Merton price). Setting stock price $P = \$40.00$, strike price $K = [\$35.00, \$50.00]$, time to maturity $\tau = 7$, 14, 30, 91 days, annualized compound risk-free rate $r = 5\%$. Parameter values $\lambda = 0.1$, $\sigma^2 = 0.3 \times (0.02)^2$, $\nu^2 = \sigma_Y^2/2\xi$. The conditional volatility of jump size process: $\sigma_Y^2 = (0.02)^2$, and the mean-reversion parameter: (a) $\xi = 0.5$; (b) $\xi = 0.25$; (c) $\xi = 0.1$; and (d) $\xi = 0.05$

from a model specification and selection point of view, it is important to investigate the impact of certain specification of the underlying asset price processes on option prices. In addition, such a study is very useful in terms of linking and properly utilizing both that in the option prices and the information contained in the historical prices of underlying assets.

7.4.2 Interplay between jump and stochastic volatility

As we have mentioned, there have been many models with changing volatility, such as ARCH/GARCH and stochastic volatility (SV) models, proposed in the literature for the asset return process. Consider the following discrete-time SV model for the time-detrended asset return:

$$r_t = \sigma_t \epsilon_t, \quad t = 1, 2, ..., T \tag{7.46}$$

or

$$r_t = \sigma \epsilon_t \exp\{h_t/2\}, \quad t = 1, 2, ..., T \tag{7.47}$$

where ϵ_t is a i.i.d. random noise with a standard distribution, e.g. normal distribution or Student-t distribution. The most popular SV specification assumes that h_t follows an AR(1) process, as proposed by Taylor (1986), i.e.

$$h_{t+1} = \phi h_t + \eta_t, |\phi| < 1 \tag{7.48}$$

which is a special case of the general stochastic autoregressive volatility (SARV) model defined in Andersen (1994), where $\eta_t \sim$ iid $(0, \sigma_\eta^2)$ and the constant term is removed due to the introduction of the scale parameter σ in (7.47). One interpretation of the latent variable h_t is that it represents the random, uneven and yet autocorrelated flow of new information into financial markets. When ϵ_t and η_t are allowed to be correlated with each other, the above model can pick up the kind of asymmetric behaviour often observed in stock price movements, which is known as the *leverage effect* when the correlation is negative (see Black, 1976). The above SV model has similar implications on the unconditional distribution of the underlying asset returns as the jump-diffusion process. Namely, if η_t is normally distributed and h_t stationary and ϵ_t has finite moments, then all the moments of y_t exist and are given by

$$E[y_t^s] = \sigma^s E[\epsilon_t^s] E[\exp\{sh_t/2\}] = \sigma^s E[\epsilon_t^s] \exp\{s^2\sigma_h^2/8\} \tag{7.49}$$

when s is even and $E[y_t^s] = 0$ when s is odd. In particular, the kurtosis of y_t is $(E[\epsilon_t^4]/\sigma_\epsilon^4)\exp(\sigma_h^2)$ which is greater than $E[\epsilon_t^4]/\sigma_\epsilon^4$, the kurtosis of ϵ_t, as $\exp(\sigma_h^2) > 1$. When ϵ_t is also Gaussian, then $E[\epsilon_t^4]/\sigma_\epsilon^4 = 3$. In other words, the SV model has fatter tails than that of the corresponding noise disturbance of the return process. It is noted that the above properties of the SV model also hold true even if ϵ_t and η_t are contemporarily correlated.

It is obvious that implications of SV on option prices depends critically on the specification of the SV processes, which have been extensively studied in the literature.[22] For instance, based on the SV model specified in Hull and White (1987), they show that when the volatility is uncorrelated with the stock price, the Black–Scholes model underprices the ITM and OTM options and overprices the ATM options. The largest absolute price differences occur at or near the money. The actual magnitude of the pricing error, however, is quite small in general. When the volatility is correlated with the stock price, this ATM overprice continues on to ITM options for positive correlation and to OTM options for negative correlation. In particular, when the volatility is positively correlated with the stock price, the bias of the Black–Scholes model

[22] We mention the numerical studies by Hull and White (1987), Johnson and Shanno (1987), Bailey and Stulz (1989), Stein and Stein (1991), Amin and Ng (1993), and Heston (1993), and empirical studies by Wiggins (1987), Scott (1987), Chesney and Scott (1989), and Melino and Turnbull (1990).

tends to decline as the stock price increases. OTM options are underpriced by the Black–Scholes model, while ITM options are overpriced by it. When the volatility is negatively correlated with the stock price, the reverse is true. OTM options are overpriced by the Black–Scholes model, while ITM options are underpriced by this model.

Since the introduction of jump component and stochastic volatility into the underlying asset return process both are to feature the asymmetry and kurtosis of asset return distributions, it is not surprising to see that they have similar implications on option prices. However, while Merton's (1976a) jump-diffusion model relies on independent fat-tailed distribution due to finite-variance shocks to the underlying asset prices, the SV model assumes instantaneous lognormal asset return distribution and relies on the dynamic properties of the price process to incorporate asymmetry and kurtosis. The numerical findings in the literature as well as in this chapter have confirmed that jumps tends to have more influence on short-term options while the stochastic volatility tend to have more influence on long-term options. In practice, since the phenomenon of implied volatility 'smile' and 'skewness' are more pronounced for the short-maturity options, inclusion of jump the component may be necessary in order to explain the kurtosis and asymmetry in the underlying asset return distributions. Thus, it is important to disentangle the jump component from stochastic volatility in the underlying asset price process. Empirically, such a task proves to be challenging. On the one hand, very often the stochastic volatility could be misidentified as jumps with high frequency and small jump magnitudes, as reported in many empirical studies (see Bates, 1995). On the other hand, if investors believe that the underlying stock price process does not have jump when it actually does and estimate the Black–Scholes model based on historical data over a relatively short time period, they may be led to the inference that the parameters of the process are not constant or the underlying volatility is changing over time even though it may not be (see Merton, 1976b; Renault, 1995). Empirical results in Jiang (1997) show that with the introduction of stochastic volatility into the exchange rate jump-diffusion process, the jump-frequency tends to decrease and the jump volatility to increase. From this point of view, the introduction of stochastic volatility into the model may be helpful in removing the spurious noise which leads to misidentified jumps.

7.4.3 Estimation of diffusion processes and estimation risk

Merton (1976b) argued that if indeed we have a sample of asset price observations and the parameters of the diffusion process are truly constant over the sampling period, then for a fixed number of observations, it is unimportant for estimation of the volatility coefficient of the Brownian with drift process between long and short sampling periods. In this chapter, we argue that when the drift coefficient is also unknown and needs to be estimated, Merton's (1976b) observation is still true. However, we further argue that when the drift function is no longer a constant, the sampling observations with high frequency is preferred to sampling with low frequency in identifying the diffusion coefficient even though both samples are of the same size. Such an argument would be strengthened if one believes that the parameters of the diffusion process are not constant over a long time period. Suppose we have a set of sampling observations $\{P(t_1 = 0), P(t_2), ..., P(t_n = T)\}$ which are realizations of the stochastic process over equal intervals, i.e. $\Delta = t_i - t_{i-1}, \forall i$ and $T = (n-1)\Delta$. The ML estimators of μ and σ^2 for the Brownian motion with drift process are

$$\hat{\mu} = \frac{1}{T}(lnP(T) - lnP(0)), \quad \hat{\sigma}^2 = \frac{1}{T}\sum_{i=2}^{n}(ln(X_{t_i}/X_{t_{i-1}}) - \hat{\mu}\Delta)^2$$

It is noted that the estimate of μ depends only on the first and the last observations of the whole set of sampling observations, even though it is a consistent estimator as $\hat{\mu} \sim N(\mu, \frac{\sigma^2}{T})$. The only way to improve the estimation of μ is to extend the total sampling period T, and the convergence rate in probability is $\sqrt{T}$ or $\sqrt{n-1}$. For the diffusion coefficient estimator, we have:

$$E[\hat{\sigma}^2] = \sigma^2\left(1 - \frac{\Delta}{T}\right), \quad Var[\hat{\sigma}^2] = \frac{2\sigma^4\Delta}{T}\left(1 - \frac{\Delta}{T}\right)$$

From this we can see that the estimation of σ^2 can be improved by either increasing the sampling period T or decreasing the sampling interval Δ. In both cases the sample sizes are increasing and the convergence rates in probability are the same.

However, when the drift term is no longer a constant, sampling observations with high frequency is of advantage. Lo and Wang (1995) point out that any single realization of a *continuous* sample path over a finite interval is sufficient to reveal the true value of σ in the geometric Brownian motion process and the trending O-U process. From equations (7.29) and (7.30) we can see that

$$\sigma_{GB}^2 = \sigma_{OU}^2 + O(\tau) \tag{7.50}$$

i.e. as τ decreases, the difference between σ_{GB}^2 and σ_{OU}^2 is diminishing. That is, when the asset returns are observed over small holding periods, the conditional volatility of the arithmetic Brownian motion process and that of the trending O-U process are very close to each other and the difference falls to zero as the sampling interval decreases. In this case, if there is an allowable estimation error due to specification or identification, there is no need to distinguish between the arithmetic Brownian motion and the trending O-U process. In general, for all diffusion processes, the correlations of the increments is small and goes to zero as the differencing period decreases since the driving random force Brownian motion is increment-dependent. Therefore predictability embedded in the instantaneous drift term no longer matters. This is not contradictory to the results in Lo and Wang (1995). The fact that high-frequency observations over a small holding period give almost the same conditional volatility for the arithmetic Brownian motion and the trending O-U process does not mean that these two processes generate the observations of asset returns over a finite holding period which also gives the same or almost the same unconditional volatility. In other words, if an arithmetic Brownian motion and the trending O-U process have the same conditional volatility, i.e. $\sigma_{AB}^2 = \sigma_{OU}^2$, then the observations of the asset returns over a finite period will not have the same unconditional variance, i.e. $s^2(r_\tau^{AB}(t)) \neq s^2(r_\tau^{OU}(t))$. The claim that the diffusion function can be identified and estimated from high-frequency observations under certain regularity conditions is also true for the non-constant but time stationary function of $\sigma(\cdot)$ (see e.g. Florens-Zmirou, 1993 and Jiang and Knight, 1997). The intuition is that the drift term is of order dt while the diffusion term is of order $\sqrt{dt}$, as $(dW(t))^2 = dt + 0((dt)^2)$, i.e. the diffusion term has a lower order than the drift term for infinitesimal changes in time. Therefore, the local time dynamics of the sampling path reflect more of the properties of the diffusion term than those of the drift term, which suggests the possibility of identifying the diffusion term from high-frequency discrete sampling observations. Such a property is relevant and important in practical applications. With sampling observations of a high enough frequency, the estimation risk for the diffusion coefficient is substantially eliminated and more importantly the drift function specification now becomes really irrelevant. Not only does it not enter into the option pricing formula, but also it would not affect the estimate of the conditional volatility and the option *prices*. The above fact, however, may lead some to advocate using the most finely sampled data available so as to minimize the effects of the drift term. As Lo and Wang (1995) point out, whether or not the most finely sampled data available is fine enough is an empirical issue that depends critically on what the true model is and on the type of market microstructure effects that may come into play.

7.4.4 Estimation of jump-diffusion processes and estimation risk

Merton (1976b) also argued that even though a sample of asset return observations with a high frequency is sufficient for correct identification of the volatility coefficient of the Brownian motion with drift, it is not sufficient to identify the total volatility of the jump diffusion process. In the latter case, a sample of observations over a long time-span is required. Therefore, if indeed we have a very long history of price changes and if the parameters of the process are truly constant over this period, then it is better to use the whole history to estimate the parameters of the jump-diffusion process. In the case of the jump-diffusion model with known constant drift, it can be shown as in Merton (1976b) that the sum of squared differences of the process over equal intervals is a consistent estimator of the total variance, i.e. $\hat{V} = \sum_{i=0}^{n-1}(lnP(t_{i+1}) - lnP(t_i))^2$ where $V = \sigma^2 + \lambda\nu^2$ and

$$E[\hat{V}] = \sigma^2 + \lambda\nu^2, Var[\hat{V}] = [3\lambda\nu^2 + 2\Delta(\lambda\nu^2 + \sigma^2)^2]/T$$

Only if T increases will both the bias and variance go to zero. That is, in contrast to the case of a pure diffusion process, consistent estimation of the jump-diffusion process essentially relies on samples over a long time period. Thus, the desirable sample no longer consists of observations over a finite sampling period with a small sampling interval, instead it consists of prolonging the sampling period in order to increase the sample size with a fixed sampling interval.

Many estimation methods have been proposed in the literature to estimate jump-diffusion models. Unfortunately, all of them require stringent restrictions imposed on the model, namely simple coefficient functions so that either the likelihood function has an explicit functional form or the (un conditional) moments can be explicitly derived. Press (1967) and Beckers (1981) used the method of 'cumulant matching', a variant of the method of moments, on simplified jump-diffusion models. Ball and Torous (1985) used the ML method to estimate the jump-diffusion process as considered in Beckers (1981) through numerically maximizing a truncated likelihood function. Lo (1988) considers ML estimation of a Poisson jump-diffusion process with jump-size determined by the process itself. In addition, Powell (1989), Longstaff (1989) and Ho, Perraudin and Sørensen (1996) considered GMM to estimate the jump-diffusion processes. The problem with empirically estimating the parameters based on arbitrarily chosen moments of jump-diffusion models, such as the method of cumulants matching, the method of moments or GMM, originates from the difficulty in distinguishing whether movements in the underlying process are part of the continuous path dynamics or part of the jump path dynamics. For estimation of a general parametric continuous-time jump-diffusion process, Jiang (1997) proposed using the indirect inference approach developed by Gouriéroux, Monfort and Renault (1993) and Gallant and Tauchen (1996). The basic idea of the indirect inference approach is that when a model leads to a complicated structural or reduced form and therefore to intractable likelihood functions, estimation of the original model can be indirectly achieved by estimating an instrumental or auxiliary model which is constructed as an approximation of the original model. The consistent parameter estimator of the original model is constructed based on simulations, which also achieves small-sample bias correction (see Gouriéroux, Renault and Touzi, 1994). In Jiang (1997), the associated auxiliary model for a general parametric jump-diffusion process is an approximate discrete-time Bernoulli jump process. This model can be easily estimated via the maximum likelihood (ML) estimation method and the discretization biases of the estimators are then corrected based on simulations. To further achieve ML efficiency, a particular indirect inference approach termed the efficient method of moment (EMM) proposed by Gallant and Tauchen (1996) can be employed. The EMM approach relies on calibration of the score generator of the auxiliary model, which embeds the original process. The embeddedness can be achieved by specifying a semi-non-parametric (SNP) score generator (see Gallant and Tauchen, 1996, and Gallant and Long, 1997). It is noted that the indirect inference approach is well suited not only to the estimation of continuous-time models but also to the estimation of dynamic latent variable models, such as the stochastic volatility models, and the jump-diffusion process with predictable jump size considered in this chapter.

7.5 CONCLUSION

In this chapter, we extend the Merton (1976a) jump-diffusion model to incorporate discontinuity and predictability as well as conditional heteroscedasticity of asset returns in pricing options. We investigate the implications of asset returns' predictability, discontinuity and conditional heteroscedasticity induced by predictable jump size on option prices through comparison with the benchmark Black–Scholes model. The model pricing errors are measured by both the absolute difference and relative percentage difference, as well as implied Black–Scholes volatility. In the specific trending O-U jump-diffusion process, we study the impact of perfect predictability on option prices through comparison with the model of perfect unpredictability (the random walk with drift) and the impact of discontinuity on option prices through comparison with the continuous diffusion model. We illustrate various patterns of mispricing of the Black–Scholes and Merton models and demonstrate that the pricing errors can be significant both statistically and economically. When predictability is induced by a linear mean-reverting drift function as in Lo and Wang (1995), we provide adjustments to both the Black–Scholes (1973) and the Merton (1976a) option pricing formulas. We further show that the Merton (1976a) jump-diffusion model can be extended to allow for various patterns of predictability through alternative specification of the drift function and allow for conditional heteroscedasticity through predictable jump sizes instead of the non-jump conditional volatility. The implications of conditional heteroscedasticity induced by predictable jump size is investigated based on simulation results.

APPENDIX

Trending the O-U jump-diffusion process with exponentially decaying jump size

$p(t) = \mu t + q(t)$ and $dq(t) = -\beta q(t)dt + \sigma dW(t) + lnY(t)dQ_\lambda(t)$, with $\beta > 0$ and $lnY(t) \sim i.d.N(0, e^{-2\beta(t-t_0)}\nu^2)$, i.e. the jump size decays exponentially, where t_0 is the initial time. Let $u(t) = e^{\beta t}q(t)$: using Itô's lemma we have

$$du(t) = e^{\beta t}\sigma dW(t) + e^{\beta t} lnY(t)dQ_\lambda(t)$$

or

$$q(t) = e^{-\beta(t-t_0)}q(t_0) + \int_{t_0}^{t} e^{-\beta(t-\tau)}\sigma dW(\tau) + \int_{t_0}^{t} e^{-\beta(t-\tau)} lnY(t)dQ_\lambda(\tau)$$

This process is governed by the transition density function

$$f(q(t); q(t_0)) = \sum_{n=0}^{\infty} \frac{e^{-\lambda(t-t_0)}\lambda(t-t_0))^n}{n!} \phi(q(t);$$

$$e^{-\beta(t-t_0)}q(t_0), \frac{\sigma^2}{2\beta}(1 - e^{-2\beta(t-t_0)}) + ne^{-2\beta(t-t_0)}\nu^2)$$

with conditional mean and variance

$$E[q(t)|q(t_0)] = e^{-\beta(t-t_0)}q(t_0),$$

$$Var[q(t)|q(t_0)] = \frac{\sigma^2}{2\beta}(1 - e^{-2\beta(t-t_0)}) + \lambda(t-t_0)e^{-2\beta(t-t_0)}\nu^2.$$

Trending the O-U jump-diffusion process with i.i.d. lognormal jump size

$p(t) = \mu t + q(t)$ and $dq(t) = -\beta q(t)dt + \sigma dW(t) + lnY(t)dQ_\lambda(t)$, with $\beta > 0$ and $lnY(t) \sim i.i.d.N(0, \nu^2)$, where t_0 is the initial time. The process has a solution given in (7.17) in the integral form. We first wish to show that the second term follows a normal distribution with mean zero and variance

$\frac{\sigma^2}{2\beta}(1 - e^{2\beta(t_0 - t)})$. Then we show that the third term follows a compound Poisson process and derive its mean, variance, skewness, and kurtosis.

Let $X(t) = \int_{t_0}^{t} \sigma e^{\beta(\tau - t)} dW(\tau)$. By the definition of Itô's integration we have

$$X(t) = \lim_{n\to\infty} \sum_{i=0}^{n} \sigma e^{\beta(t_i - t)} \Delta W(t_i)$$

where $[t_i, t_{i+1}], i = 0, 1, ..., n$ are equal partitions of the interval $[t_0, t]$. Let $\phi_{X(t)}(u)$ denote the characteristic function of $X(t)$. It can be shown that

$$\phi_X(u) = E[e^{iuX}] = \lim_{n\to\infty} \prod_{i=0}^{n} E[e^{iu\sigma e^{\beta(t_i - t)} \Delta W(t_i)}]$$

$$= exp\{-\frac{1}{2}u^2 \frac{\sigma^2}{2\beta}(1 - e^{2\beta(t_0 - t)})\}$$

That is, $X \sim N(0, \frac{\sigma^2}{2\beta}(1 - e^{2\beta(t_0 - t)}))$.

Similarly, let $Y(t) = \int_{t_0}^{t} e^{\beta(\tau - t)} ln(Y(\tau)) dQ_\lambda(\tau)$. By the definition of Itô's integration we have

$$Y(t) = \lim_{n\to\infty} \sum_{i=0}^{n} \sum_{j=0}^{N_i} e^{\beta(t_i - t)} ln Y_j(t_i)$$

where $[t_i, t_{i+1}], i = 0, 1, ..., n$ are equal partitions of the interval $[t_0, t]$, N_i is Poisson distributed with intensity $\lambda(t_{i+1} - t_i), \forall i$, and $Y_j(t_i) \sim i.i.d.N(\mu_0, \nu^2)$. Let $\phi_{Y(t)}(u)$ denote the characteristic function of $Y(t)$. It can be shown that

$$\phi_Y(u) = E[e^{iuY}] = \lim_{n\to\infty} \prod_{i=0}^{n} E[e^{iu(\sum_{j=0}^{N_i} e^{\beta(t_i - t)} ln Y_j(t_i))}]$$

$$= \lim_{n\to\infty} \prod_{i=0}^{n} E_{N_i}[E[e^{iu \sum_{j=0}^{N_i} e^{\beta(t_i - t)} ln Y_j(t_i)} | N_i]]$$

$$= exp\{\lambda[\int_{t_0}^{t} (e^{iue^{\beta(\tau - t)}\mu_0 - \frac{1}{2}u^2 e^{2\beta(\tau - t)}\nu^2} d\tau - (t - t_0)]\}$$

Since $X(t)$ and $Y(t)$ are independent of each other, $\phi_{X+Y}(u) = \phi_X(u)\phi_Y(u)$, or $ln(\phi_{X+Y}(u)) = ln(\phi_X(u)) + ln(\phi_Y(u))$. For simplicity, when $\mu_0 = 0$ it is straightforward to derive

$$E[q(t)|q(t_0)] = E[q(t)^3|q(t_0)] = 0$$

$$Var[q(t)|q(t_0)] = \frac{1}{2\beta}(\sigma^2 + \lambda\nu^2)(1 - e^{2\beta(t_0 - t)})$$

$$E[q(t)^4|q(t_0)] = 3Var[q(t)]^2 + \frac{3\lambda\nu^4}{4\beta}(1 - e^{4\beta(t_0-t)})$$

The τ-period difference of $q(t)$, $\Delta_\tau q(t) = q(t) - q(t-\tau)$, can be shown similarly with

$$\Delta_\tau q(t) = e^{-\beta(t-t_0)}(1 - e^{\beta\tau})q(t_0)$$

$$+ \int_{t-\tau}^{t} e^{\beta(u-t)}\sigma dW(u) + \int_{t-\tau}^{t} e^{\beta(u-t)} ln Y(u) dQ_\lambda(u)$$

$$+ \int_{t_0}^{t-\tau} e^{\beta(u-t)}(1 - e^{\beta\tau})\sigma dW(u) + \int_{t_0}^{t-\tau} e^{\beta(u-t)}(1 - e^{\beta\tau}) ln Y(u) dQ_\lambda(u)$$

The following four moments can be derived in the steady state when $\mu_0 = 0$. That is,

$$E[\Delta_\tau q(t)] = E[(\Delta_\tau q(t))^3] = 0, Var[\Delta_\tau q(t)] = \frac{\sigma^2 + \lambda\nu^2}{\beta}(1 - e^{-\beta\tau}),$$

$$E[(\Delta_\tau q(t))^4] = 3Var[\Delta_\tau q(t)]^2 + \frac{3\lambda\nu^4}{2\beta}(1 - e^{-\beta\tau})(1 - e^{-\beta\tau} + 2e^{-2\beta\tau})$$

The co-variance between the time lagged first difference of $q(t)$ can also be shown to be

$$Cov(\Delta_\tau q(t), \Delta_\tau q(t-\delta)) = E[\Delta_\tau \Delta_\tau q(t-\delta)]$$

$$= (1 - e^{\beta\tau})e^{-\beta\delta}\sigma^2 E[(\int_{t-\delta-\tau}^{t-\delta} e^{\beta(u-t+\delta)} dW(u))^2]$$

$$+ (1 - e^{\beta\tau})e^{-\beta\delta} E[(\int_{t-\delta-\tau}^{t-\delta} e^{\beta(u-t+\delta)} ln Y(u) dQ_\lambda(u))^2]$$

$$+ (1 - e^{\beta\tau})^2 e^{-\beta\delta}\sigma^2 E[(\int_{t_0}^{t-\delta-\tau} e^{\beta(u-t+\delta)} dW(u))^2]$$

$$+ (1 - e^{\beta\tau})^2 e^{-\beta\delta} E[(\int_{t_0}^{t-\delta-\tau} e^{\beta(u-t+\delta)} ln Y(u) dQ_\lambda(u))^2]$$

$$= -\frac{\sigma^2 + \lambda\nu^2}{2\beta} e^{-\beta(\delta-\tau)}(1 - e^{\beta\tau})^2$$

That is, the τ-period difference of $q(t)$ is co-variance stationary as the above covariance depends only on the time lag δ. Its correlation can be derived as, with $\delta \geq \tau$,

$$Corr(\Delta_\tau q(t), \Delta_\tau q(t-\delta)) = -\tfrac{1}{2}(1 - e^{-\beta\tau})e^{-\beta(\delta-\tau)}$$

Cumulants of trending the O-U jump-diffusion process

Using the characteristic functions of both $X(t) = \int_{t_0}^{t} \sigma e^{\beta(\tau-t)} dW(\tau)$ and $Y(t) = \int_{t_0}^{t} e^{\beta(\tau-t)} ln(Y(\tau))dQ_\lambda(\tau)$ defined above, one can easily derive their cumulants as follows (for a definition of cumulants as well as their relationship with moments, see Kendall and Stuart (1977, pp. 69–71)). For $X(t)$

$$K_1 = K_3 = K_4 = K_5 = K_6 = 0$$

$$K_2 = \frac{\sigma^2}{2\beta}(1 - e^{2\beta(t_0-t)})$$

and for $Y(t)$

$$K_1 = K_3 = K_5 = 0$$

$$K_2 = \frac{\lambda\nu^2}{2\beta}(1 - e^{2\beta(t_0-t)}),\ K_4 = \frac{3\lambda\nu^4}{4\beta}(1 - e^{4\beta(t_0-t)}),\ K_6 = \frac{15\lambda\nu^6}{6\beta}(1 - e^{6\beta(t_0-t)})$$

Based on the expression of $\Delta_\tau q(t)$, one can derive its first six cumulants when $\mu_0 = 0$. That is,

$$K_1 = K_3 = K_5 = 0$$

$$K_2 = \frac{\sigma^2 + \lambda\nu^2}{\beta}(1 - e^{-\beta\tau}),\ K_4 = \frac{3\lambda\nu^4}{4\beta}(1 - e^{-4\beta\tau} + (1 - e^{-\beta\tau})^4)$$

$$K_6 = \frac{15\lambda\nu^6}{6\beta}(1 - e^{-6\beta\tau} + (1 - e^{-\beta\tau})^6)$$

Cumulants of the constant drift jump-diffusion process

These can be obtained by taking the limit of the cumulants for the trending O-U jump-diffusion model as $\beta \to 0$.

Bivariate trending the O-U jump-diffusion process

$$dq(t) = -(\beta q(t) - \eta X(t))dt + \sigma dW_q(t) + ln Y(t) dQ_\lambda(t)$$

$$dX(t) = -\theta X(t)dt + \sigma_x dW_x(t)$$

where $\beta \geq 0, \eta \geq 0, q(t_0) = q_0, X(t_0) = X_0$. $W_x(t)$ and $W_q(t)$ are two standard Wiener processes such that $dW_q(t)dW_x(t) = \kappa dt$, $dW_x(t)dQ_\lambda(t) = 0$, and $X(t)$ is another stochastic process that may or may not be observable. Solution for the above system of linear SDE is given by (7.21). It can be verified that $E[q(t)] = 0$,

$$Var[q(t)] = \frac{\sigma^2}{2\beta} + \frac{\eta^2\sigma_x^2}{2\theta\beta(\beta+\theta)} + \frac{\eta\kappa\sigma_x\sigma}{\beta(\beta+\theta)} + \frac{\lambda\nu^2}{2\beta}$$

and $E[X(t)] = 0$,

$$Var[X(t)] = \sigma_x^2/2\theta$$

$$Cov[X(t), q(t)] = \frac{1}{\theta+\beta}[\kappa\sigma\sigma_x + \frac{\eta\sigma_x^2}{2\theta}]$$

Since

$$\begin{aligned}\Delta_\tau q(t) &= q(t) - q(t-\tau) \\ &= (e^{-\beta\tau} - 1)q(t-\tau) + \frac{\eta}{\beta+\theta}(e^{-\theta\tau} - e^{-\beta\tau})X(t-\tau) \\ &+ \int_{t-\tau}^{t} e^{-\beta(t-s)}\sigma dW_q(s) + \frac{\eta}{\beta-\theta}\int_{t-\tau}^{t}(e^{-\theta(t-s)} - e^{-\beta(t-s)})\sigma_x dW_x(s) \\ &+ \int_{t-\tau}^{t} e^{-\beta(t-s)} ln Y(s)dQ_\lambda(s)\end{aligned}$$

we have

$$Var[\Delta_\tau q(t)] = 2Var[q(t)]((1 - e^{-\beta\tau}) + \frac{\eta}{\beta-\theta}\beta_{qx}(e^{-\beta\tau} - e^{-\theta\tau}))$$

where $\beta_{qx} = Cov[q(t), X(t)]/Var[q(t)]$, and

$$\begin{aligned}Cov[\Delta_\tau q(t), \Delta_\tau q(t-\tau)] &= -Var[q(t)](\frac{\eta}{\beta-\theta}\beta_{qx}((1 - e^{-\theta\tau})^2 - (1 - e^{-\beta\tau})^2) \\ &+ (1 - e^{-\beta\tau})^2)\end{aligned}$$

and

$$\rho_\tau(1) = -\frac{\frac{\eta}{\beta-\theta}\beta_{qx}((1 - e^{-\theta\tau})^2 - (1 - e^{-\beta\tau})^2) + (1 - e^{-\beta\tau})^2}{2(\frac{\eta}{\beta-\theta}\beta_{qx}(e^{-\beta\tau} - e^{-\theta\tau}) + (1 - e^{-\beta\tau}))}$$

when τ is small, we have

$$\rho_\tau(1) \approx -\frac{\tau}{2}(\beta - \frac{\eta\theta\beta_{qx}}{\beta - \eta\beta_{qx}})$$

When $\eta = \beta$, it is $< 0, = 0, > 0$ when $\beta_{qx} > 1$ or $\beta_{qx} < \frac{\beta}{\beta+\theta}, = \frac{\beta}{\beta+\theta}, > \frac{\beta}{\beta+\theta}$ and < 1 respectively.

Jump-diffusion with predictable jump sizes

The jump size of the jump-diffusion process defined in (7.23) follows a O-U process. It can be shown that $E[ln Y(t)] = 0$, $Var[ln Y(t)] = \sigma_Y^2/2\xi$, and $Corr(ln Y(t),\ ln Y(t-\tau)) = e^{-2\xi\tau}$ which approaches 1 as $\tau \to 0$ and 0 as $\tau \to \infty$. The solution of the process can be written as

$$p(t) = p(t-\tau) + \mu\tau + \sigma(W(t) - W(t-\tau)) + \int_{t-\tau}^{t} [e^{-\xi(u-(t-\tau))} ln Y(t-\tau) + \int_{t-\tau}^{u} e^{-\xi(u-s)}\sigma_Y dW_Y(s)]dQ_\lambda(u)$$

It can be derived that

$$E[r_\tau(t)] = \mu\tau$$

$$Var[r_\tau(t)] = (\sigma^2 + \frac{\lambda\sigma_Y^2}{2\xi})\tau$$

and

$$Corr[r_\tau(t), r_\tau(t-\delta)] = 0$$

for $\delta \geq \tau$. The conditional mean and variance on the information available at time $t-\tau$, denoted by $\mathcal{F}_{t-\tau}$, can also be derived as

$$E[r_\tau(t)|\mathcal{F}_{t-\tau}] = \mu\tau + \frac{\lambda ln Y(t-\tau)}{\xi}(1 - e^{-\xi\tau})$$

$$Var[r_\tau(t)|\mathcal{F}_{t-\tau}] = Var[r_\tau(t)] - \frac{\lambda\sigma_Y^2}{4\xi^2}(1 - e^{-2\xi\tau}) + \frac{\lambda(1 - e^{-2\xi\tau})}{2\xi} ln^2 Y(t-\tau)$$

In addition, since $X = ln Y(t-\tau) \sim N(0, \sigma_Y^2/2\xi)$ a normal distribution, the characteristic function for

$$Y = \int_{t-\tau}^{t} e^{-\xi(u-(t-\tau))} dQ_\lambda(u)$$

can be derived as

$$\phi_Y(v) = exp\{\lambda[\int_{t-\tau}^{t} e^{ive^{-\xi(u-(t-\tau))}} du - \tau]\}$$

and the characteristic function for

$$Z = \int_{t-\tau}^{t} [\int_{t-\tau}^{u} e^{-\xi(u-s)} \sigma_Y dW_Y(u)] dQ_\lambda(u)$$

can be derived as

$$\phi_Z(v) = exp\{\lambda[\int_{t-\tau}^{t} e^{-\frac{v^2\sigma_Y^2}{4\xi}(1-e^{-2\xi(u-(t-\tau))})} du - \tau]\},$$

the moments as well as cumulants of different orders for $r_\tau(t) = p(t) - p(t-\tau)$ can be readily derived.

REFERENCES

Aase, K.K. (1988) 'Contingent Claims Valuation when the Security Price is a Combination of an Itô Process and a Random Point Process', *Stochastic Processes and their Applications*, **28**, 185–220.

Amin, K. and Ng, V. (1993) 'Option Valuation with Systematic Stochastic Volatility', *Journal of Finance*, **48**, 881–910.

Andersen, T.G. (1994) 'Stochastic Autoregressive Volatility: A Framework for Volatility Modeling', *Mathematical Finance*, **4**, 75–102.

Bailey, W. and Stulz, E. (1989) 'The Pricing of Stock Index Options in a General Equilibrium Model', *Journal of Financial and Quantitative Analysis*, **24**, 1–12.

Bakshi, G., Cao, C. and Chen, Z. (1997) 'Empirical Performance of Alternative Option Pricing Models', *Journal of Finance* (forthcoming).

Ball, C.A. and Torous, W.N. (1985) 'On Jumps in Common Stock Prices and their Impact on Call Option Pricing', *Journal of Finance*, **40**, 155–173.

Bardhan, I. and Chao, X. (1993) 'Pricing Options on Securities with Discontinuous Returns', *Stochastic Processes and their Application*, **48**, 123–137.

Bates, D.S. (1996) 'Jumps and Stochastic Volatility: Exchange Rate Processes Implicit in PHLX Deutschmark Options', *Review of Financial Studies*, **9**(1), 69–107.

Bates, D.S. (1995) 'Testing Option Pricing Models', NBER working paper No. 5129.

Bates, D.S. (1994) 'Dollar Jump Fears, 1984–1992: Distributional Abnormalities Implicit in Currency Futures Options', Wharton School working paper, University of Pennsylvania.

Bates, D.S. (1991) 'The Crash of 87: Was it Expected? The Evidence from Option Markets', *Journal of Finance*, **46**, 1009–1044.

Bates, D.S. (1988) 'Pricing Options on Jump-diffusion Processes', Rodney L. White Center working paper 37-88, Wharton School.

Beckers, S. (1981) 'A Note on Estimating the Parameters of the Diffusion-jump Model of Stock Returns', *Journal of Financial and Quantitative Analysis*, **16**(1), 127–40.

Black, F. (1975) 'Fact and Fantasy in the Use of Options', *Financial Analysts Journal*, **31**, 36–72.

Black, F. (1976) 'Studies of Stock Price Volatility Changes', *Proceedings from the American Statistical Association, Business and Economic Statistics Section*, pp. 177–181.

Black, F. and Scholes, M (1973) 'The Pricing of Options and Corporate Liabilities', *Journal of Political Economy*, **81**, 637–659.

Bodurtha, J.N. and Courtadon, G.R. (1987) 'Tests of an American Option Pricing Model on the Foreign Currency Options Market', *Journal of Financial and Quantitative Analysis*, **22**, 153–167.

Bollerslev, T.R.Y. (1986) 'Generalized Autoregressive Conditional Heteroscedasticity', *Journal of Econometrics*, **51**, 307–327.

Bollerslev, T.R.Y., Chou, R.Y. and Kroner, K.F. (1992) 'ARCH Modeling in Finance: A Review of the Theory and Empirical Evidence', *Journal of Econometrics*, **52**, 1–131.

Boyle, P., Broadie, M. and Glasserman, P. (1996) 'Monte Carlo Methods for Security Pricing', *Journal of Economics Dynamics and Control* (forthcoming).

Campbell, J.Y., Lo, A.W. and MacKinlay, A.C. (1997) *The Econometrics of Financial Markets*, Princeton University Press, New Jersey.

Chesney, M. and Scott, L. (1989) 'Pricing European Currency Options: A Comparison of the Modified Black–Scholes Model and a Random Variance Model', *Journal of Financial and Quantitative Analysis*, **24**, 267–284.

Clark, P.K. (1973) 'A Subordinated Stochastic Process Model with Finite Variance for Speculative Prices', *Econometrica*, **41**, 135–156.

Clewlow, L. and Xu, X. (1993) 'The Dynamics of Stochastic Volatility', Discussion paper, University of Warwick.

Cox, J.C. and Ross, S.A. (1976) 'The Valuation of Options for Alternative Stochastic Processes', *Journal of Financial Economics*, **3**, 145–166.

Duan, J. (1995) The GARCH Option Pricing Model, *Mathematical Finance*, **5**, 13–32.

Engle, R.F. (1982) 'Autoregressive Conditional Heteroscedasticity with Estimates of the Variance of U.K. Inflation', *Econometrica*, **50**, 987–1008.

Fama, E. (1963) 'The Stable Paretian Distribution', *Journal of Business*, **36**, 420–429.

Fama, E. (1965) 'The Behavior of Stock Market Prices', *Journal of Business*, **38**, 34–105.

Fama, E. and K. French (1988) 'Dividend Yields and Expected Stock Returns', *Journal of Financial Economics*, **22**, 3–26.

Florens-Zmirou, D. (1993) 'On Estimating the Diffusion Coefficient from Discrete Observations', *Journal of Applied Probability*, **30**, 790–804.

Gallant, A.R. and Tauchen, G.E. (1996) 'Which Moments to Match', *Econometric Theory*, **12**, 657–681.

Gallant, A.R. and Long, J.R. (1997) 'Estimating Stochastic Differential Equations Efficiently by Minimum Chi-square" *Biometrika*, **84**, 125–141.

Ghysels, E., Gouriéroux, C. and Jasiak, J. (1995) 'Trading Patterns, Time Deformation and Stochastic Volatility in Foreign Exchange Markets', Paper presented at the HFDF Conference, Zurich.

Ghysels, E., Harvey, A. and Renault, E. (1996) 'Stochastic Volatility', in G.S. Maddala and C.R. Rao (eds), *Handbook of Statistics 14*, North-Holland, Amsterdam.

Gouriéroux, C., Monfort, A. and Renault, E. (1993) 'Indirect Inference', *Journal of Applied Econometrics*, **8**, S85–S118.

Gouriéroux, C., Renault, E. and Touzi, N. (1994) 'Calibration by Simulation for Small Sample Bias Correction', Discussion paper CREST.

Grundy, B.D. (1991) 'Option Prices and the Underlying Asset's Return Distribution', *Journal of Finance*, **46**, 1045–1069.

Gultekin, N.B., Rogalski, R.J. and Tinic, S.M. (1982) 'Option Pricing Model Estimates: Some Empirical Results', *Financial Management*, Spring, 58–69.

Harrison, M. and Kreps, D. (1979) 'Martingale and Arbitrage in Multiperiod Securities Markets', *Journal of Economic Theory*, **20**, 381–408.

Heston, S.I. (1993) 'A Closed Form Solution for Options with Stochastic Volatility with Applications to Bond and Currency Options', *Review of Financial Studies*, **6**, 327–344.

Ho, M., Perraudin, W. and Sørensen, B. (1996) 'A Continuous-time Arbitrage-pricing Model with Stochastic Volatility and Jumps', *Journal of Business & Economic Statistics*, **14**(1), 31–43.

Hull, J. and White, A. (1987) 'The Pricing of Options on Assets with Stochastic Volatility', *Journal of Finance*, **42**, 281–300.

Jagannathan, R. (1984) 'Call Option and the Risk of Underlying Securities', *Journal of Financial Economics*, **13**, 425–434.

Jeanblanc-Picqué, M. and Pontier, M. (1990) 'Optimal Portfolio for a Small Investor in a Market with Discontinuous Prices', *Appl. Math. Optim.*, **22**, 287–310.

Jiang, G. (1997) 'Estimation of Jump-diffusion Process Based on Indirect Inference', Manuscript, University of Groningen.

Jiang, G. and Knight, J. (1997) 'A Nonparametric Approach to the Estimation of Stochastic Diffusion Processes', *Econometric Theory*, **13**, 615–645.

Johnson, H. and Shanno, D. (1987) 'Option Pricing when the Variance is Changing', *Journal of Financial and Quantitative Analysis*, **22**, 143–152.

Jones, E.P. (1984) 'Option Arbitrage and Strategy with Large Price Changes', *Journal of Financial Economics*, **13**, 91–133.

Jorion, P. (1988) 'On Jump Processes in the Foreign Exchange and Stock Markets', *Review of Financial Studies*, **1**, 427–445.

Karlin, S. and Taylor, H.M. (1981) *A Second Course in Stochastic Processes*, Academic Press, New York.

Kendall, M. and Stuart, A. (1977) *The Advanced Theory of Statistics* (Vol.1), Charles Griffin & Company Limited, London.

Kim, S., Shephard, N. and Chib, S. (1996) 'Stochastic Volatility: Likelihood Inference and Comparison with ARCH Models', Nuffield College, Oxford.

Lo, A.W. (1988) 'Maximum Likelihood Estimation of Generalized Itô Processes with Discretely Sampled Data', *Econometric Theory*, **4**, 231–247.

Lo, A.W. and MacKinlay, C. (1988) 'Stock Market Prices do not Follow Random Walks: Evidence from a Simple Specification Test', *Review of Financial Studies*, **1**, 41–66.

Lo, A.W. and MacKinlay, C. (1990) 'When are Contrarian Profits Due to Stock Market Overreaction?' *Review of Financial Studies*, **3**, 175–206.

Lo, A.W. and Wang, J. (1995) 'Implementing Option Pricing Formulas when Asset Returns are Predictable', *Journal of Finance*, **50**, 87–129.

Longstaff, F.A. (1989) 'Temporal Aggregation and the Continuous-time Capital Asset Pricing Model', *Journal of Finance*, **41**, 871–887.

MacBeth, J.D. and Merville, L.J. (1979) 'Tests of Black–Scholes and Cox Call Option Valuation Models', *Journal of Finance*, **50**, 87–129.

Mandelbrot, B.B. (1963) 'The Valuation of Certain Speculative Prices', *Journal of Business*, **36**, 394–419.

Mandelbrot, B.B. and Taylor, H. (1967) 'On the Distribution of Stock Prices Differences', *Operation Research*, **15**, 1057–1062.

Melino, A. (1994) 'Estimation of Continuous-time Models in Finance', in C.A. Sims (ed.), *Advances in Econometrics*, Cambridge University Press, Cambridge.

Melino, A. and Turnbull, S.M. (1990) 'Pricing Foreign Currency Options with Stochastic Volatility', *Journal of Econometrics*, **45**, 239–266.

Merton, R.C. (1973) 'Rational Theory of Option Pricing', *Bell Journal of Economics and Management Science*, **4**, 141–183.

Merton, R.C. (1976a) 'Option Pricing when Underlying Stock Returns are Discontinuous', *Journal of Financial Economics*, **3**, 125–144.

Merton, R.C. (1976b) 'The Impact on Option Pricing of Specification Error in the Underlying Stock Price Returns', *Journal of Finance*, **31**, 333–350.

Naik, V. and Lee, M.H. (1990) 'General Equilibrium Pricing of Options on the Market Portfolio with Discontinuous Returns', *Review of Financial Studies*, **3**, 493–522.

Poterba, J. and Summers, L. (1988) 'Mean Reversion in Stock Returns: Evidence and Implications', *Journal of Financial Economics*, **22**, 27–60

Powell, A. (1989) 'A General Method of Moments for Estimating the Parameters of Stochastic Processes for Asset Prices', Oxford Applied Economics Discussion Paper 76, May 1989.

Press, J. (1967) 'A Compound Events Model for Security Prices', *Journal of Business*, **40**, 317–35.

Protter, P. and Dalay, D. (1996) 'The Euler Scheme for Lévy Driven Stochastic Differential Equations', *The Annals of Probability* (forthcoming).

Renault, E. (1995) 'Econometric Models of Option Pricing Errors', Invited lecture presented at 7th WCES, Tokyo.

Rubinstein, M. (1985) 'Nonparametric Tests of Alternative Option Pricing Models Using All Reported Trades and Quotes on the 30 Most Active CBOE Options Classes from August 23, 1976 through August 31, 1978', *Journal of Finance*, 455–480.

Scott, L. (1987) 'Option Pricing when the Variance Changes Randomly: Theory, Estimators, and Applications', *Journal of Financial and Quantitative Analysis*, **22**, 419–438.

Scott, L. (1991) 'Random Variance Option Pricing', *Advances in Futures & Options Research*, **5**, 113–135.

Scott, L. (1997) 'Pricing Stock Options in a Jump-diffusion Model with Stochastic Volatility and Interest Rates: Application of Fourier Inversion Methods', *Mathematical Finance* (forthcoming).

Shephard, N.G. (1996) 'Statistical Aspects of ARCH and Stochastic Volatility', in D.R. Cox, D.V. Hinkley and O.E. Barndorff-Nielsen (eds), *Time Series Models: in econometrics, finance and other fields*, Chapman and Hall, London.

Stein, E.M. and Stein, J. (1991) 'Stock Price Distributions with Stochastic Volatility: An Analytic Approach', *Review of Financial Studies*, **4**, 727–752.

Taylor, S.J. (1986) *Modelling Financial Time Series*, John Wiley, Chichester.

Taylor, S.J. (1994) 'Modeling Stochastic Volatility: A Review and Comparative Study', *Mathematical Finance*, **4**, 183–204.

Taylor, S.J. and Xu, X. (1994) 'The Term Structure of Volatility Implied by Foreign Exchange Options', *Journal of Financial and Quantitative Analysis*, **29**, 57–74.

Wiggins, J. (1987) 'Option Values under Stochastic Volatilities', *Journal of Financial Economics*, **19**, 351–372.

Chapter 8

The probability functions of option prices, risk-neutral pricing and Value-at-Risk

JOHN L. KNIGHT, STEPHEN E. SATCHELL
AND GUOQIANG WANG

ABSTRACT

The purpose of this chapter is to examine how sensitive the probability distributions of option prices are to assumptions about the distribution of asset returns. We employ the framework of Grundy (1991) and Lo and Wang (1995) where two different models of asset returns have the same risk-neutral distribution and lead to the same (current) option price formula. As we forecast forward, however, the (future) prices will reflect the differences in the distributions and we can calculate the sensitivity of the Value-at-Risk of a typical European option to the underlying asset return distributions.

8.1 INTRODUCTION AND LITERATURE REVIEW

Since publication of the Black–Scholes option formula in 1973, the risk-neutral pricing technique has become the standard regime in asset pricing, particularly for pricing options and other derivatives. The basic idea involves the following. Investors can duplicate the payoff of options via a dynamic portfolio strategy using the underlying and riskless borrowing. Combining this strategy with a short position in an option, the investor can eliminate all risk from the total position, hence to avoid arbitrage in the market, the total position must be evaluated under the risk-free interest. In other words, since under no-arbitrage conditions risk preferences do not enter into the pricing decision, we can assume risk neutrality and price all assets in a preference-free world. For the formal argument of risk-neutral pricing, we refer the reader to Cox and Ross (1976), Harrison and Kreps (1979), and Harrison and Pliska (1981).

In terms of probability, the no-arbitrage condition is essentially equivalent to the existence of a risk-neutral (equivalent martingale) measure for the stochastic process followed by the underlying. This basic result is sometimes called the *fundamental theorem of asset pricing* (see Dybvig and Ross, 1987). The theorem states that if there is no arbitrage, the true probability measure of an underlying asset, which depends on the investor's risk preference and other subjective factors, can be replaced by the risk-neutral measure under which the underlying process becomes a martingale. Consequently, the problem of fairly pricing derivatives is reduced to taking their expected values with respect to the risk-neutral measure. So from the perspective of derivatives pricing, the risk-neutral measure is more relevant than the true measure. However, it would be incorrect to infer that the true measure's role is no more than that of providing a starting point for the risk-neutral measure. It turns out that there is a more subtle relation between the true measure and derivative prices.

Lo (1987) uses the moment conditions of the true and risk-neutral underlying distribution to construct the bound on call prices. First, it is shown that for all risk-neutral distributions which have the same mean, μ, and variance σ^2, the one that maximizes the expected payoff of an option is a two-point distribution. We can write the upper bound, $\overline{C}$, in terms of μ, σ^2, and the exercise price K:

$$\overline{C} = \begin{cases} \frac{\mu(\mu-K)+\mu\sigma^2}{\mu^2+\sigma^2} & \text{if} \quad K \leq \frac{\mu^2+\sigma^2}{2\mu} \\ \frac{1}{2}[\mu - K + \sqrt{(K-\mu)^2+\sigma^2}] & \text{if} \quad K > \frac{\mu^2+\sigma^2}{2\mu} \end{cases}$$

Given the risk-neutral distribution is known, it is straightforward to calculate its mean and variance, and the upper bound for option prices, $\overline{C}$, can be readily attained. In Lo's paper, the results of the upper bound are calculated when the underlying follows either a lognormal diffusion or mixed diffusion-jump process.

However, it is not necessary to evaluate the bound only under the *risk-neutral* distribution. It is more reasonable to take into account both the risk-neutral and true distributions. Usually the moments of those two distributions are not necessarily equal as they depend on different sets of factors. The above bound formula only applies to the case where the two distributions have common moments or there is a ready transformation from the true moments to the risk-neutral moments. This is also the reason why only the lognormal diffusion and the mixed diffusion-jump process are studied in Lo's paper, as their risk-neutral variance is a simple transformation of the true variance.

Based on Lo (1987)'s result, Grundy (1991) generalizes the connection between the bounds on European option price and the non-central moments of the true underlying asset's return distribution. First he shows how the expected payoff to a call can be bounded above in terms of any chosen set of the non-central moments of the true underlying return distribution. Second, from the observed option prices, he can establish restrictions on the true underlying distribution under which the expected return on an option over its life can be bounded below by the expected return on the underlying asset. Clearly, there are intimate links between the option prices and the true underlying distribution.

Lo and Wang (1995) further develop this theme and emphasize that all competing specifications for the true Data Generating Process (DGP) must match the *unconditional* moments of discretely sampled financial data. Even two competing specifications, like geometric Brownian motion (GBM) and the trending Orstein–Uhlenbeck (OU) process, result in the same risk-neutral distribution, hence the same Black–Scholes option pricing *formul*a. When implementing this formula, taking those sample moments as given, the drift term will affect the estimated value of the diffusion term in the underlying process. So the value of the diffusion term will change with the differently specified DGPs and different option *prices* can be obtained even from the same option pricing formula. Again, the true underlying distribution plays an important role in pricing derivatives.

Ncube and Satchell (1997) make this point more clearly from a statistical perspective. European option prices depend on five factors: the current underlying price $P(t)$, exercise price K, volatility σ, risk-free interest r and time to maturity τ. There is no randomness in K, τ and r (if we do not consider the stochastic interest rate case). However, the randomness arising from either price uncertainty or estimation error of volatility is of great interest, as we do not know the underlying price in the future and true volatility, and they must be estimated from historical data or via other methods. Certainly, the distribution of the true option price conditional on the true volatility and the predicted option price conditional on the current underlying price will reflect the information contained in the true underlying distribution.

As the distributional properties of option prices have become of fresh interest as a result of risk management calculations involving Value-at-Risk (VaR), it is worth while to pursue further the sensitivity of option price distributions to different specifications of the underlying distribution. In practice, there is no consensus about which distribution should be used in risk measurement. In the calculations of VaR, it seems that the true distribution of asset return play a dominant role, for example see Engel and Gizycki (1999). Also for regulatory purposes, as in the Basle Committee (1996), the banks are usually required to use the true distribution to calculate their VaR.

At the same time, the risk-neutral distributions are also important in risk evaluation and management. They are used in the calculation of forecasted changes in position, of option prices in VaR calculations, in the calculation of margin requirements in derivative markets (see the Span System used in LIFFE), and by central banks to assess changes in the underlying riskiness in a market. They are often based on implied volatility calculations rather than estimates of historical asset volatility. On the other hand, risk-neutral distributions do not necessarily imply that investors are risk-neutral. Indeed the actual risk incurred to a position typically differs from that represented in risk-neutral models.[1] So it may not be appropriate to use only risk-neutral measures in evaluating such risk measurements as VaR.

Duffie and Pan (1997) argue, for purposes of measuring VaR at short time horizons such as a few days or weeks, that it makes little difference whether we use the risk-neutral distribution or the true distribution. However, this does not imply that one can draw a significant amount of information for risk-measurement purposes from one's derivative pricing models, because these models are not correct all the time. For example, there has been an enormous amount of literature discussing the drawbacks of the Black–Scholes formula, even though it is still the cornerstone of modern derivatives trading and risk management.

This chapter intends to analyse the potential error of misspecification associated with the underlying return distributions in calculations of VaR for European options. We use the framework of Lo and Wang (1995) along with the approach of Ncube and Satchell (1997) and examine both the distribution of the current option price and that of its forecast when the underlying log price process is either a geometric Brownian motion (GBM) or a trending Orstein–Uhlenbeck (OU) process. We show how the distributions of forecasted option prices depend on the underlying processes, the forecasting time and other parameters. We compare the exact distribution of the forecasts to that generated via the delta approximation and consequently show that the error in the delta approach can be substantial. Since all the work described in the previous paragraph is related to forecasting derivatives, we hope that our results will help us to understand how sensitive the distributions of our option forecasts are to the 'true' nature of the underlying return process. We present the models along with our approach in Section 2 while Section 3 contains our results. A brief conclusion is given in Section 4.

---

[1]For example, Ncube and Satchell (1997) note that the probability that a European call option will finish in the money is $\Phi(\ln(P_0/K) + \alpha\tau)/(\sigma\sqrt{\tau}))$ under the true measure, but under the risk-neutral measure, the corresponding probability is $\Phi(\ln(P_0/K) + (r - \sigma^2/2)\tau)/(\sigma\sqrt{\tau}))$.

8.2 MODELS AND APPROACH

As in Lo and Wang (1995), we wish to examine the distribution of option prices where the log price of the underlying is either GBM or a trending OU process, that is, letting $P(t)$ be the price at time t of the underlying asset, we consider the two competing processes:

(a) GBM:

$$d \ln P(t) = \mu dt + \sigma dW_t \tag{8.1}$$

(b) Trending OU:

$$d \ln P(t) = (\mu - \gamma(\ln P(t) - \mu t))dt + \sigma dW_t \tag{8.2}$$

where $\gamma > 0$. That means when $\ln P(t)$ deviates from its trend μt, it is pulled back at a rate proportional to its deviation where γ measures the speed of adjustment. The trending OU process can then model the well-addressed stylized fact of mean-reversion in asset prices.[2] The associated Risk-Neutral (RN) process is given by

$$d \ln P^*(t) = rdt + \sigma dW_t \tag{8.3}$$

The solution of the three stochastic differential equations is straightforward. For equations (8.1) and (8.3) we get respectively, that

$$\ln P(t) \mid \ln P(0) \sim N(\ln P(0) + \mu t, \ \sigma^2 t) \tag{8.4}$$

and

$$\ln P^*(t) \mid \ln P^*(0) \sim N(\ln P^*(0) + rt, \ \sigma^2 t) \tag{8.5}$$

For equation (8.2) we first note that, letting

$$y(t) = \ln P(t) - \mu t$$

we have from Ito's Lemma

$$dy(t) = -\gamma y(t)dt + \sigma dW_t$$

with

$$y(t) \mid y(0) \sim N(e^{-\gamma t} y(0), \ \sigma^2(1 - e^{-2\gamma t})/2\gamma)$$

---

[2]Fama and French (1988) show that there is significant negative autocorrelation in long-run returns. Lo and Mackinlay (1988) find that stock returns are positively correlated, using weekly observation. The trending OU process only admit the first-order autocorrelation with value $\in (-1/2, 0)$, if $\gamma > 0$.

and thus

$$\ln P(t) \mid \ln P(0) \sim N(\mu t + e^{-\gamma t} \ln P(0),\ \sigma^2(1 - e^{-2\gamma t})/2\gamma) \qquad (8.6)$$

We observe that all the parameters in these distributions are assumed to be positive. That implies the mean of OU process is the smallest among the three processes, so is its variance. This is not coincidental as the trending OU process is trend stationary. As time goes to infinity, the variances of both GBM and RN process are infinite, while the variance of the OU process approaches $\sigma^2/2\gamma$.

In the following analysis, we may condition on time t or time 0 information, we refer to the latter as unconditional. We present these results in Proposition 1.

Proposition 1. *The unconditional distributions of log price under the geometric Brownian motion, risk neutral and trending OU process are all normal, with the forms given in equations (8.4)–(8.6). The variance in (8.6) is the smallest, and is an increasing function of t.*

Proof. By inspection.

The reason that the GBM and trending OU process can be competing specifications for the underlying is that in the short run, the processes are indistinguishable. We also note that, for the purpose of risk measurement, the most relevant horizon is short, such as a few days or weeks. However, in the long run the differences between these two processes can be quite pronounced. Chan *et al.* (1992) discuss the model specification issue of the short-term rate interest rate process. They show how different specifications can be nested into a general form, with specific models determined from hypothesis tests on relevant parameters. Although we could employ a similar method here to distinguish the two processes from an empirical econometric perspective, our focus is to examine the issue of the effect of different underlying specifications on the probability function of option prices.

Even though all the underlying distribution specifications have the normal form, their difference is not negligible. We will explain this point further when discussing the calculation of VaRs. Now the meaning of the probability function of option prices is worth exploring in more detail, as usually option prices are regarded merely as fixed numbers, not random variables. It is true that the Black–Scholes option price at the *current* time is a fixed number conditional on the current information. However, when we look forward at the starting time, 0, the future option price $C(P(t))$, is unknown as the future underlying price $P(t)$ is an unknown random variable. Because the Black–Scholes option price is a non-linear function of the underlying random variable, it is, as a consequence, also a random variable. As the Black–Scholes option price is a monotonically increasing function of the underlying price, it is easy to implicitly derive the probability function of option price from that of the underlying price, as argued clearly in Ncube and Satchell (1997).

In this chapter, since the distribution of underlying returns is assumed normal, someone the effectiveness of our approach may be questioned. As is now well known, the distribution of actual asset returns have heavier tails than a normal distribution. However, it turns out that the methodology of this chapter is still valid for more general cases. Bergman *et al.* (1996) show that whenever the underlying prices follow a diffusion whose volatility term depends only on time and the concurrent underlying prices, then a call price is always *increasing* and convex in the underlying prices. Many underlying distributions besides the normal can be admitted into this general class of diffusions, and we can implicitly derive the probability function of option prices from those underlying distributions. Our methodology only fails when volatility is stochastic, or the underlying price process is not a diffusion, as in these cases a call price can be a decreasing, concave function of the underlying price over some range.

In this chapter we are concerned only with the randomness arising from uncertainty of the underlying price in the future, not the randomness from estimation error in the unknown volatility. In other words, we assume that the true volatility is known. The complexity of unknown volatility justifies another independent chapter discussing its effect on risk measurement.

When considering forecasting we will need to examine the distribution of $\ln P(t+s) \mid \ln P(t)$. For the three processes above we have

$$\text{GBM}: \ \ln P(t+s) \mid \ln P(t) \sim N(\ln P(t) + \mu s, \ \sigma^2 s) \tag{8.7}$$

$$\text{RN}: \ \ln P^*(t+s) \mid \ln P^*(t) \sim N(\ln P^*(t) + rs, \ \sigma^2 s) \tag{8.8}$$

$$\text{OU}: \ \ln P(t+s) \mid \ln P(t) \sim N(\mu(t+s) + e^{-\gamma s}(\ln P(t) - \mu t), \ \sigma^2(1 - e^{-2\gamma s})/2\gamma). \tag{8.9}$$

As shown by Grundy (1991) and Lo and Wang (1995), the two processes in equations (8.1) and (8.2) will generate the same option price formula but the distribution of the option price associated with each of the three process will be different. How different these distributions are will be examined in the next section. The approach we use to calculate the distribution is that detailed in Ncube and Satchell (1997) which we now briefly outline.

As shown by Ncube and Satchell (1997), it is straightforward to determine the distribution of any option price at time $t+s$, given today's price $P(t)$ and assuming any of the three processes (8.1), (8.2) or (8.3). It follows from

Theorem 1 in Ncube and Satchell (1997) that if

$$\ln P(t+s) \mid \ln P(t) \sim N(a, b)$$

and letting $C(P(t+s))$ be the Black–Scholes option price at time $t+s$, which is a function of $P(t+s)$, then

$$\begin{aligned}\Pr(C(P(t+s)) < q \mid I_t) &= \Pr(P(t+s) < C^{-1}(q) \mid I_t)\\ &= \Pr(\ln P(t+s) < \ln C^{-1}(q) \mid I_t)\\ &= F(q \mid I_t)\end{aligned}$$

and $F(q \mid I_t)$ can be determined as follows.

First, since $C(P(t+s))$ is the Black–Scholes price of a European call option at time $t+s$ with maturity at time $t+s+\tau$ and exercise price K, we have

$$C(P(t+s)) = P(t+s)N(d_1) - K\exp(-r\tau)N(d_2)$$

where

$$d_1 = \frac{\ln(P(t+s)/K) + r\tau}{\sigma\sqrt{\tau}} + \frac{1}{2}\sigma\sqrt{\tau}$$

$$d_2 = d_1 - \sigma\sqrt{\tau}$$

Second, as $C(P(t+s))$ is a monotonically increasing function of $P(t+s)$, there exists an inverse function, say $C^{-1}(\cdot)$ and thus for $q > 0$

$$\begin{aligned}\Pr(C(P(t+s)) < q \mid I_t) &= \Pr(P(t+s) < C^{-1}(q) \mid I_t)\\ &= \Pr(\ln P(t+s) < \ln C^{-1}(q) \mid I_t)\\ &= \Phi((\ln C^{-1}(q) - a)/\sqrt{b}) = F(q \mid I_t) \qquad (8.10)\end{aligned}$$

where $\Phi(\cdot)$ is the cumulative distribution function of the standard normal distribution. Therefore, $F(q \mid I_t)$ can be readily calculated for each of the three processes specified earlier by merely replacing a and b in equation (8.10) by the relevant values in equations (8.7), (8.8) and (8.9).

It is worth emphasizing that the probability function of option prices is not normal, although we can numerically solve this function from a standard normal distribution. For example, given a critical value, q^*, we can numerically solve $C^{-1}(q^*)$, then substitute it into the standard normal cumulative distribution function to get the corresponding probability. Inversely, given some probability level, from the standard normal distribution function we can find the corresponding critical value, then solve for the relevant q value.

Up to now, we have mainly discussed the probability function of a European call price. Because of its monotonic property with respect to the underlying price, we can obtain a pseudo-closed form for that function. As the basic nature of VaR is the quantile corresponding to given a confidence interval, the value of VaR can be easily calculated when we know the probability function. However, in practice, the measure of VaR is usually aimed at a portfolio which may consist of different options and/or underlying assets, and in this case, we cannot get the exact probability function via the method we use above. However a local approximation based on the so-called delta method has been developed to deal with a portfolio with derivatives. Such methods amount to approximating derivative prices as first-order Taylor expansions in the changes in the underlying prices.

Consequently even for a simple European call option, we also wish to compare the exact distribution with that derived from a delta approximation. That is, taking a Taylor series expansion of $C(P(t+s)$ around $P(t)$ we have

$$C(P(t+s)) = C(P(t)) + \frac{\partial C}{\partial P}(P(t+s) - P(t))$$

and since

$$\ln P(t+s) \approx \ln P(t) + \frac{1}{P(t)}(P(t+s) - P(t))$$

giving

$$(P(t+s) - P(t)) \approx P(t)(\ln P(t+s) - \ln P(t))$$

We can approximate the probability in equation (8.10) as

$$\begin{aligned}\Pr(C(P(t+s)) < q \mid I_t) &= \Pr(C(P(t)) + \delta P(t)\triangle \ln P(t+s) < q \mid I_t)\\ &= \Pr(\triangle \ln P(t+s) < \frac{q - C(P(t))}{\delta(t)P(t)} \mid I_t)\end{aligned}$$

where

$$\delta(t) = \frac{\partial C}{\partial P}|_{P(t)} = \Phi(x_1) \text{ with}$$

$$x_1 = \left[\ln\left(\frac{P(t)}{Ke^{-r(T-t)}}\right) + \frac{\sigma^2}{2}(T-t)\right] / \sigma\sqrt{T-t}$$

For each of the three processes $\triangle \ln P(t+s) \mid \ln P(t) \sim N(a - \ln P(t), b)$ and so the above probability can again be easily calculated as follows:

$$\Pr(C(P(t+s)) < q \mid I_t) = \Phi\left(\frac{\frac{q-C(P(t))}{\delta P(t)} + \ln P(t) - a}{\sqrt{b}}\right) \tag{8.11}$$

Now we can compare the difference between the exact distribution of option prices with their delta approximation. Both the true distribution and approximation can be calculated in terms of standard normal, the only difference is due to the critical argument in $\Phi(\cdot)$.

Six VaR measurement can now be calculated: three result from substituting the inverse Black–Scholes formula into the three specifications of the underlying distribution; the delta approximation produces the other three. The natural question to ask now is: which VaR measurement should be used? In other words, the decision maker needs to pick one specification about the distribution of the underlying. From the risk-neutral pricing paradigm, it seems that only the risk-neutral distribution is relevant in the case of pricing and hedging options. Furthermore, given the simple setup of the Black–Scholes complete market, the risk-neutral measure is unique. However, as argued by Ncube and Satchell (1997), the probability of the option finishing in, at or out of the money should be regarded as an *objective* probability, thus the true measure is appropriate. In reality, the risk-neutral measure is just some artificial measure from which we do not observe data. (With the basic forecasting character of risk measurement, it is interesting to ask whether agents can agree on the distribution of tomorrow's underlying price. In fact one could consider an equilibrium where the agent's disagreement about the structure of future prices of the asset and the option also have an impact on the current price.)

Another reason why the risk-neutral measure cannot dominate the true measure lies in the theory of incomplete markets, where the risk-neutral measure may not be unique. In these cases, we do not even know how many measures we can have, consequently it is an impossible task to pick the appropriate measure. On the other hand, there is not so much controversy about the true measure, with which, naturally, the risk measurement starts. In summary, unlike pricing derivatives, both the true measure and the risk-neutral measure play significant roles in measuring risk contained in the derivatives.

Although the arguments in $\Phi(\cdot)$ of equations (8.10) and (8.11) look very different at first sight, they are actually quite closely correlated. The only relevant parts in these arguments are:

$$c_1 = \ln C^{-1}(q), \qquad \text{for the true distribution of option price}$$

$$c_2 = \frac{q - C(P(t))}{\delta(t)P(t)} + \ln P(t), \quad \text{for the delta approximation}$$

If we take $C(P(t))$ as the value of q, the values of c_1 and c_2 are:

$$\ln C^{-1}(C(P(t)) = \ln P(t)$$

$$\frac{C(P(t)) - C(P(t))}{\delta(t)P(t)} + \ln P(t) = \ln P(t)$$

and in this case c_1 and c_2 coincide.

However, besides the current option price $C(P(t))$, all other values taken by q will make c_1 and c_2 different, hence the calculation of VaR. This point can be clarified by checking $\partial c_1/\partial q$ and $\partial c_2/\partial q$. To simplify, write

$$C^{-1}(q) = P(q)$$

That is, the future stock price is a function of the chosen critical value of option q. As $C(P(t))$ is a monotonically increasing function of $P(t)$, the inverse function of $C(\cdot)$ exists and

$$\frac{\partial C^{-1}(q)}{\partial q} = \frac{1}{\partial q/\partial P} = \frac{1}{\partial C/\partial P}$$

Putting all the above results together, we get

$$\frac{\partial c_1}{\partial q} = \frac{1}{\delta(t+s)P(t+s)}$$

$$\frac{\partial c_2}{\partial q} = \frac{1}{\delta(t)P(t)}$$

As $\delta(\cdot)$ and $P(\cdot)$ are positive, both c_1 and c_2 are linearly increasing with q. The difference in $P(t+s)$ and $P(t)$ will determine the values of the two derivatives as $\delta(\cdot)$ changes only with P. If $P(t+s) > P(t)$, then c_1 increases less quickly than c_2. The delta approximation will overestimate the true VaR. If $P(t+s) < P(t)$, although c_1 will now increase faster than c_2, we have $(q - C(P(t)) < 0$, c_1 is still less than c_2 approximately. In summary, the delta approximation is likely to be larger than the true VaR.

8.3 RESULTS

As the two competitive specifications of the true DGP, the GBM and trending OU process are associated with the same risk-neutral process, there is potential misspecification error in the risk measurement. Since the probability function of option prices under these two processes are different, so will be the risk measurement VaR.

By choosing the confidence interval α, and denoting by Z_α the corresponding quantile for the standard normal distribution, we can use equation (8.10) to solve the critical value of the option price, q_α, i.e.

$$q_\alpha = C(\exp(Z_\alpha \sqrt{b} + a)) \tag{8.12}$$

Substituting the exact forms of b, a from equations (8.7) and (8.9) into (8.12), we have

$$q^1_\alpha = C(\exp(Z_\alpha \sqrt{\sigma^2 s} + \ln P(t) + \mu s)) \equiv C(\exp(v_1))$$

$$q^2_\alpha = C(\exp(Z_\alpha \sqrt{\sigma^2/2\gamma(1 - e^{-2\gamma s})} + \mu(t+s) + e^{-\gamma s}(\ln P(t) - \mu t)))$$

$$\equiv C(\exp(v_2))$$

respectively for the GBM and trending OU process. It is easy to show when $\gamma \to 0$, $q^1_\alpha = q^2_\alpha$. However, when γ takes positive values, q^1_α and q^2_α will be different, and $q^1_\alpha > q^2_\alpha$ in most empirical applications.

Having outlined our basic theoretical framework, we now explore empirically what the probability function of option prices looks like, and also examine the size of the potential misspecification error.

We calculate the VaR associated with a European call option on the S&P500 Index using data from 1 January 1996 to 31 December 1998. First we estimate the unconditional sample mean, variance and first-order autocorrelation coefficient, and then following Lo and Wang (1995) we match the drift and volatility parameters in the underlying process with these unconditional moments. Substituting these parameters into equations (8.8)–(8.10), the exact values of VaR and its delta approximation can then be calculated.

We have the following results: $\mu = 0.00088$, $\sigma = 0.011$, $\rho_1(1) = -0.0066$, giving $\gamma = 0.013$. Moreover, in the calculation of VaR two important parameters must also be specified first: the loss probability (or confidence interval), α, and the holding period (or forecasting horizon), s. The typical values of α are 1%, 2.5% and 5%, and the holding period, s, of 1, 7, and 30 days. As we wish to compare the exact VaR with its delta approximation, and since the delta approximation is only accurate for short periods, we restrict the

Table 8.1 The comparison of exact VaR : $s = 1$

	0.01	0.025	0.05	0.1	0.9	0.95	0.975	0.99
GBM	15.77	17.16	18.42	19.96	33.35	35.62	37.66	40.12
RN	15.54	16.92	18.17	19.70	32.97	35.23	37.26	39.70
OU	1.22	1.39	1.56	1.78	4.17	4.66	5.12	5.71

forecasting horizon to 1 or 14 days. Tables 8.1 and 8.2 summarize the values of VaR for a hypothetical European call option under the three processes, whose contract characteristics are: $P(t) = 986.39$, $t = 15$, $T = 59$, $K = 1000$, $r = 0.00023$.

In Tables 8.1 and 8.2, given $K = 1{,}000$, the hypothetical option is in the money. However, the basic result that the exact VaR under the OU process is much smaller than that under the GBM and RN still holds no matter what the moneyness of the option.

From Tables 8.1 and 8.2, it is clear that there are significant differences in the VaR under the three distributional specifications. If the underlying is believed to follow GBM, but the true process is OU, the resultant VaR under GBM will be much higher than the true one, no matter which horizon is used. Furthermore, the VaRs under the OU process turn out be extremely small in the longer forecasting horizon. It would appear that the distribution in this case is virtually degenerate at zero. The reason is that the value of γ has a dramatic effect on the distribution of $P(t+s)$ under the trending OU process.

Consider the future underlying price $P(t+s)$:

$$P(t+s) = \exp(Z_\alpha \sqrt{\sigma^2 s} + \ln P(t) + \mu s), \qquad \text{under GBM}$$

$$\begin{aligned} P(t+s) &= \exp(Z_\alpha \sqrt{\sigma^2/2\gamma(1-e^{-2\gamma s})} + \mu(t+s) + e^{-\gamma s}(\ln P(t) - \mu t)) \\ &= P(t)^{\exp(-\gamma s)} \exp(Z_\alpha \sqrt{\sigma^2/2\gamma(1-e^{-2\gamma s})} + \mu(t+s) - e^{-\gamma s}\mu t) \end{aligned}$$

$$\text{under OU}$$

Table 8.2 The comparison of exact VaR : $s = 14$

	0.01	0.025	0.05	0.1	0.9	0.95	0.975	0.99
GBM	1.65	2.86	4.43	7.05	63.06	73.36	88.64	103.60
RN	1.14	2.03	3.23	5.28	55.18	67.81	79.60	94.11
OU[a]	0	0	0	0	0	0	0	0

[a]As the VaR under the OU process is so small in this example, from 10^{-6} to 10^{-100}. We put zero for all the values of VaR under the OU process. This does not mean that the VaR under the OU process is a single number.

Table 8.3 The value of $P(t)^{\exp(-\gamma s)}$ when $P(t) = 1000$

$s \backslash \gamma$	0.0001	0.001	0.01	0.015	0.03	0.07
1	999.31	993.12	933.58	902.27	815.34	626.88
14	990.38	908.43	405.58	270.24	93.57	13.36

The first term in the expression for $P(t+s)$ under the OU process is basically a double power. Even for a small positive value of γ, it dramatically decrease the value of $P(t+s)$ when s is greater than one. Table 8.3 demonstrates this property. Since the call is a monotonically increasing function of $P(t+s)$, much smaller values of $P(t+s)$ will drive the option price to zero.

Certainly, if γ is small enough, its effect on $P(t+s)$ will not be so dramatic even given some bigger s, for example, when $\gamma = 0.0001$, $P(t)^{\exp(-\gamma s)} = 990.38$ not far from 1000 for $s = 14$. In other words, the evaluation of VaR under the OU process depends crucially on the estimation of γ from actual financial data.

Unfortunately, if we simply follow the Lo and Wang (1995) suggestion, and derive the value of γ directly from the first-order autocorrelation coefficient, we always find that γ is not small enough and its magnitude is larger than 1%. Using our daily stock prices of IBM and Dell, the value of γ is 3.4% and 18.5% respectively. Lo and Wang (1995) also briefly discuss other estimation methods for γ, using the fact that the detrended log price $q_t = p_t - \mu t$ can be approximated by the following discretized AR(1) process:

$$q_k = e^{-\gamma} q_{k-1} + \varepsilon_k, \ \varepsilon_k = \sigma \int_{t_{k-1}}^{t_k} e^{-\gamma(t_k - s)} dW_s$$

The ordinary least squares estimator is asymptotically equivalent to the maximum likelihood estimator, so we can use the OLS estimator to get another estimation of γ. However, the result from OLS is similar to that obtained from autocorrelation. For the SP500 index, it is 2.3% as opposed to 1.3% used in the above example. The associated VaR will be quite different using this alternative estimate.

As far as estimation of the diffusion process is concerned, recently statisticians have shown an increasing interest in and have developed some estimators based on the score function (Sorensen, 1997). Following this method, the estimated value of γ is surprisingly small. It is -0.000032, -0.000065 and 0.000032 for SP500, IBM and Dell data respectively. On the other hand, the estimation of σ^2 is very close to the unconditional sample variance. It seems that the empirical estimation of γ will be quite different with different methods employed. However, we will not pursue the estimation problem further in this chapter. Rather, we hope only to choose the value of γ which makes the VaRs under the three processes comparable, and is also consistent with some empirical estimation results.

We now abandon empirical analysis and compare the distributions of option price and VaR in a controlled experiment. First we choose the stylized yearly values for μ, σ, and $\rho_1(1)$ as follows: $\mu = 0.26$, $\sigma = 0.20$, $\rho_1(1) = -0.1$. These are consistent with typical empirical estimates based on stock index data in developed countries. We then transform these yearly values into daily values by assuming that there are 260 trading days in one year. The daily values are as follows: $\mu = 0.001$, $\sigma_1 = 0.0105$ (for the GBM and RN process), $\sigma_2 = 0.0111$ (for the OU process[3]), $\gamma = 0.0061$. We also specify the current underlying price, $P(t) = 420$, risk-free interest rate $r = 0.0006$, expiry date $T = 59$, and the current date $t = 15$. Tables 8.4 and 8.5 summarize our empirical results with different forecasting horizons and exercise prices.

From Table 8.4, in the short forecasting horizon ($s = 1$), it is clear that the delta approximation is very accurate under the GBM and RN distribution for the out-of-the-money option. For example, the 2.5% true VaR is 1.98 with a delta approximation at 2.01 under GBM. Because r is much smaller than μ, there is a non-negligible difference in VaR under GBM and RN. The average difference between them is about 15%. The true VaR under OU is the smallest among all three specifications, being less than half that under GBM and RN. If we misspecify the dynamics of the underlying, large errors may arise in measuring VaR. The delta approximation under OU is negative, but its absolute values are still larger than those exact VaRs.

For an at-the-money option, the delta approximation is quite accurate under all three specifications. The delta approximation is a little larger than the exact VaR under GBM and RN, but it is smaller than the exact VaR under OU, which is still much smaller than those under GBM and RN.

For an in-the-money option, the delta approximation is accurate under all three specifications as the at-the-money case. Also the exact VaR under OU is not so different from that under GBM and RN as the out-of-the-money case. There is now no negative values for the delta approximation under OU, mainly because the current call price dominates the value in the delta approximation.

When the forecasting horizon increases from 1 to 14 days, some new empirical results appear. In Table 8.5, we can see that, for an out-of-the-money option, the delta approximation is much larger than its exact VaR under GBM, and is much smaller than its exact VaR under RN and OU, except

[3]According to Lo and Wang (1995)'s methodology, in order to match the unconditional sample moments, the drift term will affect the estimated value of diffusion term in the underlying process. That is why we get different values for σ under the OU process from that under the GBM and RN processes.

Table 8.4 Comparison of the exact VaR and their delta approximation with $s = 1$

Moneyness	Out-of-the-money ($K = 480$)				At-the-money ($K = 420$)				In-the-money ($K = 360$)			
Confidence Interval	0.01	0.025	0.05	0.1	0.01	0.025	0.05	0.1	0.01	0.025	0.05	0.1
Exact VaR under GBM	1.77	1.98	2.19	3.51	24.93	26.20	27.31	28.62	77.40	78.99	80.36	81.94
Delta approximation	1.69	2.01	2.28	2.60	25.25	26.64	27.83	28.20	77.89	79.50	80.88	82.48
Exact VaR under RN	1.50	1.69	1.86	2.08	23.17	24.40	25.47	26.74	75.15	76.73	78.09	79.66
Delta approximation	1.23	1.55	1.82	2.14	23.27	24.66	25.85	27.22	75.59	77.20	78.58	80.18
Exact VaR under OU	0.68	0.77	0.86	0.98	14.84	15.83	16.70	17.75	62.30	63.90	65.28	66.88
Delta approximation	−1.44	−1.10	−0.81	−0.48	11.74	13.19	14.45	15.89	62.17	63.86	65.32	67.00

Table 8.5 Comparison of the exact VaR and their delta approximation with $s = 14$

Moneyness	Out-of-the-Money ($K = 480$)				At-the-money ($K = 420$)				In-the-money ($K = 360$)			
Confidence Interval	0.01	0.025	0.05	0.1	0.01	0.025	0.05	0.1	0.01	0.025	0.05	0.1
Exact VaR under GBM	1.10	1.85	2.79	4.31	25.77	31.14	36.04	41.95	80.95	87.08	92.41	98.65
Delta approximation	3.84	5.04	6.07	7.25	34.57	39.75	44.20	49.34	88.73	94.76	99.94	105.91
Exact VaR under RN	0.03	0.07	0.12	0.24	5.82	8.26	10.85	14.40	49.73	55.37	60.30	66.07
Delta approximation	−2.56	−1.36	−0.33	0.85	6.89	12.07	16.53	21.66	56.53	62.56	67.74	73.71
Exact VaR under OU	0	0	0	0	0	0	0	0	0	0	0	0
Delta approximation	−37	−36	−35	−33	−141	−136	−132	−127	−116	−110	−105	−99

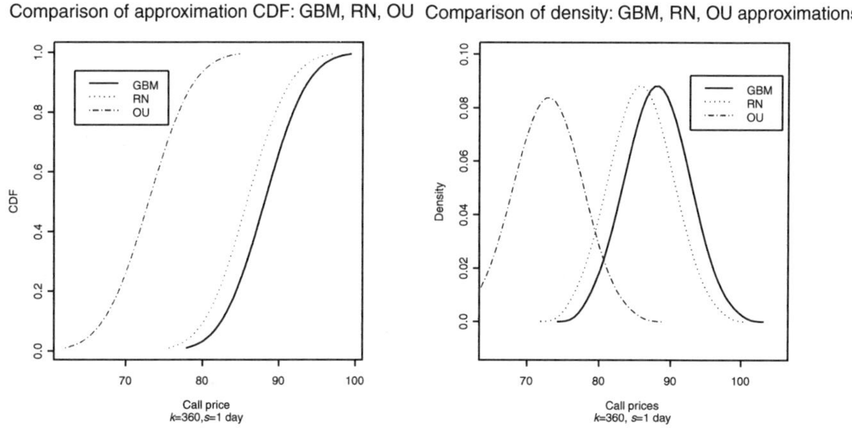

Figure 8.1 CDF and PDF of the delta approximation, in-the-money

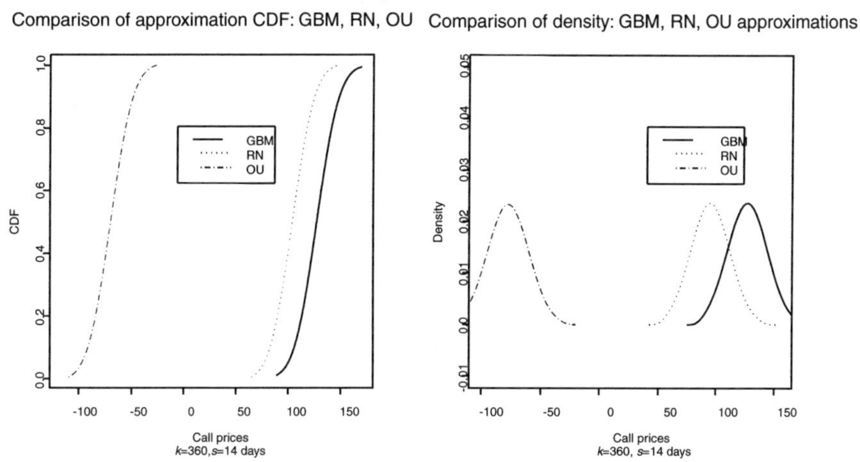

Figure 8.2 CDF and PDF of the delta approximation, in-the-money

for the 10% VaR under RN. The negative values now result for the delta approximation under both OU and RN.

For an at-the-money option, the delta approximation is much larger than the exact VaR under GBM, and much smaller than the true VaR under OU (negative values appear again). The true VaR differs quite significantly under the three specifications, which implies a significant model misspecification error with a long forecasting horizon. For an in-the-money option, a similar conclusion for at-the-money option applies.

The above results can be further illustrated by examining the graphs of the distribution (CDF) and density (PDF) functions. For the delta approximation, the Figures 8.1–8.6 show that the graphs of the CDFs under the three

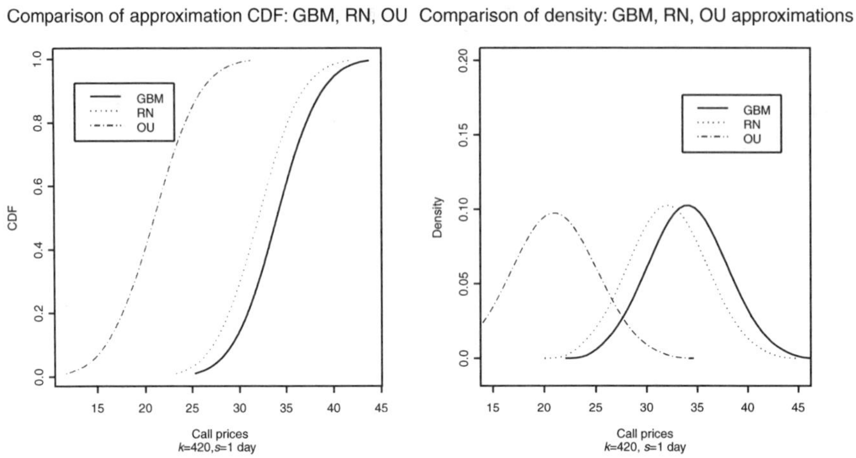

Figure 8.3 CDF and PDF of the delta approximation, at-the-money

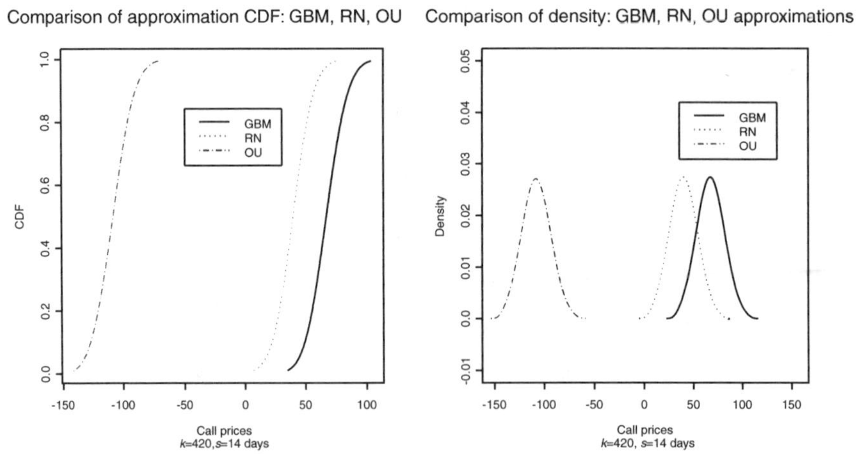

Figure 8.4 CDF and PDF of the delta approximation, at-the-money

specifications have almost the same shape, but different locations, as do the graphs of the PDFs. In particular, the GBM distribution lies to the right of the other two. This observation is true no matter how long the forecasting horizon. For the exact VaR, Figures 8.7–8.12 show that the shapes of the CDFs and the PDFs are quite different under the three specifications. In particular, when the horizon $s = 14$, the CDF and PDF of the OU process are almost straight lines.

8.4 CONCLUSION

In this chapter, we have studied the potential misspecification error associated with asset return distributions in the calculations of VaR for European options.

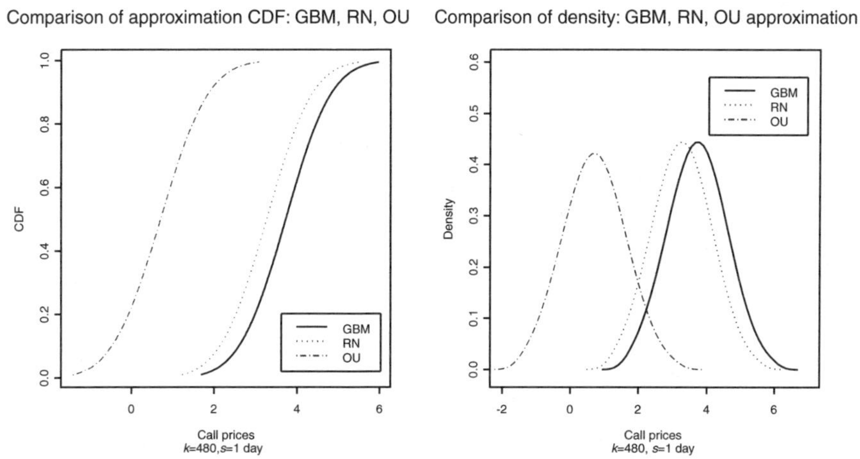

Figure 8.5 CDF and PDF of the delta approximation, out-of-the-money

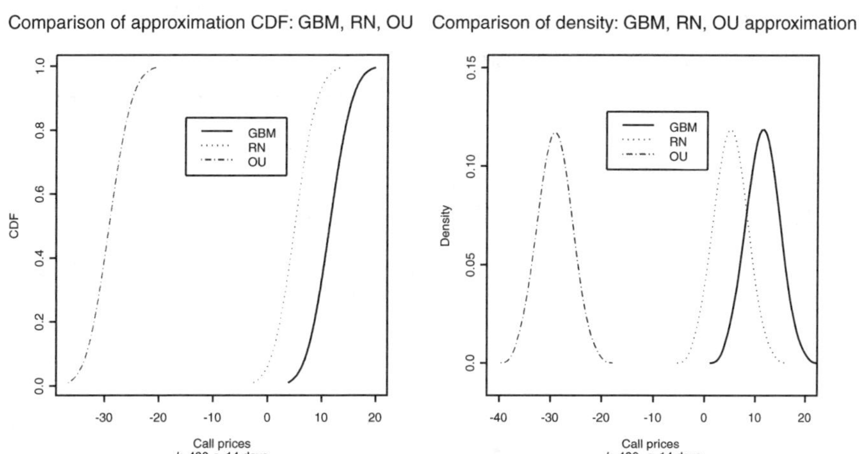

Figure 8.6 CDF and PDF of the delta approximation, out-of-the-money

If the asset return process is either the geometric Brownian motion or trending Orstein–Uhlenbeck process, the true asset return distributions are different even though they lead to the same risk-neutral distribution and hence the same option price formula. Employing the property that the option price is an increasing function of the underlying price, the probability function of the option price has been derived for the GBM, OU and RN distributions. We also derived the probability function of the option price via the delta approximation.

Based on these theoretical results, we empirically calculated the exact VaR from the probability functions under the three distributions. When the forecasting horizon is short, there is little difference in VaR under the GBM

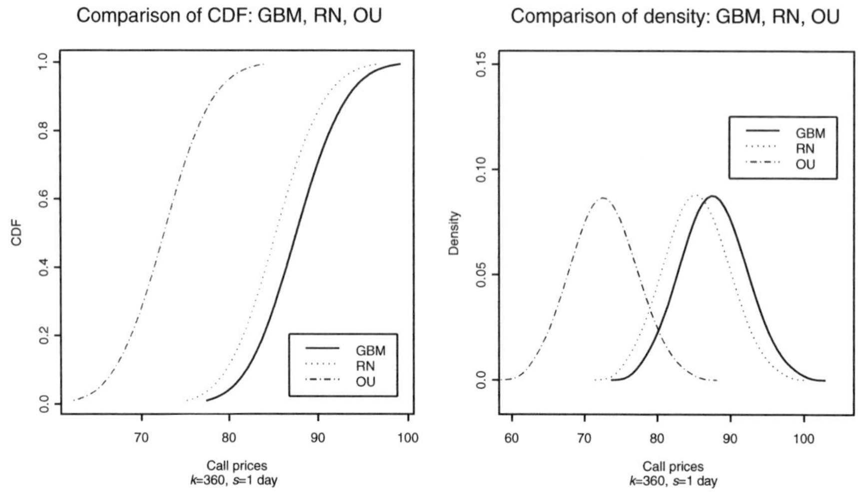

Figure 8.7 CDF and PDF of the exact VaR, in-the-money

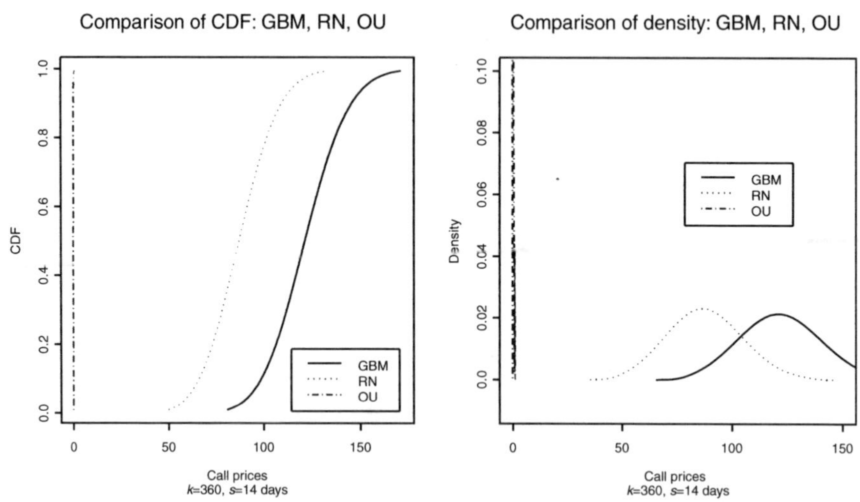

Figure 8.8 CDF and PDF of the exact VaR, in-the-money

and RN distributions, no matter whether the option is in, at, or out of the money. However, the VaR under the OU distribution is much different from the other two, often a third to a half the size.

When the forecasting horizon becomes longer, even the difference in VaR under the GBM and RN distributions is not negligible. The VaR under the OU distribution is almost degenerate at zero. All these results imply that the misspecification error can be substantial even in the simple Black–Scholes framework.

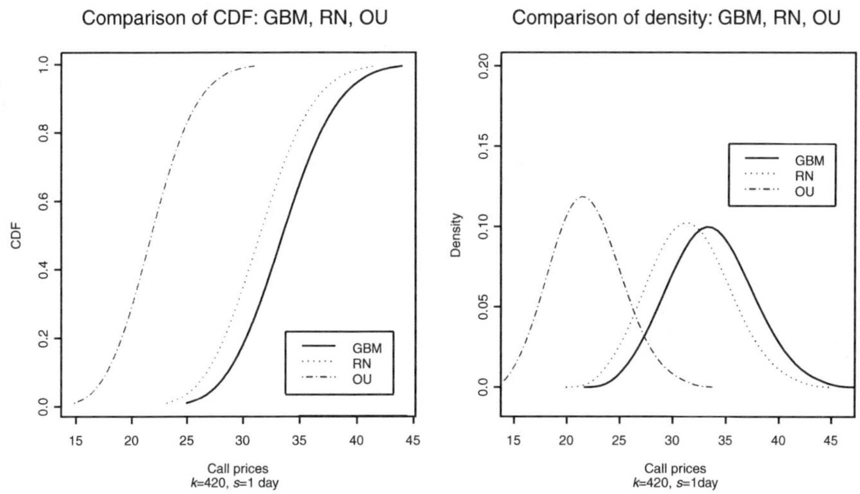

Figure 8.9 CDF and PDF of the exact VaR, at-the-money

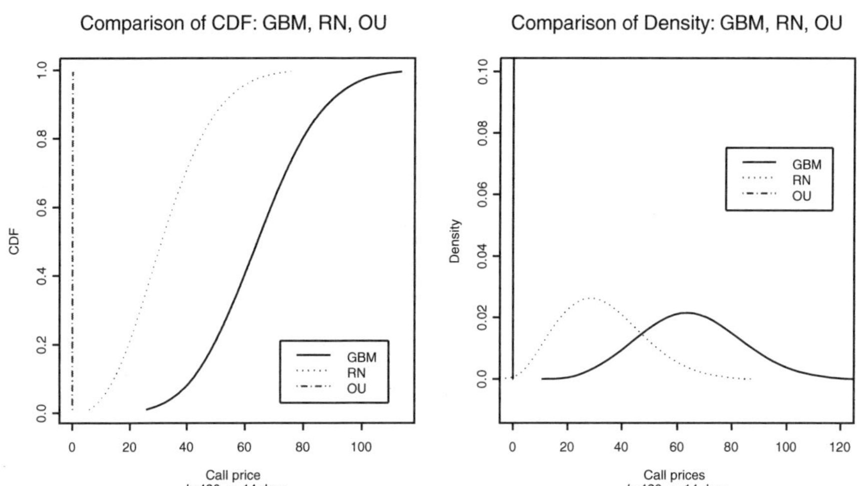

Figure 8.10 CDF and PDF of the exact VaR, at-the-money

We also compared the exact VaR with its delta approximation. Consistent with the other empirical study on this topic,[4] usually, the delta approximation overestimates the exact VaR. The discrepancy increases with the forecasting horizon.

Based on these empirical findings, we concluded that the distributions of our

[4]For example, two recent papers (Lina *et al.*, 1999; Britten-Jones and Schaefer, 1999) discuss how to calculate the VaR for derivatives such as options via delta-gamma approximation and inverse Fourier transformation.

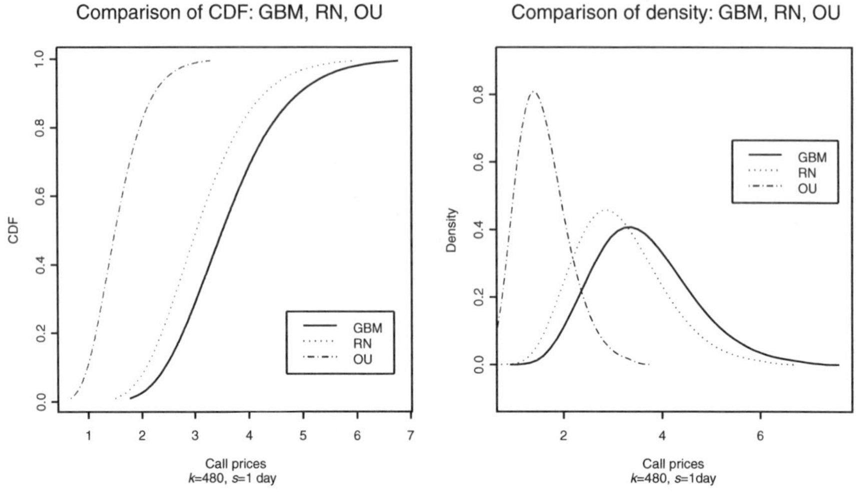

Figure 8.11 CDF and PDF of the exact VaR, out-of-the-money

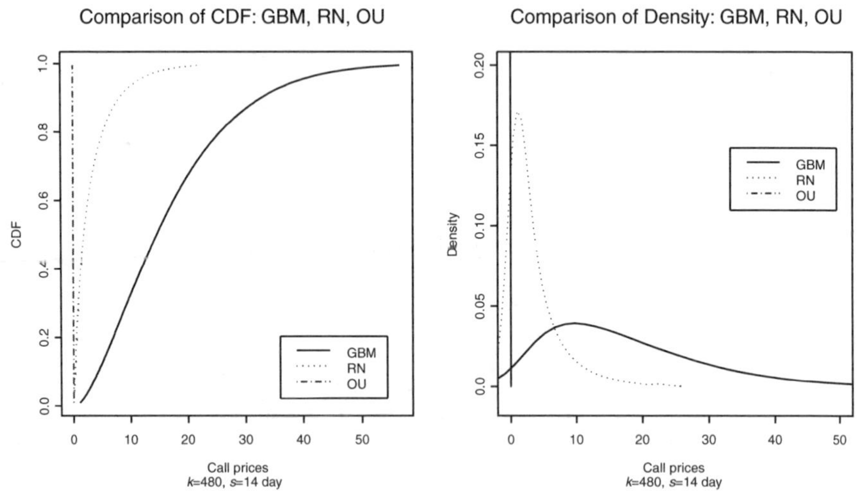

Figure 8.12 CDF and PDF of the exact VaR, out-of-the-money

option forecasts are very sensitive to the true asset return distribution. In the future, we wish to study more complicated specifications of the underlying process such as those containing jumps and stochastic volatility.

REFERENCES

Basle Committee on Banking Supervision (1996) Amendment to the Capital Accord to Incorporate Market Risks, Basle, Switzerland.

Bergman, Y.Z., Grundy, B.D. and Wiener, Z. (1996) 'General Properties of Option Prices', *Journal of Finance*, **51**(5), 1573–1610.

Britten-Jones, M. and Schaefer, S.M. (1999) 'Non-Linear Value-at-Risk', *European Finance Review*, **2**.

Chan, K.C., Karolyi, G., Longstaff, A. and Sanders, A.B. (1992) 'An Empirical Comparison of Alternative Models of the Short-Term Interest Rate', *Journal of Finance*, **47**, 1209–1227.

Cox, J.C. and Ross, S.A. (1976) 'The Valuation of Options for Alternative Stochastic Processes', *Journal of Financial Economics*, **3**, 145–166.

Duffie, D. and Jun, P. (1997) 'An Overview of Value at Risk, Journal of Derivatives', **4**, 7–49

Dybvig, P. and Ross, S. (1987) 'Arbitrage', in *The New Palgrave Dictionary of Economics*, Macmillan, London, pp. 100–106.

Engel, J. and Gizycki, M. (1999) 'Conservatism, Accuracy and Efficiency: Comparing Value-at-Risk Models', Working paper, Australian Prudential Regulation Authority.

Fama, E.F. and French, K.R. (1988) 'Permanent and Temporary Components of Stock Prices', *Journal of Political Economy*, **96**, 246–273.

Grundy, B.D. (1991) 'Option Prices and the Underlying Asset's Return Distribution', *Journal of Finance*, **46**, 1045–1069.

Harrison, M. and Kreps, D. (1979) 'Martingales and Arbitrage in Multiperiod Security Markets', *Journal of Economic Theory*, **20**, 381–408.

Harrison, M. and Pliska, S. (1981) 'Martingales and Stochastic Integrals in the Theory of Continuous Trading', *Stochastic Processes and Their Applications*, **11**, 215–260.

Lina, El-Jahel, Perraudin, W. and Sellin, P. (1999) 'Value-at-Risk for Derivatives', *Journal of Derivatives*, Spring.

Lo, A.W. (1987) 'Semi-Parametric Upper Bounds of Option Prices and Expected Payoffs', *Journal of Financial Economics*, **19**, 373–387.

Lo, A.W. and Jiang Wang (1995) 'Implementing Option Pricing Models When Asset Returns Are Predictable', *Journal of Finance*, **50**, 87–129.

Lo, A.W. and Craig, M.A. (1988) 'Stock Market Prices Do Not Follow Random Walks: Evidence from a Simple Specification Test', *Review of Financial Studies*, **1**, 41–66.

Ncube, M. and Satchell, S. (1997) The Statistical Properties of the Black–Scholes Option Price', *Mathematical Finance*, **7**, 287–305.

Sorensen, M. (1997) 'Estimating Functions For Discretely Observed Diffusion: A Review', Working Paper, Department of Theoretical Statistics, University of Aarhus.

Chapter 9

Pricing derivatives written on assets with arbitrary skewness and kurtosis

JOHN L. KNIGHT AND STEPHEN E. SATCHELL

ABSTRACT

This chapter provides formulae and a methodology for pricing an asset whose returns have known (or estimated) moments up to order four. The methodology allows one to price derivatives written on the asset. This chapter differs from previous papers based on Hermite expansions in that we do not assume risk-neutrality. We compute prices for European options and deduce the appropriate risk-neutral valuation density for the case of a representative agent with power utility. We find that pricing does not depend upon the preference parameters, nor the parameters that govern the distribution of consumption but it does depend upon expected returns in the equity market. We find that our representation leads naturally to greeks, psi and chi which are the changes in the option price with respect to changes in kurtosis and skewness. Furthermore, attempts to calibrate this model with UK aggregate data brings us back to the equity premium puzzle in a different guise.

9.1 INTRODUCTION

The purpose of this chapter is to present a framework for the risk-neutral valuation (RNVR) of assets whose distributions exhibit arbitrary skewness and kurtosis. This represents an extension of results on risk-neutral valuation relationships presented by, among others, Rubinstein (1974), Brennan (1979) and Stapleton and Subramanyan (1984). The need for such an extension follows from the paper by Hull and White (1997) who investigate the pricing of FX options where the underlying returns exhibit positive kurtosis. Their approach assumes the underlying returns follow a mixture of normals which lacks the generality required to properly model higher moments. They also assume risk-neutral valuation is available without investigating what conditions are needed. In particular, their greeks are defined with respect to functions of fundamental parameters rather than the fundamental parameters themselves. Other recent papers that use a mixture of lognormals include Bahra (1996), Campa *et al.* (1997), and Melich and Thomas (1997).

The chapter can also be seen as an extension of a literature on option pricing using Gram–Charlier expansions that begins with Jarrow and Rudd (1982), is further developed in Madan and Milne (1994) and Corrado and Su (1996), and has been recently extended by Backus *et al.* (1997). Backus *et al.* concentrate on pricing exchange rate options and explaining smile effects. They assume risk neutrality so that the risk premium is zero.

Our work also represents an extension of interesting research by Camara (1997) who presents theorems on RNVRs for arbitrary transformations of normals and log-normals. While his results are impressive, they are not suited to answer the question as to how the price of an option might change due to changes in higher moments in the distribution of the underlying asset. The question we investigate is interesting because of the recognition that, first, many long-term investments have option-like features, and second, while volatility has decreased in many mature markets in recent years, kurtosis has often increased. Furthermore, while defenders of the Ito approach might claim that a particular pattern of returns could be modelled by a diffusion process, which would give us mean–variance results, the standard mean–variance approach would be a very poor approximation over holding periods of even moderate length.

The specific approach we use is to take the bivariate two-period pricing model of Rubinstein where aggregate consumption and the asset price have a known joint distribution and assume that the marginal distribution of the asset follows a Gram–Charlier type A series (Kendall and Stuart, 1969). This allows us to specify explicitly the skewness and kurtosis of the equity market as fundamental parameters to our model. We further assume that the conditional distribution of consumption given the asset price is normal and compute the price of an option in Proposition 3. By inspection of the price we see that, for plausible parameter values, RNVR occurs. In Proposition 2 we present a formula for the RNVR distribution which turns out to be a mean-adjusted Gram–Charlier series. Furthermore, the greeks introduced by Hull and White (1997), namely, chi and psi, can be easily computed for our model since skewness and kurtosis are explicit parameters.We end the chapter with some numerical calculations applied to UK equity data. Section 9.2 presents the theory, applications and conclusions follow in Section 9.3 and proofs are relegated to the Appendix.

9.2 RNVR RELATIONSHIPS

In this section we will define a RNVR. An economy is defined to have a RNVR relationship if the price of an asset at time t, P_t, can be written as

$$P_t = \frac{1}{1 + r_f} E_t^Q (V_{t+1}) \tag{9.1}$$

where r_f is the riskless rate of interest, V_{t+1} is the (stochastic) payoff of the asset at time $t + 1$ and $E_t^Q(\cdot)$ its expectation, conditional upon time t with respect to the risk-neutral measure Q. Establishing the existence of a RNVR reduces to finding Q for a given economy. Different authors define the RNVR in different ways. Camara (1997), for example, defined it to be independent of preferences parameters while Duan (1993) defines it in terms of shifted mean parameters.

As is standard in the literature, we consider a representative agent in a two-period securities market economy. We assume the representative agent has power utility functions

$$u_t(C_t) = \frac{1}{(1 - \beta)} C_t^{1-\beta} \tag{9.2}$$

and

$$u_{t+1}(C_{t+1}) = p \frac{1}{(1 - \beta)} C_{t+1}^{1-\beta}$$

where p is the time-preference parameter, β is a parameter and C_t and C_{t+1} are (real) consumption at time t and $t + 1$ respectively.

It is well known (see Huang and Litzenburger, 1988, for example) that the above assumptions are consistent with a Pareto-optimal market equilibrium and with an appropriate theory of aggregation.

Defining, for the moment, only the first two moments of our variables we shall follow Huang and Litzenburger (1988) in parameterizing our variables appropriately, where we need to model aggregate consumption, the stock market (equity), which is measured in units of consumption, and a riskless asset whose one-period rate of return is the known constant r_f. Let $\tilde{x}_j$ and $\tilde{c}$ be respectively, the payoff on equity and the level of consumption in time $t + 1$.

Furthermore, assume that

$$E(\ell n(\tilde{x}_j)) = \hat{\mu}_j$$

$$E(\ell n(\tilde{c})) = \hat{\mu}_c \tag{9.3}$$

and

$$cov\begin{pmatrix} \ell n(\tilde{x}_j) \\ \ell n(\tilde{c}) \end{pmatrix} = \begin{pmatrix} \sigma_j^2 & K'\sigma_j\hat{\sigma}_c \\ & \hat{\sigma}_c^2 \end{pmatrix}$$

If we now consider the new variables

$$X = \ell n(\tilde{x}_j/p_t),$$

$$Y = \ell n(p(\frac{\tilde{c}}{c_t})^{-\beta}),$$

these have transformed means

$$(\mu_x, \mu_y) = (\hat{\mu}_j - \ell n(p_t), -\beta\hat{\mu}_c + \ell n(p) + \beta\ell n(c_t)) \tag{9.4}$$

and

$$\begin{pmatrix} \sigma_x^2, & K\sigma_x\sigma_y \\ & \sigma_y^2 \end{pmatrix} = \begin{pmatrix} \sigma_j^2, & -\beta K'\sigma_j\hat{\sigma}_c \\ & \beta^2\hat{\sigma}_c^2 \end{pmatrix}$$

For future reference, we note that β is assumed positive, so that $u_{t+1}(\cdot)$ has $u''_{t+1}(\cdot)$ negative, and that K' is assumed positive, since it is the correlation between $\ell n(\tilde{c})$ and $\ell n(\tilde{x}_j)$ which should be positive since large payouts in the stock market should be associated with more consumption. It then follows that K should be negative, a result we note as a lemma.

Lemma 1. *The correlation K, defined by equation (9.4) is negative.*

Proof: See above discussion.

Our next definition is concerned with Gram–Charlier (GC) expansions of probability density functions (pdf). These are representations of pdfs that are frequently used by statisticians because of their tractability and simplicity.

A GC expansion of the pdf of X, pdf(x), is defined to be

$$pdf(x) = \phi(x)\left(1 + \frac{\lambda_3}{3!}H_3(x) + \frac{\lambda_4}{4!}H_4(x)\right) \tag{9.5}$$

where $\phi(x)$ is a standard normal ($N(0,1)$) i.e. $\phi(x) = \frac{1}{\sqrt{2\pi}}\exp(\frac{-x^2}{2})$ and

$$H_3(x) = x^3 - 3x$$

$$H_4(x) = x^4 - 6x^2 + 3$$

The polynomials, $H_j(x)$, are called Hermite polynomials. The assumption in equation (9.5) is that $E(X) = 0$, $\sigma^2 = var(X) = 1$,

$$E\left[\left(\frac{X - E(X)}{\sigma}\right)^3\right] = \lambda_3$$

$$E\left[\left(\frac{X - E(X)}{\sigma}\right)^4\right] = \lambda_4$$

so that λ_3 is the skewness of X and λ_4 is the excess kurtosis of X.

It is straightforward to check that if $X \sim N(0, 1)$, then $\lambda_3 = 0$ and $\lambda_4 = 0$.

In addition, we will calculate the moment-generating function (mgf) of X, $\phi_X(s)$, which can be shown to equal the following:

$$\phi_X(s) = \exp\left(\frac{1}{2}s^2\right)\left(1 + \frac{\lambda_3}{6}s^3 + \frac{\lambda_4 s^4}{24}\right) \tag{9.6}$$

The variable X whose pdf is given by equation (9.5) will be denoted by $X \sim GC(0, 1, \lambda_3, \lambda_4)$. It is immediate that if $Y = a + bX$, then $Y \sim \left(a, b^2, b^3\lambda_3, b^4\lambda_4\right)$ since one can manipulate the mgf in equation (9.6). We next prove the following lemma.

Lemma 2. *If $X_1 \sim N(\mu_1, \sigma_1^2)$ and $X_2 \sim GC(\mu_2, \sigma_2^2, \lambda_3, \lambda_4)$ and X_1, X_2 are independent then $Y = X_1 + X_2 \sim GC(\mu_1 + \mu_2, \sigma_1^2 + \sigma_2^2, \lambda_3, \lambda_4)$.*

Proof. See the Appendix

Having presented our preliminary definitions and results, we now wish to model our joint pdf of (x, y) whose mean and covariance matrices are given by equation (9.4).

Changing notation, we wish to construct

$$\begin{pmatrix} X \\ Y \end{pmatrix} \sim \left[\begin{pmatrix} \mu_x \\ \mu_y \end{pmatrix}, \begin{pmatrix} \sigma_x^2, & K\sigma_x\sigma_y \\ & \sigma_y^2 \end{pmatrix}\right] \tag{9.7}$$

in terms of GC variables.

It seems natural that X, equity, should be modelled to have a GC distribution since the parameters of interest in our model are λ_3 and λ_4. It is a fact that these parameters are often significantly non-zero, and empirically, that motivates our chapter along with the observation that often the essential information about an equity market is in the first four moments. For mathematical convenience, we shall assume that pdf($y|x$), the conditional pdf, should be normal. To ensure that our correlations are consistent with equation (9.7), we shall start with X' and Y' such that they satisfy the following assumptions:

(A1) pdf(x') $\sim GC(0, 1, \lambda_3, \lambda_4)$
(A2) pdf(y') $\sim N(0, 1)$ and
(A3) X' and Y' are independent.

Our desired variables $(X, Y)'$ are also related to $(X', Y')'$ by the following relationship:

(A4) $$\begin{pmatrix} X \\ Y \end{pmatrix} = \begin{pmatrix} \mu_x \\ \mu_y \end{pmatrix} + A\begin{pmatrix} X' \\ Y' \end{pmatrix}$$

where $A = \begin{pmatrix} \sigma_x & 0 \\ K\sigma_y, & \sigma_{y\sqrt{1-K^2}} \end{pmatrix}$.

It follows immediately from (A1) to (A4) that we can compute *pdf*(x), *pdf*($y|x$), *pdf*(x, y) and *pdf*(y) which we present in Proposition 1.

Proposition 1. *Under Assumptions (A1) to (A4) the pdfs of Y and X are given by the following:*

(i) $pdf(x) \sim GC(\mu_x, \sigma_x^2, \sigma_x^3\lambda_3, \sigma_x^4\lambda_4)$
(ii) $pdf(y) \sim GC(\mu_y, \sigma_y^2, K^3\sigma_y^3\lambda_3, K^4\sigma_y^4\lambda_4)$
(iii) $pdf(y|x) \sim N(\mu_y + \frac{K\sigma_y}{\sigma_x}(x - \mu_x), \sigma_y^2(1 - K^2))$
(iv)

$$pdf(x, y) = pdf(y|x)pdf(x) = \frac{1}{2\pi\sigma_x\sigma_y(1 - K^2)}$$

$$\exp(-\frac{1}{2(1 - K^2)}\left(\left(\frac{x - \mu_x}{\sigma_x}\right)^2 - 2K\left(\frac{x - \mu_x}{\sigma_x}\right) \times \left(\frac{y - \mu_y}{\sigma_x}\right)\right.$$

$$\left. + \left(\frac{y - \mu_y}{\sigma_y}\right)^2\right) \times (1 + \frac{\lambda_3}{\sigma}H_3\left(\frac{x - \mu_x}{\sigma_x}\right) + \frac{\lambda_4}{24}H_4\left(\frac{x - \mu_x}{\sigma_x}\right))$$

Proof. See Appendix.

It may seem contrived that while equity has skewness and kurtosis, consumption, conditional on equity, is normal. We note, however, that our marginal for y has a GC distribution. Our aim is to construct a joint pdf whose marginals are GC distributions; Proposition 1 achieves this aim.

9.3 COMPUTING THE RNVR

We now turn to the computation of a RNVR. In terms of our previous notation, an asset will be priced in our model in terms of a RNVR, for P_t' a price and V_{t+1}' a payoff, as follows:

$$P_t' = \frac{1}{1+r_f}\int V_{t+1}' pdf_Q \tag{9.8}$$

or, in terms of the representative agent,

$$P_t' = \int\int V_{t+1}' \exp(y) pdf(x,y)dxdy \tag{9.9}$$

Thus, from equation (9.8) and (9.9), we see that

$$pdf_Q = (1+r_f)\int \exp(y) pdf(x,y)dy \tag{9.10}$$

Furthermore, pdf_Q will have two restrictions imposed on it due to the presence of two primitive observable assets: equity and bonds.

In particular, for the bond

$$\frac{1}{1+r_f} = E(\exp(y)) \tag{9.11}$$

which, from equation (9.10) is just the requirement that $\int pdf_Q = 1$.

For equity, using equation (9.11), we see that

$$1 = E(\exp(x+y)) \tag{9.12}$$

Both of these restrictions can be calculated by using Proposition 1.

In particular, since $E(\exp(x+y))$ is the joint *mgf* of x and y evaluated at (1,1) and $Y|X$ is normal from Proposition 1, and X is $\mathrm{GC}(\mu_x, \sigma_x^2, \sigma_x^3\lambda_3, \sigma_x^4\lambda_4)$,

$$\begin{aligned}
E(\exp(x+y)) &= E_X(\exp(x)E(\exp(y)|x)) \\
&= E_X\left(\exp\left(x + \mu_y + \frac{K\sigma_y}{\sigma_x}(x-\mu_x) + \frac{1}{2}\sigma_y^2(1-K^2)\right)\right) \\
&= \exp\left(\mu_y - \mu_x\frac{K\sigma_y}{\sigma_x} + \frac{1}{2}\sigma_y^2(1-K^2)\right)E_X\left(\exp\left(x\left(1+\frac{K\sigma_y}{\sigma_x}\right)\right)\right)
\end{aligned}$$

Thus, using Proposition 1 and equation (9.12), we see that

$$\begin{aligned}
1 = \exp&\left(\mu_y - \frac{\mu_x K\sigma_y}{\sigma_x} + \frac{1}{2}\sigma_y^2(1-K^2) + \mu_x\left(1+\frac{K\sigma_y}{\sigma_x}\right) + \frac{1}{2}\sigma_x^2\left(1+\frac{K\sigma_y}{\sigma_x}\right)^2\right) \\
&\times\left(1+\frac{\lambda_3}{6}(\sigma_x+K\sigma_y)^3 + \frac{\lambda_4}{24}(\sigma_x+K\sigma_y)^4\right)
\end{aligned}$$

or

$$1 = \exp\left(\mu_x + \mu_y + \frac{1}{2}\sigma_y^2 + \frac{1}{2}\sigma_x^2 + K\sigma_x\sigma_y\right)\left(1 + \frac{\lambda_3}{6}(\sigma_x + K\sigma_y)^3 + \frac{\lambda_4}{6}(\sigma_x + K\sigma_y)^4\right) \tag{9.13}$$

From similar calculations, using Proposition 1

$$\frac{1}{1+r_f} = E(\exp(y)) = \exp\left(\mu_y + \frac{1}{2}\sigma_y^2\right)\left(1 + \frac{\lambda_3 K^3\sigma_y^3}{6} + \frac{\lambda_4}{24}K^4\sigma_y^4\right) \tag{9.14}$$

These two restrictions can be imposed on pdf_Q in two stages.

First, using equation (9.14), along with (9.10) we can rewrite

$$pdf_Q = \int \frac{\exp\left(y - \mu_y - \frac{1}{2}\sigma_y^2\right) pdf(x, y)dy}{\left(1 + \frac{\lambda_3\psi^3}{6} + \frac{\lambda_4\psi^3}{24}\right)} \tag{9.15}$$

The second restriction, (9.14), can be used to eliminate ψ, since we can rewrite (9.13) using (9.14) as

$$1 = \frac{\exp\left(\mu_x + \frac{1}{2}\sigma_x^2 + \sigma_x\psi\right)\left(1 + \frac{\lambda_3}{6}(\sigma_x + \psi)^3 + \frac{\lambda_4}{24}(\sigma_x + \psi)^4\right)}{(1 + r_f)(1 + \frac{\lambda_3}{6}\psi^3 + \frac{\lambda_4}{24}\psi^4)} \tag{9.16}$$

Equation (9.16) can be used to eliminate ψ as a function of $r_f, \mu_x, \sigma_x^2, \lambda_3$ and λ_4.

It is worth noting that while we can eliminate μ_y, σ_y^2 and $\psi(= K\sigma_y)$ from pdf_Q it will still depend upon μ_x, in much the same way that occurs with power utility and Garch volatility for X (see Satchell and Timmermann, 1996).

Evaluating the integral in equation (9.15), we can readily find an expression for the pdf_Q. The final expression is given in Proposition 2.

Proposition 2. *The pdf associated with the RNVRs pdf_Q is given by*

$$pdf_Q = \frac{1}{\sqrt{2\pi\sigma_x^2}}\exp\left(-\frac{1}{2\sigma_x^2}(X - \mu_x - \sigma_x\psi)^2\right)\left[1 + \frac{\lambda_3}{6}H_3\left(\frac{x - \mu_x}{\sigma_x}\right) + \frac{\lambda_4}{24}H_4\left(\frac{X - \mu_x}{\sigma_x}\right)\right]\left[1 + \frac{\lambda_3}{6}\psi^3 + \frac{\lambda_4}{24}\psi^4\right]^{-1}$$

Proof. See Appendix.

9.4 OPTION PRICING

In this section we use our results in Section 3 to price an option. We shall consider a call option on units of real aggregate consumption in period 2.

Following Huang and Litzenburger (1988, equation 6.10.3), the price of the European call option $f(S, E)$, where S is the current price of the asset and E is the exercise price, is given by the sum of the two integrals:

$$f(S,E) = S\int_{-\infty}^{\infty}\int_{a}^{\infty} e^{x+y}pdf(x,y)dxdy$$

$$- E\int_{-\infty}^{\infty}\int_{a}^{\infty} e^{y}pdf(x,y)dxdy \tag{9.17}$$

where $pdf(\cdot)$ is the joint pdf on future consumption and asset returns, and $a = \ell n(E/S)$.

We present the valuation of $f(S, E)$ in Proposition 3.

Proposition 3. *The option price, $f(S, E)$ is given below by:*

$$f(S,E) = S\Phi(z+\sigma_x) - E\Phi(z)/(1+r_f)$$

$$+ S\Phi(z+\sigma_x)D(\lambda_3,\lambda_4;\psi+\sigma_x)$$

$$- E\Phi(z)D(\lambda_3,\lambda_4,\psi)/(1+r_f)$$

where $z = \psi - b, \psi = K\sigma_y$ and $D(\cdot,\cdot,\cdot)$ is defined in the Appendix.

Remark 1. *The above formula could be programmed straightforwardly and needs as inputs only the following parameters, other than the five used in Black–Scholes, μ_x, λ_3, λ_4, and ψ. One can solve for ψ from equation (9.15).*

Remark 2. *When we now come to compute our greeks, our task is much easier than Hull and White (1997) who, because they use a mixture, have no natural parameter for λ_3 and λ_4. We can define chi $= \partial f/\partial\lambda_3$ and psi $= \partial f/\partial\lambda_4$.*

Proposition 4. *From the option price specified in Proposition 3 and under the assumption that $K = 0$ i.e. $z = -b$ we can easily obtain expressions for psi and* *chi given by*

$$psi = \frac{\partial f(S,E)}{\partial \lambda_4}$$

$$= S \cdot \phi(\sigma_x - b) \frac{(24P_2(\sigma_x) + 4\lambda_3\sigma_x^3(b^3 - 3b))}{(24 + 4\lambda_3\sigma_x^3 + \lambda_4\sigma_x^4)^2}$$

$$- \frac{E \cdot \phi(-b)}{(1 + r_f)} \frac{(b^3 - 3b)}{24}$$

$$chi = \frac{df(S,E)}{\partial \lambda_3}$$

$$= 4S \cdot \phi(b - \sigma_x) \frac{24P_1(\sigma_x) - \lambda_4\sigma_x^3(b^3 - 3b))}{(24 + 4\lambda_3\sigma_x^3 + \lambda_4\sigma_x^4)^2}$$

$$- \frac{E \cdot \phi(b)(b^2 - 1)}{6}$$

where $P_1(\gamma) = \gamma^2 + b(b + \gamma) - 1$ *and* $P_2(\gamma) = \gamma^3 + b\gamma^2 + (b^2 - 1)\gamma + b^3 - 3b$.

Proof. See Appendix.

9.5 CONCLUSION

In this section we present some calculations for our RNVR in Section 9.3 based on recent UK data.

We take for our asset series (monthly returns on the FTA. This is based on data from February 1976 to December 1994 (227 observations). We also have a 3-month British Government Treasury Bill measured over the same period. We report the four moments for the full period and over the two sub-periods in Table 9.1.

Table 9.1

	Mean	Standard deviation	Skewness λ_3	Excess kurtosis λ_4
Whole FTA	0.0141	0.0541	−1.1009	5.1628
FTB	0.0087	0.0024	−0.1641	−0.6288
Feb. 85 FTA	0.0169	0.5190	−0.4571	1.5180
FTB	0.0093	0.0023	−0.0326	−0.5563
Post Feb. 85 FTA	0.0113	0.0563	−1.5960	7.7345
FTB	0.0082	0.0025	−0.1954	−0.9364

For the consumption of the RNVR, values of $\mu_x, \sigma_x^2, \lambda_3, \lambda_4$ and r_f are required and are chosen from Table 9.1. For example, the monthly RNVR uses the parameters 0.0141 for μ_x, 0.0541 for σ_x, -1.1009 for λ_3,5.1628 for λ_4 and a TB (monthly) rate of 0.0087. Clearly, we would have preferred a monthly bill rate but we could not find one.

We solved equation (9.16) for ψ using the package Macsyma and obtained the following values: -0.1217 for whole FTA, -0.1678 for Feb. 85 FTA and -0.0811 for post Feb. 85 FTA. Comparing these values with their λ_4 for each period we notice that as λ_4 increases, ψ decreases.

It is instructive to see what these values of ψ are measuring. We know that $\psi = -\beta K \sigma_y$. For example, if $\psi = -0.1217$, then knowledge of σ_c (the monthly standard deviation of consumption) and K (the monthly correlation between the real consumption growth rate and (real) return on the FTA) allow us to infer a value of β. Taking values from Damant *et al.* (1997)), who use real quarterly consumption expenditure on non-durable goods plus services divided by the UK population from 1976:1 to 1995:4 gives an approximate annual standard deviation of 2%. The correlation coefficient between this series and quarterly FTA returns was -0.1344. Solving the above for β, which is the coefficient of relative risk aversion gives us a value of $\beta = 156.84$. This is enormous and illustrates in a novel way a manifestation of the equity premium puzzle; see Mehra and Prescott (1985). Essentially, we need an enormous amount of risk aversion to use power utility to fit the empirical data. The inadequacy of power utility is known to hold across most mature markets; see Campbell (1996). Nevertheless it is a useful tractable utility function when extending asset pricing models to incomplete markets where utility will enter into pricing formulae.

APPENDIX

Proof of Lemma 2

Since $X_1 \sim N(\mu_1, \sigma_1^2)$ and $X_2 \sim GC(\mu_2, \sigma_2^2, \lambda_3, \lambda_4)$ with X_1 and X_2 independent we have

$$E[\exp(t(X_1 + X_2))] = E[\exp(tX_1)]E[\exp(tX_2)]$$

where

$$E[\exp(tX_1)] = \exp(t\mu_1 + \frac{1}{2}\sigma_1^2 t^2)$$

and

$$E[\exp(tX_2)] = \exp(\mu_2 t + \frac{1}{2}\sigma_2^2 t^2) \cdot [1 + \frac{\lambda_3}{6} t^3 + \frac{\lambda_4}{24} t^4]$$

Consequently,

$$E[\exp(t(X_1 + X_2))] = \exp\left[(\mu_1 + \mu_2)t + \frac{1}{2}(\sigma_1^2 + \sigma_2^2)t^2\right] \cdot \left[1 + \frac{\lambda_3}{6}t^3 + \frac{\lambda_4}{24}t^4\right]$$

and the result follows.

Proof of Proposition 1

Since X' and Y' are independent we have from Assumption (A4) that

(i)

$$\begin{aligned}
[\exp(tX)] &= E[\exp(t(\mu_x + \sigma_x X'))] \\
&= \exp(t\mu_x)E[\exp(t\sigma_x X')] \\
&= \exp(t\mu_x)\exp\left(\frac{t^2\sigma_x^2}{2}\right) \cdot [1 + \frac{\lambda_3}{6}(t\sigma_x)^3 + \frac{\lambda_4}{24}(t\sigma_x)^4] \\
&\Rightarrow X \sim GC(\mu_x, \sigma_x^2, \sigma_x^3\lambda_3, \sigma_4^x\lambda_4)
\end{aligned}$$

(ii)

$$\begin{aligned}
E[\exp(tY)] &= E[\exp(t(\mu_y + K\sigma_y X' + \sigma_y\sqrt{1-K^2}Y')] \\
&= \exp(t\mu_y)E[\exp(tK\sigma_y X')]E[\exp(t\sigma_y\sqrt{1-K^2}Y')] \\
&= \frac{\exp(t\mu_y) \cdot \exp(t^2\sigma_y^2(1-K^2)}{2} \\
&\quad \cdot \exp(\frac{t^2K^2\sigma_y^2}{2})[1 + \frac{\lambda_3}{6}t^3K^3\sigma_y^3 + \frac{\lambda_4}{24}t^4K^4\sigma_y^4] \\
&= \exp(t\mu_y + \frac{t^2}{2}\sigma_y^2)[1 + \frac{\lambda_3}{6}t^3K^3\sigma_y^3 + \frac{\lambda_4}{24}t^4K^4\sigma_y^4] \\
&\Rightarrow Y \sim GC(\mu_y, \sigma_y^2, K^3\sigma_y^3\lambda_3, K^4\sigma_y^4\lambda_4)
\end{aligned}$$

(iii)

$$\begin{aligned}
E[\exp(tY)|X] &= E[\exp(tY) \mid X'] \\
&= E[\exp(t(\mu_y + K\sigma_y X' + \sigma_y\sqrt{1-K^2}Y')) \mid X'] \\
&= \exp(t(\mu_y + K\sigma_y X'))E[\exp(t\sigma_y\sqrt{1-K^2}Y') \mid X'] \\
&= \exp(t\mu_y + K\sigma_y X')\exp(t^2\sigma_y^2(1-K^2)/2)
\end{aligned}$$

Substituting for $X' = (X - \mu_x)\sigma_x$ we have

$$E[\exp(tY)|X] = \exp(t(\mu_y + \frac{K\sigma_y}{\sigma_x}(X - \mu_x)) + \frac{t^2\sigma_y^2}{2}(1 - K^2))$$

$$\Rightarrow Y \mid X \sim N(\mu_y + \frac{K\sigma_y}{\sigma_x}(X - \mu_x), \sigma_y^2(1 - K^2))$$

$$pdf(x, y) = pdf(y \mid x)pdf(x)$$

$$= \frac{1}{\sigma_y\sqrt{2\pi(1-K^2)}}\exp\left[-\frac{1}{2\sigma_y^2(1-K^2)}\left(y - \mu_y - \frac{K\sigma_y}{\sigma_x}(x - \mu_x)\right)^2\right]$$

$$\cdot\frac{1}{\sigma_x\sqrt{2\pi}}\exp\left(-\frac{1}{2\sigma_x^2}(x-\mu_x)^2\right)\left[1 + \frac{\lambda_3}{6}H_3\left(\frac{x-\mu_x}{\sigma_x}\right)\right.$$

$$\left.+\frac{\lambda_4}{24}H_4\left(\frac{x-\mu_x}{\sigma_x}\right)\right]$$

$$= \frac{1}{2\pi\sigma_x\sigma_y\sqrt{1-K^2}}\exp\left(-\frac{1}{2(1-K^2)}\left(\left(\frac{x-\mu_x}{\sigma_x}\right)^2\right.\right.$$

$$-2K\left(\frac{x-\mu_x}{\sigma_x}\right)\left(\frac{y-\mu_y}{\sigma_y}\right)$$

$$\left.\left.+\left(\frac{y-\mu_y}{\sigma_y}\right)^2\right)\right)\cdot\left[1 + \frac{\lambda_3}{6}H_3\left(\frac{x-\mu_x}{\sigma_x}\right) + \frac{\lambda_4}{24}H_4\left(\frac{x-\mu_x}{\sigma_x}\right)\right]$$

Proof of Proposition 2

From equation (9.15) we have

$$pdf_Q = \frac{\exp\left(-\mu_y - \sigma_y^2/2\right)}{\left(1 + \frac{\lambda_3}{6}\psi^3 + \frac{\lambda_4}{24}\psi^4\right)}\int e^y pdf(x, y)dy$$

Now replacing $pdf(x, y)$ by $pdf(y|x)pdf(x)$ and noting that $y|x$ is normal we have

$$pdf_Q = \frac{\exp\left(-\mu_y - \sigma_y^2/2\right)}{\left(1 + \frac{\lambda_3}{6}\psi^3 + \frac{\lambda_4}{24}\psi^4\right)} pdf(x) \int e^y pdf(y|x)dy$$

$$= \exp\left(-\mu_y - \sigma_y^2/2\right) \exp\left(\mu_y + \frac{K\sigma_y}{\sigma_x}(x - \mu_x) + \frac{1}{2}\sigma_y^2(1 - K^2)\right)$$

$$\frac{pdf(x)}{\left(1 + \frac{\lambda_3}{6}\psi^3 + \frac{\lambda_4}{24}\psi^4\right)}$$

$$= \frac{1}{\sqrt{2\pi\sigma_x^2}} \exp\left(-\frac{1}{2\sigma_x^2}(x - \mu_x - \sigma_x\psi)^2\right)$$

$$\left[1 + \frac{\lambda_3}{6} H_3\left(\frac{x - \mu_x}{\sigma_x}\right) + \frac{\lambda_4}{24} H_4\left(\frac{x - \mu_x}{\sigma_x}\right)\right]\left(1 + \frac{\lambda_3}{6}\psi^3 + \frac{\lambda_4}{24}\psi^4\right)^{-1}$$

Proof of Proposition 3

Considering the two integrals in $f(S, E)$ given by equation (9.17) we have (i)

$$\int_{-\infty}^{\infty} \int_{a}^{\infty} e^y pdf(x, y)dxdy$$

$$= \int_{-\infty}^{\infty} \int_{a}^{\infty} e^y pdf(y|x) pdf(x)dxdy$$

$$= \int_{a}^{\infty} pdf(x)\left(\int_{-\infty}^{\infty} e^y pdf(y|x)dy\right)dx$$

$$= \int_{a}^{\infty} pdf(x) \cdot \left(\exp\left(\mu_y + \frac{K\sigma_y}{\sigma_x}(x - \mu_x) + \frac{1}{2}\sigma_y^2(1 - K^2)\right)\right)dx$$

(from Proposition 1 where $y|x \sim Normal$)

$$= \exp\left(\mu_y + \frac{1}{2}\sigma_y^2(1 - K^2)\right) \cdot \int_{a}^{\infty} \exp\left(K\sigma_y\left(\frac{x - \mu_x}{\sigma_x}\right)\right) pdf(x)dx$$

Examining just the integral we have

$$\int_a^\infty \exp(K\sigma_y(\frac{x-\mu_x}{\sigma_x})) \cdot pdf(x)dx$$

$$= \int_a^\infty \exp(K\sigma_y(\frac{x-\mu_x}{\sigma_x})) \cdot \frac{1}{\sigma_x\sqrt{2\pi}}\exp(-\frac{1}{2}(\frac{x-\mu_x}{\sigma_x})^2)$$

$$[1+\frac{\lambda_3}{6}H_3(\frac{x-\mu_x}{\sigma_x})+\frac{\lambda_4}{24}H_4(\frac{x-\mu_x}{\sigma_x})]dx.$$

Changing variables $x \to \omega = \frac{x-\mu_x}{\sigma_x}$ we have

$$= \int_{\frac{a-\mu_x}{\sigma_x}}^\infty e^{K\sigma_y w}\frac{1}{\sqrt{2\pi}}e^{-w^2/2}[1+\frac{\lambda_3}{6}H_3(w)+\frac{\lambda_4}{24}H_4(w)]dw$$

$$= e^{K^2\sigma_y^2/2}\int_{\frac{a-\mu_x}{\sigma_x}}^\infty \frac{1}{\sqrt{2\pi}}\exp(-\frac{1}{2}(w-K\sigma_y)^2)[1+\frac{\lambda_3}{6}H_3(w)+\frac{\lambda_4}{24}H_4(w)]dw$$

To solve this integral we require the moment generating function of a truncated Normal distribution. In particular, consider the integral:

$$M(t) = \frac{1}{1-\Phi(b-K\sigma_y)}\int_b^\infty e^{tw}\frac{1}{\sqrt{2\pi}}\exp(-\frac{1}{2}(w-K\sigma_y)^2)dw$$

$$= \frac{1}{1-\Phi(b-K\sigma_y)}\int_b^\infty \frac{1}{\sqrt{2\pi}}\exp[-\frac{1}{2}(w^2-2w(K\sigma_y+t)+(K\sigma_y+t)^2$$

$$+(K\sigma_y)^2-(K\sigma_y+t)^2)]dw$$

$$= \frac{\exp(-\frac{(K\sigma_y)^2}{2}+\frac{(K\sigma_y+t)^2}{2}}{1-\Phi(b-K\sigma_y)}\cdot\int_b^\infty \frac{1}{\sqrt{2\pi}}\exp(-\frac{1}{2}(w-K\sigma_y+t))^2)dw$$

$$= \exp(-[(K\sigma_y)^2-(K\sigma_y+t)^2]/2)\cdot\frac{(1-\Phi(b-K\sigma_y-t))}{1-\Phi(b-K\sigma_y))}$$

i.e.

$$M(t) = \exp(K\sigma_y t+\frac{t^2}{2})\frac{(1-\Phi(b-K\sigma_y-t))}{(1-\Phi(b-K\sigma_y))}$$

Therefore we now have that the required integrals are:

(a)

$$\exp((K\sigma_y)^2/2) \cdot \int_{\frac{a-\mu_x}{\sigma_x}}^{\infty} \frac{1}{\sqrt{2\pi}} \exp(-\frac{1}{2}(w - K\sigma_y)^2)dw$$

$$= \exp((K\sigma_y)^2/2)(1 - \Phi(\frac{a - \mu_x}{\sigma_x} - K\sigma_y))$$

(b)

$$\exp((K\sigma_y)^2/2) \cdot \int_{\frac{a-\mu_x}{\sigma_x}}^{\infty} H_3(w)\frac{1}{\sqrt{2\pi}} \exp(-\frac{1}{2}(w - K\sigma_y)^2)dw$$

$$= \exp((K\sigma_y)^2/2)(1 - \Phi(\frac{a - \mu_x}{\sigma_x} - K\sigma_y)) \cdot \int_{\frac{a-\mu_x}{\sigma_x}}^{\infty} \frac{(w^3 - 3w)e^{-(w-K\sigma_y)/2}}{\sqrt{2\pi}(1 - \Phi(\frac{a-\mu_x}{\sigma_x} - K\sigma_y))}dw$$

$$= \exp((K\sigma_y)^2/2)(1 - \Phi(\frac{a - \mu_x}{\sigma_x} - K\sigma_y)) \cdot \{M'''(0) - 3M'(0)\}$$

Similarly

(c)

$$\exp((K\sigma_y)^2/2) \int_{\frac{a-\mu_x}{\sigma_x}}^{\infty} H_4(w)\frac{1}{\sqrt{2\pi}} \exp(-\frac{1}{2}(w - K\sigma_y)^2)dw$$

$$= \exp((K\sigma_y)^2/2)(1 - \Phi(\frac{a - \mu_x}{\sigma_x} - K\sigma_y))\{M''''(0) - 6M''(0) + 3$$

For the derivatives of $M(t)$ we have:

$$M(t) = \exp(\psi t + t^2/2)\frac{(1 - \Phi(b - \psi - t))}{(1 - \Phi(b - \psi))}$$

$$M'(t) = (\psi + t)M(t) + \frac{(\phi(b - \psi - t))}{(1 - \Phi(b - \psi))}\exp(\psi t + t^2/2)$$

$$= (\psi + t)M(t) + Q(t)$$

$$M''(t) = (\psi + t)[(\psi + t)M(t) + Q(t)] + M(t)$$
$$+ (\psi + t)Q(t) + (b - \psi - t)Q(t)$$
$$= (1 + (\psi + t)^2)M(t) + (2(\psi + t) + b - (\psi + t))Q(t)$$
$$= (1 + (\psi + t)^2)M(t) + (b + \psi + t)Q(t)$$

$$M'''(t) = (1 + (\psi + t)^2)[(\psi + t)M(t) + Q(t)]$$
$$+ 2(\psi + t)M(t) + Q(t)$$
$$+ (b + \psi + t)Q'(t)$$
$$= ((\psi + t)^3 + 3(\psi + t))M(t) + (2 + (\psi + t)^2)Q(t)$$
$$+ b(b + \psi + t)Q(t)$$
$$= ((\psi + t)^3 + 3(\psi + t))M(t) + (2 + (\psi + t)^2) + b(b + \psi + t))Q(t)$$

$$M''''(t) = (3(\psi + t)^2 + 3)M(t)$$
$$+ ((\psi + t)^3 + 3(\psi + t))[(\psi + t)M(t) + Q(t)]$$
$$+ (2(\psi + t) + b)Q(t)$$
$$+ b(2 + (\psi + t)^2 + b(b + \psi + t))Q(t)$$
$$= ((\psi + t)^4 + 6(\psi + t)^2 + 3)M(t)$$
$$+ ((\psi + t)^3 + 5(\psi + t) + 3b + b(\psi + t)^2 + b^2(b + \psi + t)]Q(t)$$

Thus

$$M'(0) = \psi + Q(0) = \psi + \frac{\phi(b - \psi)}{1 - \Phi(b - \psi)}$$

$$M''(0) = 1 + \psi^2 + (b + \psi)Q(0)$$

$$M'''(0) = \psi^3 + 3\psi + (\psi^2 + b(b + \psi) + 2)Q(0)$$

$$M''''(0) = \psi^4 + 6\psi^2 + 3 + (\psi^3 + 5\psi + 3b + b\psi^2 + b^2(b + \psi))Q(0)$$

giving

$$M'''(0) - 3M'(0) = \psi^3 + (\psi^2 + b(b+\psi) - 1)Q(0)$$

$$\begin{aligned} M''''(0) - 6M''(0) + 3 &= \psi^4 + (\psi^3 - \psi - 3b + b\psi^2 + b^2(b+\psi))Q(0) \\ &= \psi^4 + (\psi^3 - \psi - 3b + b\psi^2 + b^2\psi + b^3)Q(0) \end{aligned}$$

Consequently, (b) and (c) above now have the expression:

$$(b)\exp(\frac{\psi^2}{2})(1 - \Phi(b-\psi))[\psi^3 + (\psi^2 + b(b+\psi) - 1)Q(0)]$$

$$(c)\exp(\frac{\psi^2}{2})(1 - \Phi(b-\psi))[\psi^4 + (\psi^3 - \psi - 3b + b\psi^2 + b^2\psi + b^3)Q(0)]$$

Therefore letting

$$\begin{aligned} A &= \int_{-\infty}^{\infty}\int_{a}^{\infty} e^y pdf(x,y)dxdy \\ &= \exp(\mu_y + \frac{1}{2}\sigma_y^2 - \frac{\psi^2}{2}) \cdot \exp(\frac{\psi^2}{2}) \cdot (1 - \Phi(b-\psi)) \\ &\quad \cdot [1 + \frac{\lambda_3}{6}(\psi^3 + (\psi^2 + b(b+\psi) - 1)Q(0)) \\ &\quad + \frac{\lambda_4}{24}(\psi^4 + (\psi^3 - \psi - 3b + b\psi^2 + b^2\psi + b^3)Q(0))] \\ &= \exp(\mu_y + \frac{\sigma_y^2}{2})(1 - \Phi(b-\psi))[1 + \frac{\lambda_3}{6}(\psi^3 + (\psi^2 + b(b+\psi) - 1)Q(0)) \\ &\quad + \frac{\lambda_4}{24}(\psi^4 + (\psi^3 - \psi - 3b + b\psi^2 + b^2\psi + b^3)Q(0))] \\ &= \exp(\mu_y + \sigma_y^2)(1 - \Phi(b-\psi))[1 + \frac{\lambda_3}{6}\psi^3 + \frac{\lambda_4}{24}\psi^4 \\ &\quad + \frac{\lambda_3}{6}A_1(\psi) + \frac{\lambda_4}{24}A_2(\psi)] \end{aligned}$$

with

$$A_1(\psi) = (\psi^2 + b(b+\psi) - 1)\frac{\phi(b-\psi)}{(1 - \Phi(b-\psi))}$$

and

$$A_2(\psi) = (\psi^3 - \psi - 3b + b\psi^2 + b^2\psi + b^3)\frac{\phi(b-\psi)}{(1-\Phi(b-\psi))}$$

From result (9.14) we have

$$(1+r_f)^{-1} = \exp(\mu_y + \frac{\sigma_y^2}{2})[1 + \frac{\lambda_3}{6}\psi^3 + \frac{\lambda_4}{24}\psi^4]$$

Thus A may be written compactly as:

$$A = \frac{(1-\Phi(b-\psi))[1 + D(\lambda_3, \lambda_4, \psi)]}{(1+r_f)}$$

where

$$D(\lambda_3, \lambda_4, \psi) = \frac{(\frac{\lambda_3}{6}A_1(\psi) + \frac{\lambda_4}{24}A_2(\psi))}{(1 + \frac{\lambda_3}{6}\psi^3 + \frac{\lambda_4}{24}\psi^4)}$$

(ii) Next we consider the other integral in equation (9.17) given by

$$\int_{-\infty}^{\infty}\int_{a}^{\infty} e^{x+y} pdf(x,y)dxdy$$

$$= \int_{a}^{\infty} e^x pdf(x)(\int_{-\infty}^{\infty} e^y pdf(y \mid x)dy)dx$$

$$= \int_{a}^{\infty} e^x \exp(\mu_y + \frac{K\sigma_y}{\sigma_x}(x-\mu_x) + \frac{\sigma_y^2}{2}(1-K^2))pdf(x)dx$$

$$= \exp(\mu_x + \mu_y + \frac{\sigma_y^2}{2}(1-K^2))$$

$$\cdot \int_{\frac{a-\mu_x}{\sigma_x}}^{\infty} \exp((\sigma_x + \psi)z)\frac{1}{\sqrt{2\pi}}e^{-z^2/2}[1 + \frac{\lambda_3}{6}H_3(z) + \frac{\lambda_4}{24}H_4(z)]dz$$

Noting that the integral is of the same form as in (i) above, we can readily specialize the results by substituting $(\sigma_x + \psi)$ in place of ψ in the expression for

A above. That is, we have:

$$\int_{\frac{a-\mu_x}{\sigma_x}}^{\infty} \exp((\sigma_x+\psi)z)\frac{1}{\sqrt{2\pi}}e^{-z^2/2}[1+\frac{\lambda_3}{6}H_3(z)+\frac{\lambda_4}{24}H_4(z)]dz$$

$$= \exp(\frac{(\psi+\sigma_x)^2}{2})(1-\Phi(b-\sigma_x-\psi))[1+$$

$$+\frac{\lambda_3}{6}((\psi+\sigma_x)^3((\psi+\sigma_x)^2+b(b+\psi+\sigma_x)-1)Q_1(0))$$

$$+\frac{\lambda_4}{24}((\psi+\sigma_x)^4((\psi+\sigma_x)^3-(\psi+\sigma_x)-3b+b(\psi+\sigma_x)^2$$

$$+b^2(\psi+\sigma_x)+b^3)Q_1(0))]$$

where

$$Q_1(0)=\frac{\phi(b-\psi-\sigma_x)}{1-\Phi(b-\psi-\sigma_x)}$$

Consequently,

$$\int_{-\infty}^{\infty}\int_{a}^{\infty} e^{x+y}pdf(x,y)dxdy$$

$$= \exp(\mu_x+\mu_y+\frac{\sigma_x^2}{2}+\frac{\sigma_y^2}{2}+\sigma_x\psi)(1-\Phi(b-\sigma_x-\psi))[1+\frac{\lambda_3}{6}(\psi+\sigma_x)^3$$

$$+\frac{\lambda_4}{24}(\psi+\sigma_x)^4+\frac{\lambda_3}{6}A_1(\psi+\sigma_x)+\frac{\lambda_4}{24}A_2(\psi+\sigma_x)]$$

$$= B$$

Using result (9.16) i.e. that

$$1=\exp(\mu_x+\mu_y+\frac{\sigma_x^2}{2}+\frac{\sigma_y^2}{2}+\sigma_x\psi)[1+\frac{\lambda_3}{6}(\psi+\sigma_x)^3+\frac{\lambda_4}{24}(\psi+\sigma_x)^4]$$

we can rewrite B as:

$$B=(1-\Phi(b-\sigma_x-\psi))[1+D(\lambda_3,\lambda_4,\psi+\sigma_x)]$$

Therefore since

$$f(S,E)=S\cdot B-E\cdot A$$

we have

$$f(S,E) = S(1-\Phi(b-\psi-\sigma_x)) - \frac{E(1-\Phi(b-\psi))}{(1+r_f)}$$
$$+ S(1-\Phi(b-\sigma_x-\psi))D(\lambda_3,\lambda_4,\psi+\sigma_x)$$
$$- \frac{E(1-\Phi(b-\psi))D(\lambda_3,\lambda_4,\psi)}{(1+r_f)}$$

Since

$$b = \frac{a-\mu_x}{\sigma_x}$$
$$= \frac{\ell n(E/S)-\mu_x}{\sigma_x}$$

and $1-\phi(b-\psi) = \Phi(\psi-b)$ we note immediately that the first term in $f(S,E)$ is merely the price under log-normality given in Huang and Litzenberger (1988, pp. 165–166, equations 6.10.10 and 6.10.11). The remaining terms are the corrections for non-normality.

Proof of Proposition 4

From Proposition 3, with $K=0$ i.e. $\psi=0$ we have

$$\frac{\partial f}{\partial \lambda_k} = S\cdot\Phi(\sigma_x-b)\frac{\partial D}{\partial \lambda_k}(\lambda_3,\lambda_4,\sigma_x) - \frac{E\cdot\Phi(-b)}{(1+r_f)}\frac{\partial D}{\partial \lambda_k}(\lambda_3,\lambda_4,0), \quad k=3,4$$

Now

$$D(\lambda_3,\lambda_4,\gamma) = \frac{4\lambda_3 A_1(\gamma)+\lambda_4 A_2(\gamma)}{24+4\lambda_3\gamma^3+\lambda_4\gamma^4}$$

with

$$A_1(\gamma) = (\gamma^2+b(b+\gamma)-1)\frac{\phi(b-\gamma)}{(1-\Phi(b-\gamma))}$$
$$= \frac{\phi(b-\gamma)}{(1-\Phi(b-\gamma))}\cdot P_1(\gamma)$$

and

$$A_2(\gamma) = (\gamma^3 + b\gamma^2 + (b^2 - 1)\gamma + b^3 - 3b)\frac{\phi(b-\gamma)}{(1-\Phi(b-\gamma))}$$

$$= \frac{\phi(b-\gamma)}{(1-\Phi(b-\gamma))} \cdot P_2(\gamma).$$

Thus

$$\frac{\partial D(\lambda_3, \lambda_4, \gamma)}{\partial \lambda_4} = \frac{A_2(\gamma)}{(24 + 4\lambda_3\gamma^3 + \lambda_4\gamma^4)} - \frac{\gamma^4 D(\lambda_3, \lambda_4, \gamma)}{(24 + 4\lambda_3\gamma^3 + \lambda_4\gamma^4)}$$

$$= \frac{\phi(b-\gamma)}{(1-\Phi(b-\gamma))}(24 + 4\lambda_3\gamma^3 + \lambda_4\gamma^4)^{-1}$$

$$\cdot \left[P_2(\gamma) - \frac{\gamma_4(4\lambda_3 P_1(\gamma) + \lambda_4 P_2(\gamma))}{24 + 4\lambda_3\gamma^3 + \lambda_4\gamma^4}\right]$$

$$= \frac{\phi(b-\gamma)}{(1-\Phi(b-\gamma))}(24 + 4\lambda_3\gamma^3 + \lambda_4\gamma^4)^{-1}$$

$$\cdot [24P_2(\gamma) + 4\lambda_3\gamma^3(P_2(\gamma) - \gamma P_1(\gamma))]$$

$$= \frac{\phi(b-\gamma) \cdot (24P_2(\gamma) + 4\lambda_3\gamma^3(b^3 - 3b))}{(1-\Phi(b-\gamma))(24 + 4\lambda_3\gamma^3 + \lambda_4\gamma^4)^2}$$

Consequently,

$$\frac{\partial D(\lambda_3, \lambda_4, \sigma_x)}{\partial \lambda_4} = \frac{\phi(b-\sigma_x)}{(1-\Phi(b-\sigma_x))}\frac{(24P_2(\sigma_x) + 4\lambda_3\sigma_x^3(b^3 - 3b))}{(24 + 4\lambda_3\sigma_x^3 + \lambda_4\sigma_x^4)^2}$$

and

$$\frac{\partial D(\lambda_3, \lambda_4, 0)}{\partial \lambda_4} = \frac{\phi(b)}{(1-\Phi(b))} \cdot \frac{24P_2(0)}{(24)^2}$$

$$= \frac{\phi(b)}{(1-\Phi(b))} \cdot \frac{(b^3 - 3b)}{24}.$$

Thus

$$psi = \frac{\partial f}{\partial \lambda_4} = S \cdot (\sigma_x - b)\frac{(24P_2(\sigma_x) + 4\lambda_3\sigma_x^3(b^3 - 3b))}{(24 + 4\lambda_3\sigma_x^3 + \lambda_4\sigma_x^4)^2}$$

$$- \frac{E \cdot \phi(-b)}{(1 + r_f)} \cdot \frac{(b^3 - 3b)}{24}$$

Similarly,

$$\frac{\partial D(\lambda_3, \lambda_4, \gamma)}{\partial \lambda_3} = \frac{4A_1(\gamma)}{24 + 4\lambda_3\gamma^3 + \lambda_4\gamma^4} - \frac{4\gamma^3 D(\lambda_3, \lambda_4, \gamma)}{24 + 4\lambda_3\gamma^3 + \lambda_4\gamma^4}$$

$$= \frac{4\phi(b-\gamma)}{(1-\Phi(b-\gamma))}(24 + 4\lambda_3\gamma^3 + \lambda_4\gamma^4)^{-1}$$

$$\cdot \left[P_1(\gamma) - \frac{\gamma^3(4\lambda_3 P_1(\gamma) + \lambda_4 P_2(\gamma))}{24 + 4\lambda_3\gamma^3 + \lambda_4\gamma^4} \right]$$

$$= \frac{4\phi(b-\gamma)}{(1-\Phi(b-\gamma))} \frac{(24P_1(\gamma) - \lambda_4\gamma^3(b^3 - 3b))}{(24 + 4\lambda_3\gamma^3 + \lambda_4\gamma^4)^2}$$

with

$$\frac{\partial D(\lambda_3, \lambda_4, \sigma_x)}{\partial \lambda_3} = \frac{4\phi(b-\sigma_x)}{(1-\Phi(b-\sigma_x))} \frac{(24P_1(\sigma_x) + \lambda_4\sigma_x^3(b^3 - 3b))}{(24 + 4\lambda_3\sigma_x^3 + \lambda_4\sigma_x^4)^2}$$

and

$$\frac{\partial D(\lambda_3, \lambda_4, 0)}{\partial \lambda_3} = \frac{4\phi(b)}{(1-\Phi(b))} \cdot \frac{24(b^2-1)}{(24)^2} = \frac{\phi(b)}{(1-\Phi(b))} \frac{(b^2-1)}{6}$$

so

$$chi = \frac{\partial f}{\partial \lambda_3} = 4S \cdot \phi(b-\sigma_x) \frac{(24P_1(\sigma_x) + \lambda_4\sigma_x^3(b^3 - 3b)}{(24 + 4\lambda_3\sigma_x^3 + \lambda_4\sigma_x^4)^2}$$

$$- E \cdot \phi(b) \cdot \frac{(b^2-1)}{6}$$

REFERENCES

Amin, K.J. and Ng, U.N. (1993) 'Option Valuation with Systematic Stochastic Volatility', *Journal of Finance*, **48**, 881–910.

Backus, D., Foresi, S., Li, K. and Wu, L. (1997) 'Accounting for Biases in Black–Scholes'. Discussion paper presented to the FMG Empirical Finance Conference (November).

Bahra, B. (1996) 'Probability Distributions of Future Asset Prices Implied by Option Prices', *Bank of England Quarterly Bulletin*, August, 299–311.

Brennan, M. (1974) 'The Pricing of Contingent Claims in Discrete Time Models', *Journal of Finance*, **34**, 53–68.

Camara, A. (1997) 'Doctoral Dissertation in Finance', University of Lancaster.

Campa, J. C., Chang, P.H.K. and Reider, R.L. (1997) 'ERM Bandwidths for EMU and After: Evidence From Foreign Exchange Options', *Economic Policy*, 55–87.

Campbell, J. (1996) 'Consumption and the Stock Market: Interpreting International Evidence',' Harvard University and NBER Discussion Paper No. 1763.

Corrado, C.J. and Su, T. (1996) 'Skewness and Kurtosis in S and P 500 Index Returns Implied by Option Prices', *Journal of Financial Research*, **19**, 175–192.

Damant, D.H., Hwang, S. and Satchell, S. (1997) 'An Integrated Risk Measure with Application to U.K. Asset Allocation', University of Cambridge, DAE Discussion Paper No. 9714.

Duan, J.C. (1993) 'The Garch Option Pricing Model', mimeo, Faculty of Management, McGill University.

Hull, J. and White, A. (1997) 'Evaluating the Impact of Skewness and Kurtosis on Derivative Prices', *Net Exposure*, **3**, 81–90.

Huang, C. and Litzenberger, R. (1988) *Foundations of Financial Economics*, North-Holland. Amsterdam.

Jarrow, R. and Rudd, A. (1982) 'Approximate Optional Valuation for Arbitrary Stochastic Processes', *Journal of Financial Economics*, **10**, 347–369.

Kendall, M.G. and Stuart, A. (1969) *The Advanced Theory of Statistics* **1**, C. Griffin and Co., London.

Madan, D.B. and Milne, F. (1994) 'Contingent Claims Valued and Hedged by Pricing and Investing in a Basis', *Mathematical Finance*, **4**, 223–245.

Mehra, R. and Prescott, E.C. (1985) 'The Equity Premium, A Puzzle', *Journal of Monetary Economics*, 145–161.

Melick, W.R. and Thomas, C.P. (1997) 'Recovering an Assets Implied PDF From Options Prices', *Journal of Financial and Quantitative Analysis*, **32**, 91–116.

Rubinstein, M. (1976) 'The Valuation of Uncertain Income Streams and the Pricing of Options', *Bell Journal of Economics*, **7**, 407–425.

Satchell, S.E. and Timmermann, A. (1996) 'Option Pricing With GARCH', *Derivatives Use, Trading and Regulation*, I, 1(3), 279–293, II 1(4), 353–367.

Stapleton, R.C. and Subrahmanyam, M.G. (1984) 'The Valuation of Multivariate Contingent Claims in Discrete Time Models', *Journal of Finance*, **39**, 207–228.

Chapter 10

The distribution of realized returns from moving average trading rules with application to Canadian stock market data

ALEXANDER FRITSCHE

ABSTRACT

We describe the probability density of realized returns for a moving average trading rule, given that the underlying structure of asset returns is a two-scale Gamma process. Analytical results are derived, given specific parameters of the underlying returns distribution. We find that the probability density of realized returns is skewed extremely to the left for most reasonable parameter values. Furthermore, we show that it is in general not possible to assign a preference ordering over the distributions of asset returns and realized returns from the trading strategy. An application of the theory to Canadian stock market data reveals that, in contrast to other studies, these rules cannot generate positive profits.

10.1 INTRODUCTION

It is well known that, in practice, fund managers and traders use technical analysis in order to help them with their buying and selling decisions. The conventional view among economists is to regard this practice as inefficient and resulting in a certain loss of money. Recently there have been a number of studies which challenge this particular view, resulting in a substantial increase in the literature on trading rules. The common hypothesis of these studies is that simple trading rules cannot generate above-normal profits. However, LeBaron (1991) and Levich and Thomas (1993) all find in empirical studies of exchange rate markets that some simple trading rules can generate statistically significant profits. Kuo (1998) and others arrive at similar findings using stock market data. These results are striking, given the conventional wisdom from efficient market theory that publicly available trading strategies cannot generate above-normal profits.

Knight, Satchell and Tran (1995) develop a process to model asset returns using a mixture distribution of scale gamma functions. Based on this framework, Kuo (1998) derives the characteristic functions and basic properties of realized returns from two specific moving average trading rules. He applies his results to the estimations of Knight, Satchell and Tran (1995) for British stock market data with the conclusion that a moving average trading rule can generate positive average returns of up to 6% per month.

The purpose of this chapter is to extend the results derived by Kuo (1998). In particular, this research addresses the following three questions: What is the probability density of realized returns generated by the simple trading rule? Is it possible to assign a preference ordering over the distributions of asset returns and realized returns from the trading strategy? Can one show that moving average trading rules generate significant profits over the long run and thereby substantiate the results of the earlier studies? Answering these questions is important for several reasons. First, having specific functional forms for the probability density makes the estimation of realized returns a straightforward exercise in maximum likelihood estimation. Even when analytic results are not available, it is generally useful to have a picture of the probability density. People are accustomed to looking at a random variable in the form of a density function and make inferences based on its graph. They cannot, in general, relate to three-dimensional characteristic functions. Second, it is not enough to judge the usefulness or practicality of moving average trading rules solely on the basis of positive or negative expected realized returns. People might use these types of trading strategies, simply because they prefer the lottery presented by them, over the lottery presented by the buy-and-hold strategy of just buying the underlying asset. This would be a perfectly rational explanation of why people use these trading rules even when markets are efficient and even though the rules might not be able to generate the same type of profits as the buy-and-hold strategy. Finally, the selection of a time period for the application of a trading rule is crucial to the resulting realized returns. Thus, if simple trading rules are indeed capable of generating positive profits over the long run, then they must somehow capture something elementary in financial markets. This would again strengthen the result of the above-mentioned studies and imply that financial markets are not even weak form efficient.

To answer these questions, we first derive analytical expressions for the inverse of the characteristic functions, given specific parameters of the underlying distribution of asset returns. We then test for first- and second-order stochastic dominance. From a series of graphs, we describe some of the qualitative characteristics of the densities, and, when it is not possible to find analytic expressions for the asset return process, use numerical methods to graph the density. Finally, we estimate the model by Knight, Satchell and Tran (1995) for the TSE35 Index over a period of roughly $8\frac{1}{2}$ years.

Our findings are as follows. Generally, the density of realized returns from the moving average trading rule is skewed extremely to the left and its tails become fatter as we increase the probability of positive and negative shocks to asset returns. For returns less than zero, the density of asset returns lies below the density of realized returns, but for returns greater than zero, there exist returns where the density of the trading rule lies above the density of asset returns. Given these results, we show that in general it is not possible to assign a preference ordering over the two probability distributions. However, when people only care about not losing money, they will always prefer the buy-and-hold strategy of asset returns. Finally the application shows that the rule is not able to generate profits over the entire period. Thus this result affirms the conventional theory.

The structure of the paper is as follows. Section 10.2 describes moving average trading rules in more detail, while section 10.3 describes the theoretical framework of the asset return process and the statistical properties of the trading rule. Section 10.4 forms the main part of the paper. Here we describe the probability densities in detail. In Section 10.5 we explain the estimation process and apply the model to the Canadian data. Finally, Section 10.6 concludes with a brief summary and suggestions for future research.

10.2 MOVING AVERAGE TRADING RULES AND TECHNICAL ANALYSIS

Moving average trading rules are simple trading rules from the domain of technical analysis. Technical analysis is a method for trying to predict the appropriate time to buy or sell a stock. At the heart of this analysis lies the belief that a security's 'worth' is determined simply by the amount a potential buyer is willing to pay for it and not necessarily by its underlying fundamental value. Reasons why a person might be willing to buy a security certainly may include beliefs that it is undervalued, but more importantly, they include beliefs about the future direction of price changes. For the technical analyst, it is those beliefs which drive the market. Thus, the primary determinant of security prices is individual and crowd psychology. Fundamental factors are,

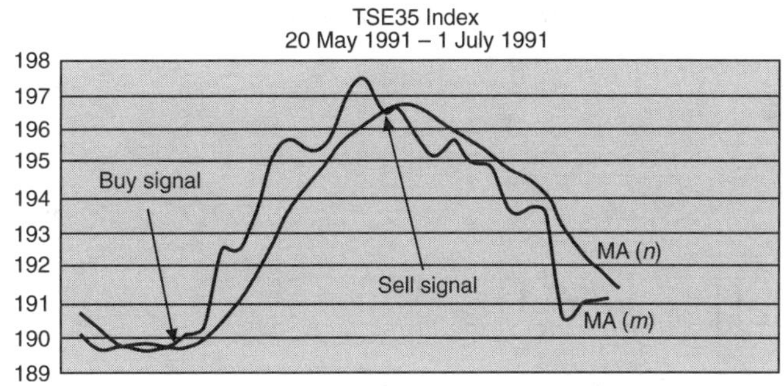

Figure 10.1 Moving average trading rule: $(m < n)$

at best, secondary. With well-informed market participants, technical analysts argue that prices reflect all important information and hence looking for undervalued securities is an unprofitable exercise. Instead, they argue, one can only try to use historical data on prices and volumes etc. in order to find repetitive patterns which one can exploit.

The main methods of technical analysis often consist of applying various charting techniques (such as *support* and *resistance* levels, *head-and-shoulders* or *double bottoms*) to the data and then representing the results on a graph. Because of its seemingly unscientific character and the difficulty of formalizing the rules of technical analysis, academics have traditionally frowned on this type of analysis. There is, however, a class of technical trading rules which does not lack this type of formalism: moving average trading rules. The basic structure of these rules is very simple. In order to generate a trading signal, they only require the graph of two moving averages of different lengths, taken over a single series. Typically the type of average used is either arithmetic, geometric or some combination thereof. The rule then issues a buy signal when the moving average of shorter length penetrates the one of longer length from below and generates a sell signal when the penetration occurs from above. This process, which can be easily formalized, is illustrated in Figure 10.1.

Definition 1 *An Arithmetic Moving Average (n, m) Rule is a signal S_t such that:*

$$S_t = \begin{cases} 1 & \text{if } D_t \geq 0 \Longleftrightarrow \text{buy} \\ 0 & \text{if } D_t < 0 \Longleftrightarrow \text{sell} \end{cases}$$

where:

$$D_t = \left(1/m \sum_{j=0}^{m-1} P_{t-j}\right) - \left(1/n \sum_{j=0}^{n-1} P_{t-j}\right)$$

Definition 2 *A Geometric Moving Average* (n, m) *Rule is a signal* S_t *such that:*

$$S_t = \begin{cases} 1 & \text{if } D_t \geq 0 \Longleftrightarrow \text{buy} \\ 0 & \text{if } D_t < 0 \Longleftrightarrow \text{sell} \end{cases}$$

where

$$D_t = \left(\prod_{j=0}^{m-1} P_{t-j}\right)^{1/m} - \left(\prod_{j=0}^{n-1} P_{t-j}\right)^{1/n}$$

It is clear that this rule is mathematically well defined. More importantly, it is Markov time. As Neftci (1991) shows, in order for a rule to have well-defined statistical properties, it must be Markov time. In his terminology, for an event (such as a major market downswing) to be Markov time, it must be I_t-measurable on the sequence of information sets $\{I_t\}$. In other words, it cannot incorporate information not contained in the relevant information sets. Moving average trading rules are clearly Markov time, since they are based only on historical moving averages. As Neftci shows, these rules are one of the few classes of technical trading rules which satisfy the criterion of Markov time. Most other technical trading rules somehow implicitly incorporate information about future prices and are thus not Markov time. The importance of this concept is that trading rules which can generate signals that are Markov time have well-defined statistical properties. Hence it becomes possible to test their predictive power and to derive their implications on asset returns and realized returns.

10.3 THEORETICAL FRAMEWORK

10.3.1 The asset return process

The theoretical foundation of all the work in this chapter is the model of asset returns proposed by Knight, Satchell and Tran (1995) (from now on KST). Their approach addresses the lack of a tractable model of asset returns able to differentiate between upside risk and downside risk.[1] The model is a method for accounting appropriately for asymmetric risk in financial markets. The process by itself is one of a straightforward mixture distribution. They assume that the return on an asset has a long run mean of μ,and can be described as follows:

$$R_t = \mu + Z_t \varepsilon_t - (1 - Z_t)\, \delta_t \tag{10.1}$$

[1] Upside 'risk' is the risk of a positive shock to the asset return, whereas downside risk is the risk of a negative shock to the asset return.

where $Z_t = \{0, 1\}$ is an indicator variable and ε_t and δ_t are two non- negative random variables. Thus, when $Z_t = 1$, a positive shock occurs and a sample is taken from the ε-distribution. When $Z_t = 0$, a negative shock occurs and the process samples from the δ-distribution. It is important not to confuse the behaviour of asset prices with that of asset returns. A positive or negative shock occurs with respect to returns and not with respect to prices. Thus two negative shocks to prices can still be a positive shock to returns, simply when $P_t > P_{t-1}$.

It is assumed that, over time, Z_t follows a stationary two-state Markov process, described by the following transition probabilities:

$$\begin{aligned}
&\Pr[Z_t = 1 | Z_t - 1 = 1] = p \\
&\Pr[Z_t = 0 | Z_t - 1 = 1] = 1 - p \\
&\Pr[Z_t = 1 | Z_t - 1 = 0] = q \\
&\Pr[Z_t = 0 | Z_t - 1 = 0] = 1 - q
\end{aligned} \tag{10.2}$$

Here, p and q are conditional probabilities such that $0 \leq p,\ q \leq 1$. The unconditional probability of being in state 1, i.e. drawing from the ε-distribution is

$$\Pi = \frac{1 - q}{2 - p - q}$$

Note that for Π to be well defined, we need to rule out the special case where $p = q = 1$.

In order to describe the probability density of returns any further, one needs to assign a distribution function to both ε_t and δ_t. KST specify the density functions for the process as two-scale Gamma functions:[2]

$$pdf_{\varepsilon_t}(r) = \begin{cases} \frac{\lambda_1^{\alpha_1} r^{\alpha_1 - 1}}{\Gamma(\alpha_1)} \exp(-\lambda_1 r) & \text{if } r \geq 0 \\ o & \text{otherwise} \end{cases} \tag{10.3a}$$

$$pdf_{\delta_t}(r) = \begin{cases} \frac{\lambda_2^{\alpha_2} r^{\alpha_2 - 1}}{\Gamma(\alpha_2)} \exp(-\lambda_2 r) & \text{if } r \geq 0 \\ o & \text{otherwise} \end{cases} \tag{10.3b}$$

Since Z_t is stationary, the probability of having a return above the long-run

---

[2]The scale Gamma function is useful, because it has as special cases:
1 Exponential Distribution: $\alpha = 1$
2 Erlang Distribution: α is an integer
3 $\frac{1}{2}\chi^2_{2\alpha}$ when 2α is an integer

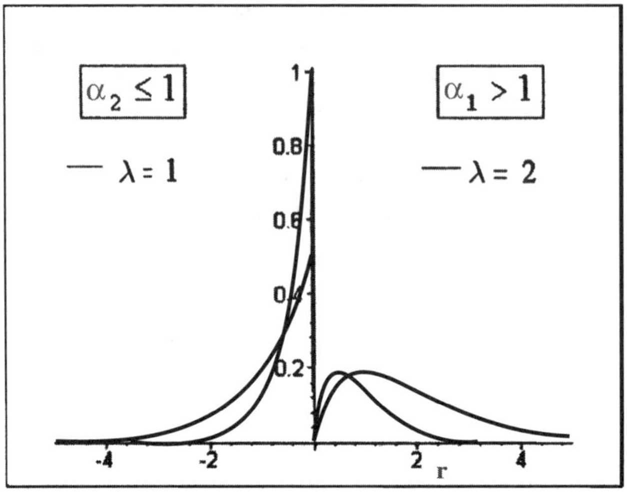

Figure 10.2 Distribution of asset returns

mean is Π. Conversely, the probability of having a return below the long-run mean is 1-Π. Given these probabilities we can write the density for returns generated by the KST process as:

$$pdf_R(r) = \begin{cases} (1-\Pi)f_{\delta_t}(\overline{\mu}-r) & \text{for } r < \overline{\mu} \\ \Pi f_{\varepsilon_t}(r-\overline{\mu}) & \text{for } r > \overline{\mu} \end{cases} \tag{10.4}$$

The corresponding probability distribution function is

$$F_R(r) = \begin{cases} (1-\Pi)F_{\delta_t}(\overline{\mu}-r) & \text{for } r < \overline{\mu} \\ \Pi F_{\varepsilon_t}(r-\overline{\mu}) & \text{for } r > \overline{\mu} \end{cases} \tag{10.5}$$

where $f_{\varepsilon_t}(r)$ and $f_{\delta_t}(r)$ are the scale Gamma functions defined above and F is the cumulative distribution function respectively.

Thus, in the KST model, the distribution of ε describes the upside risk, whereas the distribution of δ describes the downside risk. Obviously, both ε and δ need not be distributed the same. In fact, the point of the model is for the two functions to differ, in order to capture potential asymmetry in financial markets. Figure 10.2 depicts the basic shape of the density, given asset returns follow the process in equation (10.4). The picture illustrates the asset return process for a long-run mean of zero. The right side of the graph depicts f_ε, whereas the left side of the graph depicts f_δ. The shape of each side depends on the parameter α_i. As seen for f_δ, if $\alpha_2 \leq 1$, the density is monotonically decreasing. For f_ε, on the other hand, $\alpha_1 > 1$, and thus it has a maximum at $r = (\alpha - 1)/\lambda$. Lambda is the scale parameter with the property that for a scale Gamma distribution function $\gamma(\alpha, 1/\lambda) = \frac{1}{\lambda}\gamma(\alpha, 1) \equiv \frac{1}{\lambda}\gamma(\alpha)$. The expected value of asset returns given this process is:

$$E_R(r) = \mu + \Pi\mu_\varepsilon - (1 - \Pi)\mu_\delta$$

or

$$E_R(r) = \mu + \Pi\frac{\alpha_1}{\lambda_1} - (1 - \Pi)\frac{\alpha_2}{\lambda_2}$$

10.3.2 The statistical properties of specific moving average trading rules

In Kuo (1998) the geometric moving average trading rule [GMA(2,1)] is investigated. Using characteristic functions, Kuo is able to derive some of the statistical properties of realized returns from the above rules, given asset returns follow the KST process. We now briefly review some of these results.

The geometric moving average (2,1) rule

Note that from Definition 2, a geometric moving average(2,1), $D_t \geq 0$ iff $P_t \geq (P_t P_{t-1})^{1/2}$ and $D_t < 0$ iff $P_t < (P_t P_{t-1})^{1/2}$. Hence it as follows that:

$$\begin{matrix} D_t \geq 0 & \text{iff} & R_t \geq 0 \\ D_t < 0 & \text{iff} & R_t < 0 \end{matrix} \qquad \text{where } R_t = \ln(P_t/P_{t-1})$$

Thus, the action prescribed by the GMA(2,1) rule is:

$$A_t^{GMA(2,1)} = \begin{Bmatrix} \text{buy if} & R_t \geq 0 \\ \text{sell if} & R_t < 0 \end{Bmatrix} \Longleftrightarrow \begin{Bmatrix} 1 \\ 0 \end{Bmatrix} = S_t \tag{10.6}$$

It is obvious that this rule generates a buy signal only when $P_t \geq P_{t-1}$. Thus this rule says nothing more than: 'Buy every time the price goes up, sell every time the price goes down'.[3]

Kuo (1998) now derives the characteristic function for this trading rule. From equation (10.6), a buy signal is generated if and only if $R_t \geq 0$. Suppose for now that $\mu = 0$, then we know from equation (10.1) that $R_t \geq 0$ iff $Z_t = 1$ and $R_t < 0$ iff $Z_t = 0$. Thus the sequence of trading signals $\{S_t\}$ is identical to the sequence of the indicator variable $\{Z_t\}$. Kuo (1998) then uses the information contained in the Markovian structure of $\{Z_t\}$ in order to characterize the statistical properties of realized returns from applying the

[3]Note that saying 'Buy when the price goes up' is true for any moving average $(n, 1)$ rule.

trading rule. He derives the characteristic function[4] $\Phi_{RR_T}(t)$ for the realized returns from a GMA(2,1) to be

$$\Phi_{RR_T}(t) = (1 - \Pi)\,\Phi_\delta(-t) + \Pi(1-p)\frac{\Phi_\delta(-t)}{1 - p\,\Phi_\varepsilon(t)} \tag{10.7}$$

where $\Phi_\varepsilon(s)$ and $\Phi_\delta(s)$ are the characteristic functions associated with the distributions of ε and δ respectively. Given the characteristic function, Kuo also derives the expected realized return generated by the rule:

$$E(RR_T) \equiv \Phi'_{RR_T}(0) = \frac{1}{1-p}\{\Pi p\mu_\varepsilon - (1-p)\mu_\delta\} \tag{10.8}$$

10.4 CHARACTERISTICS OF THE PROBABILITY DENSITY FUNCTIONS

From the characteristic functions for the moving average trading rule, i.e. GMA(2,1), we will now examine the probability density of realized returns by inverting its characteristic function. However, since it is not always possible to perform the inversion analytically, we will approach the problem in two ways. First, we will derive some explicit analytic expressions for the pdf, given specific parameters of the underlying distribution of asset returns. From these results, we will discuss and graph the densities for some specific parameters. Second, we will invert the characteristic functions for a number of specific values using numerical methods and then present the resulting densities in graphical form. We now introduce two important concepts which will be used to derive the results.

Definition 3 *Let F be a function from $R \to C$. The Fourier Transform[5] of F is the function $f: R \to R$ given by*

$$f(x) = \frac{1}{2\pi}\int_{-\infty}^{\infty} e^{-itx}F(t)dt \equiv \frac{1}{2\pi}Fourier(F(t), t, x)$$

[4]A characteristic function is a complex function defined as:

$$\Phi_X(t) = \int_{-\infty}^{\infty} e^{(itx)}pdf_X(x)dx \tag{16}$$

This function is unique given any probability density. Furthermore, Levy's inversion theorem proves that there exists a one-to-one correspondence between the characteristic function and the probability density of a random variable.

[5]Sometimes this definition is referred to as the Inverse Fourier Transform.

Theorem (Fourier Inversion Theorem) *The probability density function of a random variable X is the Fourier Transform of its characteristic function.*

$$pdf_X(r) = \frac{1}{2\pi} \int_{-\infty}^{\infty} e^{-itr} \Phi_X(t) dt \tag{10.9}$$

10.4.1 The probability density of realized returns from a moving average (2,1) rule

Double exponential distribution

In the case where $\alpha_1 = \alpha_2 = 1$, the density of asset returns in equation (10.4) reduces to:

$$pdf_R(r) = \begin{cases} (1-\Pi)\lambda_2 e^{-\lambda_2(\overline{\mu}-r)} & \text{for } r < \overline{\mu} \\ \Pi\lambda_1 e^{-\lambda_1(r-\overline{\mu})} & \text{for } r > \overline{\mu} \end{cases} \tag{10.10}$$

Given this set-up, one can derive the probability density of realized returns from the geometric moving average (2,1) rule.

Result 1 *Let $\mu = 0$, then, given asset returns are distributed as a double exponential distribution, the probability density of realized returns from a geometric moving average (2,1) rule is:*

$$pdf_{RRT_{(2,1)}}(r) = \begin{cases} (1-\Psi)\lambda_2 e^{\lambda_2 r} & \text{for } r < 0 \\ 0 & \text{for } r = 0 \\ \Psi\widetilde{\lambda}_1 e^{-\widetilde{\lambda}_1 r} & \text{for } r > 0 \end{cases} \tag{10.11}$$

where: RRT is the realized return of the trading strategy,

$$(1-\Psi) = \left(\frac{\widetilde{\lambda}_1 + \lambda_2(1-p\Pi)}{\widetilde{\lambda}_1 + \lambda_2}\right), \Psi = \left(p\Pi\frac{\lambda_2}{\widetilde{\lambda}_1 + \lambda_2}\right) \text{ and } \widetilde{\lambda}_1 = \lambda_1(1-p)$$

To prove Result 1 we first need the characteristic functions for ε and δ.

Definition 4 *The characteristic function associated with a scale Gamma distribution is:*

$$\Phi_{\Gamma(\cdot)}(t) = \left(1 - \frac{it}{\lambda}\right)^{-\alpha} \tag{10.12}$$

Proof of Result 1. We need to invert the characteristic function:

$$\tilde{\Phi}_{RRT}(t) = (1 - \Pi)\,\tilde{\Phi}_\delta(-t) + \Pi(1 - p)\frac{\tilde{\Phi}_\delta(-t)}{1 - p\,\tilde{\Phi}_\varepsilon(t)}$$

where $\tilde{\Phi}$ indicates that asset returns are distributed as a double exponential. Applying the Fourier inversion theorem, we want to find:

$$pdf_{RRT}(r) = \frac{1}{2\pi}\int_{-\infty}^{\infty} e^{-itr}\left((1 - \Pi)\tilde{\Phi}_\delta(-t) + \Pi(1 - p)\frac{\tilde{\Phi}_\delta(-t)}{1 - p\,\tilde{\Phi}_\varepsilon(t)}\right)dt \tag{10.13}$$

Since the Fourier transform is additive, we will split up equation (10.13) into two parts.

Part 1. We define Part 1$\equiv pdf1_{RRT}(r) = \frac{1}{2\pi}\int_{-\infty}^{\infty} e^{-itr}(1 - \Pi)\tilde{\Phi}_\delta(-t)dt.$

Note that in this case, $\Phi_R(-t) = \int_{-\infty}^{\infty} e^{-itr}f_R(r)dr = \int_{-\infty}^{\infty} e^{-itr}f_{-R}(r)dr = \Phi_{-R}(t)$. Thus the first term in the above equation becomes

$$(1 - \Pi)\frac{1}{2\pi}\int_{-\infty}^{\infty} e^{-itr}\tilde{\Phi}_\delta(-t)dt = (1 - \Pi)\frac{1}{2\pi}\int_{-\infty}^{\infty} e^{-itr}\tilde{\Phi}_{-\delta}(t)dt = (1 - \Pi)f_{-\delta}(r)$$

We have

$$f_{-\delta}(r) = \begin{cases} \frac{\lambda_2^{\alpha_2}(-r)^{\alpha_2 - 1}}{\Gamma(\alpha_2)}\exp(\lambda_2 r) & \text{if } r < 0 \\ o & \text{otherwise} \end{cases}$$

and thus,

$$pdf1_{RRT}(r) = \begin{cases} (1 - \Pi)\lambda_2 e^{(\lambda_2 r)} & \text{if } r < 0 \\ o & \text{otherwise} \end{cases}$$

Part 2. We now turn to the second term in equation (10.13) which we define as $pdf2_{RRT}(r)$. Solving this part is more difficult because of the quotient involving the characteristic functions. First we substitute $\alpha_i = 1$ into Definition 4 and rearrange to get

$$pdf2_{RRT}(r) \equiv \Pi(1 - p)\frac{1}{2\pi}\int_{-\infty}^{\infty} e^{-itr}\frac{\tilde{\Phi}_\delta(-t)}{1 - p\,\tilde{\Phi}_\varepsilon(t)}dt$$

$$= \Pi(1 - p)\frac{1}{2\pi}\int_{-\infty}^{\infty} e^{-itr}\left(\left[\frac{\lambda_1 - it}{\lambda_1(1 - p) - it}\right]\left[\frac{\lambda_2}{\lambda_2 + it}\right]\right)dt$$

We now need to distinguish the two cases: $r < 0$, $r > 0$.

For $r < 0$, we can show that the expression above evaluates to

$$\Pi(1-p)f_{-\delta}(r)\frac{\lambda_1+\lambda_2}{\lambda_1(1-p)+\lambda_2}$$

for $r > 0$, we can show that the expression evaluates to[6]

$$\Pi(1-p)\lambda_1 pe^{-\lambda_1(1-p)r}\frac{\lambda_2}{\lambda_1(1-p)+\lambda_2}$$

we thus have

$$pdf2_{RRT}(r) \equiv \begin{cases} \Pi(1-p)\lambda_2 e^{(\lambda_2 r)}\dfrac{\lambda_1+\lambda_2}{\lambda_1(1-p)+\lambda_2} & \text{if } r < 0 \\ \Pi(1-p)\lambda_1 pe^{-\lambda_1(1-p)r}\dfrac{\lambda_2}{\lambda_1(1-p)+\lambda_2} & \text{if } r > 0 \end{cases}$$

Finally, adding the two parts and adding a point mass at zero, we have the result

$$pdf_{RRT_{(2,1)}}(r) = pdf1_{RRT}(r) + pdf2_{RRT}(r)$$

$$= \begin{cases} \lambda_2 e^{\lambda_2 r}\left(\dfrac{\lambda_2(1-p\Pi)+\tilde{\lambda}_1}{\tilde{\lambda}_1+\lambda_2}\right) & \text{for } r < 0 \\ 0 & \text{for } r = 0 \\ \tilde{\lambda}_1 e^{-\tilde{\lambda}_1 r}\left(\dfrac{\lambda_2\Pi p}{\tilde{\lambda}_1+\lambda_2}\right) & \text{for } r > 0 \end{cases}$$

Corollary 1 *Given asset returns are distributed as a double exponential distribution, the probability distribution of realized returns from a geometric moving average (2,1) rule is:*

$$F_{RRT}(a) = \begin{cases} \left(\dfrac{\lambda_2(1-p\Pi)+\tilde{\lambda}_1}{\tilde{\lambda}_1+\lambda_2}\right)e^{\lambda_2 a} & \text{for } a < 0 \\ 1-\left(\dfrac{\lambda_2\Pi p}{\tilde{\lambda}_1+\lambda_2}\right)e^{-\tilde{\lambda}_1 a} & \text{for } a \geq 0 \end{cases} \tag{10.14}$$

■

[6]We omit the arithmetic involved in the proof here. Even though straightforward, it is quite tedious and of no particular value. Furthermore, the result can very easily be checked using Maple. The corresponding worksheets are available from the author upon request.

Proof. *By definition, the distribution function* F_X *of a density* f_X *is given by* $F_X(a) = Pr(x < a) = \int_{-\infty}^{a} f(x)dx$. *Hence,*

$$F_{RRT}(a) = \begin{cases} \left(\dfrac{\lambda_2(1-p\Pi)+\widetilde{\lambda}_1}{\widetilde{\lambda}_1+\lambda_2}\right)e^{\lambda_2 a} & \text{for } a < 0 \\ 1-\left(\dfrac{\lambda_2 \Pi p}{\widetilde{\lambda}_1+\lambda_2}\right)e^{-\widetilde{\lambda}_1 a} & \text{for } a \geq 0 \end{cases}$$

■

Result 1 is a very nice result. Having a closer look at the structure of the density of realized returns, we see that the density is a mixture of two densities, $\lambda_2 e^{-\lambda_2 r}$ for the downside and $\widetilde{\lambda}_1 e^{-\widetilde{\lambda}_1}$ for the upside. Furthermore, the density $\widetilde{\lambda}_1 e^{-\widetilde{\lambda}_1 r}$ is just the origial density of positive shocks where we have reduced the scale parameter by a factor of $(1-p)$. Since we have two densities on each side, the terms

$$\left(\frac{\lambda_2(1-p\Pi)+\widetilde{\lambda}_1}{\widetilde{\lambda}_1+\lambda_2}\right)$$

and

$$\left(p\Pi\frac{\lambda_2}{\widetilde{\lambda}_1+\lambda_2}\right)$$

have to sum to 1, and they can thus be viewed as the probabilities with which we sample from either distribution. Thus the probability density of realized returns from the geometric moving average (2,1) rule can be modelled in exactly the same way as the probability density of asset returns. Namely,

$$pdf_{RRT_{(2,1)}}(r) = \mu + Z_t f_{\tilde{\varepsilon}} - (1-Z_t) f_\delta$$

$$\text{where}\begin{cases} \text{prob}(\ Z_t = 1) = \left(p4\dfrac{\lambda_2}{\widetilde{\lambda}_1+\lambda_2}\Pi\right) \\ \text{prob}(\ Z_t = 0) = \left(\dfrac{\lambda_2(1-p\Pi)+\widetilde{\lambda}_1}{\widetilde{\lambda}_1+\lambda_2}\right) \end{cases}$$

and $f_{\tilde{\varepsilon}} = (f_\varepsilon | \lambda_1 = \lambda_1(1-p))$

Since (1-Ψ) is a probability weight, the term

$$\left(\frac{\widetilde{\lambda}_1+\lambda_2(1-p\Pi)}{\widetilde{\lambda}_1+\lambda_2}\right)$$

on the downside of the density is less than or equal to 1. A natural question to ask is whether the downside of realized returns lies above or below the density of original returns. In other words, we want to know whether

$$\lambda_2 e^{\lambda_2 r}\left(\frac{\lambda_2(1-p\Pi)+\lambda_1(1-p)}{\lambda_1(1-p)+\lambda_2}\right) \begin{matrix}<\\=\\>\end{matrix} (1-\Pi)\lambda_2 e^{\lambda_2 r}$$

We can show that this reduces to the inequality $\Pi(1-p)(\lambda_1+\lambda_2) \begin{matrix}<\\=\\>\end{matrix} 0$. Since $0 \leq p,\ \Pi \leq 1$ and $\lambda_1,\ \lambda_2$ are both positive, we know that the downside of realized returns never lies below that of asset returns. Similarly, for the upside, we must have that the term

$$\left(\frac{\lambda_2 \Pi p}{\lambda_1(1-p)+\lambda_2}\right)$$

is always less or equal to 1. Unfortunately, we cannot show that one upside density lies above or below the other. One can show, however, that the density of realized returns lies above the density for returns when

$$r > \frac{\ln(\lambda_2+\widetilde{\lambda}_1)}{\lambda_1 p \ln p(1-p)}$$

and below for

$$r < \frac{\ln(\lambda_2+\widetilde{\lambda}_1)}{\lambda_1 p \ln p(1-p)}$$

Furthermore, recall that Π is the unconditional probability of sampling from the ε-distribution. Thus, from the definition of Ψ we see that Ψ is always less than Π, except for the extreme case where $p = 1$ and Ψ and Π are equal. If we conjecture that the probability of sampling from both distributions should be 1/2, one can show that $\Psi \leq \frac{1}{2}$ if

$$p \leq \frac{\lambda_1+\lambda_2}{\lambda_1+2\Pi\lambda_2}$$

even if $\Pi \geq \frac{1}{2}$. Combined with the above result this means that, in general, the distribution of realized returns from the trading strategy is always more skewed to the left than the distribution of asset returns.

We now want to make some comparisons between the density of realized returns and the density of asset returns. we will first discuss the three extreme cases $(p = 0,\ q)$, $(p,\ q = 1)$, $(p = 1,\ q)$. In the first case, note that when $p = 0$, the upside of the density of realized returns from the trading strategy collapses. The resulting density is the reflection of the density of the negative shocks along the vertical axis. This result makes sense given our trading strategy. Remember that p is the probability of two positive shocks to succeed each other. Hence, when $p = 0$, this will never happen. Every time the price goes up, the rule issues a buy signal. But since $p = 0$, we know for certain that the price will fall. Thus one can only lose money and the way by which it is lost is described by the distribution of negative shocks.[7] In the second case, we see that $q = 1$ implies $\Pi = 0$. Thus the distribution collapses in the same way. The reasoning for this collapse is the same as before except that, once we are in the bad state, we never leave. The third case where $(p = 1,\ q)$, the distribution of realized returns collapses completely. We know that the rule will not generate a buy signal until there is at least one positive shock. However, once this happens, we will never leave the good state. Thus the reason why the distribution collapses is that the rule will never issue a sell signal again and there is no return realized. More precisely, the length of time the asset is held in the model is first defined by the rule and then determined by the asset return process. Thus, time is a random variable in the model. But when $p = 0$, this is no longer the case, and hence the density collapses.

We now turn to the question of whether we can assign a preference ordering over the distribution of asset returns and the distribution of realized returns from the trading strategy. In order to say something about the utility of the trading strategy, it is not enough to only look at its expected return. Instead, one also needs to consider the risk involved in realizing that return. As we have seen above, we can model the two random variables R and RRT in the same way, but with different probability weights. If we view the distributions as lotteries over wealth, then it is clear that the lottery involving the trading strategy is quite different from that of the buy-and-hold strategy of asset returns. Thus, on the surface, it is not clear which of the two strategies an agent would prefer. In order to answer this question, we thus introduce the concepts of first- and second-order stochastic dominance.

Definition 5 *A probability distribution F dominates another probability distribution G according to first-order stochastic dominance (FSD) if*

$$F(a) \leq G(a) \text{ for all } a \in \mathbb{R}$$

Theorem *F dominates G by FSD if and only if:*

$$\int_{\mathbb{R}} u(a)dF(a) \geq \int_{\mathbb{R}} u(a)dG(a)$$

for all strictly increasing expected utility indices u(a).

[7]Knowing that $p = 0$ we might just want to change our trading strategy and short-sell the asset.

Definition 6 *A probability distribution F dominates another probability distribution G according to second-order stochastic dominance (SSD) if*

$$\int_{-\infty}^{x} F(a)\ da \leq \int_{-\infty}^{x} G(a)\ da \quad \text{for all } a \in \mathbb{R}$$

Theorem *F dominates G by SSD if and only if:*

$$\int_{\mathbb{R}} u(a)dF(a) \geq \int_{\mathbb{R}} u(a)dG(a)$$

for all increasing and concave expected utility indices u(a).

First-order stochastic dominance is the most general way of comparing two lotteries. It means that if F dominates G by FSD, expected utility-maximizing agents with strictly increasing utility would prefer the lottery F over the lottery G. Hence, in order to compare lotteries, it is enough to order probability distributions by FSD. Once we add the assumption of concavity to preferences, we have the concept of second-order stochastic dominance. Thus, if people have increasing concave preferences, it is sufficient to rank probability distributions according to SSD.

Result 2 *As long as asset returns are non-degenerate, the distribution function of realized returns from the geometric moving average (2,1) rule never dominates the distribution of asset returns by FSD.*

Proof. *When* $\Pi = p = 1$, *we do not have a density for realized returns. When* $\Pi \neq 0$,*we have seen that the downside of asset returns always lies below the downside of realized returns from the trading strategy. This implies that* $F_R(a) \leq F_{RRT}(a)$ *for* $a < 0$ *and thus the distribution of realized returns cannot dominate the distribution of asset returns by FSD.* ■

Result 3 *The distribution function of asset returns dominates the distribution function of realized returns by FSD if and only if* $p = 0$

Proof. *We only need to compare the upside of the distributions. If* $p \neq 0$, *in order for asset returns to dominate realized returns by FSD, all we need to show is that*

$$1 - \Pi e^{-\lambda_1 a} \leq 1 - e^{-\tilde{\lambda}_1 a}\left(\frac{\lambda_2 \Pi p}{\tilde{\lambda}_1 + \lambda_2}\right)$$

This can be rearranged as

$$\frac{\lambda_1(1-p)+\lambda_2}{\lambda_2 p} \geq e^{\lambda_1 pa}$$

since this is an increasing function in a, we can always find an a such that the inequality does not hold, namely let

$$a = \frac{1}{\lambda_1 p} ln\left(2\frac{\lambda_1(1-p)+\lambda_2}{\lambda_2 p}\right)$$

Then

$$\frac{\lambda_1(1-p)+\lambda_2}{\lambda_2 p} \geq e^{ln(2\frac{\lambda_1(1-p)+\lambda_2}{\lambda_2 p})}$$

$$1 \geq 2$$

which is a contradiction, and hence $F_R(a)$ does not dominate $F_{RRT}(a)$ by FSD when $p \neq 0$.

On the other hand, when $p = 0$, the upside of realized returns collapses and $F_{RRT}(a) = 1$ for $a > 0$, and hence $F_R(a) \leq F_{RRT}(a)$. ■

Result 4 *As long as asset returns are non-degenerate, the distribution functions of realized returns from the geometric moving average (2,1) rule and asset returns never dominate each other by SSD.*

Proof. *For realized returns from the trading strategy to dominate asset returns by SSD, the downside of realized returns has to dominate the downside of asset returns by SSD.*

$$\int_{-\infty}^{x} F_{RRT}(a)\ da \leq \int_{-\infty}^{x} F_R(a)\ da$$

$$\int_{-\infty}^{x} (1-\Pi)e^{\lambda_2 a}\ da \leq \int_{-\infty}^{x} (1-\Psi)e^{\lambda_2 a}\ da$$

This reduces to the inequality

$$(1-p)(\lambda_1+\lambda_2) \leq 0$$

which would only be true when $p = 1$, but this has been ruled out.

For asset returns to dominate realized returns from the trading strategy by SSD, we still have to check the upside. We need the following inequality to hold:

$$\int_{-\infty}^{0} (1 - \Pi)e^{\lambda_2 a} + \int_{0}^{x} \left(1 - \Pi e^{-\lambda_1 a}\right) da \leq \int_{-\infty}^{x} (1 - \Psi)e^{\lambda_2 a}\, da + \int_{0}^{x} \left(1 - \Psi e^{-\widetilde{\lambda}_1 a}\right)$$

Again, in the case of p = 1, this inequality holds as equality, but otherwise it can be shown to be violated for any

$$x > \frac{ln(\Psi\lambda_2) - ln(\Pi(p\lambda_2 - 2\widetilde{\lambda}_1) - ln(\Pi\widetilde{\lambda}_1)}{\widetilde{\lambda}_1}$$

■

At this point, one could check even higher degrees of stochastic dominance. There are, however, two problems with doing so. First, as we refine the ordering of probability distributions, i.e. as we increase the degree of stochastic dominance, the requirements on the utility function become increasingly stringent. Thus the set of agents whose utility function fits into these increasingly special classes becomes smaller and smaller and hence the result increasingly specialized. The other problem is that it seems fairly unlikely that we will be able to differentiate the two probability distributions according to even higher degrees of stochastic dominance. Looking at the structure of the density of realized returns, the upside is scaled by $(1 - p)$. The term $(1 - p)$ in the exponent will not disappear in repeated integration. We are thus always forced to compare an exponential quantity with an additive quantity. It should be no surprise that this will continue to be violated.

In summary, we can say that we are unable to assign a preference ordering on the probability distributions of the trading strategy and the buy-and-hold strategy of asset returns. Whether or not the agent prefers one over the other depends on the individual expected utility. We might, however, note that the reason why we are unable to differentiate the distributions by FSD or SSD lies in the fact that there is always a small probability that the trading strategy will generate a very large profit. However, as we have mentioned previously, the upside 'risk' is not so much a risk, but rather an extra bonus. An investor might be primarily concerned about not losing money. If this is the case then as we have seen, the investor is always better off with the buy-and-hold strategy of the asset returns since its downside always dominates the downside of the trading strategy.[8]

We now turn to the graphical description of some of the features of the density. Figure 10.3 illustrates the two extreme cases $\Pi = 1$ and $\Pi = 0$ for the

[8]There exists an entire literature on semi-variance, which deals with exactly this kind of problem. This might be an interesting area of future research.

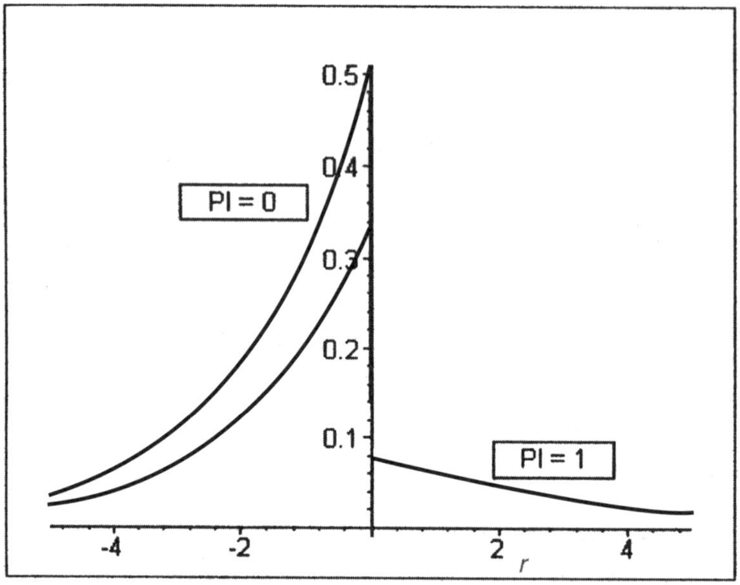

Figure 10.3 Realized returns from the geometric moving average (2,1)

density, given that $p = 0.5$, λ_1 and λ_2 equal 1/2. Note that the distribution of realized returns is skewed extremely to the left. We can see from above that when $\Pi = 0$, the right side of the distribution disappears completely. Even when the stationary probability of the good state is 1, the density remains extremely skewed. This skewness is still apparent even though the expected realized return from the strategy is positive. As we know from equation (10.8), if $\mu_\varepsilon = \mu_\delta$, the expected return on the trading strategy is positive if and only if $\Pi p > (1 - p)$. If we assume that the stationary probability is 0.5 then this implies that $p = q > 2/3$. Figure 10.4 depicts the probability density of realized returns given these assumptions. The leftward skewness is clearly apparent. Furthermore, we can see that the downside of the density is 'pushed' down as we increase p and q, corresponding with a fattening in the right-hand tail. This can better be seen in Figures 10.5 and 10.6 where we only depict the upside of the density.

Notice from these two graphs that when we increase p, we take out some weight from the centre of the distribution and put it out in the right tail. This can be easily verified by looking at the density. As we increase p, we reduce the scale parameter and hence fatten the tail. Furthermore, given that $\Pi = 0.5$, increasing p unambiguously increases Ψ, adding to the effect of the scale parameter.

Note that this result makes perfect sense given our trading strategy. If both p

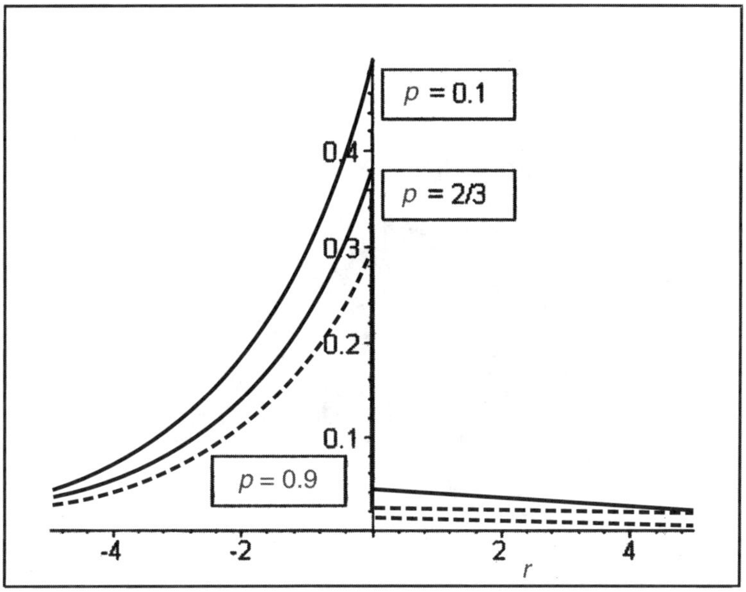

Figure 10.4 Realized returns when PI = 0.5

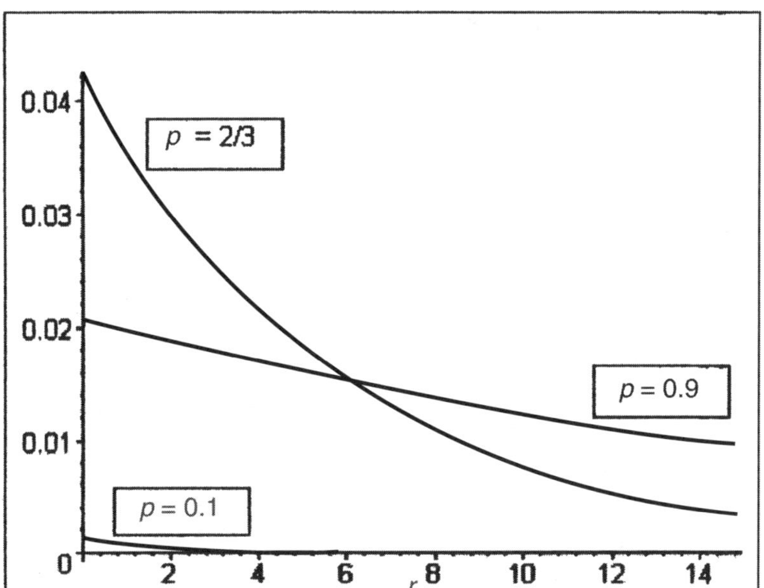

Figure 10.5 Upside of realized returns (2,1) rule

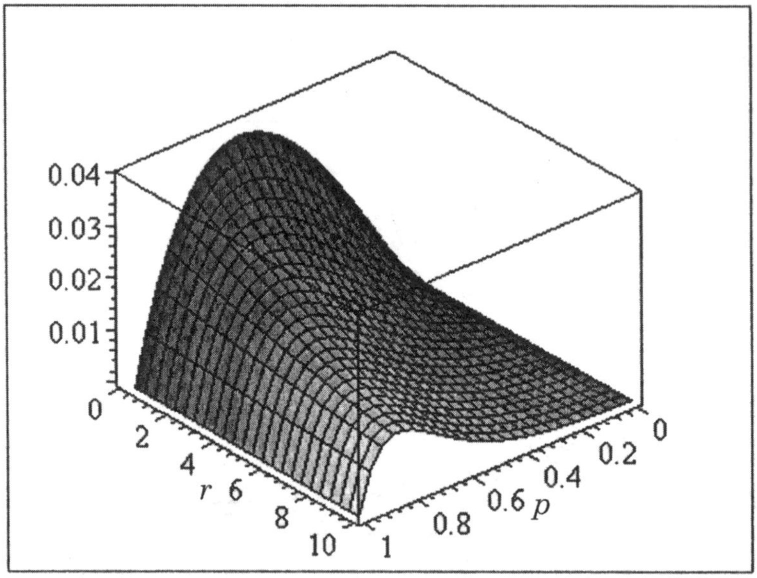

Figure 10.6 Realized returns and changes in p

and q are fairly large, it means that we have prolonged market 'cycles'. Thus we have fewer buy/sell signals but with each signal being more important. This is, however, exactly the kind of structure that moving averages are exploiting. Remember that moving average rules try to predict trends in the market. The more persistent these trends are, the more useful the rule will be. Thus when the trading signal is becoming more pronounced we would expect to earn more money from the strategy, or in other words, the probability of a loss should go down and the probability of profit should go up. This is exactly the result we get from the graph and it makes perfect sense given the rationale behind moving average trading rules.

10.4.2 Numerical inversion of characteristic functions

It is only possible to find closed-form expressions for the geometric moving average (2,1) for a small set of characteristic functions, namely those where α_1 and α_2 are specific integers. Given the generality of the asset return process, it seems limiting to describe the probability densities where the shape parameters of the underlying distributions are composed only of integers. Looking at Figure 10.2 we see that we might very well be interested in the graph of the distribution when alpha < 1. Furthermore, since we have already seen that the geometric moving average cannot generate positive profits on average, it would be useful to see what the density of realized returns of the moving average (2,1) rule looks like when we know we have positive profits on average. To get around this problem we need to use numerical methods and then plot the probability density given certain parameter values.

It is, of course, impossible to integrate a function numerically from -∞ to ∞. Hence, it is useful to rewrite the Fourier Inversion Theorem from equation (10.9) in the following way:

$$pdf_{RRT}(r) = \frac{1}{2\pi}\int_0^\infty \left(e^{itr}\Phi_{RRT}(-t) + e^{-itr}\Phi_{RRT}(t)\right)dt \tag{10.15}$$

We know that any complex function $\mathcal{Q}:\mathbb{R}\to\mathbb{C}$ can be expressed as $\mathcal{Q}(t) = \Re(t) + i\Im(t)$ where $\Re(t)$ and $\Im(t)$ are the real and imaginary parts respectively. Thus,

$$\begin{aligned} pdf_{RRT}(r) &= \frac{1}{2\pi}\int_0^\infty ((\cos(tr) + i\sin(tr))(\Re(t) - i\Im(t)) \\ &\quad +(\cos(tr) - i\sin(tr))(\Re(t) + i\Im(t)))dt \\ &= \frac{1}{\pi}\int_0^\infty (\Re(t)\cos(tr) + \Im(t)\sin(tr))dt \\ &= \frac{1}{\pi}\int_0^\infty \left(\Re\left[e^{-itr}\Phi_{RRT}(t)\right]\right)dt \end{aligned} \tag{10.16}$$

Since the characteristic function is a periodic function with decreasing amplitude, we use the following method to calculate the numerical integral in equation (10.16).

$$\begin{aligned} pdf_{RRT}(r) &= \frac{1}{\pi}\int_0^\infty \left(\Re\left[e^{-itr}\Phi_{RRT}(t)\right]\right)dt \\ &\approx \int_0^1 (\cdot)dt + \int_1^2 (\cdot)dt + \int_2^4 (\cdot)dt + \ldots \int_{2^i}^{2^{i+1}} (\cdot)dt \end{aligned} \tag{10.17}$$

The periodicity of the integrand guarantees that, as t becomes increasingly larger the small positive and negative areas more or less cancel each other out. This makes the computation of the integral much easier and more accurate.

Note that in this approximation, the degree of accuracy of the integral is set by i, where $i + 1$ is the total number of integrals that are computed in equation (10.17). We have increased the degree of accuracy of the computation up to the point where there was no change in the integral up to the first eight decimals. In general, in order to achieve the desired degree of accuracy we did not need to increase the number of computed integrals past 12.

Note also, that we would have to compute the above integral for every value of r. But since the entire exercise is for illustrative purposes only, it suffices to compute the integral over a small range, say from -0.02 to 0.02 in increments of 0.004. Then the entire process can be summarized as follows:

$$Graph[pdf_{RRT}(r)] = \left[\frac{1}{\pi} \int_0^1 \left(\Re\left[e^{-itr}\Phi_{RRT}(t)\right]\right) dt + \sum_{i=0}^{10} \frac{1}{\pi} \int_{2^i}^{2^{i+1}} \left(\Re\left[e^{-itr}\Phi_{RRT}(t)\right]\right) dt \right]_{r=-0.02..0.02} \tag{10.18}$$

We now apply this process to the results of KST.

The results of KST

KST estimate the asset return process for UK futures and stock prices using the model described in Section 10.3.1. They find that asset returns are described fairly well by the process. Since this chapter is grounded on their results it is only natural to ask what the probability density of realized returns looks like, given the parameters they estimate for the UK stock market. Furthermore, since for the FT100 Futures $\alpha_1 > 1$ and $\alpha_2 < 1$, and for the FT100 Index, $\alpha_1 > 1$ and $\alpha_2 > 1$, their results from their estimations fit well in the overall description of the different types of densities generated by varing α_i. The parameters from the KST estimation are given in Table 10.1.

Table 10.1

	FT100 Futures	FT100 Index
α_1	1.3775	1.364
λ_1	168.36	204.4
α_2	0.7499	1.4399
λ_2	99.074	214.04
μ	0	0.00042
$\widehat{p}$	0.4812	0.4816
$\widehat{q}$	0.4882	0.5080

Table 10.2

	FT100 Futures	FT100 Index
$\tilde{p}$	0.5188	0.5184
$\tilde{q}$	0.5118	0.492
$\tilde{\Pi}$	0.4966	0.4870

Note that in the model estimated by KST $p = \text{prob}[Z_t = 1, Z_{t-1} = 1]$, as it is in the Kuo (1998) model. However, in Kuo's setup, when $Z_t = 1 \Longrightarrow R_t \geq \mu$, whereas in the KST when $Z_t = 1 \Longrightarrow R_t \leq \mu$. Thus if we have to convert the probabilities accordingly, i.e. $p_K = 1 - p_{KST}$; $q_K = 1 - q_{KST}$ and hence,

$$\Pi_K = \frac{q_{KST}}{p_{KST} + q_{KST}}$$

The new probabilities can be summarized as in Table 10.2.

The probability densities associated with the FT100 Futures and the FT100 Index are depicted in Figures 10.7 and 10.8 respectively.

The first point to note is that the qualitative relationship of the graphs of the trading strategies with respect to the graph of asset returns is the same regardless of the difference in shape parameters for the two series. However, when we compare the realized returns from the geometric moving average (2,1) and the $(\infty, 1)$ rule for the two series, we see that when $\alpha_2 < 1$, the downside of the $(\infty, 1)$ rule crosses the (2,1) rule and lies below it at the centre of the distribution. On the other hand, when $\alpha_2 > 1$ then the downside of the $(\infty, 1)$ rule always lies above the downside of the (2,1) rule. Second, as we have seen in the previous sections, the graph exhibits extreme skewness and asymmetry of

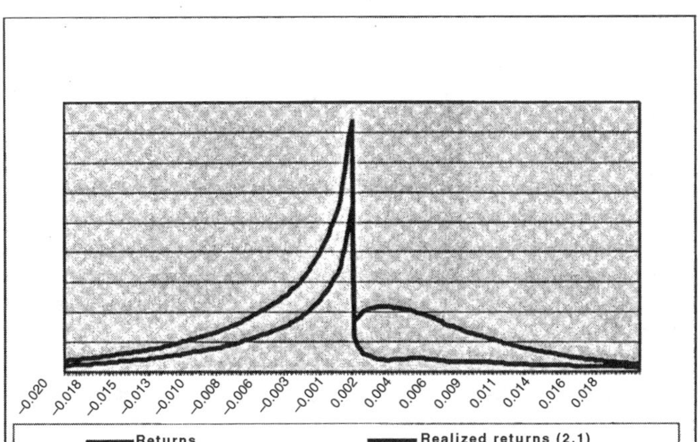

Figure 10.7 Returns and realized returns from FT100 Futures (KST, 1995)

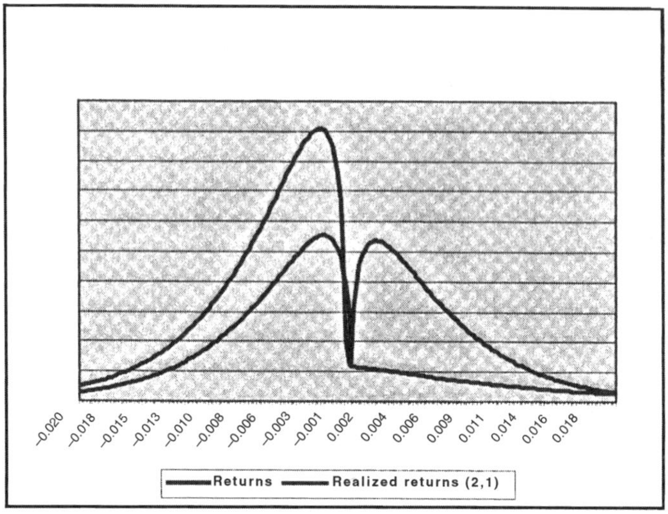

Figure 10.8 Returns and realized returns for FT100 Index (KST, 1995)

the densities. Both rules exhibit these kind of characteristics. Even though the returns distribution is 'fairly' symmetric for the FT100 Index, the graph of resulting realized returns is still extremely skewed to the left.

At this point it is also useful to cross-reference the picture of the densities for the two series with the results obtained in the special case of the exponential distribution. Namely, we clearly see that the downside of asset returns lies well below the downside of realized returns. Hence we can conclude again that distribution of realized returns from the trading strategy will never dominate that of the buy-and-hold strategy of asset returns by FSD. Similarly, for the upside, we see that as r increases, the density of realized returns from the moving average (2,1) rule lies above the density of asset returns. Here too we can then conclude that asset returns do not dominate realized returns by FSD.

10.5 APPLICATION TO TSE35

In this final section we apply the model of asset returns to the TSE35 Index. As we will see, this allows us to graph the density of realized returns when $\alpha_1 < 1$, and $\alpha_2 < 1$, thus completing the description of the graph of the probability densities given different values for α_i. However, before presenting the results of the estimation we will first describe the estimation process and the data.

10.5.1 Estimation of the asset return process

Given that asset returns follow the process from equation (10.1) and Z_t follows the two-state Markov process, we can write down the likelihood in period t, conditional on information at time $t-1$:

$$L(R_t, Z_t \mid I_{t-1}) = \left[p^{Z_{t-1}}(1-q)^{(1-Z_{t-1})} f_\varepsilon(r-\mu)\right]^{Z_t} \times \left[(1-p)^{Z_{t-1}} q^{(1-Z_{t-1})} f_\delta(\mu - r)\right]^{(1-Z_t)} \quad (10.19)$$

Hence, the total likelihood is given by $\mathbb{L} = L(X_1, Z_1)\prod_{t=2}^{T} L(R_t, Z_t \mid I_{t-1})$, with the log likelihood

$$\begin{aligned}
\ln \mathbb{L} &= \ln L(R_1, Z_1) + \sum_{t=2}^{T} \ln L(R_t, Z_t \mid I_{t-1}) \\
&= Z_1[\ln \Pi + \alpha_1 \ln \lambda_1 + (\alpha_1 - 1)\ln(r_1 - \mu) - \lambda_1(r_1 - \mu) - \ln \Gamma(\alpha_1)] \\
&\quad + (1 - Z_1)[\ln(1 - \Pi) + \alpha_2 \ln \lambda_2 + \\
&\quad + (\alpha_2 - 1)\ln(r_2 - \mu) - \lambda_2(r_2 - \mu) - \ln \Gamma(\alpha_2)] \\
&\quad + n_{11} \ln p + n_{01} \ln(1 - q) + n_{10} \ln(1 - p) + n_{00} \ln(q) \\
&\quad + n_1 \alpha_1 \ln \lambda_1 + (\alpha_1 - 1) S_1 - \lambda_1 S_2 - n_1 \ln \Gamma(\alpha_1) \\
&\quad + n_0 \alpha_2 \ln \lambda_2 + (\alpha_2 - 1) S_3 - \lambda_2 S_4 - n_0 \ln \Gamma(\alpha_2)
\end{aligned}$$

where n_{ij} is the number of pairs of the form $(Z_t = i, Z_{t-1} = j)$, n_0 is the number of Z_t's which are zero excluding Z_1, n_1 is the number of Z_t's which are one excluding Z_1. Furthermore,

$$S_1 = \sum_{t=2}^{T} Z_t \ln(r_t - \mu)$$

$$S_2 = \sum_{t=2}^{T} Z_t (r_t - \mu)$$

$$S_3 = \sum_{t=2}^{T} (1 - Z_t) \ln(\mu - r_t)$$

$$S_4 = \sum_{t=2}^{T} (1 - Z_t)(\mu - r_t)$$

The estimation of the parameters $\alpha_1, \lambda_1, \alpha_2, \lambda_2$ is straightforward. In order to estimate μ, we estimate the above likelihood function using grid search over the range from -0.02 to 0.2 and in increments of 0.0001. The procedure for the estimation is as follows. Given μ, we calculate the series of indicator variables $\{Z_{t},\}$, which in turn allows us to calculate the number of pairs of the form n_{ij}.

Table 10.3

	Mean	Std. dev.	Min.	Max.	Skewness	Kurtosis
TSE35	0.0003433	0.0086197	−0.0768518	0.0519045	−0.6848879	10.85788

The sample probability $\widehat{p}$ and $\widehat{q}$ can then be computed as

$$\widehat{p} = \frac{n_{11}}{n_{11} + n_{10}} \quad \text{and} \quad \widehat{q} = \frac{n_{00}}{n_{00} + n_{01}}$$

These estimates are then inserted into the log likelihood function which in turn is maximized. The process is then repeated for the entire range and returns the parameters corresponding to the highest value of the likelihood function.

10.5.2 Description of the data

The data is taken from the Toronto Stock Exchange 35 Index. This index includes 35 companies which together are supposed to track the Canadian economy. Historically, the correlation between the TSE35 index and the TSE300 index has been around 98% (CSI, 1998). The data covers the period from 25 February 1991 to 13 August 1999 for a total of 2209 observations. Note that we are considering a much longer time period than KST. Obviously, for a trading strategy or rule to be useful in predicting market behaviour, it has to do so *a priori*. Namely, it is well known that one can always find time periods during which certain trading rules work. However, when the same rules are applied to different or longer time periods, the rule often fails to work. Table 10.3 presents basic summary statistics.

From the summary statistics and Figure 10.9, we can see that the data is somewhat kurtotic. The line drawn on the histogram represents a normal distribution with the same mean and variance than the empirical distribution. From it we can see that the normal distribution does not provide the best fit with the data and that instead the KST process might provide a better fit.

10.5.3 Results of the estimation

Having estimated the likelihood function, the maximum likelihood is characterized by the parameter estimates in Table 10.4.

From the table we can compute the mean of positive and negative shocks,

Table 10.4

	$\widehat{\alpha}_1$	$\widehat{\lambda}_1$	$\widehat{\alpha}_2$	$\widehat{\lambda}_2$	$\widehat{\mu}$	$\widehat{p}$	$\widehat{q}$
TSE35	0.53717	94.648	0.94044	153.768	0	0.6046	0.5205

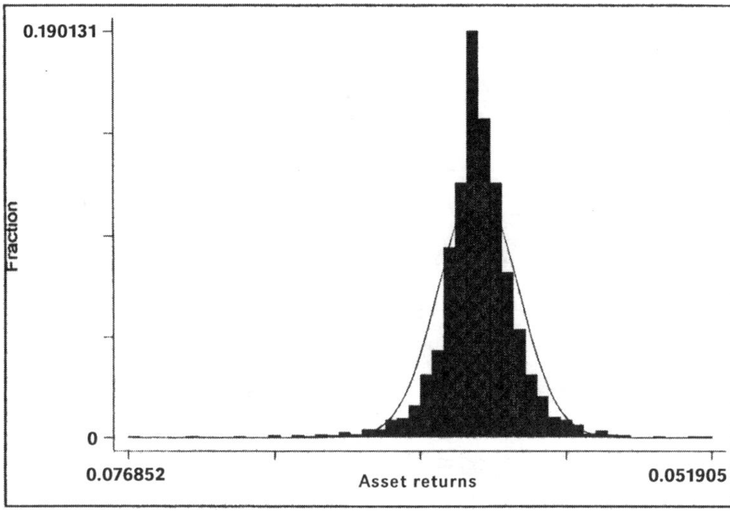

Figure 10.9 Histogram of returns from TSE35 Index

i.e. $\mu_\varepsilon = \alpha_1/\lambda_1 = 0.0056755$ and $\mu_\delta = \alpha_2/\lambda_2 = 0.0061160$. These in turn imply that the expected realized return from the geometric moving average (2,1) rule is

$$\begin{aligned} E_{RRT(2,1)}(r) &= \frac{1}{1-p}(\Pi p\mu_\varepsilon - (1-p)\mu_\delta) \\ &= \frac{1}{1-0.6046}(0.452 \times 0.6046 \times 0.0056755 - (1-0.6046) \times 0.0061160) \\ &= -0.0021933 \end{aligned} \tag{10.20}$$

we can compare this with the expected return on the TSE35

$$\begin{aligned} E_R(r) &= \mu + \Pi\mu_\varepsilon - (1-\Pi)\mu_\delta \\ &= 0.452 \times 0.0056755 - (1-0.452) \times 0.0061160 \\ &= -0.000786 \end{aligned}$$

We can see from the above that realized returns from the GMA (2,1) rule perform worse than asset returns and that it is not possible to generate positive profits when applying the rule to Canadian data.

Using the same process as in Section 10.4.3, we can graph the density of returns and realized returns from the trading strategies. The results are depicted in Figure 10.10.

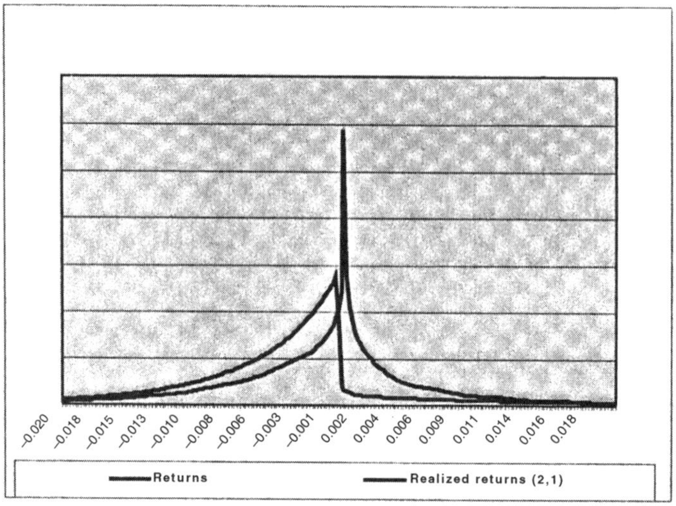

Figure 10.10 Returns and realized returns for TSE35

Notice again the skewness of the distribution of realized returns. As we have seen analytically for the special case of the double exponential distribution, for large values of r, the density of realized returns from the trading strategy lies above the density of asset returns. The picture also confirms that this is the case here. However, we know from the calculations above that the expected value of realized returns is negative. Thus, for large r, the density of realized returns does not lie enough above the density of asset returns such that it could make up for the large probability mass on the downside of the density.

10.6 CONCLUSION

In this chapter, we have tried to describe the densities and the distribution functions of the geometric moving average (2,1) rule. We have also tried to compare the asset returns distribution with the distribution of realized returns to see if we can prescribe a preference ordering over the distributions. Finally, we wanted to see if it was possible to generate positive profits using a geometric moving average rule in the long run, given Canadian data. The overall finding is that the distribution of realized returns is skewed extremely to the left. This was shown analytically for the special case of the double exponential distribution and seems to carry over to general distributional forms as shown by the numerous graphs. Similarly, it seems to be the case that preference orderings over the distributions also carry over from the special case of the exponential distribution to general types of distributions. Namely, we showed that, except for a few extreme cases, the distributions of asset returns and realized returns from the geometric moving average (2,1) rule, never dominate each other by first- or second-order stochastic dominance. This finding seems to be confirmed by the graphs since as r becomes larger, the value of the density of realized returns lies above that of asset returns. Finally, estimating the asset return process for Canadian data, we find that it is not possible to generate positive profits using a geometric moving average rule over the long run. This result is comforting to some, as it agrees with the conventional understanding that such rules cannot generate above normal profits. Hence the result stands in sharp contrast to the recent empirical results of Kuo (1998) and Brock, Lakonishock and LeBaron (1992), which conclude that one can indeed make positive profits with these rules.

Finally, in future research it would be useful to apply a series of statistical tests to the estimation of the asset return process. Specifically, the fit of the returns distribution could be compared with the fit of the normal distribution. Furthermore, an important hypothesis is that of symmetry and whether returns might be modelled by the exponential distribution. Finally, it would be useful to contrast the empirical distribution of realized returns from the trading strategy with that obtained by inverting the characteristic function.

ACKNOWLEDGEMENTS

I would like to thank Tilman Klumpp for his assistance. I would also like to thank Professor John Knight for his help and for suggesting this research topic. Any errors that remain are, of course, my own.

REFERENCES

Brock, W., Lakonishok, J. and LeBaron, B. (1992) 'Simple Technical Trading Rules and the Stochastic Properties of Stock Returns'. *Journal of Finance*, **47**, 1731–1764.

The Canadian Securities Institute (1998) *The Canadian Securities Course*, Vol. 3, Chapters 9–12, April.

Eichberger, J. and Harper, I.R. (1997) *Financial Economics*, Oxford University Press, New York.

Hida, T. (1993) *Gaussian Processes*. American Mathematical Society, Providence, RI.

Karr, A.F. (1993) *Probability*, Springer-Verlag, New York.

Knight, J.L., Satchell, S.E. and Tran, K.C. (1995) 'Statistical Modelling of Asymmetric Risk in Asset Returns'. *Applied Mathematical Finance*, **2**, 15-172.2.

Kon, S.J. (1984) 'Models of Stock Returns: A Comparison'. *Journal of Finance*, **2**, 147–65.

Kuo, G.W. (1998) 'Some Exact Results for Moving Average Trading Rules with Applications to UK Indices', in *Advanced Trading Rules*, edited by E. Acar and S. Sachell (eds), Butterworth-Heinemann, Oxford, pp. 81–102.

LeBaron, B. (1991) 'Technical Trading Rules and Regime Shifts in Foreign Exchange', Working Paper, Department of Economics, University of Wisconsin-Madison.

Levich, R.M. and Thomas, L.R. (1993) 'The Significance of Technical Trading-rule Profits in the Foreign Exchange Market: A Bootstrap Approach', *Journal of International Money and Finance*, **12**, 451–474.

Neftci, S.N. (1991) 'Naive Trading Rules in Financial Markets and Wiener–Kolmogorov Prediction Theory: A Study of Technical Analysis', *Journal of Business*, **64**, 549–571.

Pinkus, A. and Zafrany, S. (1997) *Fourier Series and Integral Transforms*, Cambridge University Press, Cambridge.

Index